12/03/12

Pipo

*A Son's Recollection of Those
Unique, Eternal and Magical
Moments with His Father*

Mike (Miguel) Garcia

D1529220

MIKE (MIGUEL) GARCIA

ISBN: 1467999741
ISBN 13: 9781467999748

Acknowledgments

This book is a tribute to my father, Gerardo Garcia, better known to me as "Pipo." He was and always will be my true hero.

The ultimate honor is reserved for God, our Creator and maker, who gave us life, the ultimate gift! Without him, this book, or anything else, for that matter, would not exist.

My beloved mother, Maria Garcia, who has stood by me all my life and whom I love very much, was indispensable in her input in this manuscript.

A special thanks goes to my brother, Gerardo Garcia Jr., for taking valuable time away from his own family to proofread and add content to this manuscript.

To my aunt Genoveva Hermida, who was there for all of us and who will never be forgotten, as well as to my grandfather Domingo and his lovable wife, Pepilla—thank you.

Also, want to mention, Antonio Lopez, who was a godsend to me growing up in Cuba.

Many thanks also go to the people listed below, who contributed immensely in making this project a reality:

Barbara Garcia, Gerry Garcia Jr., Shaun Garcia, Nelly Soto, Joshua Soto, Rayniell Soto, Anthony Santana Sr., Andrew Louis Santamaria, Josephine Santana, Josie Weber, Daniel Walker,

Theodore Christie, Frank Escalante, Thomas Smith and Jon Carman.

Also, Staci Goddard '04, Stephanie Dawn Crnkovic '08, and Randy Richardson '10, from Princeton University; Robert Vidal (author of *Bloodcaine*); John Vidal, who inspired me in obtaining my bachelor's degree.

I would be amiss not to mention Princeton University, a place where dreams do come true. I received so much encouragement and support from faculty, administrators, and colleagues alike. Without its stern commitment to empowerment through education and nurturing of employees through various programs, I would not have had the resources or the time to embark upon and complete my book. In particular, I would like to thank Chad Klaus, who started the ball rolling by picking me for the Excelling at Princeton Program, and my boss, Tom Myers, who facilitated my absence from work during class time. Also, I would like to mention, last but certainly not least, a special gratitude to Paul Breitman, who was the inaugural director of the Frist Campus Centre and responsible for hiring me.

There are none greater than the many fabulous students at this university. They have helped me succeed and are the lifeblood of Princeton University. I will always be grateful to all of them.

Finally, I would like to give the highest kudos to all the missionaries, past and present, who have given everything they have to help those afflicted with starvation, diseases, poverty, etc., and to try to prevent those conditions from happening. These are the great people of the world who are often marginalized and unnoticed by the masses.

Introduction

It has been a persistent, lifelong aspiration of mine to write a narrative of my beloved father, Gerardo Garcia, whom I also called *Pipo*. This book is a tribute to Pipo, the kind-natured person he was to all of us, and all that he meant to me. Furthermore, this book conveys the positive impact that my father had on my life and the important role he played in building my character.

Nevertheless, the most difficult aspect of this joyous journey is to set sail or simply begin writing his amazing story once and for all. It sounds easy, but, let me tell you, it is a monumental task in scope, requiring a significant amount of time and effort. I give thanks to God for guiding me all the way to the end. I have had the greatest force in the universe at my side along the course of this journey. Hallelujah!

After the death of my father on July 24, 1985, I was not only mourning the incredible loss, but was also overwhelmed with the many bills for all the arrangements while helping my mother to stay afloat. I was working over eighty hours a week at the time, and that was just the beginning of my struggles.

During this time, in my mid twenties, I was enrolled at Middlesex County College in Edison, New Jersey, to jump-start my dreams of obtaining a bachelor's degree. Each semester, I commuted from Alcan Ingot & Powders in Union, New Jersey, for two evening classes. Two years later, I had to commute from my new employer at Welsh Farms Ice Cream in West Caldwell, New Jersey, where it took me over two hours just to get there on time for classes.

My days began each morning at 3:30 a.m. and lasted until 10:00 p.m. I was overwhelmed by the incredible pace, but I never complained—I was making hard-earned money, which we needed to keep our bills from overtaking us. My mom was content, and I had a renewed sense of purpose. I was focused on the job at hand, working in order for all of us to survive; however, it was taking a physical toll on me. I noticed that I was suffering from hair loss. No one else mentioned this, but to me, it was clearly a result of all the stress I was experiencing.

I was also somewhat perplexed and happy at the same time. I was going to school, which I enjoyed, and studying deflected much of the impact of what was going on with my family.

To make things even worse, my grandfather Domingo (my mother's father) and his wife, Pepilla (my mother's stepmother), both passed away within a year of my father's death. Then, a few months later, another devastating bombshell occurred. My aunt Genoveva fell down and broke her hip. Several months after that, she died of bed sores. She was a very charismatic and vibrant person with unlimited passion for life. It was heart-wrenching to see her reduced to lying in bed. She did not respond to any rehabilitation treatment, despite daily visits from professional physical therapists and regular visits from all of us across many months. She was battling incredible pain and constantly shared with us that she was ready to finally exit this world, for she could not take the pain anymore. It was an emotional inferno for all of us, but especially for my mom.

On March 5, 2002, I was fortunate enough to find employment at the Frist Campus Center at Princeton University after being laid off by Continental Airlines in the aftermath of the September 11, 2001, terrorist attacks on our nation. In my current position at the Frist Campus Center, I have had unlimited access to unmatched resources, ample downtime to do my research, and the solitude to concentrate fully on this book. The environment has been quite conducive to my work because I am constantly surrounded by brilliant people who are more than willing to help me succeed simply by agreeing to whatever is asked.

Once I finally began writing this manuscript, I came to a significant roadblock There was a daunting question that I needed to answer satisfactorily before I went on any further. The question was simple in nature, you might think, but I was drawing constant blanks. I could not think of what title to give the manuscript. I even sought divine intervention to enlighten me with any idea for the title. I needed a title which captured the essence of my deep and loving relationship with my father. After contemplating this conundrum for a few days, the crystal-clear answer finally struck me like divine lightning! Thanks be to Almighty God! The title had to be the name I called my father from my earliest recollection as a young child to his final days. There could be no other title more fitting than Pipo, a simple Cuban way of saying "father, dad, pop," etc. Every time I say "Pipo," I know for certain my father is near me. This is the closeness I want to portray to everyone reading the story of Gerardo Garcia—who will always be Pipo to me!

Our journey together will take us to Spain, Cuba, Mexico, and America. Pipo was born in Spain, in a small village called Valle De Las Casas, in the Castilian Province near Leon, about 120miles northwest from the capital city of Madrid. I will cover his life from his birth to his arrival in Cuba, where I was born, and begin to share my first memories of Pipo, while I was growing up during the revolution of Fidel Castro in 1959 as well as during the Missile Crisis of 1962, leading up to our departure to Mexico City. I will share the transforming experiences which shaped my future relationship with Pipo. I will convey the turning point that I have labeled "the Chiclets incident," which occurred at the concourse of Mexico City International Airport. From that point on I was on a secret personal mission to help Pipo economically and in every other possible way I could imagine when we would eventually arrive in America.

Once we landed on American soil, we settled in the Ironbound section of Newark, New Jersey (a.k.a. "Down Neck"), in an apartment we dubbed "the North Pole" after enjoying a three-week sojourn in Miami.

I will also enumerate some of Pipo's many interests and pleasures. For example, he was a passionate reader of Spanish poetry and loved to recite poems both in private and in public. In addition, he adored and had an affinity for Spanish, Cuban, and other eclectic sounds that he would mesh smoothly together in his singing and dancing, while hosting legendary parties at homes and in the *barrios*. Pipo also loved the drama of bullfighting because of the brevity and sheer elegance in pursuit of the kill, which he felt imitated the courage and hardness of life. *Ole*, Pipo! He was a big fan of Manolito, the greatest Spanish bullfighter who ever lived. Pipo often spoke about the hidden meaning in bullfighting and how it related to life and death. It would take years before I finally understood what he meant, having fully matured and experienced life and death firsthand. Pipo was also a semipro wrestler in Spain and often wrestled in the many villages there to earn a little cash, but mostly because he loved the strategy and energy that it brought to his spirit.

Pipo was a trendsetter. His taste for fine clothes was immeasurable, and he loved to wear tailor-made, double-breasted suits that were in high fashion during the 1940s. With his black hair combed straight back, he reminded me of the great New York Yankees' baseball player Joe DiMaggio, but better looking. Always with a perfect demeanor and not a hair out of place, that was my Pipo.

What distinguished Pipo from others was his very core—he was a simple man who was truly devoted to God (without being pretentious one bit) and kept it to himself, to his family, friends, and acquaintances. His zest for life and sensitivity were self-evident by his kind behavior toward others. He worked very hard at everything he did and never had any grievances toward anyone. Pipo had a remarkable disposition.

I often recall running into people in Newark who knew Pipo. They would always speak of their fondness toward my father. I have never personally encountered or heard anything negative either through a third party or through gossiping. He was truly respected and admired by so many individuals.

However, Pipo was very firm with my brother, Gerardo Jr., and me when it came to discipline. Each time we veered onto or near the wrong path, he would give us a stern look while reaching for his belt buckle. He would loosen his belt a little bit at a time until we straightened ourselves out, usually before the entire belt was in his hand for a well-deserved unleashing of his wrath. I was never too happy with the punishment because it hurt so much, so I would quickly cry out for my mother to make him stop. She would always intervene on my behalf. Often, she too would get stung by the belt herself. I did not think so at the time, but I tried to play my poor mother against my father.

In closing this introduction, I would like, through one seemingly simple phrase, to honor my father for being the best father a son could ever dream of having:

"Pipo te quiero para siempre, tu hijo Miguel"
"I love you forever father, your son Mike"

While simple on the surface, the statement above is so emotionally charged for me. I had to take several breaks to gather myself before I could complete writing it. The sentiment touched my innermost being, bringing to my eyes tears which slowly ran down my face before dropping onto my writing pad. Tears are hard to keep in check sometimes. They also cleanse and purify us. This was a blessing in disguise, a catharsis if you will, because after releasing my emotions clearly and visibly on these wet writing pages, I have turned the page and have confronted head on my biggest foe—*myself!* Self-doubt was and always will be our worst demon that hides in the darkness of our soul, destroying us. These tears represent a form of expression that is by far the most powerful human display of that which carries our lifeline for one another and the real purpose in living…encompassing an eternal, *loving relationship!*

Preface

Who was Pipo? Gerardo Garcia was my father. "Pipo," meaning "father, pop, or dad" in the Cuban dialect of Spanish, is the name I called him when I was little boy in Cuba. That name has never left me. It is dear to me for so many reasons that it would simply take an eternity to list them all. Even as I grew older, I always referred to my father as Pipo. It is a simple identification with the person I loved and cared for the most in my life.

Growing up in Cuba was the best time of my life because of Pipo. He was one of the most liked people in all the surrounding towns, provinces, and cities where we lived. In addition, it seemed that every time I went out with Pipo, he always attracted a large crowd. I was overwhelmed by his magnetic personality.

On several occasions we were approached by a number of policemen who were investigating what was going on. Shortly after, the police officers themselves became engulfed in my father's stories, jokes, poetry, singing, and Spanish folk dancing, and they became part of our universe. But it was not merely the storytelling that made Pipo unique—it was also his humanity. He had an affinity for going beyond the casual social greetings we are all conditioned to in society and making some type of connection to the higher needs of others, whatever they may have been.

On one occasion, I was very proud to learn of how many people he had helped during Flora, one of the most destructive hurricanes that had ever struck Cuba and the Dominican Republic, killing over fifteen thousand people in October of 1964. Even though I was only five-and-a-half years old, I remember this incident with absolute clarity because of the many downed trees, light polls blocking streets, homes without roofs, and people running around searching for family members and friends. I was Pipo's little assistant, helping unload all kinds of water, soft drinks, and beer from his truck. In Cuba, my father had a beverage distribution business even while Fidel Castro was in charge. In a two-day period, we must have unloaded over ten fully loaded trucks of free beverages.

Pipo taught me a very important life lesson in the wake of this act of nature—never, ever turn your back on anyone who needs help, no matter who he or she is! This remark by my father has defined who I am today. I have remained humble in the realization that helping a fellow human being is the highest plateau to reach in the entire universe. Thanks, Pipo!

Pipo was born in Valle De Las Casas, a small village about twenty miles away from Leon ("lion" in Spanish) in the Castille Province of Spain, on April 23, 1909. I remember Valle De Las Casas well because far in the horizon you could see this beautiful, panoramic view of a mountain with three recognizable peaks called Peña Corada, where my father would play, explore, and work as a young boy.

I can still remember the radiant glow in my father's eyes as he shared his fond memories of this mountain, the region, and the surrounding villages, where we had a large family presence. I enjoyed seeing these special places with Pipo on a family trip back to his birthplace. It was like he was reliving his childhood days again through me.

After our first family dinner near the mountain, I left with my female cousins, who introduced me to their many friends, including one Spanish girl that I fell in love with at first sight. She was simply adorable. We left the confinement of the village and walked toward Peña Corado to explore the area that Pipo had spoken about with me. It felt like time stood still that day. We were away from the village until darkness set in, which was almost 11:00 p.m. in that era in Spain. I was trying to be very brave with this local girl, who knew the terrain so well, but I knew there were many wolves in the valley that let out haunting howls at irregular intervals. I managed to maintain a cool demeanor in front of the girl, but inside was a different story. By this time, my mother had sent my other cousins to look for us. She knew the mountain surrounds were dangerous because she had walked in them herself with Pipo more than twenty years before. The memory of being with Pipo and then meeting that pretty girl that day still brings a smile to my face. I had stood directly in the steps of my father's childhood. I also knew then, and looking back now, that it was a monumental point in my life. It was my first step toward becoming a man. I felt ready for the future, no matter what it held.

Pipo had ten siblings. At the age of eighteen he joined the military and stayed there for ten years. He never forgot to send money home to his parents. After leaving the military, he opened a bar near his former base in the port city of Ferrol. It was there that he began to recite Spanish poetry in public, his passion. Pipo's bar became a trendy place for meeting new people, having good conversations, and partying. Another one of Pipo's rules was to never abuse alcohol. He told me he never drank at his bar unless it was a special occasion. The pressure from his navy buddies to overindulge was high at times, but he overcame it.

Pipo then emigrated to Cuba and worked for his two older brothers in beverage distribution for four years. He returned to Spain a married man and started a pig, chicken, and cattle farm. Shortly after, his business went bust due to a severe virus which affected the entirety of his livestock. Needless to say, he lost every penny he had and went back to Cuba to work for his brothers again, but this time after one year he bought their business and succeeded.

Another important lesson Pipo taught me is that life is always going to throw heavy obstacles, but don't ever be too discouraged, because if not for them, life would not be worth living. One of my secret goals in life was to help Pipo, especially after leaving Cuba for America. In 1968, at the young age of nine, I decided to provide my father with money from all types of work that I was doing after school to help out with the family finances. I proudly shined shoes, carried groceries, sold lemonade, and so on. I was the happiest person in the world because this time I was helping my true hero—my Dad. My commitment to him was absolute. It continued not only until his death, but beyond. I also promised to help my mother, brother, friends, and strangers, just like Pipo.

In addition to the Cuban hurricane disaster relief, my father was a courageous man who fought in three wars, including the Spanish Civil War.

At the age of fifty-seven, he and my mother decided to leave Cuba and come to America, via Mexico, to provide a better life for my brother and me. Over the years, I have wondered whether I would have had enough courage to start a new life along with two young children and no money in a new country where I couldn't speak the language.

My father and I shared many great memories. Among the many, three always come to mind the most: Pipo's birthplace home in Spain, a family visit to Mexico's pyramids, and attending baseball games at Shea Stadium.

We arrived in Spain in July of 1974, almost twenty years after my father and mother had left. It was a tiring trip because we had fifteen suitcases full of presents for our family. We had to rent two taxis just to transport our entire luggage. Not to mention the inconvenience of it all. Sometimes I would play a joke on Pipo. I hid some of the bags, and he stated to get a little frustrated and blamed my mother and me, but it was all in fun.

Arriving at Pipo's birthplace felt like traveling back to the beginning of time. It was a desolate area. There were no roads, just dirt and mud. Our taxi got stuck several times with its heavy load. Pipo's eyes lit up with joy upon arriving at his home, but to me it was torture. I hated it. I just wanted to get out of there. First, before entering the property, a heavy wooden door needed to be opened about one hundred feet away from the front door. The courtyard looked and felt like quicksand as we trekked toward it. I told Pipo, "I don't want to stay here long."

He replied, "Son, just give us a hand with all the bags."

I said, "Hold the taxi, Pipo!" but before I realized it, the taxi had driven off and left me stranded.

After meeting aunt Rosario, I asked her for directions to the lavatory. I couldn't seem to find it anywhere in the house. Pipo interjected and said, "Come here I'll show the way." He opened the front door and said, "You see the big tree two hundred feet away?"

I said, "Yeah...."

"Well, make a right past the green bushes and lift the wooden cover of the hole, and that's your lavatory for the next week... so get used to it." I was in disbelief. I could not be angrier at this new predicament. I was like a reactor ready to explode on Pipo or whoever was standing near me. I was a city kid from Newark, New Jersey, one of the toughest cities in America! I was not going to succumb to this ancient environment where you could be prey to all kinds of wild animals, especially wolves. You could hear their hungry calls at night, which was so pitch dark that you could hardly see your own hand six inches away. Man, that was scary! I was totally out of my comfort zone. I was practically shitting bricks every time I went outdoors to get water for cooking from the well. I felt like a lamb ready to be sacrificed.

As I approached the hole, I looked back and saw about a dozen white chickens following me in a straight line. It was crazy; they were in perfect formation. It was like a drill sergeant was leading them on a military operation. At the same time, I caught Pipo's face lit up with joy at seeing me endure the hard facts of life that he had to face growing up there forty years earlier. This daily ritual of providing lunch for my new best friends became fun. I even had some names picked out for them and would yell, "Chow time, come and get it while it's fresh...." Yummy, yummy.

The above snippets and other magical accounts with my father's people will be covered more in depth in the upcoming chapters. So sit back and relax and enjoy this amazing narrative ride with me.

He will always be my true hero...Pipo.

CHAPTER 1

The Early Years in Spain

Gerardo Garcia (Pipo) was born on April 23, 1909, in a small village called Valle De Las Casas, a province of Leon, Spain. He was the son of Joaquin Garcia and Elena Garcia, who were also born in the same village. His parents were simple people full of humility and were well loved by everyone in their small community.

Pipo's father worked the land, planting many crops and taking care of the livestock while his mother was at home raising the children. There were ten children altogether, five boys and five girls. The oldest was Manuel, followed by Radigundus, Marcelino, Susana, Fidel, Juentina, Gualupe, Gerardo (my father), Justiniano, and Rosario, who is the only surviving sibling. She currently lives in a senior citizens home in the town Cistierna Spain, where her niece is employed and takes great care of her.

Valle De Las Casas was a tiny town in Spain. The local inhabitants called it *Aldea,* which means "village" in Spanish. At that time it had a population of about four hundred people living in approximately forty houses. There were no structured roads at all. Most roads were one lane of dirt with barely enough room for one *coche* (vehicle) or horse and carriage to pass through. There was only one main road to enter and exit the village. The houses had no electricity (just lanterns or candles for lighting), no water, and no sanitation on the premises. For refrigeration, they used giant ice bricks to preserve the food.

I remember my first trip to Aldea n 1974 with Pipo and my mom, Maria. We travelled there by taxi, and before I even thought of getting out of the car, I told him that there was no way I'd stay in this ancient Aldea for more than a couple of hours at the most. He quickly tried to put me at ease by assuring me that he would hold the taxi for three hours until we got the fifteen bags of luggage unloaded into the home and sorted out the various gifts for his sister Elena, whom he hadn't seen in over twenty years. He promised me that afterward, we would leave for the city of Leon as soon as possible. I reluctantly agreed to step out of the safe confinement of the taxi into the "lion's den" and help unload the bags into the house.

Before we entered the home of Pipo's birthplace, we had to unlock and open a huge, old, wooden door. It resembled a door from a fortress, but was a lot more eerie, like something from the sixties TV show *The Munsters*. Let me tell you, that was not a good first impression. From there, we then had to navigate the grounds, maneuvering around the dirt and mud to get to the house itself, which was about one hundred and twenty feet away from the taxi. It was a struggle not to fall and become buried alive in all the slimy mud.

After surprising aunt Rosario with many hugs and kisses, we distributed the gifts. I immediately went outside to talk to the taxi driver, but he was long gone. I quickly ran back inside in total despair to tell Pipo that I didn't want to stay in this dreadful environment anymore. He assured me that we would leave soon. Well, soon was about five days later, or an eternity to me! No wonder Pipo left this place and joined the military. I would have done the same, too, in a heartbeat.

This experience was a real wake-up call for me. I felt incredibly blessed to live in America after witnessing such a scenario in person. I vividly recall my first night in that house. It was both a nightmare and night *terror*, full of suspense and with dangers lurking in the nearby plains—much closer than my comfort zone. For starters, there was obviously no light in the house. We had to use a lantern to navigate at night. The house was also infested with spiders. I could see them running amok everywhere I turned. For the life of me, I could not think of ever going to sleep and risking having these creatures crawl all over me while I slept. It simply was not going to happen.

The bed that we all slept in was elevated about four feet high to keep the rodents from biting us while we slept. Just imagine that scenario for a moment. To make matters even more disturbing (if that was remotely possible), the bed was made out of hay. I was itching so much that I had to put my pants and shirt on to stop myself from practically peeling off my skin to keep the insatiable, unwarranted itch from driving me insane.

The very worst part came when my mom turned off the lantern in the room. The darkness was so complete that I could not even see my hand five inches away from my face. It was pitch dark like a solar eclipse! At this time I was becoming nervous, starting to hear weird sounds coming from nearby. It sounded like a herd of wolfs and coyotes on the prowl looking for food. I yelled across the room to my mom, Maria, to turn the lantern back on. After twenty minutes of my shouting, she finally gave in.

In the meantime, Pipo was in his natural element and slept like a baby—unlike his sleepless nights in America, where he was stressed out and had to take pills for just a couple of hours of unnatural sleep.

As an adult looking back, I now believe that the harsh life that I witnessed there looks a lot more desirable than our current, fast-paced, in-your-face lifestyle, which is rampant and killing us all. I have drawn well on those experiences, seeing my father so relaxed in the environment when I though he was crazy. In retrospect, I would've preferred for us to stay there at that time and live a simpler life.

The next morning, I asked aunt Rosario, a slim but strong fifty-five-year-old woman, for onother lavatory. She told me yes we have onother one, next to the one you went yesterday about fifty feet away.Just walk again outside the house past the biggest tree and the bushes and look out for a hole covered with wood. "That's the same type of lavatory, Miguel (Mike)."

"You've got to be kidding," I said. My mom was standing nearby and heard my comments. She even started laughing at my expense.

Then Pipo joined in the fun and said, "You are going to have company...."

I replied, "What company?"

He said, "The chickens will line up right behind you as you approach the hole."

I turned around, completely confused. At this point, Pipo and the rest of them were hysterical, focusing on my reactions as I headed over to my newfound hole in the ground to return to nature what nature had given me. I was not amused as a young, typical, know-it-all teenager. On my way to the depository hole, I noticed about dozen chickens around the front of the house start to make noise and go wild with enthusiasm, following each other and quickly lining up right behind me in formation. They seemed to be more disciplined than most soldiers following orders. I think the military should've used these highly disciplined chickens to teach their new recruits how to follow proper decorum in a straight line without ever skipping a single beat in their marching routine. What a memorable site for me as an impressionable teenager. It was feeding time for the chickens as I got closer to the hole. They surrounded me, watching closely, but with respect until I was done. On the way back, I noticed my family outside waiting for my return to tell them all about it, since it was my inaugural ball with nature's calling. I wouldn't have any of it. You know, in nature nothing goes to waste, and I saw and learned this firsthand. In the days that followed, the chickens became my buddies, and when I was about to depart for good on my last day, I made sure I overate to give them one last final big meal for being so good to me and welcoming me into their family!

To obtain water, you had to go the center of Aldea to a large fountain near the church and the school. There were a lot of activities in the area, with people selling all types of goods. There was plenty of bartering or going to the small general store (which was the only one in town) to purchase necessities which could only be found there. It sold meats, fish, bread, and milk. However, these items were only trucked in to Aldea twice a week. The town center area served as an important gathering area for meetings and staying in contact with villagers and visitors alike. The church and the fountain are two relics that still remain intact from those days.

Pipo stayed in this village until the age of eighteen, helping his mother and sisters, as his father had died when he was only six years old. The older brothers—Manuel (sixteen years older), Marcelino, and Fidel—emigrated to Cuba to avoid being drafted into the Spanish military.

Meanwhile, my father, Pipo, remained behind and dedicated himself to working in the dirt fields, planting corn, garbanzo beans, and many assorted vegetables with his five sisters. He also worked in a nearby town called Oviedo in the province of Asturia as a coal miner. At other times, he worked in towns like Prado De La Guzpena, Cistierna, and Mataporquera. Mataporquera was a very far commute. It took about three hours by train each way to get there, but to save money he would bike instead, pedaling for more than ten hours a day. You can imagine how exhausting this must have been for him. Usually, he didn't make it home before midnight and had to bike through a dangerous forest that contained many wild animals, waiting and hiding for their prey in the dark. The forest was home to wolves, coyotes, snakes, and wild dogs, all battling each other for food.

Pipo once told me a story about the time a hungry wolf chased him through the heavy forest for nearly an hour, despite Pipo's nonstop pedaling trying to get away from him. Pipo said he could hear it making all types of wild growling sounds from its mouth during the chase. The wolf was no more than twenty feet behind him for most of the chase. Pipo told me, "I was lucky to survive that ordeal! I got lucky from the friendly terrain that I had traveled so often, and my familiarity with it helped me enormously during the chase. In addition, most of it was downhill, and I knew all the curves, roads, and tracks that I needed to follow in order to outrun him. Plus, I was in great physical shape and was not ready to be eaten by any wolf that day!"

What a great story! I was at the edge of my seat the whole way through his tale. That's why I was a little bit worried about my own safety and the possibility of wolves seeking me out in revenge because of my father being the one that got away! I knew I wouldn't be as brave or lucky as he had been that night.

In between Aldea of Valle De Las Casas, there is a mountain that gives the Province in Castile and the nearby city of Leon a challenge for thrill seekers. Many people try to climb it, but only the true professionals are ever successful in reaching the very top of one of Spain's highest mountains. The mountain is called Peña Corada and it has a unique shape. The upper part has three separate peaks, which remain covered in snow all year round. It is one of those rare natural treasures that belong on everyone's must-see list.

I was very fortunate to spend one afternoon with Pipo, walking and listening intently as he described everything about this imposing mountain. He pointed his finger several times for me to look up as he went into microscopic detail about the terrain. In the midst of a beautiful rainbow, he said, "Son, this is where I spent many hours thinking about the present and what the future held for me. One thing I knew for sure was that I wanted to leave this place and see other parts of the world, but my mother and sister needed my help, so I was trying to figure out what was best for them and me. Sometimes, I would lose track of time just thinking, but the reality was I had to provide for my mother and sisters or they would not be able survive." I could see Pipo's face light up with inner happiness and serenity remembering the soothing nature of this mountainous environment in his past. This time around, with me, he was thinking not only about those old days and the hard living, but also how his future had actually turned out. By this time, his mother had already passed away a couple years before. I spotted his eyes glazing over with emotion;

I knew he was very happy to have me with him at that special place. The true meaning of that moment did not sink in for me until later in life!

I tried to change the tone of the conversation slightly by asking Pipo if he had ever attempted to climb the mountain. He said, "Yes, three times, but I was so busy with work that every time I started my climb, I would think of my mother and my sisters, and then I'd stop because it was not practical to continue, even though I yearned for it. Even so, I climbed it several times in my mind, and that's what really counts, don't you think?"

I said, "Yes, Pipo. Yo comprendo (I understand)."

Then he said, "Miguel, what I want you to do is always remember Peña Corada, son! Will you do that for me? Esta bien (Is that okay)?"

"Si padre, para siempre (Yes, father, forever)!" What an incredible day to have spent with my true hero. I will always cherish that day with him.

Afterward, we went on to visit other family and friends at nearby Aldeas. Upon returning back to Valle De Las Casas, we stopped at the home of Benedict, my father's nephew. Benedict was a giant of a man. My father said, "Miguel, I'm going to introduce you to "the Gorilla," professional wrestler. His job is to wrestle for money. It's not a bad living around this area, getting paid for what you enjoy doing." I was in awe; I couldn't say a word at first. Benedict was so intimidating; he had such a big head and a very dark moustache. I was afraid that he would pummel me to death with his Popeye forearms if I said anything stupid. Within a second, he put me at ease and started to tell me how Pipo was one of the best natural wrestlers in the region during his youth. Unfortunately, Pipo was so busy tending the fields that he was not able to devote the time and effort to develop into a champion like Benedict. It was a travesty not to see him wrestle in the region and beyond at his prime. According to Benedito (Benedict), as an amateur and semipro wrestler, Pipo was highly regarded as one tough *hombre* (man) with a dynamite personality, and everyone cheered for him during the outdoor matches. Even the losing wrestlers would always make their way to Pipo after the matches for some great storytelling and plenty of jokes as he kept busy entertaining the crowd. "They loved your dad, Miguel. As a young kid, your dad inspired me to become a wrestler. I followed the path that he was not able to due to his family obligations. He was my hero!" explained Benedito.

I asked Pipo if he ever wrestled Benedito for fun. Laughing, he said, "No, he was just too big, about six feet six inches tall and 290 pounds, and I was only five feet nine inches tall and 175 pounds. He would've crushed me to death, son."

Then Benedito said, "The crowd would've jumped on me to defend your father way before a fight could've taken place. He was the people's champion, and he was my uncle, whom I love so much!"

After that, we walked in the pitch-dark night back to aunt Rosario's house for dinner. Minutes later we had company at the house as a bunch of cousins arrived to reunite with Pipo. All of a sudden, this pretty young girl walked in with her family. She was about my age with beautiful long black hair. She was my distant third cousin whom I had never met or knew I had until now. Wow! I kind of like it here now, I thought to myself. After dinner, she invited me outside for a walk around Aldea with her. I said, "Sure, let's go!" We walked until we got tired, and I suggested we stop and sit on a small peak which had a pleasant, unobstructed view of the plains below. I really did like this girl a lot for some unfathomable reason. That being said, she did have a lot of class, and she was really smart, both of which helped. Just when things were about to become more heated, darkness began to settle in and I lost my nerve upon hearing the wild wolves in the foreboding night. I suddenly made an excuse to leave when she was moving in to kiss me. I jumped up and told her that it was late and I had to be back at Aunt Rosario's house before my mother started to worry and came looking for me. She gave me a confused look and tried her best to convince me to reconsider my decision, but she didn't have a chance, especially with all those wild animals on the prowl that I could hear (even if I couldn't see them!). Not even that pretty girl was going to allay my fears about being eaten by one of those hungry predators. Those wolves destroyed my potential night of romance big time. I quickly got up and we both ran back to our families. She led the way because I had no knowledge of how to go back and would've gone the wrong way if she was not with me. I think she really like me right away. A few days later I met another girl. However, this girl was more aggressive than the other one. She gave me a big hug and a kiss, and later on the train she came over to say goodbye with the same passion she had shown when we first met, but I was more interested in the other girl. She was so much fun to be with and a lot prettier, while this one was husky with short, blondish hair. The deal breaker for me was the first girl I met was a really classy girl. She had "a touch of class," just like the wonderful comedy movie hit of 1973 starring George Segal and Glenda Jackson with the same title that I chose to give to this special girl.

At the age of eighteen, my father was notified by the Spanish government authority to report for obligatory military service in the port city of Ferrol. Upon reporting, he was told to be ready for combat as soon as he reported. This was a time of crisis in Spain as a strong division arose within the country, which was engulfed in a bloody civil war. My father fought valiantly for the Republicans, who were in power, against General Francisco Franco in the Spanish Civil War.

At the very beginning of the war, Pipo and his brother Justi were taken prisoners by Franco soldiers in the province of Austuria. He was released after a meticulously thorough background investigation. His brother, however, was falsely accused of wrongdoing by a military tribunal and sentenced to death. My father appealed for a second review of the case. Luckily, Pipo had good working relationships with top government officials because he had worked as an assistant to these officers. The appeal was put in front of the military court, and the new verdict came back innocent. Justi was immediately set free. My father was an angel of justice throughout his whole life, helping family, friends, and even enemies.

The incident with his brother is but a small example of what Pipo did during his life to make this world a better place. It would take me too many pages to write a comprehensive list of all the other things he did, but this incident was a very serious one whereby he saved his brother's life, and his humanity played a monumental role in this most happy outcome.

I remember asking Pipo if he ever knowingly killed anyone in combat. He always gave me the same short answer, "No!" but my mother told me many years later that he had.

After the war was over, Pipo was incorporated in the new government of Spain, led by Franco at that point, when he joined the navy. Pipo was stationed in the port city of Ferrol, where he decided to live during his military obligations after being discharged from active duties.

Today, Valle De Las Casas has come a long way; most of the old homes are remodeled with many of the modern amenities that you find in most homes today.

The youth that once lived there have for the most part left for the larger cities like Madrid, Barcelona, and Seville, or for other European countries. However, when they have their vacations or a long weekend free, they return for the solitude and the simplicities of life that my father savored as he slept like a baby that night on the high bed in my aunt's house.

Nowadays, the residents have also furnished their homes with beautiful and luxurious objects and installed satellite dishes and outdoor pools. Furthermore, all the roads are paved now, so they can drive their fancy Mercedes Benz *coches* (cars) into their automatically opening garages. The most important characteristic of Valle De Las Casas today is that life is slower and there is more humanity, just as it was when my father grew up there.

Henry David Thoreau said it best in his most famous book, *Walden,* calling for simplicity and harmony with nature. This calling is at the core of Aldea. Valle De Las Casas was a most precious place for Pipo, family, and friends to unwind and be restored in this oasis of a sacred ground.

As for the wolves, they are still around today, but on a much smaller scale in terms of numbers. So don't be too comfortable if you ever visit there!

CHAPTER 2

Port City of Ferrol

The port city of Ferrol was the birthplace of Dictator General Francisco Franco and Pablo Iglesias, founder of the Socialist Party. Quite a dichotomy of political views was home grown in this vibrant region of Spain, located on the Atlantic coast in the province of La Coruna in Galicia. By the time Pipo completed his military services, there was an abundance of work available in Ferrol. Rather than work in the major naval shipbuilding center, which supported much of the local economy, Pipo decided to go into business with a friend of his from the navy days. They opened a bar in Ferrol to cater to the large military population that was stationed there. The city's naval base was and still is the most important naval base in western Spain.

Living and working in Ferrol was so much easier than back home that Pipo spent nearly fourteen years in the city. Many of his shipmates and former military friends resided in the city and always dropped by the bar for some fun. My father was a born leader. Even though he never realized this, others did. He was a trendsetter who would wear the latest fashions that arrived from Paris. He loved to dress in the finest garments available, but he never overspent or took money from the bar or pennies earmarked for the family's expenses. Only after everything was paid for did he allow himself to indulge his fine taste in clothes. This cosmopolitan taste was well catered to in Ferrol, which attracted a myriad of high-fashion boutiques to quench the demand of this vibrant and energetic region. It was an exciting time to be young and thirsty for life, and for Pipo, it was as good as it could be. Compared to life in Valle De Las Casas, it was an entirely different planet.

My father's bar was always packed and he was at the epicenter of the reason why it was standing room only. Since my father loved to dance and tell jokes, people flocked to be around him. What made my father so popular, above anything else, was his unabashed humor that he shared with everyone he came across. The ability to self-deprecate and laugh at himself was an irresistible God-given characteristic that he possessed. This trait made him very approachable to the many local ladies as well, who would spend countless hours in the bar just to be around him.

He was very generous with his clientele at the bar and made people feel like they were part of his family. In many ways, this was because they really were family to Pipo. His kindhearted actions distinctively proved this every single day. He would even buy many customers drinks out of his own pocket. However, he was always very conscious of the fine line between business and pleasure. He never allowed himself to get intoxicated in his bar. After the bar closed at night, he would take long walks with friends and stop at coffee shops for a social nightcap.

According to my mom, my father had a daughter in Ferrol before they met. This idea is not totally farfetched, considering the atmosphere which was prevalent in the city at that time. After my father passed away, my mom found a small photo inside his wallet of him and a little girl, riding on the handle bars of his bike. I now have that very same photo in my wallet, even as I write this sentence. No one in the family has ever confirmed or seems to know anything about how valid this claim is. If it is true, it's a secret which my father took to his grave, never sharing any details with family or friends, with the possible exception of his brother Justiniano (Justi), whom he was very close to. During those days, conceiving a child out of wedlock was considered a reprehensible taboo. The entire scenario is a mystery to all of us. I honestly think Pipo would have shared this information with us in his later years if it was true, allowing himself to be free of a dark secret which surely would have burned him inside all those years.

In 1944, Pipo left the city of Ferrol behind. He embarked on a cruise ship called *Magallanes* and headed for the paradise island of Cuba. Based on my mom's recollection, he left from the port of Virgo in Spain, near Northern Portugal, although she cautioned that is was also possible he left from the port of Gijon or from the city of Bilbao in the bay of Biscaya. Point of origin aside, Pipo arrived at the capital city of Habana (Havana) after twenty-two days at sea.

CHAPTER 3

Pipo's Early Days in Cuba

In Cuba our father took over a distribution company, which he got from his brother, Marcelino. He distributed soda, beer, malt, and a stronger beer that was dark. As his business grew, other distributors in town could not compete with him and he ended, with the other brands of beer.because they went out of business in the summer and on the weekends my brother would help him deliver the beer throughout town and onto the farms where there were small bodegas. Our father also had a helper he called "Son." Son came to be like part of the family.

When the beer and soda trailers came in to deliver beer, my father would hire a few workers who worked at the sugar mill to unload the beer into our warehouse, and then my father would get up early and deliver the beer through town. Around noon he stopped to go home for lunch and take his siesta for two hours. Before he fell asleep, he had all the bills ready so that while he was sleeping my brother could go and collect them. Usually the bills would be a few thousand dollars. God forbid if my brother was missing any money! After all this work, my father would give my brother one Cuban peso, but at that time that was a lot of money.

Well, this went on for a few years, until the revolution. There were rebels and government troops all over. On one particular night, my father went across the street to talk to his friend when, all of a sudden, my mother started screaming at my father to come back home. She noticed that from one side of the yard there were soldiers coming in and from the other side rebels were also arriving to fight. At last my father realized and came running in, and we locked the doors, shut off the lights, and went into a shelter that my father had built to protect us from the bullets and bombs that had hit the town a few times.

On one occasion we had to get out of bed because there were a lot of bullets and bombs in the area and run to the shelter in the middle of the night. Everybody went into the shelter, including some of our neighbors, too. Everybody got in except my father. He was the last one in and there was no more room. Bullets start flying, but all he could do was put half of his body in and leave his rear end out with all of this going on.

There is always room for a laugh. My aunt Genoveva said that the only thing he didn't care about was his butt. We all started laughing.

After a few of those nights and days came word that the government was going to bomb the whole town. So, that night Pipo told us that we were going to the sugar mill, since it was safer there. More than half of the town was there. We all went into the smoke stacks of the sugar mill for the night, and the next day we went back home. A few days later, word again came that the same thing was going to happen. This time Pipo decided we were leaving and going to this farm that belonged to a distant cousin and staying there until this the fighting was over. When we got to the farm, there was only this old wooden house, no electricity, and the toilet was outside. The house had been in the middle of nowhere. We were trying to get away from this fighting because Pipo wanted us to be safe. After a few days of being there, our cousin came back and said everything was over, so we could go back home, so there was Pipo, packing the car and going back home. When we got home, everything was there—our house, the warehouse, everything was safe.

So Pipo went back to his business, and we started our routine again. Not long after Castro came to power, he decreed that any private business would be taken over by the government and jobs would be given out working for them. One afternoon Pipo was taking a shower and two government agents showed up at the house while we were sitting in front. One agent asked where Pipo was because they had to talk to him. My mother told them he was taking a shower, and they said, "Tell him to come out." My mother again told them where he was, but they insisted, so my mother went to get him out of the shower. There comes Pipo with a towel wrapped around himself and dripping wet. Well, one of the agents told him to be at the bank in the morning with all the paperwork and bank accounts that belonged to the business, and they would meet him there at 9:00 a.m.

Well, the next morning Pipo and my mother went to the bank, and there the agents were, waiting for him. They asked him for everything that belonged to the business, and they looked it over and said to him, "The business is no longer yours; it belongs to the government. From today on you will be working for us." My father felt like the whole world came to an end, but he didn't have a choice. Even though a lot of people liked him in town and felt really bad for him, there was nothing they could do for him, so he went to work for the government. But this time, instead of working next to the house, he had to travel to the next town, which was about thirty-seven kilometers away. He had to take the bus in the morning, go to the next town, go to this warehouse, and pick up the truck that used to be his and that was already loaded. He would then drive back to our town to deliver the beer and soda that at one point used to belong to him. That really bothered him, but he never said anything because he had to support his family.

On another occasion, they came to the house, these soldiers, and asked where my father was. Again he was in the shower, and the soldiers said, "Bring him out now." My mother went and got him to come, and they told him, "Put something on and come with us; we have something to talk about."

My father got in the car with them and asked, "Where are you taking me?" because he noticed that they were driving out of town, not to the police station. He asked them again and by this time he had a bad feeling that something wasn't right. He started to think they were driving out of town because they were going to kill him in the woods, and at that point he was thinking, "The only thing to do is if I am going to die, they are, too."

Finally the one in charge said, "The reason you were picked up was because you took a box of contraband to this house and somebody saw you."

My father said, "You take me to this so-called house. That box was a box of crackers that I was bringing to this party that they are having, so take me there," which they did. When they arrived at this house, the soldiers got out with him and went into the back yard of this house, and there was a lot of people there. The owner of the house had known my father for many years, and he was a captain in the police department. When he saw my father walk in, he asked, "What's the problem?"

My father told him, "Well, you'd better not eat those crackers, because they said that was contraband." At this point the police captain got up and told the soldiers and the man that was in charge to apologize to my father and take him home and he would see him in the morning.

After a couple of years, my aunt Genoveva said, "Why don't we move to another town and I will buy a house?"

After talking it over, everybody agreed and we moved. Things went along well for a while, but all our family had left Cuba and they were sending kids to fight in Africa as soon as they became of military age, which at that time was sixteen years old. My brother was getting close to that age, my father said, "No way he's going there," so we decided that we had to come to the United States. He told them at work that he had applied for a visa to leave the country, but as soon as he told them that, he was terminated from his job there. He had no job, nothing, but we had a 1954 Chevrolet Impala, and he decided that he was going to use it as a taxi, especially on the weekends to take people to the beach. So every Sunday he would have somebody going to the beach, which gave him some extra cash. On these trips he would take my older brother with him, so while he was waiting for the people, my father and my brother would spend the day at the beach. That was something special to him; he used to enjoy it very much.

Then, because he used this car for so many trips and there was no way to get any parts or tires, the tires were wearing out. Someone stole two tires from the government and sold them to him. Well, he was happy again until he found out the tires were stolen, and that was it for him. He couldn't take it. Pipo almost had a nervous breakdown. He couldn't live with knowing that those tires that he bought and put on his car were stolen; he didn't even want to leave the house, thinking that somebody was watching. By this time his guilt was so great that my mother had to call the guy and tell him to take the tires back. The man came and took the tires off the car, and my father ended up with some used tires. After that he was back to normal again.

Everything was working out fine. My mother and my aunt decided that instead of my father making a few dollars here and there, they would start a small business selling churros and flavored ice cubes in front of the house. We were doing well, but then my brother's visa to leave Cuba arrived, and it was only for him, so we had to tell the government that he was leaving. Two months later my father and the whole family went to take my brother to Habana for the flight to go to Mexico. We stayed at this nice hotel for a few days, and then it came time to take my brother to the airport. We took him there, and once you got there, after a few minutes you had to leave this room and say good-bye. My father grabbed my brother, who was only fourteen years old at the time, and said to him, "Don't you cry, because if you do we will never get out." He gave my brother a hug and told him go, and my brother disappeared into a room. The next time we saw him, we were on top of the airport terrace to watch my brother walking to the airplane, which was parked in the middle of the runway far from the terminal. My brother walked to the plane and went up the stairs, and he listened to what Pipo said; he never shed a tear. Without even turning, he just waved good-bye just before he went into the plane. All this time my father never said a word; later on my mother told us he used to cry a lot, but we never saw that. He wanted us to grow up strong.

After almost a year in Mexico, my father arrived in 1968 in the United States, before my mother did. The first thing to do was to get a job. He stayed at his brother's house, where my older brother Gerardo Jr. had been staying for the past year. He started looking and got a job in a factory call Magnus Organ. There he started working for under two dollars an hour. He knew that my mother was coming, so he had to get an apartment and have it ready for when my mother arrived. That's where he found our first apartment, on Pacific Street in Newark, New Jersey. It was an apartment that didn't have heat throughout the house, but only in the kitchen. There was a gas heater that he had to buy from the previous tenants. The apartment was in bad shape. It needed painting and lots of cleaning, so with the first paycheck he got, he and my brother went and got some paint and some cleaning supplies and started the process of turning this rundown apartment into some kind of livable condition, so when my mother arrived we could go to our own house. After about two weeks, this old-looking apartment was our future home.

CHAPTER 4

Working in Cuba

In Cuba, Pipo's brother Marcelino and cousin Candido Sanches (who was born in Santa Aulaja in the province of Leon, about one mile away from Valle De Las Casas) placed him at La Comercial Store, located in the city of Jobabo in the province of Las Tunas.

The store was ideally situated in a central area called El Centro Del Batey De Jobabo (the Center of Batey from Jobabo). To gain access to this location, one had to carefully cross multiple train tracks at one's peril! Inside this district were the workers' homes and many stores open to the public. In the beginning, Pipo spent the majority of his time driving a truck and making deliveries to other stores and private homes. When business was slow, he would work inside the store, selling food, liquor, clothes, plumbing supplies, electrical equipment, furniture, and a whole host of other products. He also worked in the cafeteria, preparing sandwiches and serving coffee, beer, and soft drinks. One of these soft drinks was Materva, one of the most popular drinks in Cuba and one that I just loved as a kid. Pipo also served as a source of information for customers seeking advice on any products and was a calm contact for customers complaining about any faulty products. The store also had an exclusive agency for the distribution of the beer brands Tropical and La Cristal, the best sellers in town and the surrounding area. The store was a gold mine with the legal right to distribute these products, among other brands of beer, and the king of kings of the soft drink world, Quinaber, which was the single most popular beverage on the island.

Pipo worked in this job until 1954 when my parents decided to return to Spain. The move back home only lasted about two years. Upon returning to Cuba once again, it took Pipo nearly two years of doing odd jobs to make ends meet before he was able to retain his former job with the agency. By 1960, Pipo's success enabled him to buy the agency, along with its rights to distribute and sell Cristal, Tropical, and the soft drink giant Quinaber, from his cousin Candido and his brother Marcelino. However, his successful business was short lived. In 1963, the new Communist Party government nationalized all free enterprises, including Pipo's personal business. In the months ahead, he was ordered to train a newly appointed deputy to run his now-state-owned company. After several months showing the ropes to the deputy in charge of his company, Pipo departed with much sorrow. In the months ahead, the sales volumes were so low that a communist official knocked on his door one day and asked him to rejoin his former company as a government employee. After discussing this development with my mom, he accepted the new position and once again took over the operations of his beloved company under the auspices of government control officials who had no idea how to run a business. Under the directions and parameters of the officials, he was allowed a lot of flexibility, which resulted in very high sales volumes. This positive outcome was rewarded by the Socialist Party of Fidel Castro by an increase in his wages to 375 pesos per month. This was a staggering salary and one of the highest at that time. There were many reasons why the enterprise came back to life so quickly, but it was mostly Pipo's rapport with all the customers which drew them back once they knew he was at his old spot. Pipo didn't just sell beverages; he shared his upbeat attitude and warm soul with all of his customers.

In 1964, our family relocated to the city of Victoria De Las Tunas in the province of Las Tunas, approximately seven miles away. During this period, Pipo commuted to Jobabo on a daily basis to continue working at the agency until 1965, when he was notified that he was no longer needed or allowed to work at the state-owned company.

It had been decided that Pipo was no longer part of the new government's plans because he had applied to leave Cuba for America via Mexico, following his brothers Manuel, Fidel, nephews, nieces, cousins, and many friends that had already left the island legally. Life in Cuba was becoming very difficult for the average Cuban, and there were shortages of just about everything. Even the basics, like bread, milk, rice, and meats, were hard to come by. The government then implemented a rationing system for the public, using a booklet to share limited goods across the country. This new policy accelerated the mass exodus of Cubans from the island. People were going to the government building in droves to apply for exit permits, and our family was no different than any other. My parents wanted the best for us, their children. The news of Pipo being fired without any notice spread around the area like wildfire.

I clearly recall tagging along with Pipo on one of his final delivery rounds in 1965, letting people know that this was the last time he would be making a delivery to their business. Stop after stop, I witnessed grown men cry and lament about what was happening to Pipo. As usual, Pipo took a modest, upbeat view of his situation and those of so many of his country friends who were having a difficult time themselves, trying to provide for their families and resorting to the black market for relief.

The black market in Cuba thrived in those days, and it helped stave off the complete meltdown of the local economy. Even though it was illegal to purchase any goods from this unofficial source, the government did not crack down on the underground trade too harshly. The times that it did crack down were more for

show than anything else. The government needed to discourage any wild notions by the masses of runaway capitalism taking over their new socialist model of governing. This was especially the case following the recent victory of the 1959 revolution against ousted former President Fulgencio Batista.

By now, Pipo had been given a week to turn all his keys in to the deputy in charge of the agency or face prison. My father asked me to accompany him on the symbolic trip. I was so young that I had no concept of the significance of what was happening. We made the journey in his delivery truck from Victoria De Las Tunas, our home, to Jobabo for a final good-bye to the many friends whom he had worked with for nearly twenty years. What caught my attention was that the place was desolate. There was no one around as we hunted for a particular government official to give the keys to. All the walking was making me thirsty, so I asked Pipo for a Coke behind the counter where he used to serve the customers for many years. He said, "Miguel, yo no trabajo mas aqui y no puedo darte una Coca-Cola" (Mike, I don't work here anymore and I can't give you a Coke).

I said, "Porque, Pipo (Why, Pipo)?" to which he responded, "Es muy dificil de explicarte hijo, cuando yo hoy doy las llaves no puedo entrar aqui mas (It's very hard to explain, son. When I turn the keys in today, I can't enter here ever again)." Even though I was only about six years old, I sensed a real sadness in my father's voice, and this sadness was clearly reflected on his face. He was about to leave a place which he loved and cared so much about. I was at his side when this farewell took place, finally drinking a small bottle of Coca-Cola that one of his friends had snatched from the small refrigerator behind the counter and given to me. I felt like I was the happiest kid in the world. Within ten minutes the place was packed with people who had heard that my father was about to say farewell for the last time to a place whose vibrance he cultivated and cherished. It was a very poignant moment for Pipo and the entire agency as they all embraced with teary eyes, thanking my father for providing a better life for all of them. As he gave the keys to the government-appointed official, even the official was moved by the whole spectacle. On the way out of the facility, Pipo rested his right hand on the compound wall by the gate one last time in acknowledgment to himself of what that place had meant to him. I of course imitated Pipo's gesture, resulting in a brief smile from him as he said, "Vamonos, Miguel (Let's go, Mike)."

We emigrated to Mexico a few years later in 1967.

CHAPTER 5

My Mother, the Courtship, and New Family

My mother, Maria, was born on August 30, 1925, in an eastern province of Cuba in the town of Jobabo. Her parents were Domingo Viña and Filomenia Choren from the province of Galicia in the city of Lugo, Spain. Her maternal grandparents were Salvador Choren and Manuela Garcia, while her paternal grandparents were Entanislao and Manuela. I and some others also call my mother "Mima," as well as "Maruja" and "Marujita." Mima was born in the house of her aunt and uncle, Genoveva Choren and Manuel Ermida, who owned one of the best restaurants in town. They typically served over 250 people each day. Her grandparents, parents, and aunt and uncle all lived under the same roof in one house. Her father, Domingo, worked at the Central of Jobabo (center with many retail stores) and her grandfather Salvador was involved in the security of the compound. Later on in Spain, he worked as a civil guard while Manuela stayed home taking care of the house.

Filomenia died only twenty-six days after giving birth to my mother; her death a result of the plague, which had killed many others before her. Mima was raised by her grandparents until they too passed away, when she was eighteen years old. The death of Filomenia was tragic for her parents, as they had already lost a grandson just a short time before. The grandson had been like an angel, but sadly died after only four months of life. The arrival of a baby girl, Maria Filomenia, my beloved mother, was such a joy for her grandparents!

In June 1930, the family moved to a town called Palas De Rey, located in the province of Galicia in Spain. Mima tells me that she was very happy with her grandparents. I could sense and feel her love for them as she remembered those times and shared them with me for this book. Tears started to flow from her eyes as described how much they meant to her, growing up without a mother and an absent father. She called them "Papa" and "Mama." She explained, "The love I had for my grandparents was the deepest love I ever experienced in my life! The three of us were one—if we had only one sweet or a cake, we would share it equally. We never started dinner until all three of us were sitting together." Both of her grandparents died in 1942. Her grandmother died on August 13 and her grandfather died on November 10, meaning they were only separated for a short time, right to the very end.

In October 1944, Mima left for Cuba. The ship departed from the port city of Vigo. Following a quick stop the next day in the port city of Cadiz in southern Spain, the ship travelled to New York City. They stayed in New York for three days while the ship loaded and unloaded freight and supplies. Among the supplies were wines, ciders, cognac, and clothes.

The trip from Spain to the Cuban port city of Habana took twenty-five days to complete. Wow! We are spoiled today with our modern air travel. When they arrived in Habana, my mom was met by aunt Genoveva, her father, Domingo, as well as her friend Bernardina, along with her daughter Rosina. Earlier, they had rented a boat to meet her at the entrance to the seaport. The ship was not allowed to dock at the terminal until all the passengers had been cleared by Customs and Immigration.

My aunt Genoveva was the first one to spot my mom, becoming overwhelmed with joy and emotion as she jumped up and down while waiting nervously to hug her. My mom has repeated many times that their reunion was full of both incredible euphoria and melancholy following the loss of her grandparents.

Two days later they left for Jobabo by train—another long trip which would last about sixteen hours. My mother said that the two days in Habana were a godsend, allowing them to rest and enjoy the electrically charged city.

Upon arriving at the train station of Jobabo, it appears that the whole town welcomed her home. The atmosphere was similar to a presidential visit or some famous movie star rolling in for an event. There was a buzz in the air! Among this enormous gathering, my father, Pipo, was anxiously waiting for her at the train station. My aunt Genoveva was a very good friend of his and had told him about her niece and her arrival, so he was more than ready to meet her on that crazy day. My aunt Genoveva introduced him to her as they mutually embraced and kissed each other on the first meeting. From that point on, he would visit her every chance that he got. It was an every night occurrence at aunt Genoveva's home. They usually spent the evening playing Barasca, a popular Spanish card game that I also played with them frequently.

My mother settled down quite nicely with aunt Genoveva and her husband in their restaurant/home. They lived on Maximo Gomez Street, named after the famous Dominican who fought for Cuba's independence against Spain. My mother and Pipo were a very popular twosome in the community.

The courtship did not blossom until three years later when my mother and Pipo started dating officially. According to my mom, it was a wonderful time, and the marriage six years later was even more rewarding. They were married on August 5, 1951, in a civil wedding in Victoria De Las Tunas. Dr. Cuebas presided over the ceremony, which took place at Pipo's older brother's spacious home. Manuel's mansion was fit for a king; it was mostly constructed of cement, with two floors, each divided by a long corridor in the middle for easy access to at least sixteen rooms. In addition, it had two beautiful small terraces in front and a large one overlooking the enormous backyard connecting to the driveway on the side.

Upon my uncle Manuel and aunt Marciana immigrating to America in the mid sixties, this gorgeous home was taken over by the Cuban Socialist/Communist Party and converted into a government office complex. I was about six or seven years old when I witnessed this transformation, as our own home backed onto the garden of my uncle's mansion. I used to climb over the seven-foot high cement wall, spending countless hours talking to and playing games with the construction workers and government officials. They were very nice people who were simply doing their jobs. Many of them repeatedly told me how grandiose and beautiful my uncle's former home was.

At the wedding reception there were many guests having a great time dancing the night away, and Pipo and my mom were at the center of the celebrations. The alcohol, food, and music just kept coming. After the party, Pipo and Mima took a bus to Camaguey, the city where I was born, to stay one night at the luxurious Hotel Plaza. The very next afternoon, they flew to Santa Clara in the province of Villa Clara in northwestern Cuba. From there, they took a taxi to the city of Cienfuegos in the province of Cienfuego. Cienfuegos was a resort town, known for its pristine beaches and abundance of fun activities. They stayed at San Carlos, a five-star hotel, for two weeks. After their incredible honeymoon, they rented a small house in Jobabo in front of the famous La Colonia Española (a Spanish social club), near the main road that went straight to Victoria De Las Tunas.

On October 20, 1952, my brother, Gerardo Juan Ramon Garcia Vina, was born in Chamizo Clinic, in the city of Victoria De Las Tunas. Gerardo became known as Geri or Gerardito by the family, and later Gerry after we had moved to America. For the purposes of this book, I refer to my older brother as Gerardo Jr.

Four or five months after he was born, my brother was baptized one morning. That very same day, my parents prepared an altar in their Jobabo home in preparation to be married by the Catholic Church. This was of paramount importance for my mother. As a devoted Catholic, she felt that their marriage had to be sanctioned by the church in order for them to be fully married in the eyes of God. Father Acha performed the quick ceremony in front of the best man, Florentino, and the maid of honor, Tete Ermida, plus two other witnesses. The ceremony was kept secret from everyone, and it work like a charm.

Later in the afternoon and well into the evening, the street in front of our house and the whole area, including the backyard, was full to capacity, shoulder to shoulder if you will, celebrating a second time around, but with the same joy as the civil wedding a few years earlier. It was a mega party and is well remembered by those who were present for the spontaneous occasion. In small towns, news travels very fast, and when you mention a celebration, people drop whatever they are doing to join in. Add Pipo to the mix of any celebration in town and it resulted in a carnival-like atmosphere. Their unplanned wedding reception took on a life of its own. As people danced and partied, they carried my mother and father on their shoulders through the local streets, revering the happy newlyweds once again. My father's truck full of beers was parked in front of the house, with giant kegs of beer, soft drinks, and liquors being unloaded by friends in a constant, smooth, unbroken chain leading inside the house. The Cuban Afro music was heard many blocks away and drew neighbors far and wide. People flocked to our house in droves to join in on the festivities. People were dancing and drinking, and the aroma of roasting pigs made everyone's mouths water in anticipation. The roasted pig was supplemented with all the typical Spanish and Cuban cuisine that you could think of. The party lasted until the next morning, when the sun came shining down our block. As usual, Pipo loved to socialize and took it all in with delight as he made all the guests feel like this was their party. My parents pulled off a remarkable event with everyone thinking they were celebrating my brother's baptism, not my parent's secret second wedding. The logistics and planning were outstanding, and there was plenty of food and drinks to go around for the many attendees and beyond. My parents were ready for this onslaught of people. In Cuba, Pipo was called "El Hombre" (The Man), but in a humble way that he would always laugh off with sincerity, making them know how much he appreciated their friendship.

I don't know how Pipo did it, but I wish I had 1 percent of his God-given gift with people.

While in Habana, en route to embark on a ship to Spain in June 1953, my mom was notified that her uncle Manolo, the husband of Genoveva, had died. The trip was immediately postponed and they returned to Jobabo to grieve and support the family in a time of incredible loss. The trip was rescheduled for June 1954, the following year.

Shortly after arriving in Leon, Spain, Pipo was met by his nephew Santiago, who was a learned man in farming. Against the wishes of my mom, Santiago persuaded my father to purchase a farm for chicken and pigs in the town of Jarrafe, about ten miles away from the city of Leon. In just two years, the business went downhill because of a severe virus that made the animals fall sick and die at an alarming rate. He had no choice but to sell it back to Santiago, who had sold it to him two years earlier. He was probably the only person who would've taken this failed business from Pipo, because he was the one who had recommended this farm to my father in the first place. My parents lost a large amount of money because of the farm and it put them in a very precarious financial position, resulting in them returning to Jobabo, Cuba, in 1956.

Back in Cuba, my aunt Genoveva and my mother opened a new restaurant in the house. My father helped them until there was an opening in his old job with his brothers at La Comercial in 1958. My mom and aunt continued to work at their successful restaurant. Many times over the years, my aunt and mother confided in me how tired they used to get while working so many hours just to make ends meet. They did receive much pleasure from the great clientele, who kept them well balanced with funny stories.

The war in Cuba was the beginning of the end for the regime of Fulgencio Batista, the president of the country. In December 1958, Che Guevara and his units attacked the stronghold city of Santa Clara Batista, and Batista's forces crumbled.

On January 1, 1959, Batista fled to the Dominican Republic for refuge, leaving Cuba without a leader. Shortly after, this vacuum was filled by Fidel Castro. Castro took total control of the nation, proclaiming that he was now the leader of the new Cuba. Castro became head of the armed forces, "El Comandante" (the commandant). A month later, he became the prime minister, and subsequently "El Presidente" (the president) of Cuba. He had now consolidated all the power in his new reign, which would be the longes reign in the history of Cuba. Castro had an amazing forty-nine year run that ended in 2008 when presidential and constitutional authority was transferred to his brother, Raul Castro, after Fidel Castro fell very ill.

The aftermath of the Revolution resulted in another son for my parents—Miguel Angel Garcia Vina (me), born March 1, 1959, in Camaguey City in the province of Camaguey.

The birth tells me that my parents were pretty busy themselves with their own revolution. It goes without saying that I'm a by-product of both; this constitutes me a staunch revolutionary by nature! However, with the well-being of others in full mind, and to those who are impoverished by the insatiable greediness of others in their relentless pursuit of more...and more...and more...to those scoundrels, I say enough with this accumulation of wealth! Que Viva La Revolucion! (Long live the Revolution!) God is watching, my friends!

In the hospital, Pipo and Elsa Espinille kept my mom company. Pipo was ecstatic, passing the finest Cuban cigars to everyone he came in contact with in the hospital and at work, and buying cases for himself to hand out during his deliveries.

Normal life resumed for my parents, as I hardly cried for my night feedings. My mom said I was never really too much of a crybaby, which makes me happy to know. She said I was a good eater and always finished all my feedings and then some. I guess I wasn't hungry enough to cry for food by the time night came, allowing my parents to catch up on much-needed sleep. Thumbs up for little Miguel!

Soon after he purchased his business, La Agencia (the Agency), Pipo had to give the keys to a government official and was told not intervene in any matter relating to the business. After a lengthy conversation with this official, he was told to expect to come back to work as an employee of the company in the near future, pending a state review.

During Castro's first nine months in power, he passed approximately 1,600 decrees and new laws to accommodate his new vision for Cuba.

In May 1961, Castro cancelled the promised elections and declared the Constitution of 1940 obsolete. In December of that year, he broadcast that Cuba would become a new socialist nation. The new Socialist Cuba would require a reorientation of values. To achieve this goal, Castro and Che Guevara developed the New Man Theory, which called for the development of a new type of citizen. This theory held the belief that Cubans should no longer work for personal profit, but for the welfare of all. Income and benefits, such as medical services and education, would be evenly divided. Under this new political structure, the state would control all government agencies with watch groups to enforce ideological purity. This theory of utopianism was well intended, but unfortunately human beings are greedy and fallible by nature. This results in the endless, foolish cycle of topping each other with more wealth. It caused many unfortunate, dire consequences in our broken society and created much hardship between classes. Since the beginning of civilization, mankind has developed many political and economic model systems; all have failed to deliver us to the promised land of fairness. Mr. Che and others in the past, present, and future must be commended for their vision of equality, but all will come across the same stumbling block; our own irrational proclivities that defeat us every single time we try to improve our human condition. It is us and will always be us! If only we could follow the teaching of Jesus! Our hardened hearts did not even soften for Jesus; what makes anyone think they will change for anyone else?

This madness almost led to complete annihilation of the human race during the Missile Crisis of October 1962. The world was at the very brink of a nuclear war.

In our town of Jobabo, there was a chill in the air. Everyone was glued to the radio broadcasts for latest news, listening to the Voice of America, BBC, and others. During this intense period, I must have developed my first unconscious affection for radio and shortwave, because today I'm a big radio lover and I firmly believe it started with this crisis, watching Pipo intensely tuned in to these life-and-death stories making the news following many natural disasters, such as the hurricanes that frequently invaded the island.

According to my mom, when Pipo got home after making his deliveries, he said that the mood with his friends and customers was so down with concern about the impasse between the two superpowers (America and the Soviet Union) that he had never seen anything like it in his life. He had had many conversations and the common theme was that we were ground zero and likely to all be killed. This verbiage was rampant everywhere he went, he told my mom. They needed something to lift them up, and he would console them by telling them that a war was not going to happen. Nobody was crazy enough to resort to nuclear warfare, no matter how stubborn and fixated they were on their idiotic position. You will see! To distract them, Pipo would throw in a couple of lighthearted tales to loosen up the anxiety and would play a hand or two of dominoes while drinking a beer. He tried to give them a sense of normalcy in a potentially explosive situation. Such was Pipo—always the optimist, helping people cope with uncertainty.

During this period, Pipo was extremely concerned with the severity of a possible war and the impact it would have on us. He was well familiar with the ugliness of war. The crisis that started on October 14 endured two weeks further to October 28, reaching its peak on what is called Black Saturday, when they got very close to war. Pipo remained certain that confrontation would not occur. Sure enough, word came via radio that the American president, Soviet Union Premier Nikita Khrushchev, and Fidel

Castro had reached an agreement at the final hour. The missiles were removed from Cuban soil.

After hearing the greatest news in the world, the city of Jobabo rejoiced in total jubilation. Everyone came out of the houses, embracing each other and celebrating in the streets until the early hours of Monday morning, October 29, 1962.

CHAPTER 6

Life in Jobabo, Cuba

Jobabo was a small city in the province of Las Tunas with simple living at its core. It is known for the first uprising against the Fulgencio Batista government in 1958, whereby Che Guevara and Camilio Cinfuegos came in with troops and set the city free. Sixty years earlier, General Maximo Gomez led Cuba to its independence from Spain.

Our family lived in a medium-size house constructed mainly out of wood. The house had three bedrooms, a spacious living room, a cozy kitchen, two bathrooms, and a garage-type storage building on the side of the house. With many plants in hanging baskets and planted along the front, the house had a very tropical appearance, blending in well with the many trees that we shared with our neighbors in a communal garden. The setting resembled a mini rainforest with a water well in the center for our daily water requirements. The area was very convenient and useful. I would help my parents and aunt Genoveva with these fun chores, such as fetching water, whenever I was playing with my friends.

Initially, we rented the house, but after Castro took power, it was given to us by the government. Not a bad deal!

We lived on Main Street of Maximo De Gomez with our beautiful and sexy housekeeper, Catalina, who was about sixteen years old with gorgeous long black hair. What a pity that I was much too young to even go there. Catalina became part of the family. Her father was renting a small apartment across from our home where Pipo parked his 1954 black Chevy four-door sedan. It was an honest, simple way of life, but I was too young to fully comprehend what my parents already knew. What made it all possible was our unity as a family. Each one of us had our own important role that we excelled in carrying out for the betterment of our future. This is something which today's society lacks very much; the majority of family members focus on themselves, sacrificing the good of the whole family to focus on their own personal gain.

My father worked very hard at his job, making deliveries while my mother and aunt Genoveva took care of my brother, Gerardo Jr., and me. On many occasions, we would have large parties celebrating birthdays, anniversaries, holidays, etc. These festivities were always very grandiose in scale. We normally invited about two hundred guests, but when the delicious food and music got rolling, it seemed like the entire neighborhood naturally joined in our party. Given Pipo's work with spirits, there was never any challenge with the beverages running low!

Speaking about simpler times, there were days when Pipo would take me to various local circles in the city to see the circus and ride with me on the carousel pony, moving up and down as it spun round and round. When the carousel did stop, more often than not, Pipo would get back on the horse to please me, even though he might have been tired or dizzy after working all day. Other times, he told me that since I was big now, I should ride on the carrousel by myself and he would watch me from the side. Each time I went by, he would make a gesture acknowledging me as I proudly smiled and waved back at him. I remember those precious moments as if they were yesterday, and I remember those rides especially well, because it was just my father and I together. After the rides, Pipo would buy me cotton candy, which I loved so much, and we would walk around the place and watch many different shows. That is, if my father didn't get stopped to chat with so many people along the way. I enjoyed the funny clown, as he would make all kinds of weird faces, and Pipo's clowning-around nature interacted playfully with him as well. I would laugh myself silly, watching the two of them trying to top each other with expressions. The tightrope act caught Pipo's attention fully. The crowd watched in complete silence with suspense as I held onto my father's arm until the daredevil made it to the other side safely. Not to be outdone, Pipo entered the strong man competition, with the only thing I remember being the sound of the bell constantly ringing while those gathered applauded. I guess he did pretty well in this game, because at the end he won a prize, which he handed to me. The crowd cheered when he put down the big hammer and dried his sweaty face off with his white handkerchief.

Other times, we went to Bijao River, which was one of our favorite destinations for picnics with family and friends. The river was just ten minutes outside the city along the main road going to Victoria de Las Tunas. These excursions were always highly anticipated by all of us as we enjoyed each other's company. We played catch and jumped in the water, diving underneath as the cold water splashed on top of us. When it was brunch time, we all converged next to each other on the grass near the edge of the river. As we ate the best Spanish egg and potato omelet outside of Spain, we would notice snakes swimming in the water and coming on shore. More often than not, Pipo would scare them away or kill them if they got too close to any of us. This river was very popular with the locals, and at times it got a little too crowded. One thing was a certainty—you always ran into friends there, which added to the fun even more with great music and dancing in this tropical paradise.

Jobabo had a beautiful park in the center of town where one had a clear view of the sugar mill factory's smoke towers in the distance. This was where my father took me bike riding and to fly kites. It was well known by kite fanatics, and flying kites was considered a recreational sport. I spent many hours helping my brother work on his kite for tournaments or just flying it in the park for pleasure. Great times were spent at this park. We would look upward and watch as the blue sky became transformed by a flotilla of kites with intricate designs and bright colors, even attracting the gaze of other onlookers in the park. It was simply spectacular in scope, but one really had to be there to take it all in.

I always used to pass this park on my way to my grandparents' house on the other side of town, as well my uncle Marcelino's house, which was literally a stone's throw away from the famous Colonia De España social club, where my parents were members.

I vividly remember the time I was helping my grandparents at their newsstand store move this rather large and heavy old cabinet away from the wall. It must have weighed a ton; it took us several hours and many tries to untangle this big boy. After we moved it, I went behind the wall and found thousands of coins on the floor. According to some customers at the store who knew a little about coins, a good portion of these old coins were rare. What a find! It was the talk of the town for a few weeks. Pepilla, my grandfather's wife, was more concerned with the mess and wanted to shove the coins quickly back underneath the cabinet for aesthetic reasons. I also had a great time in their big yard. My brother and I used to play with this old pedal go-cart, pushing each other round and round endlessly as fast as we could get it to go, which was still slow! Grandfather Domingo would come and make it go faster by pushing it while running full speed until fatigue overcame him and he returned inside for a rest and some cold water.

One of my prized possessions at this time was a pet I had. It was really a chicken which had been given to my brother. He and I took good care of her and she was like a member of the family.

Traveling in Jobabo with Pipo was never boring, as he was known by practically the entire city. It felt like every time we got out of our automobile, we would be stopped by people for long chats. The best part was that I always seemed to get barraged with free drinks and snacks by all these people along the way. These trips with Pipo were always filled with excitement as we made our way around most of the city. Upon returning home, my mom would quiz my father on what had taken him so long!

The only unpleasant thing I remember was the time I fell down from a tree and landed on top of a glass, which punctured my sneakers and gave me a deep wound that needed twenty stitches to close. In Cuba, getting stitches done was a very painful procedure for anyone. Man, did it hurt! I can still remember the sharp pain as the doctor closed up my foot, stitch by stitch. Pipo and my mom tried to keep me under control as I screamed my lungs out! Earlier, Pipo had been very upset with me when he heard the news of my accident. This was a serious cut. He strongly scolded me for not being more careful while playing with my friends. Earlier in the week, I had fallen from my bike and badly scraped my skin off my legs and knees, resulting in a lot of bleeding. My wild tendencies had me jumping over fences and climbing trees every chance that I got, totally oblivious to the possibility of getting hurt. But when I did get hurt, I had to suffer the repercussions of not going to school or being allowed to play with my friends for some time. When I was told of this dire news of not being allowed outside, my eyes became teary. Without saying much, Pipo noticed and explained, "This happened to you because you just don't listen. You are too stubborn, Miguel!" In the house, while I was nursing my foot, I was constantly being looked after by my parents, aunt Genoveva, my brother, Gerardo Jr., and Catalina because I could not put any pressure on my foot until the stitches came out roughly two weeks later. During this time, my grandparents gave me a beautiful coloring book with some wooden crayons. For the next few weeks I stayed at home coloring, playing Chinese checkers, Parcheesi, dominos, and Barajas (a Spanish card game). I also did puzzles, watched lots of my favorite cartoons on the television, and learned to play chess with my father, Pipo. All in all, aside from my immobility and the pain of removing my stitches; it wasn't too bad being stuck at home because I had my family and friends with me.

I learned to play chess so well during my recuperation that my father took me a friendly match with friends and family. My first game was against this tall thin man who my father thought I had a good chance to beat. I was on cloud nine hearing this from my hero and onlookers alike, cheering me on with every move. At that time I was only about six years old, and the player I was against was a regular, good player himself. However, after months of playing with Pipo, I was pretty good at formulating strategy and thinking a few moves ahead, as my father had shown me. With the crowd on my side, I could hear amusing remarks being muttered toward my opponent, like, "You're getting beaten by a six-year-old kid!"

While my father, Pipo, and everyone in the room were laughing at my surgeonlike maneuvers, I was taking away my opponent's pieces one by one until I decided to go for checkmate. I ended the game with the final kill position to his king. Even though he couldn't believe what had just happened, he shook my hands and said, "The better man won." He hurried away, looking flustered. This was my first game against someone other than my father, and I had been victorious, thanks to Pipo's teaching.

After winning, I jumped up from my chair and received handshakes from those in the crowd, not to mention from Pipo, who said, "I told you guys my son Miguel could beat him with no help."

We stayed there about three hours, watching and talking about other games that were played. Before leaving, the man whom I had beaten earlier approached me and uttered the words, "I want a rematch!"

I said, "Yes!" and shook his hands again with a smile. I was glad that I beat him because I had wanted to do it for my hero, Pipo. Needless to say, we played again and again with similar results. Over time, my game improved so much that I became a top-tier player, losing only to the very best.

As we left the room that night, my father grabbed my head and patted me on the back, saying, "Let's go home and tell your mother all about it!" That night was the genesis of my passion for chess, and having my father there made the experience and the memories of that night extra special. As I got older, I excelled at the game often beating the best player in town. Unfortunately, this included my guru as well…sorry, Pipo, I had a great teacher…I'm smiling and looking up at a photo of Pipo on the wall in front of me as I write this sentence.

While we lived in Jobabo, we would often go on vacation to Santa Lucia De Gebara beach. One time there, we decided to take a long walk together to explore a region a couple of miles away from where we normally stayed. There was a beach there that we had longed to visit, but never had until now. It was a rough area, not smooth like the one we left behind with silky white sand. As we walked alongside each other on top of the wet sand, just outside the reach of the small waves, we marveled at the many exotic shells passing by our footprints. This area of the beach was abandoned and there were no people as far as the eye could see. The sand was rough with many big, boulderlike rocks buried half way into the sandy ground. It was tough going and hard on our bare feet. At times, we had to stop and soak our feet in the water because the top part of the sand was so hot that it would burn us unless we ran down to the water to cool off. As we walked farther and farther away, we started to lose sight of our beach camp behind us. At this point, we started to notice a flock of black birds flying low and circling the area. I asked what was going on out there. Pipo said, "Probably some dead animal or fish of some sort." I was mesmerized by the soothing tranquility in this area with Pipo at my side, but I also sensed some type of unknown danger out there, some form of evil lurking in this desolate beach terrain with weird-looking trees. I had an eerie feeling; I just could not shake it off for some reason. These feelings have been so innate and strong to me over my lifetime that every time I have had them, I knew that something bad would surely come to fruition. Well, keep your fingers crossed about what lay ahead in our journey…

At this point, we had to be at least four miles away from our camp. There was nothing in front of or behind us, so we might as well go to the farthest point before calling it a day. Turning back now would have been a long undertaking itself. We proceeded to increase our pace toward the area we hoped to reach. I could not believe the picturesque duplicity of this secluded region. I was very perplexed because I had those bad vibes again and they were stronger in the midst of all nature's glory. The scene reminded me of the colorful paintings inside those famous Cuban cigar boxes. As we begun to get closer to the point, we started to see all this debris washing up on the shore. We could smell the penetrating odor of dead animals. And sure enough, we started to see various types of dead fish, crabs, and birds literally lying on top of each other while these big black birds nosedived in a continue flow to yank large chunks of rotting meat from them. There had to be thousands of these black birds preying on the dead animals. It was similar to one of those scary Alfred Hitchcock or *Twilight Zone* movie scenes. This was just the beginning of our odyssey, and what we were about to experience and witness as we went forward was mind shattering and too incredible to ever forget. We started to hear even more screeching noises in the distance; it was other birds joining the many black ones already in the sky. We were dumbfounded by what was going on. They appeared to be at war with each other for territorial supremacy of some sort or some other unknown reason. It was a mystery; it was like the devil himself was in control of these savage birds above us. It was also a complete mystery to Pipo, as I constantly barraged him with questions about the cause of this phenomenon. Soon enough, all the answers to my many inquiries would be revealed.

We began to move upward past the dunes onto higher land, away from the shoreline to avoid any possible direct conflict with these rabies-infected birds. My father was concerned that they might attack us and poke an eye out if we got to close to them. Under these conditions, he felt we should stay a few hundred feet away from the water for safety reasons. Upon climbing the ten-foot sand dunes, we came to an area that looked like a wildlife refuge for migrant birds. This area was rough, with many stones, plants, bushes, ocean debris, and abandoned boats. It all looked very serene. We could almost taste the higher concentration of saltiness in the air. From this point on, we began to walk straight back to the ocean and over the elevated mountain terrain, and we came into full view of what was causing the curious situation. Standing and looking directly down, we could see the beautiful blue ocean in front of us with the horizontal sun rays bouncing off the water. Nature's beauty was unfolding before our very eyes. However, our appreciation quickly dampened when we saw an eye-shattering creature lying on top of the wet sand with small waves lapping against it. It was a whale who had died and floated to shore, or who had beached itself on the sand and died. It was goliath in size—about forty feet in length. What an imposing mammal to see up close. Our first impression was one of disbelief that I can still recall even today. The worst part was all the birds devouring this poor creature one bite at a time. As we approached the dead whale, we saw chunks of meat everywhere nearby. The feisty birds paid no attention to us at all, carrying on indulging their hearty appetites. We got to about twenty feet from the whale when Pipo and I noticed that its bottom section was all eaten away, while the top portion only had deep wounds caused by the birds we saw sitting on top and munching away. The bottom had to have been eaten by other sharks or mammals before it drifted to shore, so we thought. That still did not explain all those big chunks of fresh meat we first saw all around the area. We could even see thousands of little fish biting away at the section of the whale which lay in the water. It was an incredible sight! The entire scene looked like a slaughterhouse gone mad. It was so gory and disgusting. We left for higher ground, because I was getting sick of watching and smelling the rotting flesh. I was ready to vomit if we did not leave immediately.

About two hundred yards away, we found a nice location to pause and take a little siesta before the long four-mile hike back to our beach area, where my mom, brother, aunt Genoveva, and Catalina were waiting to catch up with us. After an hour or so we got up and wandered around the sandy terrain to pick up some stones. Pipo started throwing them toward the ocean about two hundred feet away in the distance. We played this game for fifteen minutes to see who threw the rocks the farthest and made the biggest splash in the water. During our walk, we were amazed at all the beautiful shells and pebbles surrounding us. We would pick them up and examine their contours and rainbow-colored patterns. We were so caught up with this activity we became engulfed in the hidden paradise, which seemed uninhabited by any people. It was a gem of a place. Suddenly, Pipo yelled at me and said, "Miguel, no te mueva ni mire para bajo" (Mike, don't move or look down), and before I was able to even react, my father came running at me from behind and picked me up. He ran for both our lives as I had been standing on top of a crocodile. The reptile woke up from a deep sleep, apparently startled, and went after us as Pipo zigzagged our way out of danger. He ran relentlessly for a few minutes, carrying me to safety. We had veered off to a crocodile's nest without even realizing where we were. Again, we were fortunate that the crocodile had been overstuffed with food and was in a deep sleep, resting from the eating frenzy around the whale. If not, I surely would have been eaten by that ten-foot-long animal.

The mystery of the beached whale had finally been revealed and our curiosity had been fully satisfied, but Pipo berated me for my lack of attention to my surroundings. He stressed how important it was to always be aware of my surroundings to ensure my own safety. That incident served as a very valuable lesson to me, and it is one which I have certainly incorporated in my adventures ever since. I still give thanks to Pipo's lesson that day (and for rescuing me from the jaws of death). These tendencies have helped me to avoid serious car accidents, falling rocks, and getting sucked into a jet blast at my job at United/ Continental Airlines as a ramp & customer service agent in Newark Liberty International Airport. Today, this vigilance is more indispensable than ever before, particularly following the September 11, 2001, terrorist attack on our country. I'm able to keep the flying public safer, as well as taking care of the work environment for colleagues and myself.

I clearly already had a subconscious ability for picking up bad vibes, as evidenced by my premonitions of danger during this walk. All I needed was for Pipo to cultivate this ability in me. This awareness is particularly valuable when travelling through nature, which has a constant offensive against us, not just through crocodiles, but in many other forms, too.

When we returned to the camp, I never mentioned the crocodile ordeal to my mom or anyone back there. I knew she would have flipped out and it would have poisoned our weekend vacation. It was my little secret with Pipo and we never shared it with anyone. Well, up until now—the secret is finally out of the bag!

In the months ahead, we never went back to that section of the beach. All the same, we always kept a watchful eye on the family as they often slept and rested on this public beach. It was a disconcerting thought that there were big crocs, one of which almost ate me, only four miles away. They could crawl near us uninvited at any time, looking for food.

From Jobabo, we also went on day trips to the countryside to visit friends at a farm called Caballeria. We all always looked forward to these visits. The area was about thirty-five or so miles away from our home off the central main road that connected the island from top to toe. We would leave very early in the morning in Pipo's work truck and stay late into the evening. On the way there, we saw endless fields of corn, potatoes, cotton, and sugar cane, all surrounded by coconuts and palm trees. On these trips, my brother and I helped our father load two giant silver kegs of beer, soft drinks, and some bottles of rum and cognac. Once there, the host would roast the traditional Cuban suckling pig, along with other dishes like yucca (casava), black beans, plantains, white rice, and some avocado salads. The best part was munching on the delicious crispy skin as the pig turned on the spit. My favorite part was the tail, for some unknown reason. While the pig roasted away on the fire, we took rides in the back of an open truck. It was very bumpy, but fun, as we stopped several times to talk to the local workers working in the fields. On one particular stop, we jumped off and walked deep into a sugarcane field and began to help the workers cut the crop. They showed us the proper way to use a sickle. This sickle was considered a true symbol of the working class, as evidenced by the former Soviet Union flag, which had a hammer and sickle. At first, it was a lot of fun helping the workers, but after some time beneath the hot sun, it became very tiresome. Everyone was cutting away, about ten of us in total. To quench our thirst, the locals began to peel individual sugarcane sticks and hand them to us. The sugarcane was so tasty and fresh! We went underneath several palm trees to suck in the juice to cool off from the hot sun. Our new friends gave us several sticks of cane to take back to the family. Before we left, Pipo invited the peasants to join us at the farm for the evening's festivities after work.

After a few hours, we returned to the delicious smell of roasted pork in the air. Our mouths drooled at the savory smell in anticipation. The inviting sound of Cuban music playing traditional songs was in full swing as we dismounted from our truck. You could hear the popular song "Guantanamera" in the background. With the greenish palm trees, cigar smoking, drinking rum and beer, and a crystal blue sky to go with all of it, you had the Cuba that my father Pipo and family knew and loved so dearly. It was Cuba at its finest! Sharing good times with friends and family in a communal way—this was what Cuba was like in Pipo's time. We were living life to the fullest, under the ever-present theme of simplicity and humility, and we were fully content. Living for today and enjoying each other's precious company should be our number one goal, but how often do we forget this or give credit to how fulfilling this way of life can be?

During this trip, my aunt Genoveva purchased two cows for my brother and me as gifts, and had them stay there at the farm. After they produced several calves and we had moved to Victoria De Las Tunas, she then sold them to the farmer because they had become part of their family. My aunt explained her decision to my brother and me. It was not really a big deal for me, since every time we visited my former pet cows I felt the same joy, regardless of who owned them. They were known for producing lots of milk and were well taken care of due to their cooperation. They were cash cows in all senses of the words.

One evening while we were all sitting home watching a program on our old black-and-white television set, my mom began running toward us and screaming hysterically like she had seen a ghost. After Pipo and Genoveva calmed her down a bit, she pointed to the squeaky wooden floor near the door to her bedroom and said, "Do you see what I see? It's a spider!" Not believing my mom, at first, we thought it was a small harmless frog lying on the floor. In reality, it was nothing as mundane as that, it was a killer predator spider! It was large, dark brown, and very hairy. Both my parents looked for something to kill it with. After finding a couple of brooms in the kitchen closet, they came running back quickly and started to smash this nasty-looking creature for a solid two minutes, while we all watched this drama come to a happy and safe ending (for us, at least). After it was killed, my father, Pipo, picked it up in a shovel with one scoop and disposed of it in the trash can outside, near our car garage. Looking back now, it was a hilarious spectacle. My parents were chasing after the spider like a pair of deranged lunatics, jumping up and down and shouting at each other as they pulverized the poor spider. My aunt Genoveva was trying to be helpful with directions and advice from the side of the room, all while Catalina, my brother, and I were laughing hysterically.

This uncontrollable laughter by Catalina was short lived, as a few days later she became the victim of a similar incident herself, just with a different host. If you thought my parents' episode of smashing the jumping spider was funny, this one was the ultimate event of all the ages. You couldn't make this stuff up even if you tried! The previous night, Catalina had complained to my mom that she was not able to sleep at all because of some rattling noise emanating from one of the large wooden chests that my parents had purchased to sail from Cuba to Spain and back. They contained our winter clothes, blankets, and other items for safe keeping. Upon hearing Catalina's concern about all the noise, my mom went with her to the bedroom to try and help calm her fears. After listening for five minutes together next to the two crates, they heard nothing, nada, not even a whisper. They decided to investigate further by placing the top one on the floor so that they could open it up and check for the source of the problem. After removing all the items from the first chest and finding nothing, they began to open the second chest. Suddenly, two big black rats jumped out onto the wooden floor! One ran off to the bathroom and disappeared through the drainage pipes. The other one somehow sneaked inside Catalina's pants so quickly that it caught her off guard and she was helpless to stop it. My mother screamed and ran toward the living room, grabbing the attention of Pipo and the rest of us to tell us what had happened. Catalina was trailing right behind her, screaming her lungs out and desperately trying to push down on the rat from the outside of her pants as it was stuck in her hips. At first, we were bewildered by her motions as she threw herself relentlessly on the floor. Then we found out that she had a rat caught inside her pants! She begun to loosen her pants at a fever pitch, jumping and shaking her torso until the only thing she had left on was her white bloomers. The ugly rat with the big fat tail rolled out of her pants (that now lay on the floor) and it ran across the room, disappearing into the darkness. Catalina was exhausted and frightened to death as she tried to recapture her composure by running to her bedroom to calm down and put her clothes back on. She reminded me of someone performing the rumba at the carnival, but one hundred times more intense. It was the show of all shows and we had the laugh of a lifetime at her expense. In reality, we have all had our share of bad experiences at one time or another with these different creatures that are as common in Cuba as a fly in most domestic homes in America. It was actually a miracle that Catalina did not get bitten by the rotten rat. Ten minutes later, she returned to the living room and apologized to Pipo and us for her provocative outbreak earlier. Pipo comforted her with a bright smile and said, "In all my years I've never seen anyone shake their hips and legs so fast that their pants literally flew off." Catalina smiled back before retiring to her bedroom for the night.

I guess the old saying is true—never laugh at another person's misfortune too much, because your time will come…just wait and see.

A couple of weeks later, my mom spotted some little holes in the wooden floor of our house. Through one hole in particular, she saw the head of a snake! She told our neighbor Augenio, who was visiting at the time, all about what she had seen. Augenio ran to his truck and grabbed his machete. He told my mom and us kids to leave the area as he quietly staked out the snake while sitting about five feet away from the hole. Within ten minutes, the snake popped up fully, and quick as lightning, Augenio swung downward toward the floor, cutting the snake in half before calling us to come and see! We children were fascinated, but my mom covered her eyes to avoid seeing the aftermath. The very next day, my mom went on a mission and told us to help cover every single hole in the house with cement, wood, or anything we could find. Too many of these creatures seemed to have a free pass into our home and she said this had to stop. After hearing my mom's concerned my father took upon himself to cover every possible hole he could find on kis knees. He even kidded with us serveral times of seeing these creatures trying to come inside the house while he was patching away. Something that my mom was not very amused or wanted to hear. However, my father's joking and kidding personality was so funny that my brother, aunt Genoveva and our, house keeper Catalina and I could not hold back our contagious laugh, obviously at my mom's expense.

In Jobabo, living with spiders, rats, mosquitoes, frogs, lizards, snakes, and other creatures is just part of the landscape in a tropical paradise, but let's not forget the biggest foe that nature throws at us. You guessed right if you said hurricanes… the mighty hurricanes that invade us with unrelenting wrath much too frequently.

One of my earliest childhood recollections of Pipo is centered on the epic impact of Hurricane Flora in early October 1963. It was a category five storm and it first hit land in the southeastern part of the island, about 120 miles away from Jobabo at Guantanamo Bay. (This is where the American naval base is located, housing the Al-Qaeda terrorists. It has been widely covered by the news media for the past few years for alleged human rights abuses by President Bush's administration. President Obama promised to permanently shut it down in 2010). Flora was the fifth deadliest hurricane in recorded history to hit the Atlantic and, sure enough, the deadliest to hit Cuba. About fifteen hundred Cubans lost their lives to this killer storm after it had already killed over six thousand in Haiti and almost a thousand more in the Dominican Republic. What made this category five storm even more powerful than others was that it looped around the island twice and stalled above it for three days. It brought close to two massive floods per hour. The floods combined with gale force winds, resulting in unprecedented devastation.

Before the hurricane hit land, my father, Pipo, and my brother, Gerardo Jr., were busy getting ready for the storm by going to various hardware stores around town to purchase supplies. Everywhere, you could hear constant tapping noises from the people as they hammered away, boarding up their homes to make them sturdier against the incoming heavy winds. When Pipo and Gerardo Jr. returned home, I helped them unload the plywood, boxes of nails, candles, barrels of water, food, and other essentials for our home. I was my father's proud little assistant, tagging along as he nailed plywood on all of our doors and windows to secure our home from the heavy winds that had already begun to increase in speed while we worked diligently. My main job was to give Pipo the nails when he requested them. During the rush to get done nailing as quickly as possible, he smashed his left thumb hard with the hammer. The hammer and nails fell to the ground and Pipo mumbled, "Me cago en la leche en la madre que te pario (I shit on milk and the mother who gave birth to you)." This was an old Spanish exclamation proclaiming disgust. I remember that Pipo was in severe pain after he climbed down from the ladder. I could see his thumb turning black quickly. He told me to run inside the house and get some ice to put on his finger. After a few minutes, we resumed the job at hand.

Upon completion of our home, the entire family went over to our neighbor Roberto's home, which was a one-level, solid brick dwelling with a store on the side. Roberto's house was about a hundred yards away from our home. As we hurriedly walked to our safe haven, the sky above was turning dark and ominous and the wind was starting to make a whistling sound. As we entered Roberto's home, I quickly noticed how crowded it was. People were lying all over the floor, sleeping, talking, and many babies and children were screaming in fear.

As Flora began its assault on our town, my mom yelled at Pipo several times because he insisted on running back and forth to our house, checking whether there had been any damage yet. As I was drinking milk from the bottle, my mom yelled at Pipo on his way out, "Estas loco o que (Are you crazy or what)?" My father did not pay any attention to her as she pleaded with him to stay at Roberto's house, safe with the rest of the family. Pipo was determined to follow his instincts for a while and check on the status of our house until it became too dangerous. I guess he was a little stubborn at first, but he knew his limit and nature's strength. I heard the wind blowing really hard and shaking the entire structure of the house. People began to worry and panic. At this time, Pipo yelled to grab the attention of everyone who was screaming and crying. He assured them that Roberto's house was constructed from reinforced cement and solid bricks strong enough to handle the wind and any flying debris that might slam into the exterior of the house. After this pep talk, Pipo volunteered to go outside to his car, which was in the garage, to check for any news on the hurricane, since we had no working radio in the house due to an electricity cut.

As he was walking toward the front door, I sprung loose from my mom's grasp and ran after Pipo, grabbing his hands. I said, "I want to go with you!" to which he replied, "No son, it's too dangerous for you! You can't go with me now, but maybe later on when the storm calms down a little bit more."

I was persistent in my desire to be with him and insisted, "I want to go with you, Pipo."

Despite my sad face, Pipo refused to let me join him, saying, "No! No! And no! You cannot go!" His strong affirmation that I was not allowed to go with him made me cry, because he was my hero and I did not want to be separated from him at any cost. In retrospect, he was certainly correct and I was obviously naïve and stubborn as a young child. However, my motives were so pure and innocent that Pipo lovingly understood why I wanted to be with him, no matter what dangers stood in front of us. I did everything possible to not let go of his hands. I even held on to his left leg with my two little hands in a tight bear hug. My mom, hearing me cry, came to take me away with her, but I wouldn't budge an inch. My resilience finally paid dividends despite them trying to trick me by offering me Lifesavers (my favorite candy) and a great story. However, I was not fooled. I loved Pipo so much that I did not want to be apart from him even though they kept giving me food or toys to play with. This drama went on for a good twenty-minute period before it was finally resolved to my liking. Pipo said, "Esta bien (OK), you can come with me, but listen very carefully. You must hold on to me as hard as you can, hijo (son)."

I replied, "Yes, padre (father)," with the biggest smile a kid could ever have.

My father picked me up and held me tight as three men pushed forward and opened the front door. We ran about a hundred feet very close to the ground, toward my father's car, until we reached the passenger side. Once there, he put me down and said, "Now hold on to my leg with both your hands and I will hold you with one of my hands, esta bien?"

"Si padre!" I said. He used his other hand to grab the keys out of his front pocket. It was very trying for Pipo because the wind was blowing so hard that the car was shaking and bouncing around, making it difficult to get the key in the lock.

He then handed me the flashlight and pointed to the keyhole and said, "Hold on tight!" During all this, the heavy rain blinded us completely and the streets light were flickering. We also heard nearby transformers making power surge noises. It was very scary to say the least. It took Pipo a good three minutes to finally get it in and open the door of the car parked in the open garage which had only a roof and no sides. Once inside the car, he turned on the radio, but had trouble finding a clear station to hear the news. In the meantime, we looked outside and could see electrical wires sparkling on the ground like fireworks on the Fourth of July. We also saw a big tree bending like a rubber band, ready to break in half, about two hundred feet away. My father constantly reminded me to stay down on the floor of the car because all around, flying debris was crashing into houses and trees. He was concerned, rightfully so, as it was just a matter of time before we would be hit by debris ourselves.

Finally, Pipo was able to tune into a station clearly enough to get the latest report on the storm. He told me, "Miguel, silencio por dos minutos para oir las noticias (Mike, silence for a couple of minutes so I can hear the news)." I did as he had requested and kept silent on the floor of the car. A few minutes later he said, "Hijo tenemos que estar alerto de todo eso zin de los techos de las casas que esta volando y tambien los senales de trafico que son de metales y que son muy peligroso (Son, we have to be careful of all the flying zinc from the rooftops of the houses and the metal traffic signs that are very dangerous)." The broadcasters were warning the population of decapitation by these flying objects. I acknowledged him, shaking my head fervently in agreement. We stayed in the car for about twenty minutes, listening to the news, just my hero, Pipo, and I together, as it should be. I believe this event also introduced me to my love of the radio, and I'm still hooked on listening to it up to this day. During that time with Pipo in the car, I felt very safe and protected and wouldn't have wanted to be in any other place in the world than with my father.

After Hurricane Flora was over, we embraced our family, friends, and neighbors at Roberto's home and left for our own home to return to some normalcy. The damage to our home was minimal considering the size and strength of the hurricane. We had a few zinc plates missing from our roof, collapsed trees in front of the house, and a ton of mixed debris scattered everywhere.

Pipo did a fine job in preparing for Flora, and I was proud to have helped. I remember going over the grounds inspecting the damage with my family when my friends from the neighborhood came racing toward me and told me that a big tree had fallen down about 150 feet away from our house across the backyard of our neighbor Candida. My parents wanted to chop it up into small pieces to get rid of it, but I was able to plead with aunt Genoveva and convinced her to get my parents to leave it in place until the leaves dried up. My friends and I played and climbed on that big tree for about a month until it was cut up by the city. What fun we had! That tree was like a treehouse, with so many branches that you could hide in with no one ever knowing you were in there. I wanted to preserve this fabulous tree in my memory. Long after it was gone, I took a picture with my aunt and my brother that I still cherish with fond memories.

Later on, my father and I took a walk around the neighborhood to check on our friends. There were no fatalities, only a few injuries, thanks be to God. However, there was a lot of destruction; the streets were covered with zinc plates peeled off rooftops by the heavy winds, and there were fallen trees and light poles with loose live wires creating havoc for the cleanup. My father, as always, did his part, volunteering his time to help with the cleanup, and he also donated refreshments from his business La Comercial to the community that was cut off from receiving supplies. I, as usual, followed my hero everywhere he went. I was his proud little assistant. The Bihau and Jobabo and one other river had overflown and blocked the movement of any goods and services coming in and out of our small town. I remember us looking down the street along our house into the distance and seeing one of the fields flooded. At that time, we didn't realize that our town had been completely surrounded by water from the three rivers, which had burst their banks. Nothing could get in or out of the town by the usual means, so the military had to bring food and water in with helicopters and amphibious vehicles. This lasted almost a week. My father's goal was providing shelter for the family during this time. His entire focus was on protecting us from any harm, and this showed the true essence of my great father—his first impulse was always to think about us and not himself in any time of need. We could always count on him for almost divine protection. It felt like he had an insight on what was about to hit us, as the hurricane was like no other storm that had ever hit the island before. I remember my father's stern words telling us that it was going to be a bad hurricane. As we were living in a nice wooden house with a tin roof, my father had said there was no way we could stay in it. Our friends that lived across the street had just build a nice concrete and block house, and as the winds started to pick up, they invited us to share their shelter, so we packed up and went across the street to their solid house. Finally, the hurricane hit, and you could hear the wind and trees falling over while we just sat on the floor away from the windows and doors. The rain was very hard and we could hear the tin roofs being ripped up from the houses. The loose pieces of tin were flying like flying all over town. My father had had a vision of all this, and he took immediate action. Off we went to wait out the hurricane where he thought it was safe enough for us.

Today, every time I hear about hurricanes or I'm in the middle of a heavy, torrential storm, I recall that special moment I spent with Pipo battling all the elements in that crisis, which united us even more as a community and a family. My father was a true servant back then when it really counted. It did not matter whether it was a crisis with the magnitude of Flora or just a friend needing some money to pay for something; he was always there, ready to say yes and help. How often do we today turn down a desperate request in the time of need by a brother, sister, friend, colleague, or stranger because we are only thinking about our selfish interests and no one else's? The answer is, just about always. Pipo never shared this attitude. The very core of his heart and soul was sympathetic to the struggles of those around him, and he felt their needs as if they were his own. This is why he was loved so much by everyone and never criticized, because criticizing him would have been tantamount to criticizing themselves, and nobody wants to do that because we love ourselves too much. Pipo had the ability to transcend pettiness and look at the big picture instead without missing a beat. I, as his little assistant, have tried to the best of my ability to follow in the footsteps of my hero by continuing to serve my brothers and sisters in their time of need, often without it even being solicited by them. This is the engine that makes the world jump with pure joy. So come on, brothers—let's not lose any more time. Join the Pipo express train and let's leave the biggest imprint we can by serving each other in perfect matrimony. I will, and I hope you will, too.

Hurricane Flora represented to me the very beginning of a bond which will last for eternity. In the Spanish language, if you take away the *A* in Flora, you get the word *flor,* meaning flower, representing nature's inner natural beauty in creation and vitality (as exposed to us in the many beautiful flowers). In this vastness of floweriness, my father, Pipo, was a fully blossomed flower that changed the world for the better in but one life cycle.

It's only fitting that on the day when my father was buried, it rained and rained and rained. It felt similar to the heavy rains of Hurricane Flora once again, but this time I was not four and a half; I was a grown man of twenty-six. The absence of Pipo by my side was intrinsically obvious to me on that fateful day. I was deeply saddened, as you can imagine. I tried to hold back my tears, but I could not, like the moment I held onto my father's leg to go with him to the car and started crying because he wouldn't let me go with him at first in light of the heavy rains and wind. This time, I knew that Pipo was in control of the heavy rains and I was very safe; he was telling me, "Son, I am right here with you in spirit just like I was there before in the flesh. Don't ever be afraid. I will always look out for your well-being; you are my little assistant forever." Well, maybe not so little anymore...

From that point on, I felt truly mentally liberated to move on with life. A newfound peace overcame me miraculously; it enlightened me to the very fact that Pipo would be with me in spirit twenty-four hours a day, seven days a week, an arm's length away, if I only called on him.

As we all know, water and wind are in constant flow and motion; sometimes they almost appear to be standing still, but upon closer scrutiny we see they really aren't. The spirit of my father, Pipo, is like that, always in motion in my direction and I in his.

CHAPTER 7

Drunks and a Zipper

Just about every couple of months, my aunt Genoveva, brother, Gerardo Jr., mom, Maria, my father, Pipo, and I would travel to Puerto Padre for a day, weekend, or week for some family fun and recreation. This port city is in Las Tunas Province and was known for its many sugar mills; however, that era has faded into ancient history and has given way today to one that is more dependent on tourism. It has become a modern and trendy tourist destination for many Cubans and world travelers, except for Americans, who are still prohibited to travel to the island freely because of US-imposed sanctions in the early 1960s to punish the government of Fidel Castro. In retrospect, this has hurt the Cuban people a lot more than you could ever imagine. If the idea was to remove Castro from power, it did not work. This insane policy resulted in many people going hungry and dying due to extreme shortages in essential items like medicine. I just hope that the Obama administration changes this archaic policy soon and doesn't drag its feet much longer by posturing or paying lip service in appeasing those hardliners which are crucial in any presidential election state. Treating Cuba just like any other country is long overdue; time will tell if Obama has the fortitude to lead and draw a hard line in the sand, if you will, that has been blowing in the wind for too many years over too many previous administrations.

Our trip to Puerto Padre started from Jobabo in Pipo's 1954 Chevrolet black sedan automobile. Along the way of our two-hour trip, there were amazing stories being told by my parents and my aunt Genoveva, as well as a lot of shenanigans between my brother and me. All of this was in aid of making the journey pass by quicker. Among our shenanigans was my brother constantly whispering in my ears that Pipo was driving too slowly and he should drive faster because, at that snail's pace, we would never make it there. I took my brother's message to heart and told my father to drive faster. This constant bombardment by me was relentless, as my brother kept feeding me lines with which to aggravate Pipo until his patience began to weaken. In the meantime, my brother started to laugh so uncontrollably that my mom and aunt were simultaneously making facial signs to cut out whatever we were doing. After much horsing around with Pipo, he finally erupted in a high-pitched voice and said, "Enough is enough! If this behavior doesn't stop now, I will turn this car around and go back home and the both of you will be punished and not be allowed to play with friends." After his ultimatums on many of these trips, a silence would usually spread rapidly inside the car and last for the next hour or so as we conformed to his demand. Then, to perhaps avoid getting Pipo more upset, I would go into my own little world by turning around in the backseat and placing my face near the rear window glass to look upward into the sky and follow cloud formations. This was an activity that I enjoyed doing from anywhere, growing up in Cuba. There were many images coming and going continuously in the sky as we drove to Puerto Padre. What I was always intrigued by was my earnest determination to see God peeking through the many clouds above. A couple of times, I thought I saw him reveal himself to me for a few seconds, but to no one else in the car, as I pointed to where he was in the sky to show my family. Whenever I saw him, I said, "Thank you for mommy and daddy, and sorry for making Pipo upset." I would also pledge to be a good boy for the duration of the trip. As a result of the vision I saw in the sky, the remaining time in the car was tranquil and I was well behaved to the very end, along with my brother. However, the reality was and always will be that it's a very difficult task indeed to keep a young boy, like I was, still in a compact environment for any length of time. And I was no different from any normal, restless, and explorative boy making his way through nature's maturation cycle. Sometimes as adults we are too caught up in our daily task of work and responsibility that we lose sight of what it is to be a child, who learns by trial and error. It's worth remembering our own experiences during those times as well so we can be more childlike. The truth is that we all remain a child inside anyway, but pretend to be adults in public. Never admitting to our innate dispositions of who we really are is a mistake we shouldn't make too often.

The funny thing about Pipo was that he drove like an old turtle. Man, he was slow! He has actually been stopped several times in Cuba and in America and given a warning, and on one occasion was issued a ticket for not meeting the minimum speed limits. I kid you not!

As we got closer to our destination, we started to notice sand dunes along the white rocky road, a drop in temperature, and the smell of salt water in the air. Plus, in the far horizon, as you start going downhill, you can't help but be awed by the picturesque, panoramic view of the blue ocean staring you right in the face until the road levels off and the view disappears. On most days, the water was calm, but other times it was very choppy and you could see heavy waves. As always, in the background was the rising sun, reflecting its brightness and glare in the water. During all these trips, we never took one single photo; how very unfortunate, because it was one of the most impressive views I have ever witnessed. I shall never forget the view as we were just minutes away from reaching our destination in Puerto Padre and checking in at the hotel in an area not too far away that we called El

61

Sucucho because of a few buildings with fishermen that sold the day's fresh catch around ten in the morning.

We proceeded to the pier to board a commuter boat that was always docked thirty yards away from the hotel. Sometimes it had over a hundred passengers for the crossing. It took only about ten minutes to complete the short journey over the deep bay of Puerto Padre before reaching Llanita beach. This beach was Varadero, the most acclaimed beach resort in Cuba then and now. It was described by many as the closest thing to paradise that you can get on earth.

The people, mostly locals from Las Tunas Province, were good natured and quite hospitable toward one another. We were constantly invited to share food, drinks, and good times with others. You always seemed to find someone to help you with just about everything, as my mom tells me. If you needed to know where the best fish to buy was, they would come with you and show you. If you need some rice, beach clothes, or a floating tube for me, it was the same. Afterward, we would receive an open invitation to come to their area for some traditional Cuban cuisine of delicious pork, congri (rice mixed with beans and chorizos—Spanish sausages), cassava, and Spanish tortilla. That's the atmosphere that captured my parents' heart and led them to come back to this area each and every time.

The sand was white and fine, similar to a falling snowflake. Once you entered the water, you quickly noticed the warm temperature, which was about eighty degrees; you could see crystal clear all the way to the bottom, where your toes rested on the soft wet sand. What captured my attention big time was the beauty of the many fish swimming and swirling around me. They came in all sizes, shapes, and different colors that left me mesmerized. I would play with them by myself or with my newfound beach best friends for hours or until mom called us to go and eat. I often ignored her calls and stayed playing in the water. After everything failed, she'd send her biggest gun, Pipo, waking him up to try to convince me to come and eat. When Pipo eventually came, I would plead with him enthusiastically to stay a few more minutes in the water. He would respond by giving in to me and saying, "Esta bien, un poco mas!" (Okay, a little more!). A little more turned out to be an hour as my mom scolded my father for being worse than me, all while complaining about the food getting cold.

Pipo loved the water, and it showed as we played many games together in the ocean. Among them was waiting for a wave, especially a large one, as it approached us ready to break, then jumping in unison to avoid being knocked down. Sometimes, I was a bit sneaky, trying to outfox him with the waves, but he was always one step ahead of me. I would try splashing water in his face to blind him for a couple of seconds or pulling on one leg so he would fall, but nothing worked; his feet were far apart for better balance and he was too strong. We waited in full anticipation for the next wave and the next and the next, jumping slightly backward to avoid the full thrust of the impact. The only times he ever took heavy hits were when he was distracted by nearby swimmers or rafters getting too close to us. I never got tired, but when Pipo did, I picked up my plastic shovel and bucket and started to put sand all over his body while he slept. By the time he woke up, his face was the only remaining visible part. He could hardly move and pleaded with me to remove some of the sand so we could go back in the water for some more fun. I really loved these enjoyable times, often at his expense. I also believe that he enjoyed my shenanigans as well, because he would crack a half smile in my mom's direction as both of us headed toward the water to remove the sand from our bodies; especially Pipo, who looked like an Egyptian mummy as he stood up. In the water, I helped him remove all the sand by splashing water on his back.

After the cleaning, I asked Pipo to take me to the front of the pier to see all the boats anchored there. He said, "Fetch your floating tube and we will go." I immediately ran out of the water to where my mom, aunt, and brother were, grabbed the tube, and ran back like Speedy Gonzalez across the hot sand to Pipo. I placed the plastic tube around my waist as Pipo guided me through the calm, shallow, turquoise water near the boats. This area was about five feet deep, but it quickly got much deeper if you went any farther. Pipo lifted me up and helped me climb inside one of the commuter boats as well as a couple of the fish-ermens' little boats that were there with the owners sitting inside resting and eating. I was having a ball with Pipo in these boats until I saw my tube floating away from us and decided to jump back in the water and chase it with Pipo. My tube was very easy to follow because it was bright orange on the bottom and green on top. All others were black, mostly made from the inner tubes of tires. I had the best-looking tube on the beach, and I held on to it with much pride and joy. If you don't believe me, just turn to the photo section in the book and you'll see what I mean. In that photo, I'm standing in front of my parents and brother, holding my inner tube with a feisty look in my eyes to scare off anyone thinking of taking it away from me. The same applied to my bucket and shovel, which I always kept a watchful on even as I wandered off to play with Pipo and my friends. What gave me the biggest pleasure was when Pipo took time to spend with me, hav-ing fun on the beach or taking a walk to buy fish to take home with us. I remember one time after lunch that my mom wanted to purchase the best available fresh fish before leaving. To get there, we had to travel to the northeastern section of Llanita Beach in a slightly inward curve that was not visible from our location. It was about a mile away by foot, but the temperature and the baking sand made it too hot to walk. My mom asked Pipo to try to rent a boat for this short journey. Pipo quickly returned with good news that he had found a boat to take us to the fish houses. We boarded the little blue wooden boat with my brother, Gerardo Jr., aunt Genoveva, my mom, Maria, Pipo, me, two couples, and the rower, for a total of ten passengers. The fisheries were about a mile and a half away, a little bit farther by boat because it went around the coast.

This trip was the genesis of two separate incidents that ironi-cally occurred in the same day. One was a horrific life-and-death situation with a couple of drunks, while the other recounts the pain and embarrassment I had with a most unrelenting zipper. As we departed from the pier, the water was becoming choppier; you could see and hear the waves crashing hard nearby. This was not a real problem for us on board, even though our little boat was rocking quite a lot. As we proceeded to our destination, we kept about two hundred yards away from land as people swam and played in these more isolated areas of the Llanita Beach. The first leg of the trip was uneventful, and it took us twenty minutes to reach the fisheries. These fisheries were not really structured houses; they looked more like huts built mostly with bamboo sticks placed into the ground and dry palm trees on the roof and side. After twenty minutes of trying to decide what to buy to take back with us to our home in Jobabo, a new fresh catch arrived as the fishermen pulled in to the pier to unload their catch. We waited ten minutes until the fish had been placed in these hard aluminum buckets for sale. It didn't take my mom or the other couples long to purchase about ten to fifteen pounds of large fish. Everyone was happy and talking about the wonderful fish they had bought and how they planned to cook it once home and all of that. On the way back, I could not help but notice these large ships on my right-hand side. They were so huge that they looked like cities in the ocean. As I pointed to them, Pipo would identify the ship to me and explain what it was used for. Since he had been a navy guy himself in Spain, he was very familiar with the maritime environment. I was constantly poking him with questions as everyone looked and listened to Pipo answering me. Most of these vessels were oil tankers and cargo ships, but we also saw submarines and a few military destroyers that left us in awe as we cruised in their shadows about a mile away. Pipo was having a ball reminiscing about his days in Port Ferrol when he was a cadet sailing the oceans of the world. These ships were all moving pretty fast, making lots of swishing noises in the water. A half hour earlier, that same area had been clear of any ships. On my left side I saw many people swimming, fishing, and playing Frisbee or other games in the water, as well as sleeping and relaxing. Then I told Pipo I couldn't see the bottom anymore as the water had become very dark blue and green. He said, "The water is very deep here; that's why it's so dark green, son. Hold on tight and stay low inside the boat!" This was especially important since we had no life jackets onboard. Man, it was very scary that I was not able to see the little fish any more. To take my attention off my fears, I focused on the dolphins which swam near us here and there. At times, you could even spot a predator shark by its fins as they came above the water in the far distance. These were very dangerous waters. You didn't want to fall overboard or go for a swim in this area at any cost.

Most of the trip, Pipo or my mom held my hand as they were worried I might fall overboard. About half way into our return trip, we encountered two men swimming nearby yelling and behaving very erratically in the water. It was about two in afternoon, according to my mom, when the sun was at its highest point. What then transpired was something that no one on the little blue boat would ever forget for the rest of their lives, including yours truly, even as a five- to six-year-very-young boy.

Inside our boat there was a lot of concern about the two men in the water. We thought they were in deep trouble and needed help fast, so we came to assist them with a possible rescue. Or so we thought. As we approached them, one of the men climbed into the boat without any warning or permission, causing the boat to almost capsize, possibly killing everyone. While the other man held onto the boat, a shouting match grew between us and the man inside the boat for doing what he did. The rower, who was also the owner of the boat, tried his best to reason with these two fellows to find out what the problem was, but he had no luck at all. These two were highly intoxicated and looking for trouble at any cost, and we happened to be in their environment at the wrong time. These two drunks were so out of control that they started to argue profanely with each other and were ready to unload wild punches. The one in the boat was trying to get away from the other one as the other started trying to climb onboard to fight. In a desperate voice, my mom shouted to Pipo, "These guys are drunk and crazy; they are going to flip this boat over! We are all going to drown! Do something!" Even my aunt Genoveva tried to plead with these lunatics to calm down, but the screaming and profanities only grew louder.

In the midst of all the shouting and commotion, I began to cry earnestly. In the moments that followed, the person in the water, who was even drunker than the one inside the boat, started to get angrier and angrier, forcefully shaking the boat as he circled our vessel in pursuit of a fight. The guy inside the boat kept moving away and bumping us to avoid getting hit. The boat was rocking side to side so much that it began to take in water. The other couples with us started to use a few buckets to throw water back overboard because the boat was sinking lower. There were only about ten inches between the boat and the water level. We were constantly getting splashed from the one man outside along with a mutual barrage of profanities. At one point, the boat was about to turn over when Pipo told everyone to move closer to the other side to balance the weight of the boat. Pipo's quick thinking averted a sure death to many of us in the boat. Twenty minutes into the nightmare situation, the man in the boat lowered his hands to his now-so-called buddy to bring the fight into our sphere for one last showdown. At this point, my father had had enough with these two jokers. He grabbed the man inside the boat by his neck with one hand while he used the other hand to push him off the boat completely. Everyone in the boat applauded Pipo's heroic act, but no one with greater pride than me. The man landed about ten feet away from us, with a big, welcome splash as he hit the water flat and upside down. At this point, the rower started to row furiously to get everyone back to shore as soon as possible. The other drunk in the water was separated from our boat by the two men who had accompanied us. It was a crucial time for the situation to have been defused, because the water level was nearing the upper part of the boat. We had taken too much water already and would've been at critical mass before we started to sink.

Apparently, these drunks were great swimmers as we saw them swim back to the beach safely. These two men demonstrated that they had no consideration for others as their reckless behavior almost caused our doom. This unforgettable moment only lasted for about twenty minutes, but to those who were there on the fateful afternoon boat ride, it felt like a lifetime of many twists and turns, not knowing the final outcome. My mom tells me that she still cringes just thinking about what happened that day, even after almost fifty years.

When we got back to the pier at Llanita Beach, my mom asked all of us to hold hands and thank God for bringing us back safe and for giving my father the resolve and fortitude to finally end the nightmare.

I then immediately proceeded back to the wet sand to play, making holes, castles, and fortresses with my little shovel and bucket without a care in the world. Many people congregated near our picnic area on the beach to hear about what had just transpired during our adventure to buy some fresh fish.

Three hours had passed since the incident when my mom called me to get ready to leave for our hotel across the Puerto Padre bay. Before leaving, she gave me this new, mostly blue pair of shorts with white trimming and told me to change right away. I said, "I don't want to! I like my old shorts that I'm wearing!"

To which she replied, "Those shorts are too dirty and you have to be clean for dinner tonight at the hotel restaurant. I want you to look nice. Come here, Miguel, I will change your shorts real quick!"

I said, "No! Not here, mommy, there are too many people watching." I was embarrassed to be nude in public. I was self-conscious that my buddies would see me naked and make fun of me. So, I told my mom to give me the shorts so that I could put them on myself somewhere where nobody could see me. She acquiesced. I took the new shorts, which I hated, and ran to a secluded area behind this one wide coconut tree, surrounded by palm trees and bushes. It was about forty yards away from our picnic location to the right, looking from the ocean toward the beach. Before I took my shorts off, I made sure that no one was hidden and looking at me, because on many prior occasions my friends and I had witnessed couples kissing and hugging in this area. I wasn't taking any chances and risking being caught off guard by anyone lurking in the bushes. Nervously, I took off my old shorts and reluctantly put on my new blue ones. I hurried up and pulled up the zipper, however, my penis got caught in the metal teeth (my old trunks did not had a zipper). Ouch! Ouch! Ouch! Ouch! I was in pain beyond that which any words could ever reveal. I ran at full speed holding the zipper with one hand and my private part with the other so it wouldn't hurt too much while I tried to find Pipo. Instead of Pipo, I bumped into my mom first, all while crying my lungs out. I immediately brushed her to the side and saw my father, Pipo, running toward me to find out what had happened. He took the zipper in his hands and tried to move it upward, but it wouldn't budge at all. It wouldn't move, as it had a good chunk of my skin imbedded in its teeth, which only made it more painful. Since it couldn't move upward, he tried to lower the zipper without any success. My brother who was standing nearby was making fun of me by laughing and saying that they would have to cut off my penis if they couldn't get it untangled soon. His comments only made me angrier at him, and I begged Pipo and mom to make him stop taunting me. He did stop soon after that, because he knew he would face harsh punishments once we got home. He then helped my aunt Genoveva hold a long beach towel to block the view of the many spectators converging around us as I screamed out in pain.

Finally, Pipo grabbed the zipper really hard, trying again in an upward and downward motion, but it was still stuck. At this point, I started to bleed and the wound was getting larger due to the grinding effect of the zipper. Pipo was getting frustrated after seven minutes of my loud crying and inability to stand still. Finally, my mom told Pipo to hold me down tightly, while she tried to unleash the stubborn zipper. At this point, I was so upset with my mom that I started to berate her with a barrage of comments blaming her for what had happened to me. Since I was about five years old, a big man in my own eyes, I did not want my mom to see me in those conditions, exposed, if you will. However, I relented, because Pipo was near me. My mom grabbed the zipper and pulled it down slowly as it finally unhooked my skin. The aftermath was not pretty; it was bloody and missing a sizeable amount of tissue. Pipo asked me to show him the wound, as I wouldn't let my mom see it. I also didn't want to talk to my mom anymore; it was her fault this whole thing had happened to me. I was a hard-headed little boy who had a bit of an attitude, and I did like to not compromise.

After some time, my father said, "You are a big boy now! Don't cry anymore! Go and play a little longer with your shovel and bucket."

I said, "It still hurts a lot, Pipo!"

He acknowledged this and offered to go in the water with me for a few more minutes. He smiled and he and I ran down to the water with me wearing my new blue shorts that were not so new anymore.

Today, whenever I bring up this event with my mom, she immediately starts to laugh, describing my innocent demeanor and expressions during this traumatic experienced. I'm sure my brother, Gerardo Jr., laughs just as much as my mother when he remembers that day. In retrospect, I look at it from a mixed-emotion point a view. Bottom line, the experience did hurt! I can feel the pain of it all coming back even just thinking about it.

These two events helped make me a stronger person whenever I have had to face difficult situations later on in my life. The first event in the boat left a lifetime signature of courage and valor imprinted in my mind because of Pipo's heroic actions. The second event proved his loving care for me during a very sensitive and embarrassing time when I needed him the most.

CHAPTER 8

Los Tres Reyes (The Three Kings)

In Cuba, we celebrate Noche Buena (Christmas Eve) on December 24 and the Festival of the Three Kings (or Wise Men/Magicians), Caspar, Melchior, and Balthazar, on January 6 (which is ironic, because I started to write this chapter on this very day of January 6, 2010. An amazing coincidence?!) According to an old legend based on a Bible story, these three kings saw a bright star on the night when Christ was born and followed it to Bethlehem, where they found the Christ child, baby Jesus, and presented him with gold, frankincense, and myrrh. These were the very first Christmas gifts. For me, Christmas meant toys! Lots and lots of toys, even in scarce Cuba. I couldn't wait until this day each year. It was by far one of the happiest times in my life as a child. My fondest moments with Pipo were during Los Tres Reyes Magos on the early morning of January 6, 1964, in Jobabo, Cuba. The previous day, my aunt Genoveva had suggested to me that I pick up grass and leaves and place them outside the house for the three kings' camels, because they had a long journey and might be hungry. Upon hearing this, I ran outside with a basket made of hay, filled it all the way to the top, and placed it on the right side of our front door. I asked her if it was enough for the camels, as Pipo was home from his work at La Comercial and would see my work. She said, "Yes, so you should get more toys!" Now I was on cloud nine after hearing that good news.

I went inside the house, grabbed Pipo by the hand and took him outside to show him the camel's food. He looked at me and said, "You forgot the water! They need lots of water after a long journey through the desert, son. Let's look for a bucket around the house, OK?" We searched every room in the house without finding anything. I was getting frustrated and very angry because the camels would not have any water to quench their thirst and the three kings would get upset and leave me no toys. I couldn't let that happen. No way!

All of a sudden, around the front porch of the house, I noticed flowers and plants in these wooden, clay, or cement buckets. I said, "Pipo, let's empty one and fill it with water!"

He smiled and said, "No! No! Your aunt Genoveva and your mother *nos matas a los dos* (will kill us both)."

I said, "They have so many, I just need one!"

Pipo said, "I will find one! Hold my hand while we look for your mother and your aunt Genoveva around the house." Two minutes later we found them in the yard planting more flowers in these buckets. I started to kick the buckets until my feet hurt.

Then Pipo said to them, "We looked all over the place for buckets and can't find a single empty one." Our house was like a flower garden; it had about a thousand of these buckets full of flowers hanging from the porch ceiling, as well as on the ground. My mom replied that we must have missed the buckets, because they were where we always kept them—in the storage closet! Upon hearing that, I ran as fast as I could to the storage closet and opened the door with anticipation. Bingo! I found a grey one sitting on the ground. It was made out of clay and weighed about ten pounds, but I did not care how much it weighed as I had super strength when it came to toys. Nothing was going to hold me back from filling it with water. Pipo helped me fill it with our outside hose pipe, which we used to water the plants and clean our 1954 Chevy as well as Pipo's work truck. Once I had filled it, I left it next to the food that I had put out earlier. Now, I was a happy kid.

Once I went inside the house, I was very obedient—well, somewhat. I did all the right things, like getting ready to take a shower and then eat with the family in the dining room. Following this was the most important activity of all to my brother and me on this holy night—trying to go to sleep early! Pipo and my mom told us that bedtime was ten o'clock and we shouldn't be late or else we would scare off the camels.

My beloved aunt Genoveva was in the room telling us to go to sleep as well and try not to get up in the middle of the night to check for toys, either. She said, "Tomorrow is a big day, so you must get proper rest." I said I was going to sleep straight away. I then went and kissed Pipo, mom, and aunt Genoveva with a big happy smile on my face before going to sleep in my own bed in my parents' room. On the way to the bedroom, I opened the front door and checked the status of the food and water one last time. I was concerned that a mouse or a cat might eat the food and leave nothing for the hungry camels.

After sneaking in a little more black-and-white television watching with the family sitting in the living room on our sturdy, elegant, wood-finish couch with a bamboo bottom, my mom said, "It's eleven o'clock. Put on your pajamas and go to bed, Miguel. Right now! Do you hear me? Go to bed before the three kings get upset and give your toys to other kids!"

Then my aunt Genoveva jumped in and added, "Yes, be the good little boy that you are and go to sleep. Tomorrow is Christmas and you are going to get lots of wonderful toys. You've been a good boy all year." I smiled at her and gave her a hug and a kiss. I really loved my aunt Genoveva. Off I went to bed.

Since my parents shared the bedroom with me, before I jumped into my bed, I climbed into their bed through a small opening in the mosquito net and gave Pipo and my mother another big good-night kiss. Impatiently, I then went back my bed as my mom turned off the lights. I could still see inside the room because of the bright street lights outside. I was also able to see and follow the many small stars shining in the black sky from my bedroom window. I was trying my very best to peek and see the three kings bringing my toys. No matter how much I tried to go to sleep, I just was not sleepy. Since I was not able to fall asleep in my own bed, I jumped out and went over to my parents' bed to be with them. Before I could climb inside, I had trouble opening the mosquito net that was clipped closed from the inside. My mom heard all the commotion as I was trying get in and quickly opened a small hole in the net, just big enough to let me squeeze in before any mosquitos could get inside and bite the living daylights out of all of us. I rolled in without disturbing Pipo, as I put my left hand on his arm and finally fell asleep between them.

When I woke up, it was still dark. Pipo turned over and looked at the clock on top of his night table and said, "It's only three o'clock in the morning, it's still too early, son. Go back to sleep or else Los Reyes will not come if you are still awake!"

I dozed off without realizing it, and what felt like a few seconds (but was actually three hours) later, I heard my mom's voice whispering in my ears to get up. She said, "I heard the camels outside the front of the house, Miguel." Pipo also reiterated what my mom was saying about the camels and added that he had heard loud noises coming from the living room. Before he was able to say another word, I jumped out of bed and headed straight to the living room to see what they had left for me. When I entered the living area, I saw our two sofas next to each other, as well as two chairs on both sides of the room, full of toys! Toys! And more toys! It was an incredible sight. Wow, I was in heaven. The two chairs on my right were for me and the two on the left were for my brother. It seemed like we both got there at the same time. He looked upset that I had more toys than he did. My aunt Genoveva and my mom tried to calm down my brother. He was furious. Since he was about seven years older than me, he was used to being spoiled with an abundance of toys before I arrived on the scene. He had actually had an even better time than me because his early years were spent in the pre-Castro era of free capitalism, when goods were readily available.

My mother acquiesced and said, "You have been receiving lots of toys over the years. In fact, Miguel will never have as many toys as you have! Besides, he deserves all these toys as he has been a really good boy this past year."

The first thing I saw that caught my attention was a dark blue machine gun. I immediately grabbed it, put my little finger on the trigger, and squeezed it all the way. It started to make lots of noises, and the front of the barrel lit up with a red light as well. It was my first machine gun, and I felt I could take on the world. After a few minutes scoping my toys, I went to Pipo's bed and started to rapid fire my gun at him. He woke up from the noise with a big smile as I proudly showed him my new machine gun. Since he was my hero, I naturally said, "You fire the gun, too!" He held onto it in bed, mimicking my every move and noises just like I did. We played a long time, pretending to be good soldiers. He then asked me to take him to see all the new toys that the three kings left for me. I grabbed his hand with one of my hands and held onto my machine gun with the other while we marched to the living room together. That moment in the living room was phenomenal; I think it was the happiest morning of my life. My father was at the center of the joyous feelings I was experiencing when I again saw all the toys next to him. I remember seeing trucks, soldiers, bowling balls, games, marbles, coloring books, and a bike with training wheels, just to name a few. Not too bad in Castro's Cuba! Years later, my mom told me how they were able to obtain so many gifts for us on that Christmas. Unbeknownst to my brother and me, they spent countless hours in line to get so many high-quality toys. She even sold her finest dresses to raise money for these expensive gifts for her sons. Sometimes, they paid two or three times the price of an item just to get it. This was especially true in the case of the machine gun that made me bananas when I first saw it, as well as the bike. They even paid friends to stand in line in front of stores to purchase items for us as well. My mom said that it was almost like a crusade. They had a checklist of all the toys we wanted. They worked nonstop for more than three months to fill the list and make it the best Christmas ever.

Pipo also had a major role in this endeavor as well, since he was very well liked and had many connections around town with the business community due to his own business, La Comercial. He'd asked them for a personal favor, which was very uncharacteristic of him, but for us to be happy he did what it took to make this reality happen without a second thought. Pipo was able to get one-of-a-kind toys that my mom and aunt Genoveva were not able to get themselves. He said to my mom, "I'm so overjoyed with happiness each time I hand out one of the toys that I requested from my friends during my deliveries. It's so special knowing how happy Miguel and Gerri (my brother, Gerardo Jr.) are going to be. It makes life worth living just to see their big happy smiles on this day." My father's gratitude was already in the stratosphere to begin with, but he was so appreciative of what they did for him that he gave his entire weekly delivery order of beverages for free to everyone who did him a favor.

Sometimes, Pipo would toss a comment to my mom like, "I think we are overdoing it! Don't you?"

She would reply, "I want this Christmas of 1964 to be the most memorable one in their young lives!" And indeed it was the very best.

Writing about that day brings back all the happy feelings I had. According to my mom, Pipo looked at her, shook his head, and broke into a big smile, saying, "I guess it's OK to spoil them just this one time!" It was certainly toys galore, the most toys or gifts I have ever received during this lifetime. Shortly after that memorable Christmas, the Cuban economy began to experience the first widespread signs of severe shortages. Toys, naturally, became an even more limited commodity.

The fruits of this great and memorable Christmas were that we were fully united as a strong and loving family on that very special day of January 6, 1964. That day will live in our hearts and souls forever. After I had played with all my toys, I shared them with my neighborhood friends—but not my machine gun, as that was my pride and joy and I didn't want it to get damaged! In the afternoon, Pipo took me to Maximo Gomez Street in front of our house to learn to ride a bike. As I was learning to ride my bike, my grandfather Domingo and his wife, Pepilla (my mother's stepmother), arrived with even more toys, so I stopped and went to join them in the house for about twenty minutes to open my gifts. I loved my grandparents so much as well! They were very loving and humble people. Pepilla was the most child-like person I have ever met in my life. She was simply adorable! Soon after, I rejoined Pipo on the street. My mom, aunt, grand-father, and Pepilla came outside near the curb to watch me ride my new bike for the first time. My father followed close behind me so I wouldn't fall over. At the time, the street was crowded with many kids as they showed off their new toys and a bunch of homemade scooters, to the delight of all the onlookers. I was impressed by their ingenuity and was able to ride one of them myself in exchange for a ride on my red bike. It was a real spectacle in the neighborhood, seeing entire families standing outside in the street, watching us while we played together. It must have been even more enjoyable for them, seeing us run around with so much innocence and zest for life. They may have lost those sentiments as they became adults, but they seemed to recapture them on this one special Christmas day.

As an adult now, I'm able to identify with the special feelings that they felt and go back in time and place myself fully in my parents' shoes as I watch all these smiling kids with God-given purity that engulfs our spirits beyond any words. That day, I happened to be one of those little munchkins, bringing all that joy to them.

In the following days, Pipo continued teaching me how to ride my bike until I was confident enough to take off the training wheels. When I finally took off the training wheels, I said to Pipo, "I'm a big boy now!"

He replied, grabbing my hand gently, "Yes, son, you are, but be careful, OK? Let's go home and tell your mother, aunt Genoveva, and your brother the good news. I'll race you home!"

Oh, by the way, I beat him, but I think he might have let me win! Only Pipo would really know the answer! Either way, it was the happiest day in my life with Pipo and my family.

CHAPTER 9

Beers and Cuban Cigar Boxes

Beers and Cuban cigar boxes equaled fun times with my father, Pipo, and me. It all began when I was about five years old, when he asked me to accompany him to his place of work, La Comercial, in the hometown city of Jobabo to make deliveries. It was quite a treat and I was really looking forward to the deliveries scheduled for the very next day. The following morning at about eight o'clock, I eagerly jumped out of bed and followed him all over the house. Finally, it was time to hop into his black 1954 Chevy. I was as happy as you can be—Pipo and I alone together. I remember all the sights and sounds, but none more than our small talk in the car. I was a very precocious kid, asking the usual multitude of questions while my father did the best he could to both pay attention to the road and answer me. As we crossed the railroad tracks, nearing La Comercial, I asked him what that giant factory with those tall towers was for. It was blowing out all this white smoke from the top, which was blinding us and covering the blue sky above. He said, "Son, it's El Ingenio (a manufacturing plant). It transforms raw sugarcane into powdered sugar. This plant is one of the best in all of Cuba. The sugar is always crystal white here." As we proceeded, we entered La Comercial. He showed me around the entire complex and I met many people, shaking hands with all of them. He introduced me as his little assistant for today's deliveries. Before leaving the facility, he took me to the cafeteria so I could have something to eat and drink, like a fresh Materva, which is a very popular Cuban soft beverage. In the meantime, Pipo went to the warehouse to load the truck. I waited for about thirty minutes or so and then he came and picked me up. Off we went with a truck full of all types of beverages for that day's deliveries.

This particular day started off overcast with a slight chance of rain, but by the time we got to our first stop, the weather had changed dramatically. It became clear and sunny with a beautiful dark blue sky. What a feeling! I was sitting in the passenger seat waving to passing cars as the cool wind was becoming warmer as the day went by. From the higher elevation inside the truck, I could see everything much better than in the car. Our first stop was outside Jobabo in the countryside. I remember this long two-lane road with very little traffic volume on it. There was one way for each direction, so to pass one another, you had to increase your speed and make sure there was no oncoming car on the other lane. I was told by my brother, Gerardo Jr., that this road took us to Victoria De Las Tunas, our future home, if you went to the right and Havana if you turned left. One possible explanation for the lack of traffic in this byway was because of the many shortages, especially of gasoline, that were taking their toll in Cuba. The scenery was spectacular on both sides of the road and I just could not stop looking around as I talked to Pipo. You were able to see long stretches of palm and coconut trees across the plains, as well as farms with many horses and cows. You could also see large flocks of birds filling the blue sky. It looked so serene and peaceful as we continued driving onward.

One time during our drive, Pipo got very excited after glancing at the rearview mirror and said to me, "Look quickly, son, you're about to see this beautiful car coming very fast behind us and about to pass us." As I turned to look out the rear window of the truck to check the car he was talking about, it passed us on the left at a lightning fast speed. It was like a supersonic jet, cruising the low ground so fast that no other car could keep up. Pipo marvelled at the beauty of the car we had just witnessed. He said, "Son, that fancy car is one of the newer models in Cuba and, sadly, the very last ones to be imported from America!" It was an early 1960s Cadillac. My father was mesmerized looking at the grandiose blue convertible automobile. It resembled a spaceship with its long back fins, sporting two round red lights on the bottom and two small ones on top. They looked like rocket engines. What a sight it was—my father kept pointing as it disappeared in front of us, within seconds, into the distant horizon. I asked him to go faster to try to catch up with it and he started to laugh and said, "Son, that car is going so fast that nothing less than an airplane would be able catch up with it."

I asked him how fast was it traveling, to which he replied, "I don't know exactly, but I guess it is easily going over 200 kilometers per hour. That car probably belongs to a government official who is showing off, because there is no need to go that fast on this road." Visiting Cuba today, you'll find many of those same cars I saw as a child, still rolling in the streets after nearly sixty years. They sure don't make cars anymore that are able to endure nature's wrath for so long. Shame on America's "Big Three" auto manufactures that have built so many inferior products ever since those golden days! It's like living in a giant museum, traveling back in time and reliving the fabulous fifties and sixties once again. It's an era and place where I'd like to go and visit one day and reminisce about those days spent with Pipo and family.

Just before our first stop, Pipo decided to stop and help an older man who had broken down on the road. After he was able to get him going, we shortly arrived at our first delivery on what had turned into a very hot day. I noticed him sweating quite a lot because his white under-shirt was drenched as he unloaded the heavy cases of beers and soft drinks into a handcart, which he wheeled over some steps to bring it inside the store. A few minutes later, before leaving for our next stop, he brought me a small, cold Coca-Cola bottle as he dried his forehead with a towel that he kept in the truck. Our next delivery was only a short distance away. At this stop, I got off the truck and walked inside the restaurant/bar establishment, so he could introduce me to his business associates that were in the bar drinking and eating. I shook their hands and went back to the truck to help him unload many more cases of beers and other beverages before we returned to Jobabo for the bulk of the deliveries. In Jobabo, I helped Pipo by pushing the hand truck full of cases and holding the paperwork. Upon entering various stores, Pipo asked the owners to show me various cigar boxes to keep me entertained and away from high temperatures. At first, they kidded with him about me being too young to smoke those cigars, but they knew why he wanted to show them to me. These boxes contain beautiful works of art that capture Cuba's long heritage. I was fascinated with the fine details of the painting. Better yet, I was also not in my father's way as he worked diligently to get the work done faster. I was a good boy waiting for Pipo to come where I was sitting and call me whenever he completed his order. Sometimes, Pipo would finish rather quickly and rest a little bit next to me by the counter, drinking a beer when his friends insisted he had one. On top of the counter, I would place in front of Pipo all these colored cigar boxes that the owner of the store had fetched for me from the back counter, which displayed the cigars at a safe distance from the public. My father and I would contemplate the artwork of each to decide which one was the best and had our favorite paintings. We then separated our favorites and put them in front of us while the eliminated ones were placed at the back of the counter until we had only one left to crown as the winner. Not only did my father and I participate, but strangers and his friends also took part in picking their favorite ones. It was a lot of fun going to different places and comparing the Cuban cigar boxes with each other, as well as with those from other countries, but the Cubans were by far the very best looking. These activities made the time seem like it just flew by instantly, especially when combined with the very hot sun and carrying the many heavy beer cases that we unloaded onto the hand cart.

My main job was to push the hand truck with Pipo whenever we went uphill. That was no easy task. On some occasions when it was too difficult, we would get the owner to come and give us a hand pushing it up the steep inclines. Needless to say, we had a few breakages, which my father was not very happy about. While I was with him, about ten cases of beer slipped off the hand truck and broke as they hit the hard street. Other times, we were fortunate that the street was not paved and absorbed the impact much better without losing merchandise. We were able to salvage less than half of the bottles inside the cases. You could see all the beer flowing into the streets like a mini flood. It was not a pretty picture for Pipo because it signified lost revenue. When this happened with me this one time, he immediately got over it by taking time to play with me inside the establishment with none other than the cigar boxes. If the paintings were covered with cigars, we would empty and place the cigars in other boxes until we saw the painting underneath. On one of these occasions, while I was appreciating the value of these incredible paintings, I put a Cuban cigar in my mouth from the box to mimic my father's friends who were smoking and drinking beer. One other time, I asked my father for a taste of beer while sitting on the stool and he said, while he looked at me, "Okay, just a little sip, but don't tell your mother!"

I quickly replied, "Si Pipo, yo no le digo nada a mami (Yes, Pipo, I won't tell mother anything)." After a quick sip, I realized I did not like it because the taste was too bitter. I quickly returned to my Coca-Cola.

The colorful cigar box lithographics were begun by a Galician named Ramon Allonos, who immigrated to Cuba in 1837. Among my favorite labels are La Gloria Cuba, Romeo & Julieta, La Corona, Fonseca, Quintero, Ramon Allonos, Bolivar, Truja, El Rey Del Mundo, and H. Upmann. I recommend that everyone check out these breathtaking works of art. You will not be disappointed. You could even Google them and enjoy them online, just like millions of other people have. Even though I saw many people smoking cigars in these establishments and drinking lots of beers as I travelled around with Pipo on deliveries, he was never a heavy drinker. We just enjoyed each other's companionship and love, which were our only vices, and I thank God for the predisposition we had. I can't say the same thing about American President John F. Kennedy on the eve of the Cuban embargo when he asked Press Secretary Pierre Salinger to obtain some of the best H. Upmann Cigars. This premium brand was and still is considered one of the best when it comes to Cuban cigars. Mr. Kennedy had an insatiable taste for these limited and pricey stogies that represent the ultimate status symbol, showing everyone that you've made it really big in this lifetime. Reaching the pinnacle of Maslow's pyramid of the hierarchy of our needs, this apex of actualization is what we all strive for when every other basic need has been met.

Thanks be to my father for the exposure to hard work and to the world of fine art. Those bygone moments that I spent with Pipo looking at the cigar boxes and unloading beer have helped me a great deal. They have reinforced in me the value of maintaining a balance between hard work and play. This is evident today through my affection for cultural stimuli and the need to embrace work, in large part due to the seeds that Pipo planted in me back then without my even knowing. As a result of this shaping, I have immensely enjoyed visiting many museums of all types and in many countries. I also always strive to do my very best in all my endeavors, big or small! Bravo, Pipo! Well done!

CHAPTER 10

Building Toys with Pipo

Growing up in Cuba during the Socialist Revolution of 1959 was very difficult because of the shortages we faced after Fidel Castro, Che Guevara, Camilio Cienfuegos, and many others overthrew the American-supported right-wing government of dictator Fulgencio Batista. Soon after that, America imposed an embargo on this sovereign state, and we began to feel the full pinch of this ill policy and the need to reinvent ourselves and develop strong resolve to survive this injustice.

Growing up in Jobabo was like ground zero for me, my family, friends, and our community at large. We had to challenge ourselves to be more creative than we had ever been before to repair our basic infrastructure and appliances. We had no workable alternatives but to keep them all in good working order indefinitely because we knew from the get-go that we wouldn't be able to replace the very few things we still had before the US sanctions started. This was the new lifestyle we were forced to live in Cuba. Our streets became more crowded as friends united to work together, repairing the automobiles and homes. There was a general lack of the essentials like food and medicine—the most difficult part of the sactions. We all naturally worked in a communal manner to share the limited resources as best as we could to just make it through another day. It was a hard life; "one slow day at a time" was our rallying cry. I recall seeing friends working long hours with their children, building all types of contraptions. This approach was no different with Pipo and me as we worked closely together on several of the hottest gadgets of the times. Among the most sought-after items to build were slingshots, scooters, kites, and small boats made out of empty cream cheese wooden boxes. The neighborhood kids were resilient and energetic competitors, and, most importantly, proud of what they created out of junk or trash. The only thing one had to do was just step outside one's home to observe this spirit of ingenuity. In retrospect, it was a good thing, because it kept us very busy after school and out of trouble.

The most important gadget was, of course, a slingshot, kept in one's back pocket for all types of reasons. Firstly, it was a status symbol among the kids. It also showed unity within our group as well as serving notice to others to not mess around with us or they would be fired upon at will. It was our ultimate weapon, a real treasure for protection, hunting, and for pure, unadultered pleasure. I had to build one for myself, but before that got off the ground, I needed someone to help me, and I couldn't think of a better facilitator than my father, Pipo. However, in the beginning, when I approached Pipo for assistance in constructing one of these lethal slingshots, he hesitated quite strongly because he thought (and rightly so) that it would be used for the wrong reasons. He was adamantly afraid that I would hurt someone if challenged or succumb to peer pressure challenges that would lead me to do many stupid things, like breaking windows. After a lengthy conversation with my father, I made a firm promise to never point or threaten any person with it. My emotional plea with tears in my eyes convinced Pipo to help me build my ultimate toy weapon. His remarks to me went like this: "Esta bien (OK), we will build one together, so you can learn how to build one yourself in case it breaks or you want to make an even better one! All right, son, follow me! First, we need to find a few raw materials before we can begin our project. Luckily, I know just where to locate them!" My father said we needed to look for the right tree trunk to serve as the handle for the slingshot. This was the most important piece of the entire unit. It had to be very strong and durable to handle the force as it fired away stones, marbles, rocks, and our deadliest ammunition—copper nails and wire U-shaped mini clamps.

We could find the natural raw material for our slingshots, if we were lucky, in just about any tree. Unfortunately, we were not so fortunate initially. Our search proved to be more difficult than expected. It took us almost two hours to find a suitable U-shaped tree trunk branch before we hit the jackpot. One finally met my father's criterion of having the right size U shape with a long, sturdy stem underneath, with enough room to place the hand without worrying about being hit when firing the ammo. We then proceeded to stop at an auto mechanic's garage and ask my father's friend for a piece of rubber from an old tire tube. After that, we went back home and cut a small piece of leather or cowhide from an old pair of shoes to make the pouch to load the ammunition. At this time, I was very happy that everything was coming together, ready for assembly. We now had all the parts. Pipo cut the rubber from the tube into two identical bands which measured about twelve inches long and a half an inch thick. He then tested the bands for elasticity before hooking them up to each side of the wooden handle. Only after he was satisfied with the result did he cut a small portion of leather and install the pouch. Before completion, he sanded the handles to help me avoid getting splinters in my hands. After he was done with them, they were as smooth as a baby's skin.

I commended Pipo's work, but he said that he wasn't done yet and instructed me to get four or five bottles. I pick up long-necked beer bottles and lined them up on top of the red bricks on the side of our house in the backyard. At this time, my enthusiasm was hitting critical high mass as my hero was about to test his work-of-art slingshot with different types of ammo. Needles to say, my hero, Pipo, did not disappoint me as he was hitting and breaking those bottles with the accuracy of a marksman. It was music to my ears as he said to me, smiling, "You try it now, son." I was pretty bad, missing my first twenty shots by a wide margin. He then saw me flustered and said, "Hold on for a minute and listen to me, son. You are not taking your time. Just slow down a little bit, take a deep breath, look at your surroundings, and concentrate on your shooting target. That's the first step! The second step is practice, practice, and more practice!" Sure enough, these valuable tips were a godsend. Within a half hour, I was becoming more accurate and breaking bottles at a feverish pace. I had to move farther back to conserve the bottles. I even had to partially cover the bottles by putting bricks, wood, and other obstructions in front of them to preserve my few remaining targets. My accuracy increased exponentially thanks to my guru, Pipo, who took the time to guide me.

Just as I was about to leave to look for my friends and show them my new slingshot, Pipo said, "Don't forget to clean up all the broken glasses before someone gets cut, OK?"

I replied, "Yes, Pipo," as we both looked at each other with a big grin on our faces.

After cleaning the mess, I found my buddies and proudly showed them my new slingshot. Off we went fully armed to hunt those little green lizards that were very prevalent in Cuba's terrain. They were just about everywhere you could imagine; their favorite locations were in the bushes, trees, walls, and in backyards. Sometimes, they were very difficult to spot because they blended in so naturally with the surrounding environment. However, when we did find them, they were dead meat because we often competed with each other to see who would have the highest number of kills. I remember once picking up one of these dead lizards by the long tail and showing it to Pipo for him to see what I did. He would often stress to me to be careful with the slingshot and with these little creatures. At other times, I would try to bring my mom into the mix, showing her my kills by waving them in the air as she would become frantic and hysterical, yelling at me in a loud voice to get rid of them now. I was laughing at my mom's expense, which was not very nice, until she called for Pipo to come and take them all away. I think she was afraid of them or found them repulsive, as they were severely disfigured by that stage. We also targeted the many birds that adorned the blue sky. This was more challenging and rewarding because the kills were more difficult to come by. Usually, the winner of this contest was the best shooter. I did very well among the group with the exception of the older kids who were true marksmen. After countless hours using these slingshots, they would eventually break, but it was not a problem because I knew the fundamentals of making them again—thanks to my father's emphasis on being self-sufficient in everything we did. The philosophies I learned from my father encouraged me to pursue new ways of improving my slingshots and making them last longer. I replaced the wooden handle with a strong metal wire which could bend ("borrowed" from backyards and park fences). We did this by having spotters so we wouldn't get caught in the act of removing these priceless raw materials. It was a lot of fun and filled with suspense because we would have faced a severe punishment if we were ever caught removing these items.

Speaking of fun and joy in our neighborhoods of Jobabo and in Victoria De Las Tunas, the homemade scooter was the epitome of coolness. To construct these machines, we would start by removing the wheels of roller skates and placing them on the bottom of a flat board. If we did not have skates to get the wheels from, we would try to find and use old wheelbarrows or small abandoned wheels wherever we could find them. This was not an easy task in Cuba, because nothing was considered junk or useless. After nailing or screwing them on tightly, we would get another board and connect it upright with a broom stick cut short and mounted on top to create a handle bar. What a contraption!

I was very fortunate because for Los Tres Reyes, (The Three Kings Day), Christmas in Cuba, I received a brand new scooter. However, I quickly noticed that these homemade scooters went much faster. They were blazing through the streets in bunches. The biggest problem they faced was potholes. If you hit one of those, it was the end of your scooter. It would need a complete overhaul, especially if the bearings were damaged. Bearings were just about impossible to find, so rule number one was knowing your surroundings. This was a very potent trait given to me by Pipo and one that I passed on to my buddies: avoid the pot holes. We only lost one scooter, thanks to those golden words from my father!

The other fun thing to build to keep us entertained was kites. This activity was very much a family venture where parents and siblings spent countless hours and days together, making these delicate flying paper birds. My brother always took the lead in building them because he was a natural in this area. He was so meticulous about details. For example, he made sure that the material used was strong enough to withstand the strong winds, but at the same time light enough to be able to climb faster and higher without breaking apart. It was an art that only he was able to discern fully. He would spread the materials out in front of us in our living room and assign different responsibilities to each of us to help complete this project. I helped out with the cutting and gluing of the thin sticks while my aunt Genoveva and my mother concentrated on the cutting and sewing of the fabric for the long tail. This left my father, Pipo, as the sole quality controller, enabling my brother flexibility to look at the big picture and not worry about any flaws during the construction period.

After finishing our masterpiece, we all went to Jobabo Park to test fly our kite. We were met there by my grandfather Domingo, his wife, Pepilla, and others for a pleasant day of recreation and relaxation. The hardest part of flying the kite was trying to get it off the ground and not crashing and breaking it before it ever flew. This was the most nerve-racking part of the whole day, because if it did crash, it would've be a big waste of time and back to the drawing board. To get it off the ground safely, my brother would run with the kite as fast as he could while my father held the rope on a wooden handle. Once it was slightly airborne, my brother would run back and take over control from my father to let out more rope so the kite could climber higher. This was no easy task because there were already many kites in the sky, and one's kite could easily get tangled among the others and destroyed. Furthermore, there were many electrical wires to navigate through before reaching a safe altitude. The most memorable part was standing with my family, especially my brother and Pipo, learning how to fly these family-built kites safely. The sight was awesome, looking way up into the sky and seeing all these kites parading their eclectic shapes and colors. Our kite was amazing! Firstly, it was much was larger than most and was easily distinguishable from the others because of its long length and the many colors of its tail. We also played many games with friends and strangers alike. One of the most popular games was to try reach and maintain the highest altitude despite the strong winds that could easily destroy the integrity of the kite. I could hear my father constantly yelling, and I mimicked these same utterances to my brother: "Give it more rope, more rope, and be careful with the other kite lines!" This give and take went on endlessly with everyone in our family, but sometimes it would get lost in all the yelling snippets from the large crowds in the background. We all took turns flying the kites. However, the most fun part was when Pipo was at the helm of the rope line. We infused his time with the same barrage of comments he had given my brother earlier, but increased it tenfold, saying how poorly he was flying the kite to try and rattle him for our selfish pleasure. Nobody wanted to be the one that crashed the kite that we all built. We started shouting something that went like this: "Pipo! You are getting to close to other kites, hurry up and move to the left before you get it tangled! Watch for light posts, trees, and the electrical line! Oh, don't forget the constant flock of birds coming this way."

This full attack on Pipo went on for twenty minutes until he finally said, "No mas!" (No more, just like boxing great Roberto Duran's bout against Sugar Ray Leonard, when he quit boxing and left the ring). He continued, "I can't see anymore in the hot sun. I'm sweating so much that my eyes are full of sweat and it's making me see double and triple as I try to concentrate on the kite." When he said those comments, we all broke down laughing for a solid five minutes of fun. It was payback for the wholesome good humor that was uniquely his.

We have all heard over the years the famous line "free as bird." Well, certainly that day and many others just like it encompassed the essence, from a child's perspective, of how wonderful it is to have a family that does things together. The state of being in the moment slowly left us once we joined America's high-speed culture.

The last invention of the big four involved transforming an empty wooden cream cheese box into a small little boat that could float. It sounds easy, but it took a great deal of work to make it happen. These wooden boxes were about twelve inches in length, six across, two inches upright, and the wood thickness was about a half inch. They were very hot commodities and difficult to obtain because everyone was aware of their usefulness once the cream cheese was consumed. I was very fortunate because of Pipo's connections, gained through customers of his distribution business. Pipo sometimes managed to get some boxes for me through these connections.

It was such a delight when Pipo came home flashing one of these empty boxes as he stepped out of his truck to look for me. I was like a little puppy with sheer joy and affection for my hero as he handed me the box so I could build a boat. The best part again was that we spent days together carving and molding the boxes to look like a sailboat. We incorporated everything; nothing went to waste. He also stressed to me the importance of sharing my extra boxes with my friends, which I happily did. Once we completed a boat, my friends and I showcased it in the nearby ponds, streams, and rivers, as well as when we went to the beach. We even dug lengthy holes in the ground and filled them with water to check for possible leaks before we took the boats out in deep water. At times, we had a few problems with buoyancy—sometimes the boat would lean on one side, causing it to sink. This made my friends and me all the more determined to work together as a team and fix the cause until it was perfect. This closeness created a deeper bond between my friends and me, thanks to Pipo's advice. He highlighted to me numerous times the importance of sharing each other's things, as they would then grow to become even better things. Those words rang so true with me back then and they've been with me ever since. In retrospect, Pipo was encouraging me from an early age to be more self-assured in my thinking and actions and to be humble and loving and think about others.

As a result of these life lessons from Pipo, I've come up with this equation called SSKB for fun. It's the acronym for slingshots, scooters, kites, and boats, and it is 100 percent Pipo and the magical presence he had on my life and the lives of our family and the many others he he touched profoundly. We all thank him!

CHAPTER 11

Living in Victoria De Las Tunas

In early 1965, we moved to the city of Victoria De Las Tunas in the Province of Las Tunas. This municipality is located in central-eastern Cuba along the *carretera* (highway) between the cities of Camaguey (where I was born), Holguin, and Bayamo and also serves as its capital. The city is among the top ten in population, after only Havana, Santiago de Cuba, Camaguey, Holgin, Santa Clara, Guantanamo, and Bayamo. It was named after the defeat of Spain in the Spanish-American War, where Cuba proclaimed victory.

The primary reason for our change of residency was that Pipo's state-run employer, La Comercial beverage distribution company, was consolidated into one main location in Victoria De Las Tunas. This created a longer commute for my father from our home in Jobabo. In addition, my parents had already submitted to the Cuban government the legal forms required to emigrate to America. This maneuver presented a real headache and made it imperative for Pipo and our family to leave Cuba, because he was told by government officials that his 1954 black Chevrolet had to be in good working condition upon returning it to the socialist government before leaving Cuban soil. If this provision was not adhered to fully, no exit visa would be granted to America and our application would be permanently denied. To keep this scenario from ever happening, my father kept his automobile unscathed at home and took the bus to commute to work daily. This hour-and-a-half travelling time each way became too tiresome to continue after six months. Finally, Pipo and my mom decided to accept my aunt Genoveva's generous offer to buy a house there so he wouldn't have to spend so much time commuting. (I believe she told me that it cost her six thousand Cuban pesos for the house; a very large sum of money in those days.) Upon purchasing this new home, we had to surrender our old Jobabo home, which had been given to us at no cost by the Cuban government. In Cuba, no person or immediate family members were legally able to own or possess two separate homes at one time. The newly formed Cuban Constitution made it crystal clear that all citizens were entitled to equal distribution of good and services. This law was the foundation of the 1959 revolution that swept Fidel Castro into power. Any violations of these laws by anyone resulted in a long prison sentence.

Our new home was located on 97 Angel Guardia Street near a corner garage called Gascon. Gascon was a huge facility located across the street from Victoria Elementary School, where I was about to attend class. It was great! In Cuba, school was compulsive six days a week, including Saturdays until midday, unlike America's five-day requirement. The home itself was mainly constructed from marble and cement with a zinc roof. As a result of the zinc, you could hear the raindrops knocking on the rooftops, making you feel like snuggling up in bed and going to sleep like a baby. It was very relaxing and soothing to the soul. The interior of the house was spacious, with four bedrooms, one living room, a kitchen, and one bathroom, all on the left side as you entered, as well as a long, open hallway for easy access. The hallway also served to connect the dining area to the back terrace, where we had a grape vine to shield us from the hot sun. Twenty feet into the yard, we had a *poso* (well) for our water. Our fresh start came crashing down eight months later when the new management at Pipo's work held an outdoor meeting and asked anyone who planned on leaving Cuba to raise his or her hand. They said that there would be no repercussions and they merely wanted to make sure that workers were trained and ready to take over for anyone leaving in order to maintain continuity for the betterment of the state and its people. Under this umbrella of cooperation, Pipo naturally raised his hand and informed everyone gathered of his intent to emigrate to America with the family. He indicated that it wasn't certain, as the move still hadn't been approved by the state and he didn't know how long this would take. After the meeting had drawn to a close, he was approached by another member of the management committee and requested to turn in all his keys immediately because he was no longer considered a patriot and did not warrant any more privileges from the state. As of right then, he was instructed to leave the premises and informed that his employment with La Comercial had ended forever.

This unexpected action was quite a shock to my father, because he had been so involved with the business for nearly twenty years and now he was out, just like that, without any input. The worst part was that these committed managers were too blind to realize that my father actually was a true patriot who devoted his last drop of sweat in advancing Cuba's best interest. These new managers had no business savvy. They were strictly bureaucrats who never knew what a real hard day's work was all about! They were immersed in red tape and produced absolutely nothing. These blood-sucking worms were our biggest foe. This type of bureaucrat destroys the fabric of many nations. Their mentality is prevalent in all types of political and economic systems, whether it is socialism, communism, or capitalism, and especially in Cuba, where they removed many people from the workforce like my father—people that could have enhanced the quality of life for all Cubans. This cancer is more debilitating than any enemy's invading force. It results in the raping of natural resources because it affects the country's psyche and yields total despair.

Pipo shook off this bad news as well as anyone possibly could have, based on my observations on that fateful day and based on what my mom told me about this terrible period. After my father left the company, he was constantly approached by his ex-work colleagues who had become his friends. They gave him boxes of rum, food, and other merchandise to help us survive, all at great peril given the consequences they would have faced if they had been caught. Six months later, when things became more difficult, my parents and aunt Genoveva started a home-based Spanish churros enterprise. Churros are stick-shaped pieces of dough that are fried and then sprinkled with sugar. Churros are so yummy that you can't stop eating them, especially when paired with hot chocolate. This clandestine business was a lifesaver and actually became very profitable in the black market economy. Our clientele grew so large that we could not keep up with the demand. We mostly catered to the local pool of people which even included many government officials. However, our biggest customer was from my Victoria Elementary School across the street. Many times, the teachers would place an order with me early so they would be able to get them in time for their recreation break. They would excuse me from school for five minutes to take the order to my mother and aunt. Our in-house maid, Catalina, my brother, and sometimes family and friends were imported to help us. Our front house was always crowded with people waiting an hour or two for these delicious goodies from the low, open window that we served from. In the meantime, my poor Pipo was busier than ever before, running around all over Victoria and other towns to obtain the supplies we needed to make the churros. These mainly included cooking oil, flour, and sugar. This was a very difficult task to pull off in Cuba, because everything was rationed and therefore limited. However, if anyone could do it, Pipo would be the one to do so because he was so well loved and known. He always managed to find all the required ingredients to keep the business flourishing until the city of Victoria and other nearby municipalities ran totally dry. We then had to readjust and become even more resilient. Consequently, we started to make pudding and lemon ice blocks to try to stay afloat. This *modus operandi* was the norm growing up in Cuba in the 1960s. The fighting spirit of never giving up was the way of life for us and for the many Cubans who inhabited this island paradise during the tough economic times.

One of my most dear pastimes was window shopping for toys with my father in the late evenings, four days a week, in Victoria De Las Tunas. This ritual always gave me great joy. We would hold hands as we went from store to store, checking out all the toys I wanted for Los Tres Reyes (the Three Kings). In retrospect, I tell you, he had to have the most patience in the world to spend so much time traveling about three miles until we had visited every toy store in the city. My favorite stores were the two that had a big red, yellow, and green dump truck for sale. We used to spend the most time in these stores because I wanted one so badly. I couldn't help myself from having a little tantrum when Pipo wanted to leave, winning me some extra time in the shops. However, my beloved father had to get up early to go to work and would promise me that we would come back again the next day. He always stuck to his word, so I relented and happily held his hand again as we walked back home talking about the truck. Needless to say, I did not get the truck that I wanted so much. I remember how disappointed I felt when Christmas came around and I did not see the truck with the rest of my toys. They told me that they spent days in line to get me the big truck, but there were only three of them and they were gone by the time they made it to the front of the line. I knew in my heart and mind, even as a little boy, that they had tried their best to please me. Later on in the evening, I remember how happy and lucky I felt to have such an incredible family that really loved me. Immediately upon realizing this, I gave both my parents a heartfelt apology for my poor attitude earlier in the morning, along with a big hug and a kiss.

This was the city where I first learned how to read. I hadh come down with chicken pox, a disease that was very common among children in Cuba. My case was quite severe, so I was isolated in order to protect others because I was extremely contagious. Only Pipo, my mom, aunt Genoveva, and some friends of mine who had previously contracted the disease visited me. It was very funny seeing people running away from me to avoid contracting it themselves. I specifically recall our maid, Catalina, running like a track star past me continuously with her mouth and nose covered. At one time, I yelled at her that I would jump out of bed to chase her around the house if she didn't stop. She began to scream, calling for my parents to make me stay in bed. Earlier, my parents had placed a red illuminating light on the ceiling to help alleviate my red eyes and face. This was a Cuban folklore remedy believed to help cure chicken pox, which it did five days later. My red eyes were gone due to the low light emission that penetrated right through the white mosquito net.

To keep me from getting too bored, Pipo would constantly bring me new comic books to look at, since I did not know how to read yet. However, I learned how to read within a month, mostly because of my circumstances of being on lockdown mode in my bed in my parents' bedroom. After coming home from work, Pipo would come and climb inside my bed to read to me until his eyes became so heavy that he fell asleep. While he slept, I began to poke him in the side of his ribs for about a minute before he would wake up again. He then went back to where he had left off, but it was no use—after a short five minutes or so of reading, he again started to babble sleepily, saying all kinds of things that did not follow the story line or make any sense. This had me very confused. I would jump up and down in bed to try to stop his spell of sleepiness and would also say, "Pipo, you are falling asleep without finishing the story!"

"It must be the low red light in the room that's making me sleepy," he said, but I asked, "How come I wasn't falling asleep as well then?"

"You must be used to this light, son!" And again, I think Pipo was correct, because everyone who came in to read to me was no match against the sleep-inducing power of this red light. It was frustrating and very funny watching them all fall asleep ten minutes into reading the story. They would lie there, snoring away, completely carefree. The only time I left my red room was when nature called.

I attributed my learning to read to that red light, which made my family and friends drowsy as they tried to read to me but could never get to the end of the book. This unwelcome scenario forced me to decipher each line of the comis books that lay around me, word by word, on my own as they lay next to me sleeping. This led to a happy celebration when I was finally able to read to my parents, aunt Genoveva, my brother, and friends, and I never fell asleep in the midst of the red light that was stronger than taking any pill.

Our home was full of funny stories and episodes, as you will soon learn. One of those was the time my brother, Gerardo Jr., came looking for me excitedly. He had an ulterior motive unbeknownst to me. While I was engrossed in playing games in the backyard with my best friend, Tomasito, who lived with his parents and beautiful sister, Lidia, next door, he said, "Come here, I want you to do something for fun!" I asked what he wanted me to do.

"Well, Catalina (our housekeeper) is taking a shower right now and the door is not locked! Go over there and quietly open it wide so I can see her with no clothes on!" he said. I replied angrily to his remarks by saying that I would not do it. I told my brother that she would get mad and tell Pipo, who would whip me with his belt! Catalina was about seventeen years old at the time and had a very beautiful body. My brother was about fourteen, with strong hormones that were starting to take off. Since I was only seven, he wanted me to do his dirty work as he positioned himself in view to see her completely naked once the door was opened. Somehow, he convinced me to pull off the prank by promising me toys. I was kind of scared as I got closer to the bathroom door, hearing the water splashing in the background. All this time, he was urging me in a low, whispering voice from the hallway near the terrace to open it at once, before someone came in and spoiled the whole thing. I heard him say to me repeatedly, "Don't be a chicken, open it! Open it!" I looked at him one last time before I quickly opened the door, catching our Catalina by surprise. Yelling at me, she was totally exposed in the sunlight from the hallway. This was music to my brother's eyesight, but it also left in me in shock at seeing the first naked girl in my life. She was very upset with me for what I had done, chasing me all over the house and uttering these words: "You just don't do that! You don't do that, Miguelito! How would you like me to do that to you?"

My brother was enjoying the entire show, laughing, about fifteen feet away. Upon seeing my brother, she stopped chasing me and ran back to the bathroom to get a towel to cover up. When she reappeared, she said, "I'm going to tell your mother and father the bad thing you did to me as soon as they come home!"

I quickly said, "Catalina, it was my brother's fault. He told me to do it! Blame him!"

"Both of you are going to get it when your father gets home," she said. Upon hearing these words, I began to cry because Pipo was a disciplinarian who lived up to that billing. I had to brace myself for the full impact that was heading my way very shortly. It goes without saying that when my father walked in the house, I hid in the kitchen closet, where I could hear Catalina talking to my parents about the incident. Within minutes, my father angrily shouted for me to come to him immediately. I reluctantly came out of the closet to face the music with much trepidation. As I got near him, I saw him unbuckling his belt for some good old-fashioned discipline. My mom and aunt Genoveva tried their very best to interject for me, pleading for Pipo to go soft or stop it altogether. However, my father did not change his mind, belting me on my butt for a good solid minute as I ran around the living room crying and screaming to Pipo that my brother had told me to do it all. "It's not my fault! He forced me! Hit him! Hit him!"

"Don't worry about your brother! He's going to be next after I finish with you," Pipo said. Man I tell you, I can still feel the stinging of the belt on my red legs and butt.

When he completed my well-deserved physical punishment, he called Catalina over so I could apologize to her for my misbehavior and promise never to even think about repeating it again. After I sincerely said to her, "I'm so sorry for my bad behavior" and gave her hug, I thought the case was closed, but not so fast.

I was cut off from watching my favorite cartoons and the most popular weekly program in Cuba, the adventures of the masked man himself, "El Zorro," for a month. This was a *novela* (soap opera) that had the country glued to their television sets. It was a family experience, like going to the movies. Since many homes had no television to watch it, they would come to our house or we would rotate with other families who had sets, offering food and refreshments for some great, memorable times. Even though I did not like the spankings by Pipo, they definitely laid out a loving blueprint of discipline for me to follow for the rest of my life. His tough love proved to be the magic pill. Many times today, we don't have the stomach to pursue the same techniques in raising our kids. This result, more often than not, ends up in a catastrophic consequence for modern society at large, where youths have no respect for others and are full of violent behavior.

I remember when all the characters of the hit show *Zorro* came to life and practiced in our street of Angel Guardia in preparation for the upcoming carnival, which took place about five blocks away from our home. This unexpected event took our city by storm. We all camped outside, waiting to catch a glimpse of all our heroes in person at their corner chalet, practicing and signing photos. Upon hearing this news, I ran as quickly as I could to tell Pipo all about it so he could take me there. I was so excited at meeting the masked man himself that I ran the entire distance as my father did his best to stay with me, which he did. Once we arrived, large crowds obscured my view, so Pipo picked me up and placed me on his shoulder, so I could watch the swashbuckling, intense exhibition duels. You could hear the sound of the metal swords colliding, much to the cheers of the immense crowd. The masked man did not disappoint us with his dazzling, victorious performance. It was a real treat to witness my television heroes come to life in front of my eyes, especially seeing them with my ultimate hero, Pipo, in one late-afternoon setting. This was an incredibly impressive event for a young boy like me. It was simply amazing. It was a good thing that we went to this by chance, because the next day, all three shows were sold out at Vicente Garcia Central Park. This was the biggest park in the city and the center of the carnival, as well as the place my father often took my brother and me for some good times.

The carnival in our hometown was great fun for me and my father as we spent an enormous amount of time together. It was the party of parties. Nothing can compare with the energy and the sheer vibrancy that literally sweeps you along into a virtual cloud where time seems to stop and succumb to the beat of the rhythmic Caribbean music. This wave was full of intense passion, dancing, singing, and fireworks, all in unison with family, friends, and strangers. No one stopped for days until the very end. Our trek originated from the main square of the park, following the colorful floats around the city, along with the most beautiful women pn the island displaying the fastest hip movements in their seductive dance and wearing those skimpy clothes that leave you gasping for air. Along the carnival parade, we would stop for drinks and food. Most times, I asked Pipo for a *frita* (a Cuban hamburger) and a Materva (a Cuban soft drink) while Pipo would get a *cerveza* (a beer), either La Cristal or Hatuey. After a short break, we would jump back into the parade in sync with the music as we danced and waved to the crowd. The best part was when we passed by our own home. We saw my mom, aunt Genoveva, my brother, Catalina, and many neighborhood friends on both sides of the street dancing and waving back at us. On a few occasions, they joined us en route and we celebrated the festivities together. For some reason, every time I got lost, my father knew just where to find me in the parade. The only thing he had to do was to look for the prettiest girls riding on the float and there I would be, right next to them with a big smile on my face (at least until my father came and took me with him to join the rest of the family). I think Pipo approved of my wise strategy, because he also never deviated too far away from the dancing girls and their tiny costumes. However, sometimes I would play a joke on Pipo and disappear into the large and noisy crowd to drive him nuts in his worrisome search for me. During his frantic search, I could see Pipo running around the parade crowd yelling my name: "Miguel! Miguel! Where are you?" After a short ten minutes of drama, I would suddenly stop my charade and reappear by sneaking up behind him. He would sternly warn me not to do it again or else. After his vociferous speech, we continued on the partying trail with the carnival parade to the sultry Afro Cuban beat, with me sitting on Pipo's shoulders.

Speaking about parades, I vividly recall a memorial parade to honor Argentina-born and Cuban fallen revolutionary hero Ernesto "Che" Guevara, who was captured in Bolivia and executed on October 9, 1967. This happened one month before we departed for Mexico City. Che's popularity in Cuba was equal to Fidel Castro's and in some instances even exceeded "El Comandante" himself. Today, he is an iconic figure who is widely revered by many; especially the young and disenfranchised. At Princeton University, where I'm currently employed, and other similar institutions of higher learning, Che is still very much alive. You can't help but notice, as you walk around the campus, how prevalent his image is—plastered on the walls of student dorms and on T-shirts. In addition, his signature black guerilla beret is a fashion statement with wide political activist overtones among many college students.

I remember watching this massive parade as an eight-year-old, standing outside my home. It went by for a solid five hours in tribute to him. It also served a dual purpose as a rallying cry for Cuban unity against American imperialism. You could hear the constant chanting of "Que viva la revolucion (Long live the revolution)," "Que viva Che (Long live Che)," and the constant, loud recital of "Fidel! Fidel! Fidel!" intertwined with the words "Cuba, si! Yanki, no! Cuba, si! Yanki, no!" These words were imbedded into the Cuban psyche, referring to the evilness of Americans always meddling in others countries' internal affairs. It was a very colorful parade, as the young children wore the Cuban colors of red, white, and blue and carried flags and posters of Fidel, Che, and other Cuban revolutionary heroes, such as the famous poet Jose Marti, who fought against Spain's tyranny and for Cuba's liberation in late 1895. He was killed in his struggle and eventually became a martyr and a symbol of Cuban sovereignty.

What left an enduring impression was not necessarily what went on at this historical event. It was what took place during and after the parade. My best friend, Tomasito, whom I always played with, invited me to his house to show me some new toys that his father had been able to get for him. Our two houses connected to each other via a side door on the right, near the middle of the yard, because we shared a communal well located on our property. This arrangement made our families close to one another. We welcomed each other all the time; we celebrated our birthdays and many events in unison. There was a lot of love between us. However, upon going to his home on this particular day, his father, Tomas (a committed member of the Communist Party who also served on the neighborhood commission to monitor any anti-government movement) called me over. In front of his son, Tomasito, he said, "I've got something to give you, Miguel!" We had woken him up from the usual afternoon siesta he had taken. He then handed me a black cloth memorial band about an inch wide to put on. After struggling and failing to put it on myself, he helped me tie the band onto my left arm to show my patriotism and sadness as a way to pay homage to the death of comrade Che—a hero of the revolution and a person he admired greatly—on this most sorrowful of days. Since I was so young, I really did not fully understood how big an icon Che was or what he meant to the masses. I just wanted to be part of this event with my buddy Tomasito and others who wore the bands proudly.

When I got home, my mom said, "Who gave you that band?" Before I could answer her, she took it off and told me not to put it on again because she was not a communist and was still upset about what the local officials did to remove Pipo from his business, La Comercial. Upon hearing this backdrop, I completely understood my mom's position and why she reacted so forcefully in not wanting me to wear this black armband during those days. However, I did not take her actions very kindly. I angrily revolted with resentment by running back to Tomasito's home to get another band from his father, Tomas. This back and forth played out a few times before she told me Pipo would be very upset if he saw me wearing the band. I said I wouldn't wear it anymore, shaking my head in disapproval. I learned a hard lesson that day. I wanted to march together in unison in the streets with my friends. So, my only choice was to wear the band at Tomasito's home and remove it at my home. This arrangement was a win-win situation for both my mom and Tomas, who had just run out of bands. He had to quickly cut one out of a large piece of fabric to make me one for the parade that was only minutes away. At times, my mom would exaggerate or speak for my father because she felt it was the only way I would obey her. It was a tactic that she employed to have it her way all the time, until my father's passing. This weapon of choice was often challenged by me going directly to Pipo to make sure she was telling the truth. Anyway, whether my father Pipo would get upset with me for displaying the armband was unlikely, because during the last five minutes of the parade, he was standing outside our home, next to me, as I wore the band with Tomasito, his father, and many others, cheering and waving to the very end. In retrospect, my father did not carry any grudge or resentment toward anyone or any political party. He was very much loved, even by those hardcore communists like Tomas and others who tried their best to penetrate the bureaucracy to have Pipo reinstated at his old job, without much success.

After the parade was over, I looked back and saw my mom staring out the window, shaking her head as I smiled at her while I proudly wore my black armband with Pipo next to me.

I firmly believe that Tomas was a great person who deeply aspired to his convictions to the very core, without any reservations. In Cuba, this mentality often alienated friends and neighbors who took sides or viewed each other with suspicion. In the case of my father and Tomas, this was a nonfactor. Both knew where they stood without ever compromising the truth. This was a genuine trait that should be admired by all of us, no matter whether you subscribe to a communist or capitalist ideology. Both camps knew it was not perfect, but they all firmly agreed that treason was the worst crime perpetrated against the State and it was not tolerated under any circumstances. We all loved Cuba the same and wouldn't do anything to compromise it. This commonality, just like sharing our water well, was one approach of preserving our way of life for the better; which my father did naturally. There were no pretenses here; what you saw was what you got with Pipo. This love of Cuba was entrenched in his soul and no one was able to take it away from him.

Overall, life in Victoria De Las Tunas was simple, with countless memorable moments to share. One thing I enjoyed about growing up in Cuba (as I mentioned in an earlier chapter), was falling asleep to the sound of rain hitting the zinc plates on the roof of our house. Sometimes, in the middle of a heavy rainstorm, I would get up and go to the bathroom and notice everyone sleeping like newborn babies. There was something magical and relaxing about those raindrops hitting our roof, at least until the lightning and thunder entered the scene. These devastating storms came with intense lightning and powerful thunder that shook the houses and cut off the lights for hours. During these terrifying storms, I would see aunt Genoveva and my brother in the corner of the dark house sharing a candle as the lightning strikes penetrated the entire house, resulting in loud booming aftermaths that made your skin roll up and shiver in trepidation. During the middle of these wicked storms, my father had a flashlight and would go looking for leaks and trouble spots and making sure we were all safe. My mother was hysterical and frightened to death, walking around the house carrying a lid of melting candlewax, looking and screaming for me in the midst of these loud electrical discharges from Mother Nature. I, on the other hand, was trying to wait it out in the only safe location there was—underneath my bed! We could hear lightning striking nearby areas, all the while hoping ours would not be one of the targets. In the thick of these storms, neighbors would sometimes come knocking on our front door to check on our well-being or ask us about needed supplies like candles and batteries. With all this commotion going on simultaneously, my aunt Genoveva would shout that we had a leak on the roof and get a pail and mop quickly. And before you knew it, we had multiple leaks springing everywhere inside the house. It felt like we were in a circus, running into each other, emptying pails and cleaning up the mess with very little light. It was hilariously insane, but scary at the same time. We did our best to cope with the bad weather. Our maid Catalina did not make things any better and I could constantly hear her loud screaming around the house. Many times during these storms, I heard my mom and aunt Genoveva praying to God to end the violent storms, without much success. After the storms were history, the whole neighborhood would converge in the street to unite and make sure everyone was safe and sound. At times, I saw Pipo running into homes to check how the elderly neighbors were doing. That was my Pipo—always thinking about others.

The other situation almost took a real bite at my butt. This happened when I saw my aunt Genoveva in the terrace hallway, doing needlework. She called me over to keep her company, talking to me while she worked. After a couple of minutes, I decided to sit down in a rocking chair to her left, almost at the edge of the terrace. As I was ready to sit down and rock, my aunt yelled at me, "Miguel, stop! Don't sit! There's a huge rat on the chair!" When I looked back, I was startled and I panicked big time! The rat stood up on its two legs, ready to sink its teeth into my flesh. It was the ugliest rat I've ever seen; it was foaming and spitting a whitish liquid of some sort. My aunt said, "Get away from it fast! It looks like the rat is infected, get away! You don't want to catch rabies!" In our city, there was a massive rat control problem. It was a real epidemic. These uninvited guests were carriers of all types of disease. We were literally being invaded, not by the American military as you constantly heard in the media, but by a four-legged creature that ran amok in our surroundings. It became so severe that we had over fifty mouse traps in our home alone. In addition, we had several cats to help fend off this large infestation.

We had called a state-owned pest control company, but they were too busy to help. Pipo had the odious task of trying to reduce the rat population as soon as possible before they started viewing us as their food source and attacking us, just like in the movies *Willard* and *Ben*. Pipo started by carefully placing chunks of poisoned food all over the place. I even began using my slingshot to help with the elimination. My father complimented me on several occasions; I definitely had no shortage of targets to practice with. I killed about twenty to thirty after school just in our backyard, but they still kept coming. To increase our killing rate, Father started to throw bricks at flocks of these pesky multipliers. I remember my father going around the property every morning wearing a glove, scooping up all the dead ones using a shovel and throwing them into a big aluminum can. It was so gross watching him do this unenviable task. I was ready to vomit seeing the piles and piles of dead rats. For the record, Pipo did all the shovelling. No one else had the stomach for this cleanup. As they say, someone had to do it, and it wasn't going to be me or my mother or aunt! Well, this scenario continued for over a month. What was fascinating to me was seeing Pipo in action, handling these ugly creatures without any disgust or fear. He went about getting the job done as quickly as possible. He was a total professional. Sometimes, some of the rats were still alive, so he'd use the shovel to hit them on the head to finally kill them. One time, he grabbed one by the tail and showed it to my mom as a joke. She quickly covered her eyes and vanished to avoid puking. Pipo was having a good time with Mom, and he looked at me, all smiles. When my father finished, I helped him load the four heavy cans into the back trunk of his Chevy. According to his count, each contained about fifty rotten rats. We drove to a secluded area on top of a cliff and launched them into a river that had a strong current. We stood there together, watching as they floated away.

I also took my father's advice of knowing your immediate surroundings by heart, and this came in handy when my brother was getting beaten up by two guys in front of uncle Manuel and aunt Marciana's mansion about two hundred feet away. It took place in this wide street that connected to a tertiary road and also served as a parking lot. This roomy area was where we often played in the evening as my parents, family, and friends came together to socialize. Pipo was often with us because of his concern about the many speeding cars cutting through this shortcut and possibly injuring us, but not this time. Against this backdrop, I discovered my brother being beaten up. At first, I looked around to try to find someone to help, but there was nobody in sight. I was about to take action to help him, but then I realized these guys were much bigger and stronger than my brother and I. Since I didn't want to get beaten up by them as well, I searched for anything to use as a weapon to even the playing field somewhat. Unfortunately, I couldn't find anything near me quickly, and I had left my slingshot at home. This was one of the few times that I didn't have my slingshot, as we were practically inseparable! It couldn't have come at a worse time. My brother continued screaming loudly while I grabbed a large tennis-ball-sized rock from the ground and threw it as hard as I could. I had another one in my left hand, ready to fire away as well, if necessary, to protect myself. I aimed at one of the bullies who had his back toward me. He was approximately forty feet away. Lo and behold, with Lady Luck on my side (or maybe more likely a guardian angel guiding my aim with precision), the rock I had thrown hit my intended target just like a cruise missile. Because I struck him solidly in the head with my first throw, he fell mercilessly down to the ground. This result gave my brother and me the opportunity to run away safely to my uncle's next-door neighbor, who had witnessed the entire drama. She yelled at us outside her door to come in and hide.

Upon hearing her golden words, we frantically ran past her and she closed and locked the door behind us. Again, we were very fortunate as everything went our way during this scary (but thrilling) moment. We waited out the "storm" for forty minutes until we were sure they had left the area for good. The best part for me was that they never saw who had thrown the rock. As we left the house, we diligently surveyed our surroundings before running to our home, past the large Gascon car garage facility that stood at the corner of our street. When we got home, we shared the details of what had just transpired with our parents. Unbelievably, these two kids threw a brick through our window, shattering it, in response to my brother's popularity with some of the school ladies. My brother had no choice but to go after the kid who had broken it. Then he was blindsided by the buddy of the guy he was chasing. The friend had been hiding, waiting in the wings, ready to gang up on him. Both of my parents told me that I did a heroic act in coming to the rescue of my sibling because it was in self-defense. Then Pipo shook my hands and said, "Tomorrow, we are going to the matinee to watch a great movie in celebration of your good deed." My father's words really connected with me because they revealed how proud he was of me for putting fear to the side momentarily and taking action to prevent any further onslaught against my brother.

Before any further discussions about the matinee ensued, Pipo invited me to join him and my mom grocery shopping. In Cuba, shopping for food was really "black market" shopping. This kind of practice was the only way one could obtain any meat. Unsanctioned underground shopping was very common in those days. You faced a long prison sentence if you were ever caught, but the government officials often looked the other way, as they knew the black market helped the keep the economy from totally collapsing. The economy had been on life support ever since the American embargo was imposed. My mother used me as a cover, as a woman with a child was less likely to be apprehended. Needless to say, this approach proved to be very successful for my mom and family friends, because even though we had several close calls, we never got caught. We always managed to have just enough food to eat. The state was happy to compromise and coexist with the parallel market, as long it did not threaten the formal system. In Cuba, all commodities sold were severely regulated and rationed in an official ledger for record keeping to ensure equal distribution of goods. Any discrepancy in the ledger resulted in the allocation of goods being halted pending further investigations. This created a long backlog for all types of goods and services. Only the essential items were allowed to continue being rationed out. These included milk, rice, bread, water, and limited meats. This policy was a way of life in Victoria De Las Tunas and throughout Cuba. This hard life did not dampen our spirits one bit. We were a happy and close-knit family, without much infighting. Years later in America, when money and material things became paramount, it often clouded the thinking of my inner and extended family, which was very unfortunate because we were never able to recapture that same cohesiveness again. I guess this was due to the crazy mentality of work, work, work!

In retrospect, those days in Cuba were really the best times of our life, despite the daily hardships that we faced. We sorely missed that period once we lost focus of what was really important in the big picture—family and nothing more. Those days of normalcy involved having my father, Pipo, come home from work as my mom, aunt, and the maid collaborated to ensure the house affairs were in order as my brother and I rushed home for dinner. It all ran like clockwork. After dinner, Pipo would go to either Maceo or Vicente Garcia Park to be with friends. My mom and the rest of the family sat at our home chatting with neighbors. My brother was doing his own things with friends, while I played with Tomasito and others. We always made sure we were always together about an hour before bedtime at our front doorstep. These moments were really priceless as we played Zorro using wooden sticks for swords and making our own masks out of cardboard, which we painted using black shoe polish. We also kept busy by playing hide and seek, riding our bikes, or just relaxing, watching cartoons. Not to be outdone, we often meddled in some serious games of dominoes, a Cuban tradition, or Spanish Barajas, a most popular card game among everyone, especially with the ladies. Other times, I would accompany my father to the parks with a quick stop at his older brother Manuel's house for a little get-together. Even though my uncle Manuel was more of a disciplinarian than my father, I always had a good time with him. As a matter of fact, I remember many shenanigans with him. Being the practical joker that I was, he was always on my radar and very much fair game to me. What made it extra special was the stern demeanor that he had at times. I was often afraid of him, but that did not curtail me from doing what I did best, having fun at other people's expense. I naturally did this in a genteel manner (if that's even possible). On one occasion, I jumped over into his backyard from my house and started to rattle the pigs and the other animals in the corral. The unrest in the backyard drew out my aunt Marciana to check what was eliciting such behavior in the animals. I would immediately hide until she went back into the house. A few minutes later, I would enter the house from the rear door for a quick visit. Upon hearing me, she would say something like, "Was that you making all the noise outside to scare the animals?"

I responded nervously, hoping I didn't get caught, replying along these lines: "aunt Marciana, I think it was a snake! I saw one in my yard!" This was true and I thought it was a good excuse.

Well, she said, "Oh, you did? Just be quiet, your uncle is sleeping and you know he gets upset if he doesn't get his full afternoon siesta." I told her I would be quiet, but that I was starving. aunt Marciana agreed to make me a snack, but only on condition that I would sit still. My aunt was too smart for me to fool her, but nevertheless, she went along with my devious prank without letting me know that she had me totally figured out. In the meantime, my uncle woke up, greeted me, and, to my aunt's unbelievable delight, we started to play games together for hours while she was brought us food and drinks. My uncle Manuel was a very strong-minded person indeed, but deep down, he was soft and loving. I attributed his predisposition to his role as the father figure to his nine siblings, including my own father. His own father had died at a very young age.

There were many adventures in his house, located at 60 Maceo Street. Among the many were the weddings of family members, and who could forget those big bashes where we all celebrated together? Besides the rock incident where I came to the rescue of my brother, there was another memorable situation that happened to me during this time instead of my brother. It happened in the very same vicinity. A neighborhood kid stole my parked bike while I was sitting on the front steps of my uncle's home, talking with my friends. He came out of nowhere, quickly mounted my bike, and took off. My only chance of catching up with him was to spring forward in a dive to stop him before he picked up speed. Well, my strategy paid big dividends because I was able to grab the back seat, and the kid lost control, crashing into a parked car. I, on the other hand, landed face first on the hard concrete surface, busting my lips and severely scraping my knees. My friends secured my bike as I ran back home a block away. As Pipo opened the door, I told him what I had done and why I was bleeding. I also mentioned to him that for some strange reason, every time I touched my front upper teeth with my tongue it felt so sharp that it hurt. "Come here and let me see," he said. Upon looking at it, he noticed that my front tooth was broken in half. My mom took a look herself to see the aftermath of my kamikaze stunt. aunt Genoveva, my brother and Catalina started taking turns to see my chipped tooth. I decided to see it for myself and walked over to my bedroom to take a look in the mirror. When I saw how ugly I looked, I started to go on a rampage and began to cry earnestly. I told Pipo, "All the kids at school are going to make fun of me." He said, "Miguel, tomorrow we will go to the dentist to have your tooth repaired." Well, I remember it like it happened just yesterday. We visited six dentists that day and they all had the same answer—they couldn't repair it. Their professional advice was for me to wait until I was a little older. My parents were relentless, but in the end nothing could be done to restore my tooth. Upon hearing this final bad news, Pipo calmed me down by telling me the advantage of having a sharp tooth. He said, "Now you will be able to cut into apples better, son." Pipo used to bring cases of apples home on a regular base because of his many friendships. He went to the kitchen cabinet and retrieved an apple for me, so that I could check out my new razor-edged tooth. He said, "Here's the apple, give it a try, son!" I grabbed it from him and, to my amazement, again my father was right. It worked and I became happy once again, thanks to my father thinking outside the box. Today, I'm still reminded of that misfortune every time I brush my teeth, especially in the morning. I'm able to see one tooth a quarter shorter than the rest of them.

A month earlier, I went to the doctor to get treatment for a nasty cold. During this visit, I was prescribed the wrong dosage with dire consequences. The dosage was much too high for children, and I had a very strong reaction to it. My tongue became locked and I was unable to speak. When this occurred, I was fortunate that my parents were nearby, because I became very ill and very frightened. I was then rushed to the hospital emergency room by Pipo and my mother, where I was given an injection to counteract the heavy dosage. Later on when I returned to normal, I was told that a slightly higher dosage would have killed me. Years later in America, in 1972, I fell of my bike at the corner of McWhorter Street and New York Avenue and landed on top of a piece of glass from my broken mirror. The glass penetrated the knee cap on my left leg. The worst part, besides the unbearable pain, was how I was treated at St. James Hospital Emergency Room at Newark, New Jersey. My treatment involded being given twelve stitches. For two months, I complained to my parents about how painful and infected it was. They finally took me to see my cousin Casanova, who told my parents that I had a piece of glass an inch long inside my leg. After surgery, my cousin told Pipo and my mother and then me that I had come extremely close to losing my ability to walk, permanently. This pesky glass was damaging my ligaments and arteries. It had travelled about two inches since the accident.

Unfortunately, these bad experiences with doctors have left me with enduring memories that have severely impacted my faith in doctors. Every time I have to go to see a physician, I become very tense and uptight with trepidation. This is my one Achilles heel which still haunts me today as it lingers with no end in sight. The so called Cuban witchdoctors, who are spiritual doctors that practice a religion called Santeria, are the sole exception. La Santeria is famous for its songs, rhythms, dances, and magic. Whenever I got sick, my mother asked my father to take me with him to the countryside to one of these priest's homes to have my illness removed, because I always felt protected by his presence. In the beginning, I was afraid of these rituals being performed on me by these medicine men, who dressed weirdly, wearing colorful costumes and speaking to the spiritual world in tongues with African overtones. Pipo would grab my hands tightly to help me follow the instructions of the priest as he danced and simultaneously threw water on me, chasing out my impure spirits. This healing practice normally took about forty minutes to complete. Afterward, my father asked me a series of questions about what had just taken place and how I now felt. Before he did, he would say something to allay my feelings, like "Tu eres muy valiente!" (You are very brave). These words coming from my hero really comforted me and, more importantly, made me happy as we drove home, admiring the countryside with me completely cured. The best part of these trips was the long conversations that I had with my father, who I believe had a bigger part in healing me than any of those priests. This was down to one simple factor—his deep love for me that resonated exponentially within me.

On one of these occasions, I asked him to let me drive home. He said, "Hold on for a minute or so until I pull off to the side of the road, then come sit on top of me and grab the steering wheel." My eyes lit up with joy like a shining star when I heard those words. Wow! Driving Pipo's car (a 1954 Chevrolet black four-door sedan) was like being in heaven with pure excitement. From this point on, it became a tradition that every time we went to see the priests, I would take control of the wheel on the way home. I recall that while driving, Pipo would often remind me to pay attention to the road ahead instead of looking and waving to people working in the fields. This was because, at times, I would veer off to the left or to the right of the road. He kept telling me, "Miguel, stay in the center of the road or I am going to pull over and not let you drive anymore." But he never did. Driving was my reward for behaving well and for my valor during these ceremonies to help me whenever I had any type of sickness that did not go away. My father would talk and make jokes, imparting fatherly advice to me all the way home until we entered our home city of Victoria De Las Tunas. He would only stop to concentrate on the heavy traffic. At that point, I happily went back to my passenger seat. I welcomed these outings with passion and couldn't wait for the next one to come. Visiting these doctors was a godsend and an awesome experience because it provided so much uninterrupted quality time with Pipo. Plus, taking control of the wheel was not half bad either. It was a real kicker—I simply loved it! If I could borrow the famous line from a New Jersey tourism commercial that former Governor Thomas Kean made a household phrase, "New Jersey and You, Perfect Together." Well, that was Pipo and I.

Another family outing that we often embarked on was going to the home of my uncle Fidel and aunt Clara in the city of Bartle. They had this huge orchard with four acres of fields full of oranges and tangerines at the back of their house. We took turns picking, collecting, and obviously eating these delicious fruits. Afterward, we would all walk around the forestlike enclave and play all sorts of games like hide and seek, all while admiring the pristine beauty surrounding us. As we made our way to the back of the field, there was a large, closed cage that housed all the livestock. It literally ran the entire width of the field and was humongous in size. They seemed to have everything running around inside making crazy noises. I saw pigs, chickens, rabbits, and even birds. On crossing this midsection, you had another field full of trees winding down to the farthest edge of a brook. I was not permitted to go to that area because the stream was very deep. In addition, this area contained lurking alligators and other predators that were not able to penetrate the fortified cage or beyond it.

Often, we would just relax and fall asleep in a hammock under a cool, soothing breeze after having a traditional roasted pig feast with all the fanfare that came with it. At times, it was frustrating for me because it left me by myself as my family enjoyed their siesta. To keep me from getting too restless, I would make a hole in the ground and fill it with water and start playing with my wooden boat. I had an explosive and adventurous imagination when it came to playing. I even set my boat on fire to give it a more realistic flavor, imitating cannons firing their weapons, hitting and disabling my vessel. At times, my cousin Fidelito, who is the same age as my brother, would come by and play with me for a short time. I remember the time when he said, "I just received these baseball cards from America and I want to show them to you." This first introduction to these precious cards captured my eternal curiosity, and I dreamed of one day owning some of these cards myself. Years later, thanks to Fidelito, I became a serious collector of baseball cards in America, but not before

I went to Pipo's pants and my mom's pocketbook to look for change to continually purchase baseball card packs to try and satisfy my insatiable appetite. Years later, it all paid off big time as it gave me additional money to help my parents buy our first home when I sold these cards. Today, I own just a few cards from this childhood pastimes. However, I'm still the proud owner of a mint 1967 Topps Tom Seaver rookie card. It's one of my prized possessions, along with a 1970 Johnny Bench.

My brother and cousin Fidelito were always together because of their street brawls against each other. Their historic duel started in front of our home in Victoria De Las Tunas. It continued through the streets, back into the house, and back to the streets again. This was an unforgettablly horrific fight for those who witnessed it, including myself. It lasted more than a half hour. Fidelito was staying with us to attend high school, and he and my brother had become competitors over everything, from academic success to having the prettiest girl in their camp. Their hostility blew up one afternoon, just like a tinderbox. Many people tried to stop the fight, including my aunt Genoveva and my mother, but to no avail. They punched each other continuously without listening to anyone trying to stop the fighting. They were screaming profanities and yelling at onlookers not to interfere until they settled it. Only when both of them succumbed to exhaustion did the fight end. Luckily for them, Pipo was working. However, when he came home, my brother and Fidelito got an earful from Pipo as they both shook hands in front of my father and promised never to repeat this behavior among cousins again. I was expecting them to get a bigger beating from my father, but he surprised me and gave them just a stern scolding. Pipo's nonaction was really an action. I didn't see it at the time, but looking back, he took the proper route. He had taken the high road in dealing with their exorbitant inexperience of life.

One of our main destinations for a full vacation of fun and relaxation was Guardalavaca, the most popular beach resort in the eastern province of Holgin, near Gibara, the place where Christopher Columbus first stepped foot on this paradise island of Cuba. I remember one particular vacation week that began on September 31, 1964, at this fabulous hot spot. This gateway was different than going to La Playa De Llanita. It was a special place where I learned how to walk in the sand with Pipo for the weekend because it was further and had more things to see and do. To me, what stands out about this place, among my many recollections, was the way my father attracted so many people wherever we went. This was especially evident at a fancy dinner night cabaret. It was similar to Ricky Ricardo's Tropicana Club in the television hit show of the 1950s *I Love Lucy*. He was like a magnet and people would come to greet him and shake his hand. The biggest eye opener was these beautiful Cuban showgirls with the skimpiest tropical costumes you could ever imagine. They left very little to the imagination, if you get my drift! I think my mom was not very pleased by what she saw. Sometimes, she uttered to Pipo to put a stop to all the interruptions so we could finally have dinner. I think it was just an excuse to get him away from those beautiful girls who coalesced around him after they performed and were in the intermission. Since my father was great at telling stories, they hung onto him without any sign of wanting to leave; even when they had to go back to quickly prepare for a wardrobe change for their next number.

One thing about Pipo, he was also very proud of us and always introduced our family first to anyone before going any further. While eating dinner, my mother became very upset with Pipo because one of the showgirls apparently winked at him. It was a funny turn of events because of Pipo's humorous line that I still remember. He said, "Remind me to buy you a straw hat when we go outside to cover your brain from the hot sun, because you are beginning to see things that nobody is able to see a hundred feet away except you. Never mind that I can hardly see them at all from this far distance. In the meantime, I'm going to the bar to get you an ice cold drink. This will help you cool off and stop you from seeing things that only you can see!" When we heard this, we all broke out laughing. My mother was always a little bit jealous and on guard. She would let my father know how she felt whenever ladies paid too much attention to my father. Pipo was a very devoted husband and father. He wouldn't cross the line to be with other women, but that never stopped my mother from her concerns.

What triggered all this attention to my father was that he was a very giving person. This trait was magnificently captured in the classic book *The Art of Loving*, by Erick Fromm. He defined a loving relationship as one based on care, responsibility, respect, and knowledge. We care for someone by responding to their needs based on our understanding of and respect for them as unique individuals. Fromm wrote, "In the most general way, the active character of love can be described by stating that love is primarily giving and not receiving. Giving is the highest expression of potency. In the very act of giving, I experience my strength, my wealth, my power. This experience of heightened vitality and potency fills me with joy. I experience myself as overflowing, spending, alive, and hence as joyous. Giving is more joyous than receiving, not because it is a deprivation, but because in the act of giving ties the expression of my aliveness" (Fromm, *The Art of Loving*, Thorsons, 1995, pp,17–18),

The next few days we spent countless hours at the beach, enjoying the calmness of the water and the beautiful natural scenery. The main difference between this resort and the others, besides its beauty, was it seemed like we never left the water. We were always together until our skin begun to crinkle from too many hours exposed to the salt water. This is the only beach that we still have pictures of, showing those unforgettable moments frozen in time. We were not allowed by the government to take any photos or anything with us upon leaving Cuba. Only the clothes we had on our backs. This action by the government was very invasive to me, even as a young child. We were ordered to go to a secluded room for a final body search before boarding our plane at the Jose Marti International Airport in Havana. This search was intended to make sure we did not have any possessions hidden in our clothes. We were able to send some of our precious photos by air mail only upon declaring their contents and paying a fee a few months prior to our departure. This enabled us to salvage a few of them. I have one of the photos hanging in my bedroom to constantly remind me of those days.

This vacation started off very rocky. Pipo became tired at the wheel and for a split second lost concentration on a sharp curve and almost went into a deep ditch on the side of the road, nearly flipping over the car and killing all of us. An hour later it was déjà vu again as we crossed a large river where the road was decaying on the right side. Only the left two wheels remained on the pavement of the bridge, as the rocks and dirt fell to the river sixty feet down. This was a very scary moment that we were fortunate to survive. After an hour of rest and trying to recoup from this close call, we finally arrived at Guardalavaca in one piece. Unfortunately, our streak of bad luck did not stop just then. The power station was hit by a lightning strike and it cut off the power in the little Vilas community where we were staying. We had no lights to speak of; it was a total blackout as people came out of their villas to seek information and comfort. The blackout occurred while we were on the sidewalk finishing unloading our car before taking all our belongings inside. There was no problem for us as Pipo took the initiative. He ran to his car trunk, as I followed close behind him, and pulled out two flashlights, handing me one. We walked around checking and helping vacationers, even though we didn't know them. My mother wanted him to remain with us, but after that small feud was resolved, Pipo carried on, coming to the aid of others. This was a wonderful experience for me because we met so many people that we wouldn't have been able to if not for the blackout. During our week of vacation, people were so grateful to my father for helping them out that they would come by our villa and invite us to their parties. Their generosity did not stop there; it continued at the beach everywhere we went walking in the sand.

My father was like a folk hero. Everyone knew his name and people would invite us to share their food and drinks. We had no solace if we wanted to be alone. The only time my mom, aunt, brother, Catalina, and I had Pipo to ourselves was out in the water. Outside the water, he belonged to the masses who wanted to thank him for his heroic deeds. I felt so lucky that he was my father and I wanted to be just like him when I grew up.

CHAPTER 12

Leaving Victoria De Las Tunas for Mexico City

After a long, frenzied farewell at the train station by all of our families and friends, we left our home in Victoria De Las Tunas for the last time, with the exception of my brother, Gerardo Jr., who had emigrated three months earlier to America, with a four-month sojourn in Mexico City. My brother's situation was delicate because he was approaching his fifteen birthday, an age of mandatory military consignment, and he would not be able to leave the country if this occurred. So everyone was happy that he was able to leave to avoid going to a foreign land and get killed fighting in a war. But it was also a double-edged sword because he would be by himself in a strange new land and separated from us for the first time.

The first leg of our long trip began at the Victoria Train Station as we boarded the train called *El lechero* (the milk train) because of its many stops to deliver the milk. This was our second emotional trip to Havana within three months after accompanying my brother. However, this time the mood was jubilant, because soon we would be united once again in America. I remember riding this time in a first-class private box to avoid the drunks we previously encountered, which almost resulted in a confrontation with Pipo. These drunks were insulting my mother with sexual overtones that my father was not going to tolerate. If it wasn't for the conductor who literally threw out these obnoxious, intoxicated individual at the next stop, we would have had a brawl in our hands. Pipo used to say, "Sometimes you have to take action when everything else is not working." This particular journey was so personal and very enriching. It's very difficult to put into words on what I was feeling and thinking. Knowing this was the last time I would be privileged to be in Cuba, riding with my hero, Pipo, my mom, Maria, and aunt Genoveva. The most satisfaction I remember was sitting by the window next to Pipo and sharing each other's company in our swan song as the train moved along the 460-mile trip. We did not arrive at the Havana Train Station until ten thirty in the morning, about a sixteen-hour trip. We spent most of out waking hours looking at the beautiful countryside. Along the way we saw many peasants working in the fields. Those were mostly sugarcane. One thing that kept grabbing my attention was the simplicity of regular folks just going about their daily business. Sometimes you saw people in their rocking chair and hammocks taking a snooze without a care in the world. In retrospect, it was an amazing scene,; especially with the tough living conditions Cubans were facing. This slow way of life was really full of eternal serenity in my young mind.

I also sensed the same with Pipo. At times this was quite evident to me, because as I looked out I could still see Pipo's face reflecting in the window. He was looking very relaxed, admiring this land that he loved so much. He was taking it all in one last time before leaving it behind for good. I was so fortunate to be within in this momentous train ride. This was a new beginning and he knew it would be very difficult to start over. I at times wonder if he was having second thoughts of leaving Cuba coming into his mind during this time with me. My gut feelings are that he sure did. My mother echoes my opinion that he was concerned about what we were about to face in a strange land, but that he had come around fully that this was best for the family, specially for my brother and me. He was aware that life in America was going to be faster paced, with less time for family and friends. It was his way of having a lasting imprint of Cuba in his mind for whenever he needed to grasp the simpler days. He wanted an image were he could go back and reminisce about this soothing multiple train ride (philosophically speaking) without missing a bump on the tracks.

At dawn I woke up Pipo to point out all the people riding their bikes, tractors, cars, and walking outside. He said, "Son, these people are going to work!" But it's too early, I said. He quickly replied, half asleep, "It's too early for you as well! Go to sleep! In five hours we will be in Havana!"

I said, "Okay, Pipo, I will." Shortly after, I felt asleep next to him, while my mother and aunt Genoveva were sleeping on the opposite side, facing us. Speaking about my mom, en route toward Havana (the capital city of Cuba), I remember this episode with Pipo of almost getting left behind. This happened when she suggested to Pipo to get as something to eat and drink, after he had missed the previous station because he was too busy talking to other passengers in the corridor of the train. He was able to disembark quickly at the next stop in Camaguey City Station. Ironically, this was the city of my birth. To waste no time, Pipo ran quickly to the food court, knowing time was short. In the meantime my mother, aunt, and I left our private box and went to the corridor window of the train to get a better look. We opened it and stuck our heads out to have more of a linear view of the station area and Pipo; after ten minutes of being planted in this position, my mother really began to panic big time. She said, in a very worried tone of voice, "This man (my father) is going to be left behind if he doesn't hurry up and return immediately!"

I quickly put an end to the notion by harshly criticizing her pessimistic comments. I said something to her like this: "No! He's not going to be left. You'll see him come back on time!"

My aunt Genoveva also tried calming my mom down. She said, "Don't worry! He's going to make it back, trust me!" These stops are normally fifteen minutes in duration. Our imaginary sand clock was about to run empty. At this time you could see other passengers making their way back, except, of course, Pipo. My mom flipped out completely. "He is going to ruin it all! He knows quite well, this is the most important trip of our lifetime! If he doesn't come on time, our trip to America will be no more. I know what happened, he probably started talking to someone, yapping away like he always does, and lost track of time," she said. Figuratively, as the last grain of sand fell, we still saw no Pipo anywhere in sight. My aunt then said, "I see the conductor telling everyone to board the train, because we are leaving the station in one minute." My mother began to cry as the train blew its loud horn and started to slowly roll out of the station without Pipo. With our heads still out the window, we saw Pipo running as fast as he could from behind as the train passed by the food court where he was. Now with one hand full of food and drinks, it was a race with the train to the finish line. He looked like a world-class sprinter for the last ten yards as he jumped inside the box car, holding to the little steel step rail with his left hand, without dropping the food. This memory of seeing my father running and smiling all the way to our cab was quite an enriching experience for me, one that I will never forget. We were all very happy to see Pipo safe and sound—none more relieved than my going-out-of-her-mind mother. She lamented to us and then to Pipo, "He made it in the nick of time this time! Are you crazy? You almost missed the train!"

He said, "The food court was very crowded and had very little food left."

"You should know better than to take chances that would've put our trip at risk and jeopardized going to America," she said. "I don't understand why you waited so long to buy food in the first place?"

My father replied, "We brought enough with us to last until we get to Havana but you were too stubboen to ever listen!"

She said, "I wanted to save it for later in case we run out early on."

He said, "Okay, enough talking for a while. Let's all eat now."

My mom said, "Fine, but what do you have?"

"Just cheese sandwiches on white bread. That was the only food left, and I had to pay extra just to get these," he said.

"I can't believe you took a risk for cheese sandwiches. What's wrong with you?!" she replied.

"It's your fault, because once you get an idea you never put it to rest."

Not to take sides but on this point my father was absolutely correct. My mom has done the same thing to me ever since he passed away. She is unfortunately unable to let things just go. She has always been unyielding with me. I have to give my father the highest kudos for putting up with her fixed stubbornness. This back-and-forth exchange went on for another ten minutes until it finally ended. During the peak of the donnybrook, I was trying my darnedest, along with my aunt, not to laugh, which I must admit was a daunting task. I immersed myself in the middle of this verbal assault to change the subject at hand and return to a state of normalcy. Now we all were focusing our attention where it should be, on our pending trip to Mexico City, rather than squabbling and bickering.

As we arrived at the Havana main train terminal, I could not help but notice how slowly we were traveling inside this massive rail yard facility. It took us about a half hour before reaching the platform to deboarding. My father told me the reason for this delay was the heavy traffic and the fact they had to switch locomotives to the back of the train for the return trip back east. At the station we were met by my father's cousin Theodore, who chauffeured us around the spectacular city for one week before we left for Mexico City. We stay at the most symbolic hotel in all of Havana, Habana Libre. After the fall of Batista, Fidel Castro chose this one-year-old hotel, the Habana Hilton, as it was originally named in 1959, to serve as the temporary headquarters of the revolutionary government. This famous hotel is located at the nerve center of the Rampa; it is the ideal hotel for business travelers and tourists. It is not too far away from the Malecon and its wonderful view of the bay, and it's a half hour away from Varadero Beach, the most heralded beach resort in Cuba, along with the many pristine eastern beaches. It's also a close drive from Jose Marti International Airport. Without sounding too biased, there are few places in the world with as many beaches as Cuba and as beautiful as this surreal paradise on a Caribbean island. So if Cuba is in your future travel plans, don't procrastinate any longer to see these treasures for yourself.

Among the must-see sights are the island of Cayo Santa Maria's Beach a seven-mile-long island of virtually untouched beach with memorable wildlife; Cayo Coco, one of the most stunning coral reefs in the world, encompasses this island and Cayo Largo Beach with its beautiful, white, fine sand. From this perfect strategic location we had the time of our lives, visiting just about everything we could possibly see in Havana before leaving for good. Much of the architecture is similar to what you find in the US capital in Washington, DC. The most striking buildings, to me, were the Presidential Palace, the awesome Cathedral Square, and Habana University. I also remember going to this famous restaurant called Bodeguita Del Medio, a place where the famous writer and adventurer Ernest Hemingway spent much time. But nothing can compare with the El Malecon. The Malecon is the mile-long oceanfront boardwalk that runs along the main downtown street. It has three lanes in each direction on this heavily trafficked street. This oceanfront is a spectacular experience. I remember driving by and seeing the waves breaking along the concrete wall and splashing people as they ran for cover. Of the seven days we spent in Havana, according to my mom, we visited El Malecon each day. I loved being there with my father, Pipo, and looking at the blue water and the many ships crossing over the horizon or entering the bay. We also would turn our backs to El Malecon to see the Havana skyline and the beauty of the sunset. Sometimes while looking at this view or just talking with others and strangers, we would be surprised by the force of the waves and get drenched and have to go to our hotel nearby to change oru wet clothes. Man, that was a lot of fun! I remember this one vivid, long conversation with Pipo that went something like this: "You know, son, if you look straight ahead beyond the horizon, that's America, the place we are going to live soon and our new home."

I noticed for a split second a moment of sadness in his face and voice. Even though I was only eight years old, I was smart enough to realize that I had to distract him somehow, and that's what I did. I said, "Pipo what is the big tower all the way to the right?"

He said, "Son, that's the former Castle of the Three Kings of El Morro and the fortress of San Carlos De La Cabana. Now it is mostly a historic military park museum."

I commented, "It looks so big and old, Pipo."

My mother, aunt Genoveva, cousin Theodore, Pipo, and I were enjoying the ocean breeze when we were caught off guard by a big wave that hit the giant boulders before the wall and soaked us. But this time it was great, because it cooled us from the hot sun. Getting splashed is a tradition that the locals often enjoy to escape the heat. The Malecon is a strip similar to what cruising was in America in the 1950s—a place to see and be seen and to feel the pulse of the city. It was an escape, an oasis, as the mist of the ocean waves remained airborne and kept coming endlessly. I loved sitting on top of the two-foot high wall listening to my father speak to me about so many things. No matter how chic or famous this landmark was, this was most memorable, because of Pipo and the rest of the family together, with the exception, of course, of my brother. For those who want to know more about El Malecon, you could go to You Tube and watch a bunch of videos on it.

One of our last stops in Havana was at the world-famous Club Tropicana. At one time no club in the world matched the Tropicana for sheer entertainment. It was the club for the rich and famous. I remember the ambience and extravagance was still in high gear even after its peak years in an earlier time, featuring lovely Cuban ladies coming with all the trimmings, if you know what I'm alluding to. As most old timers could tell you, Cuba in its heyday was the Paris of North America. Everyone at our table was having a great time as Pipo and my mother danced to many great Latin, hot songs, the club resembled more of a carnival feast. To get a better look, I left our table and made my way to the front of the dance floor. There I was able to see them much better on the crowded dance floor. I remember when the large orchestra with those big bamboo drums started to hack away nonstop to the rumba beat, and the place almost exploded with pure excitement. I was so happy watching my parents shake and move their hips and everything else feverishly to those unique, wonderful sounds the Caribbean has to offer.

During that time I also was clamoring at the sheer beauty of those showgirls wearing those glittering costumes that shone like bright stars. Suddenly I got pulled into the dance by this strange, pretty young girl to dance with her. Well, she was a lot older than me, or so I thought. Later on I found out that she was only three years older than I was. I danced a few numbers with her. However, the apex of my dancing was really when Pipo saw me and came over to dance next to me. We were having a great time. You could see it in the facial expression of my parents that they were having the time of their lives. In the midst of an uncertain future, they were living life to the fullest, grabbing each second at a time and holding it as long as they could. It was like they were living outside of the curse of time. This was also obvious in the crowd that was converging on the dance floor with them and later on around our table. My father's God-given personality and humor were on full display, making everyone feel like this was his or her party and he or she was the invitee on this particular night. Some people called it the "it" factor; others called it charisma. Whatever it was, my father always shared it. This unselfish mannerism and behavior, this duality if you will, was never clearer to me than on that night. I just happened to be too young to understand it fully. But it left a residue of positivity within me that I will never let go. Amen to that!

The night before departing from Havana to Mexico City, we all went to the hospital to see one of the best human beings that I have ever known God to place on earth, along with Pipo. He was family more so to us than most of our own blood relatives.

His name was Antonio Lopez. He loved our family so deeply that he was a frequent visitor at our home in Jobabo. He and his wife, Zoila, gave my brother and me two calves, which we kept at our uncle Marcelino Colonia's twelve-family ranch, where he kept all his livestock. I often visited this farm with Pipo and my family to see all the animals. I enjoyed their company immensely and I always thanked them for being so good to me by giving lots of hugs and kisses to them. Upon arriving at the lobby of the hospital, my parents were told that I was not allowed to enter Lopez's room. After my parents, aunt Genoveva, Zoila, and Theodore were allowed to visit him, I wanted to go also with them. I told them, "I'm not going to America if I don't see Lopez," in an unyielding, loud voice (I was crying my life out without stopping until they let me in). My mother then suggested to Zoila, "Let's try to sneak him in the room. Lopez is very sick, and we are leaving tomorrow, so this will be the last time he would ever see him again! We have to get him inside somehow."

Zoila replied, "How are we going to do it? There are too many nurses and security all over the place."

"Well, we have to put him in the middle of us when we make another visit to his room and have Gerardo (my father) distract them."

My mother was correct in using the biggest so-called weapon for this task, as Pipo worked his magic one more time. He was able to distract the staff until I got close to Lopez's room. I got too excited and broke my cover, running the last fifteen feet to his room. However, Pipo, along with my mother, was able to convince the nurses to let me stay ten minutes. Well, the plan worked, although not like they invisioned it. When I saw Lopez, he was extremely ill, but I remember how happy he became when he saw me. I was like his son that he never had, since they never had kids of their own. I ran to his side of the bed, and he reached over and gave me a big hug and a smile and told me the following words: "You do me a favor (as he grabbed me tight next to him). Always be good to your Mom and Dad."

I said, "Yes, I promise, Lopez." And with that strong affirmation, I gave him one last hug. Shortly afterward, he passed away.

I was just so glad that my persistence paid off big, because I was able to see our beloved Lopez one more time.

My father said afterward, "I'm very proud of you, son, for not taking no for an answer. Tonight you did the right thing in wanting to see Lopez; he is a wonderful man and a great man." I will always relish those few minutes with Lopez, as well those comforting words from my father, because they meant I was forming a moral scope to handle difficult decisions that we all have to come to terms with in our daily life.

The next morning November 10, 1967, Theodore took us to Jose Marti International Airport to get ready for our long-awaited departure to Mexico City. On the night before, we all were very appreciative to Theodore for being so wonderful to us during our stay in Havana. We took him to a great restaurant for one last time, finally, or so we thought. Well, after dinner he took us back to our Habana Libre Hotel. Outside the hotel my father and all of us embraced him. My father then pulled out from the inside pocket of his sports jacket a stack of bills, held by a wide rubber band two inches thick, and handed it to him.

Once inside the airport concourse, I grabbed Pipo by the hand and took him with me to this corner souvenir shop to look around. I was flabbergasted at what I saw. These items were exclusive for sale at the airport only and not available anywhere else in the country. For starters, I loved these two drum sets. One was small, while the other was almost a carbon copy of the ones used at the Tropicana Club. Pipo said, smiling, "You like these, don't you, son?"

I said, "These are what I always wanted, Pipo. Let me look at them a little longer."

"In America these drums are plentiful, son, and if you still want one, we will get it for you." Those gentle and loving words went a long way in making me happy.

We were urged by my mom and aunt to come out to head for the gate to board our flight. But before we left, I asked my father to buy me a pack of Chiclets chewing gum and a roll of Lifesavers candy. As he checked his pocket looking for some change, he said, "Son, I can't buy you both! It's one or the other." After a slight hesitation on my part, I said, "Los Salvavidas (Lifesavers)."

"Okay, go and get them while I pay the lady," he said.

I was so excited; I said, "Gracias (thanks), Pipo!" When I opened the candy, the first thing I did was give one to Pipo. His was a red one, mine was a yellow one. My favorites were green and yellow. I also shared them with my mom and my aunt, as well as a new friend who I had just met who was flying with us. We became buddies really quickly and playmates in Mexico City, and his parents and mine became very close also in Mexico City. We then went to the gate and gave the attendant our tickets. However, before boarding the plane, every one of us was led to a secluded room for final clearance by the authorities. In this room they told us if anyone was caught smuggling any jewelry, money, precious diamonds, or anything of value, he or she would be apprehended and immediately taken into custody. "In the following room we will do a body search for confiscation of these unlawful items," they said. "It's in your best interest to come forth now and disclose any such items before proceeding any further." These dire warnings were never carried forward in our group. It was just a scary ploy. There was no next room, so we went right through to the ramp, boarded a four-engine propeller plane from Cubana De Aviacion (the national airlines of Cuba), using a portable stepladder to climb up.

I was very enthusiastic about my first airplane ride and couldn't wait to get off the ground and fly just like the birds. I had a window seat next to Pipo and my nervous-wreck mom, while my aunt had an aisle seat across from us. I remember the flight attendants, giving the emergency instructions as the plane was taxiing to the runway. I said to Pipo, "How long is the flight to Mexico City?"

"About three and a half hours," he said.

I commented, "That's a long time to be in the air...do you think we might see birds flying alongside the plane?"

He said, laughing, "Maybe, but if you see a flock of birds too close to our plane, tell me quickly!"

"But why, Pipo?" I said.

"Because the captain needs to know to avoid them. Too many birds could damage the propeller and make the plane not fly anymore," he said.

"You mean little birds could make this big plane crash?"

He looked at me with a bemused face and said, "Yes, son, those little birds, if there are too many, could do that."

"Okay, Pipo, I will keep looking for birds."

"Don't forget to wake me if you see anything, even if I fall asleep!"

I said, "Don't worry, Pipo, I will protect this plane from those ugly birds."

Meanwhile, my mother was looking very nervous. I said, "Mom, what's wrong?"

She said, "I always get nervous on takeoff and landing, but don't worry. After we are airborne I will keep you company because your father and your aunt will be sleeping, and I can't sleep on planes."

"Okay, Mom," I said as the plane lifted off.

Once in the air, I noticed how high we were. I could see little boats in the big ocean. They looked like my wooden boats from those cream cheese boxes that we made. But my task was to keep my eyes open all around the sky, looking for birds, not look down at the boats. It was frustrating because I was getting tired, with no birds in sight. The only thing I was seeing were the propeller engines making noise as the blades spun. A few minutes later, since I saw no birds, I started reading and looking at magazines my mom gave me. While I was reading, I noticed on my right that building structures were coming closer to our plane. It appeared that we were descending very fast and ready to land. I woke up Pipo right away and asked him, "Are we there yet?"

He looks at his watch and said, "No! We just left about twenty minutes ago!" My father was puzzled by this occurrence, but then the captain announced that a mechanical issue had arisen and that we had returned back to Havana to check it out; nothing serious, but he wanted to be certain before we were too far away. As the plane landed, my mother made the timeliest waggish remark on why we had returned. She said, referring to Pipo,

"We came back because they are looking for you! That's why! Don't you get it or what?! Why would they bring us back? For some little airplane problem, not in Cuba! You answer the question now!"

I could see on Pipo's face that he was getting a little apprehensive and not thinking straight after just waking up and getting bombarded from all sides inside this small metal tube. My mom's capricious comment caught my father off guard for one of the rare times. "You know I haven't committed any infractions or said any derogatory words toward anyone or least of all the government," he said.

"I know that and you know that, but do they know that?!" she replied.

"What am I going to do now?" My father said. In the middle of this melodrama, my Mom said,"I finally got you even for the past episodes you bestowed on me."

The captain announced the mechanical problem (this time Pipo was awake) and assured us we would be departing again in forty minutes pending clearance from the mechanics. He told us to remain seated because we wouldn't be deplaning. Pipo quickly, after hearing the captain's update, realized it was all a fabrication by my mother. He was good natured with a great smile rallying back with these comments: "Aha, aha! You think that was funny, getting me worked up like that?! Well, I deserved it."

As they both laughed it off with pure love, she said, "I really had you going, right?"

I said to Pipo, "She played a real good one on you!" Even my aunt Genoveva and passengers alike were amused by my mom's shenanigans.

Forty minutes later, just like the captain stated, we were ready for takeoff once again. We taxied slowly back for departure, sitting patiently, waiting for our turn. Once we made it to the beginning of the runway, he cranked the engine for maximum power for takeoff. (I again sat by the window.) As the plane sped down the runway, I looked out the window and told Pipo that the plane was not flying. And as he looked, the captain put the brakes on and aborted the takeoff once again. It was a hard stop, and we were lucky not to get hurt. Then Pipo said to my mom jokingly, "This time they are coming for you!" She was not amused, but realized it was Pipo trying to help her with what just happened, a very scary moment. Upon deplaning, we were told the flight was rescheduled for the next morning. Hearing the good news, my father called his cousin and told him to come back and pick us up. An hour later he showed up, taking us back to our Habana Libre Hotel and paying for the night, since Pipo had given him all his money. As we walked into the lobby of the hotel, I noticed this great smell coming from the bakery on the side, which was making fresh *palitrocos* (Cuban thin bread sticks). I immediately told my mother to buy me one. However, she was told that they were unfortunately sold out due to their limited quota for the day. Upon hearing this bad news I was very disappointed, because of that penetrating aroma that was making my tongue turn to water.

Then my father returned from the front desk, after securing a room with Theodore. We sat in the dining lounge area for some snacks and drinks. He then went to the bar and surprised me, bringing me the famous little six-ounce contoured Coca-Cola bottle with a fancy glass. He made my day. I tell you, in Cuba that was not an easy thing to do. (These were in extremely limited supply.) I don't know how he did it, but he did! I decided since it was my first Coca-Cola ever to drink it straight from the bottle. I drank it very slowly, savoring each gulp as it quenched my thirst and admiring this little unique bottle that I wanted to keep so bad for myself after I drunk it. A few minutes later, I asked Pipo for some *palitrocos*, and he said, "How many do you want, son?" My eyes lit up when he asked me that question.

I said, "Pipo I want two!"

He said, "Give me a few minutes to say hello to some friends, okay?"

Ten minutes later, I saw him coming toward me, holding in his hand two of these wonder sticks. I was ecstatic and overjoyed and said, "Gracias, Pipo, te quiero mucho!" (Thanks, Pipo, I love you very much.) I don't know how you do it."

Then my mother jumped into the conversation and said, "Gerardo (Pipo), the baker told me he was completely sold out!"

Pipo responded, "Yes, he was, but he had a few of them left in a bag to take home to his family. And after I got to know him, I asked him if he would be kind enough to let me buy two for my son, but he just gave them to me without wanting any money." My mother just shook her head in disbelief about what she just heard.

Needless to say, we went to sleep early to be well rested for the next day's flight. After the second farewell to Theodore at the Jose Marti Airport, and hopefully our last one, we went straight to the ramp exit door to wait in line to have our Cuban passports restamped with a new date of November 11, 1967, and gave the attendants our airline tickets. (I still have those original tickets in mint condition. You can view them in the photo section.) But before leaving Cuba I dragged my mom, aunt Genoveva, and Pipo to the souvenir store for a final quick stop to look at my drum and all those toys on display. We were then again checked and cleared by all security officials and led to the ramp, where we boarded the plane. This time the plane took off without a hitch, and we circled Havana and started to fly over the blue ocean en route to Mexico City. However, at midpoint of the flight I woke up Pipo and told him, "The sky is bird free, but the propellers' blades are not spinning anymore. Why, Pipo?"

He immediately then awakened and leaned toward me to get a better angle so he could more closely look through the window to see the engines. After he saw nothing wrong, he gave me a big smile and said, "You thought you had me, too, didn't you?"

"Yes, Pipo!" I said with a big, drooling smirk on my face.

He said, "Son, you are right! You got me once again!"

We landed at Mexico City International Airport at 11:30 a.m. on a sunny day. Inside the plane I was mesmerized, along with my family, by how big this airport was. We were all looking intensely from the small windows as we were taxiing to our gate. During this unforgettable moment of arriving on new soil, we kept hugging each other, with tears running down the face of my mom, aunt, and many others. We had become very close with the other passengers and closer in Mexico City. It was a really jubilant occasion with so much emotion. This outburst of euphoria being let loose would've filled the inside of the plane with our tears and drowned us if we had stayed any longer. That's how big of an impact it was. I was in awe, in suspended animation, if you will. My face was glued to the window looking at rows of Aeronaves De Mexico (Air Mexico) planes taking up the entire terminal. These were big planes with no propellers, nothing like our little plane. It was a sea of planes lined up next to each other with no end in sight, no matter how hard I tried to look from different vantages. But the most striking thing that I couldn't figure out until we were almost at the gate to try to see one of these artistic colorful bird painted on the Aeronaves De Mexico aircrafts; which was the corporate trademark logo of this company on its tail. Even Pipo was no help this time, as he and I were running a game in real time to see who would be the first to fully identify this mysterious, intriguing logo in the midst of blinding sun that reflected from the aluminum color exterior of the fuselages, obstructing our view. Finally, we were able to satisfy our curiosity—well, more like mine, which was burning inside my belly like a fire coming from Godzilla's radioactive mouth. It was a man's face appearing inside an eagle's mouth. From this point on, this airline, because of the unusual corporate logo, became my favorite airline in my formative years in Mexico and in America. It served as the genesis for my love affair with airplanes and was a truly benchmark moment that has not changed one bit. This love of these machines is in full bloom today because of the result of the meshing experiences of family and metal. I have remained close to these amazing flying wonders. I am a proud team member of Continental and United Airlines at Newark Liberty International Airport, working on the ramp to remind me of the impactful day. This has been a hobby of mine ever since. I have never really looked at it as work or a job. It's more of a passion of reaching out to yesteryear, if you will, each time I go to play with these metal birds.

Before stepping out into the jetway, my father, standing in the aisle opposite my mother, while aunt Genoveva and I were standing in front of our seats, said the following words: "We are in a new country now! Everything we had in a physical sense is no more. It is left behind and there is no need to ever visit. What we take only is family and friends and those special memories. Today is a new beginning for us. Let's keep celebrating together and never stop, just like we always have." After this emotional moment, we all kissed and embraced each other as my mother and my aunt Genoveva said a prayer thanking God for a safe journey to Mexico City and beyond. And off we went thought the jetway and into the hands of the Mexican Customs Authority. You couldn't help but noticed as you walk in how concentrated this area was, plastered with many 1968 Olympics banners and paraphernalia of the upcoming Summer Games.

CHAPTER 13

Mexico City, Mexico, 1967–1968

When we left Cuba, we were the second wave of three that immigrated to America from 1959 to 1980, mostly to avoid political unrest. The first wave was mostly middle class, highly educated professionals, such as doctors, engineers, teachers, lawyers, accountants, etc. Our wave was called "the freedom flights," which permitted families to unite with loved ones through the third countries of Mexico and Spain before entering the United States. The third wave was known as the Mariel boat lift, concluding with a semiwave in the 1990s of *balseros* (boat people).

Before I go on any further, let me go back and revisit that fascinating logo that I was so fixated to find out what it was and why it was painted on the Mexican flagship airline, Aeronave de Mexico, the airline we would travel in a few months to Miami. This symbol, called Cuauhtémoc-El Caballero Aquila, is a tribute to the Aztec. Among this culture, the eagle was a revered animal, always regarded in high value. Warriors known for their courage were often selected to join the elite corps of the Eagle Warriors and dressed themselves resembling eagles to hunt for their prey.

After clearing customs, we were met by Pedro. He was my cousin Elena's husband's (Segisberto) uncle who lived in Mexico. My cousin Elena is one of ten children of my uncle Manuel and aunt Marciana, who had immigrated to America one year earlier. After we left Mexico, Elena's home was our nine days' transient stay in Miami, Florida, on route to settling in Newark, New Jersey. She and her husband were very courteous and did everything humanly possible to makes us feel very welcome. They took us everywhere, including a Catholic-run facility where we were able to get some free winter clothes for the frigid weather waiting for us up north. I picked up a thick winter coat. I have the deepest gratitude for her genuine hospitality during those difficult days when we had no money to speak of. They paid for all of our expenses.

As we were walking the concourse of the Mexico City International Airport (now named Benito Suarez for the nineteenth president of Mexico, who was adored by his people; he was to Mexico what George Washington and Abraham Lincoln are to America), I spotted a convenience store. This store had even more stuff than the one I adored in Cuba's airport. It was an amazing discovery. I saw *sombreros* (hats), magazines, candy, cigars, and the centerpiece of my naïve irresistible indulgence: Chiclets. In Cuba, having chewing gum was not a reality at all. If you were able somehow to get your hands on some, you were worshipped by your friends and foes alike in hopes of getting a piece. I recall the time I received two sticks of gum inside a letter sent by my brother, Gerardo Jr. I was pursued everywhere I went. It did not stop until I divided and distributed the gum equally to all my friends. I think I was happier for them than myself, because I enjoyed the pleasures of giving, just like my hero, Pipo, did. This euphoric spirit of doing what is right has been branded in my psyche since I was born, due to my parents' teaching. The only drawback, if there was one, was I had only a tiny piece for me to chew. Even the empty aluminum foil and the outside brand-name wrapper were sought out. These sometimes were filled with some sort of glue to be passed on or to show you had the goods to be popular *en la calles* (in the streets). Like I said earlier, we had resolve and creativity. This last example showed the lengths we went to in order to satisfy our insatiable craving for chewing gum.

From this backdrop, imagine for a second what I was feeling upon seeing pack after pack just lying on shelves in front of my eyes. I was a little boy caught in a candy store with my hands full of candy. But in this case it was not figurative; it was literally true. I was holding in my little hand a pack of something that I wanted more than anything in the world. So I jetted to the store and grabbed a yellow pack of Chiclets from the middle shelf and yelled to Pipo, "Chiclets! Chiclets! Chiclets!" Upon hearing my loud screaming, my parents, aunt Genoveva, and Pedro increased their walking pace and headed toward me. I was jumping up and down, waiting with anticipation for Pipo to buy me this particular pack, while the store manager looked on with dismay. But I couldn't wait any longer for Pipo to get there. I told the store owner, "That's my father coming this way; I'll get the money for you right away!" He just shook his head in an approval mode, as I ran with my pack to meet Pipo and the rest of the family, who were engaging in small talk on the concourse about hundred and fifty feet away.

I said, "Pipo, I have this pack of Chiclets I am holding in my hands and I want you to buy it for me!"

He followed, looking a bit sad, and said, "Son, we just arrived in this country and I don't have any money right now (emptying all his pockets). I don't even have *kilo* (in Cuban it refers to a penny), do you see? What do you want me to do? I will buy it for you soon, but not right now."

In the meantime, my mom and my aunt did their best to calm me down, because I was not being reasonable. I was so disappointed; I was not buying anything that they had to say to me. I then began to cry so hard that I started making a really bad scene, turning many heads. Pipo was not very pleased with my selfish behavior, which I had never displayed before. After a few minutes, I was able to settle down a bit and apologize to everyone. I then, somewhat reluctantly, took the gum back to the store and placed it back in the box. This was quite a reality blow for me. It was going to be my first-ever full pack of chewing gum. When I returned, my mother wiped the tears from my face with Pipo's white handkerchief. I also noticed something different in Pipo's demeanor from the one he always had in Cuba. He seems less alive, if you will, less energetic, and more worrisome. Deep down in his heart, he was concerned about the future, especially in a strange land, with only the clothes on our back and no money. I have to give Pipo the highest kudos in a million lifetimes. Beginning a new life in a foreign country without speaking the language (later on in America), coupled with two young kids, and his biggest nemesis was that he was already fifty-nine years old. He was a man of strong character, with unmatched fortitude in positive thinking and in action. This mentality of going forward was a godsend and what kept us together, confronting many challenging obstacles. Even with all this perseverance, he still needed some help.

This self-discovery by me became my central mission in my life, without Pipo or anyone else privy to my little secret. I became very happy with this incredible revelation that I was given by God at this young age. And for that, I give the ultimate gratitude to God for guiding me to this most rewarding conclusion in reversing roles as I grew older. It seemed to me from this point that I knew what Pipo was thinking and feeling. I honestly felt his deepest pain, as if it were my very own, because it was. The best part of this spiritual connection was that it was not one way. Pipo also seemed to know my soul as well. This was a great honor bestowed on me to be a facilitator for Pipo and my family in times of need. I did this always with adoration, without ever skipping a beat, even during those tumultuous teenage years. This wrenching incident with the Chiclets was a stone-hard transformation for me, because when we arrived in America, I took it upon myself to work hard so I made enough money to hand it weekly to Pipo. This odyssey began when I was nine years old carrying groceries at Food Fair Supermarket (that became Foodtown) on Lafayette Street in Newark, New Jersey. Now this first location where I earned my first monies is inhabited by a Portuguese local vendor called Seabra's supermarket. I also shined shoes on Ferry Street and made lemonade around our community, especially in front of our North Pole home. How could I not! This was my ultimate hero that gave me everything a son ever needed and then some. He gave me his love, time, and his value system, which prevented me from ever going astray, especially in the world of illicit drugs to which I was heavily exposed.

These life lessons of knowing your environment and doing what's right are a hallmark of his legacy to me. To his credit, I never experimented with any drugs in my lifetime, having come close many times because of stupid peer pressure and beautiful ladies. I remember this one time when I came very close. It happened in the early eighties in the parking lot at a famous nightclub called the Playpen in Sayreville, New Jersey, where my brother regularly hung out. I was trapped in the middle of the back seat with two girls next to me; trapped as they passed around some white powder. Now, being squashed in this setting, I had no choice but to follow the crowd and indulge or be forever labeled as a sissy or not cool anymore every time I was seen there. So the easy choice would've been to take it and put it up my nose, right? But I thought about how disappointed my father would be if I did this and possibly followed the curse of this path that so many have taken and ruined their life. This pursuit of what initially appeared to be an innocent high was in full gear that night from my perspective. What made it more difficult for me was that the powder was passed by a two hot-looking, seductive girls who were feeling no pain, and I also had a few drinks in me as well, plus they were in heat. This moment of truth was finally confronted by me by dropping the powder to the floor, as they all scrambled to look for it. This gave me the out that I needed to step out of the car to return to the club and save face with everyone. But I learned a good lesson: never put yourself in such a position in the future.

Now, it was my time to step up economically, to try to keep the ever-present pressure that he inherited somewhat manageable for my hero. That frame of mind was my goal.

As we were leaving the concourse, again filled with Olympics banners, en route to the parking lot to hop in his car, Pedro called me over and said, "Miguel, take this money and get your Chiclets." I was on cloud nine as I looked at my parents. Then my mom quickly interjected and said to me, "Take it, but what do you say, son?"

I said to Pedro, "Gracias, muchas gracias (Thank you very much)." I ran back and picked up the same pack I had before. I was elated with this turn of events. I came back skipping and going side to side, until I united with everyone and gave Pedro his change and everyone a Chiclet. I also cherished this pack, constantly looking at it while I chewed the gum. I even saved it for many years later, until I misplaced and lost it for good.

After the airport, Pedro invited us to a small Mexican restaurant for lunch and to spend some time with each other. He also loaned some money to Pipo to help out with our expenses. Then we left for a hotel called Pal for temporarily shelter a twenty-five minute walk from the Centro Historico area. I remember walking or taking numerous cabs rides in the vicinity, which included the Avenida Arcos de Belen as Avenidas Balderas, to name just a few, with my parents and friends. This hotel was called by many the mecca for Cuban refugees. While waiting to check in at the front desk, Pipo went to Western Union to pick up a wired fifty dollars from Rosina, a good friend of the family. When he came back, we were inside our hotel room unwinding and settling down. When he walked in, he said, "It's time to eat!"

I said, "What do you have inside the bag, Pipo?" (He was all happy and smiling now that he had a few dollars and pesos his pocket. This outlook made me happy once again.)

He said, "I got ham, bread, potato chips, cheese, apples, pears, sausages, and bottles of Pepsi-Cola."

My mom said, "You overdid it, didn't you?"

He smiled and said, "Enough talking. Let's enjoy it together like before."

I said to Pipo, "This is the best ham I ever tasted and the only one I ever had in my life!"

"Well, I'm glad that you like it, son. Now keep eating, okay?" he said.

Well, I kept eating so much that I was too stuffed to play with my new friend from Cuba who was staying at this hotel. I remember my aunt Genoveva asking me, "Miguel, pass the ham and the Pepsi bottle to me."

I said, "How about the bread?"

"No, thank you," she replied, "just a little more of this delicious cured ham."

Even my mother got into the act. She said, "I don't know if it's because I haven't eaten ham in a very long time, but this is the best-tasting ham I've ever eaten!" I could see the smiles on everybody's face while we ate in the small kitchen with the strong aroma of coffee brewing in the background. It was a most joyous time in an unpredictable situation. In the meantime, Pipo's brother Marcelino, my uncle, came into the room and greeted us and joined in our first food fest in Mexico City. (He had immigrated a few weeks earlier.)

A few minutes later a commission representing the Catholic Church arrived to ascertain to what denominations we belonged. Upon a lengthy interview process with my mother, we had qualified for free shelter and food, excluding meats, because of my mother's heavy involvement with the church in Cuba. It wasn't just any shelter; it was a spacious mansion in appearance. This refugee home was located at Anatole France in the Polanco District, the most affluent residential and business section in Mexico City. When I heard this news, I was very disappointed, because I had made new friends in the large Cuban community at this Hotel. But in retrospect it was a miracle gift from God to our family. This welcome change of fortunate alleviated a substantial economic burden on all of us, none greater though than on Pipo. In addition, we had a great time with the people we met there while waiting for legal approval from the American State Department to enter the United States. We were given a rooftop apartment called the doll house that had been converted into a small three bedroom and a tiny kitchen. It was given this name because the owner's daughters kept all their dolls and toys in this most secluded area. On the opposite side of our apartment was a large, roomy apartment with all the amenities you would find in a four-star hotel. It was occupied by a brother of the owner with two young kids about my age. We were separated by an open rooftop terrace about one hundred feet long. This open cement ground provided a launching pad for our wooden assembled planes that were very popular because they were inexpensive— less than a peso. They were not very sturdy and were vulnerable to total breakage, but, notwithstanding this, we had a ball throwing them from the roof, watching them glide down three hundred feet to the long front courtyard of the compound. This fun was not limited just to the many young kids, as the adults, including my father, often participated in this thrilling activity in this home.

Pipo also helped me with obtaining valuable knowledge about airplanes. We would spend countless hours together before going to sleep in the bedroom, cutting out all the articles in *Reader's Digest* magazine about airplanes. I had a foot-high stack of articles well protected beside me. Every night before I succumbed to sleep, I eagerly re-read them and looked at the various new technologies coming to these flying machines. The best story was from a different magazine that Pipo had given me, featuring a front cover photo of an airplane with no propeller. Wanting to know more about this weird plane, I asked Pipo multiple questions so he could explain to me how it could fly without any propellers. I was so enthusiastic, I did not give him a chance to fully answer. Man, I was out of breath. After I calmed down a bit, my father said, "Miguel, this plane is called a jet! It has no propeller, but inside the engines, it has high-speed rotating blades that jettison the air in front and it comes out very hot through the back. All planes in the future will be jets because of higher speeds. This is the coming of the jet age, son."

I was hooked, listening to Pipo while looking at him read the magazine in standard Spanish. He was able to break it down for me in simple layman's terms, so I could understand its content fully. This mannerism by Pipo pulls me even closer to him, sharing my interest for airplanes. This insatiability was the starting point, because in Mexico City we did not work or go to school, so we had lots of leisure time to find a productive and a fun activity to do with each other. One of those during the 1960s was collecting military airplane models that came inside the Kellogg's Corn Flakes boxes. This was the hottest hobby among everyone who stayed in this dormlike mansion. The most sought after and cherished in the set of about thirty seven planes was the fortress-like B-52. These corn flakes boxes were distributed equally weekly to each family, about twenty-five people. Sometimes Pipo was in charge, along with the designated caretakers, who were a couple. At times, I was inside this supply room with just Pipo. I would be a prevaricator if I said I wasn't tempted to open boxes and take out the planes. However, Pipo was always closely monitoring every move while he did a running inventory. One thing about Pipo is that his integrity was impeccable, beyond any reproach. This rock-solid, fundamental principle was nonnegotiable, not even for me to satisfy my longings. So I had to come up with a plan to sneak inside the supply room without Pipo or anyone ever finding out...

What I did when I was inside with my father on one of those times was to bring a piece of Scotch tape with me and placed it between the door and the lock when it was open. Later on, when everyone was asleep, I came back with a small flashlight to search, open, and pocket these amazing models. Once inside, I started quietly and carefully to open a corn flakes box, but within seconds, I began to feel very guilty and ashamed, and I quickly stopped and left the room. I was also worried that I might get caught and get the punishment of my life. Later on I heard that someone was sneaking in, going through the boxes, and exchanging or taking out all the B-52s. What a bizarre turn of events. We had an unscrupulous thief, and I knew who it was, but before I got my revenge, I informed Pipo and he immediately fortified and changed the lock. The person doing this act was the oldest of the seven kids in the house. He also, naturally, had the largest, most envied collection by far, more than everyone else combined. He did everything in his power to complete the set of thirty-seven models. He was never satisfied, always showing it off in a spectacular display case in his room. To achieve his goal, he broke into our room and took one of my planes that he needed for his set. He had a bad reputation of doing crazy things, even making tiny holes in the walls so he could get a peep at two beautiful eighteen-year-old girls dressing, for which he got in big-time trouble. Upon hearing this, I angrily ran like a bullet to his apartment room and retrieved my plane. But I wasn't finished with my outrage just yet; I dismantled his prize display and threw all the planes to the floor, where I stepped on them in disgust. I did not want any of those planes; I wanted justice, and nothing more. Later on he confronted me and apolgized to me for doing such a bad thing. He later on changed his tune and let us play with his planes. We even helped him complete his set. After the hunt to complete his set was over, he volunteered to display the set on a platform that we built in the corner of the communal living room so everyone could enjoy them together. My father suspected that someone was entering the room, without permission. Because he mentioned it one evening while playing dominoes with the other men in my present.One thing about my father he was one sharp guy when it came to knowing your surrounding. He was on the trail to the perpetrator from the moment he realized that this was happening.What gave it away that someone was stealing, was the way he placed and stack meticulously the food supply.He mentioned that this person who was doing this was not taking any of the food supply, but was opening the corn flake boxes and closing them up again.He was quite aware of who was doing this act and for what purpose; which was taking out the inserted airplanes.He was laughing as he was telling the story to us on the table.Then he ask me, "Miguel do you know anything about it?"No Pipo!His good natured did not mean he was weak at all but somehow knew I will transmit the message crystal clear that my father was on to him if he did not stop breaking in.Well, that was Pipo always finding the best method in getting his point acros in a proper measure respond.

Aside from these competitive spirits, among us kids, we were all good buddies and well behaved. This attitude was reenforced constantly by all the parents in the house, especially my own parents. This brings to mind an incident that occurred while I was walking toward the front door to play with my friends in the spacious courtyard. When this elegantly dressed older woman whom I had never met before walked in with her many belongings, I offered to help carry a shitload of stuff inside the house. She was so taken by my politeness and how well educated I was that she offered me a one-hundred peso bill for my good deed. In 1967 that was a lot of money. The exchange rate at the time was twelve and one-half pesos for one American dollar. However, I told her I could not accept her generous offer without the approval of my parents. Within a minute or so, my parents came to see what was going on with me and introduced themselves to her. The older women then said to my parents, "I've never met a more educated and well mannered young child in my life. How nice and refreshing it is to come across your son."

My mother very much appreciated her kind remarks and said to her, "Muchas gracias, señora" (Thank you very much). Then the lady explained to my parents how she tried to give me this money for helping her, but that I had refused to take it. In the midst of this conversation, the two caretakers of the home came near us to introduce my parents and me to lady, who was the owner of this beautiful home. She then reiterated to my parents, "Please ask your son Miguel to take this money from me."

Pipo said, "Son, go ahead, take the gift from this generous woman. But don't forget what to say...and give her a big hug and a kiss."

"Yes, Pipo," I said. I took the money, but not before I took one last glance at Pipo for reassurance. Then my mom, shaking her head in approval, said, "Si...si, coge el dinero" (Yes...yes, take the money). I finally took the money and put it in my pocket. In leaving, the lady commented on her genuine liking of me and thanked my parents for raising such a disciplined child. She also invited me to her nephew's big bash birthday party at her home a week later, two blocks away. It was the biggest birthday party celebration I ever been asked to attend. I was told that over two thousand people attended this gala. Once there, I was toy struck; I couldn't believe what I saw. It was like I was in a Toys 'R' Us and sports store, all in one. I played for the next six hours without relenting. The most fun was the multiple piñatas (animals that we could crack open, stuffing our pockets with toys and candy). However, the very best fulfilling moment was not the party; it was when I called Pipo over and took out the one hundred pesos and gave it to him. That was my numero uno moment for me, bar none. Later on, we learned that she was one of the wealthiest people in Mexico. She had a soft spot in her heart for Cubans, because when she was growing up, her parents were helped a great deal by many Cubans. She was hands on, always making sure we and those who came before and after were taken care of properly. My father was precisely correct when he used the word "generous" to describe her steadfast contributions to the Cuban community in a time of crisis. We owed her endless gratitude for sticking with us.

This time period in Mexico City in the refugee mansion felt like we were in a cocoon in perfect harmony. This was indicative and synonymous with Pipo's adventurous outlook about life in general, which permeated all of us. Even though our stay in this country was rather short, five months in duration, it never slowed down one bit. We were always in a transient mode, exploring the great treasures of this ancient Aztec civilization and the lasting influences of Spanish colonization. Among the places that we visited, the ones that should be on everyone's must-see list were the Pyramids, Guadalupe, and Chapultepec and its fabulous cultures, which encompass this large city. I will go more in depth on these sites later, but for now I want to go more in detail, on what we did to keep busy, fun busy.

For starters, my father and most of the men in the evening played, what else, dominoes, which is imbedded and anchored in our roots. The games were held on the first floor, between our communal living room and the first dorm room. The more serious games were contested at the end of the dorms, near the supply room. These games were generally played for money, mostly chump monies; wages were much less than a peso per hand, since no one had much of it to speak of, and typically lasted till dawn. At times, to loosen up the atmosphere, they let us partner with one of them for friendly matches. I was a partner with Pipo and we kicked some heavy butt, let me tell you. Other times we partnered with the ladies and my buddies. What I liked best was seeing Pipo having a ball intermingling with the other players. He made everything around him seem to come alive by telling funny stories that made everyone forget his or her turn. He was literally and figuratively the master of ceremonies. I would sit quietly about three feet behind him to observe and learn as the drama unfolded. It was lots of fun, never boring, and always entertaining! The ups and down of the game were thrilling, compounded with cigar smoking and loud, chatting outbursts; add great food to the mix, finish it off with some cold Corona beers, and you are approaching an unmatched sphere of nirvana from a genuine Cuban perspective.

My biggest nemesis was my curfew of eleven thirty in the evening during the weekdays. The weekends were pretty much open until I fell asleep, at which time my father would pick me up and take me to bed. Now, the question you might ask yourself is, why erect any curfew if you did not have to attend school? Well, I also posed the very same question to my mother and Pipo. Their reason was that I had to get used to going to sleep early so that when I enrolled in school in America, this rudimentary conditioning would get me ready for doing well. My mom said, "Discipline is for your own good, Miguel."

Growing up in this household was terrific, especially when we all gathered in the living room to watch television on a black-and-white console TV that had issues with picture clarity. Sometimes we had to take turns holding the small portable rabbit-ear antenna to tune in to our favorite shows. This was very annoying and tiresome, but compared to what we had in Cuba, it was a big-time upgrade. But nevertheless, it made for great kidding-around comments by those yelling to keep a steady hand while holding the antenna. It was a comedy circus to remain still for the never-ending one-more-minute pleads. The most challenging job was evenly dividing among the twenty-five people the viewing schedule to prevent an ugly war. We did this by pulling numbers from a large sombrero, with the lowest numbers picking first. We practiced this successful arrangement for the duration of our stay. We even bartered each other for time slots to watch our favorite TV shows. The adults always wanted to watch the news, soap operas, and old movies, while the teenagers and the kids were interested in cartoons, comedies, music, and sports. However, my father, besides having a keen interest in viewing the news, was open to giving away his allocation with the sole exception of his adamant love affair with bullfighting. He looked forward to tuning in to this weekly spectacle, along with me. I sat next to him, screaming continuously, as we shouted "Ole!" in unison. I wouldn't miss it for the world. This was also my first exposure to popular shows like *The Avengers*, *The Monkees*, *Bewitched*, *Speed Racer*, *Gigantor*, *The Man from U.N.C.L.E*, *Tarzan*, etc. The most talked-about event was the premier showing of the Beatles' "Yellow Submarine" musical video. I remember being so disappointed, because I was expecting a cartoon with submarines and instead got something unexpected. Years later, I was able to really appreciate the brilliance of this masterpiece.

The most heralded show, one not to be skipped, was the weekly performance of the Mexico City University Orchestra, which left us each time in awe. They sang their hearts out with so much sheer emotion that it made the ladies' hearts melt. It was the show event to watch, and everything came to a complete stop in our refugee compound for two hours. We all gathered around, similar to what had transpired in the 1967 "Summer of Love celebration" in America a few short months earlier. It was a social phenomenon during a most colorful period and was sweeping America. It was the cry-out movement of "Give Peace a Chance". This most perfect, harmonious attitude was in full swing within those walls, and beyond that we coalesced.

My mother and aunt Genoveva cooked, cleaned and babysat the owner's two kids while he was away on business trips. During his absence, I was fortunate to watch my favorite cartoons on his portable television. It was my parents' and my first exposure to such bizarre and revolutionary new television technology, which was in its infancy. I was so bewildered with enthusiasm that I really looked forward to helping my mom and aunt with the cleaning, as long as she turned on the television. But before she put it on, I received a stern warning to be extra careful and keep a safe distance so I wouldn't damage it.

A couple of weeks later, my mom was able to convince the Catholic Commission to grant my father's brother, uncle Marcelino, permission to relocate to our doll room apartment to stay with us. This made everyone very happy and it really showed, for none greater than for Pipo, who had a glow on his face. My uncle also was very well liked and friendly. He was always on the go, though going somewhere, never comfortable with standing still, made him extremely transient in nature. This disposition made him a target for barrages of jokes, innuendos, and lots good humor aimed at him, mocking his eccentric proclivities. I tell you one thing: Uncle Marcelino was a sweet man with an innate sense of humor that you just wanted to bottle up and give out as a remedy to improve the human condition. It was never a dull moment for sure, having uncle Marcelino mixing with Pipo. We all loved them; they both had the natural knack to tell jokes, stories, and laugh at themselves, encapsulating our friends and family. It was a great tag-team combination, a one-two punch, if you will, but again, it was with no effort whatsoever, it was just God-given ability. No pretentiousness or anything like that.

Speaking about humorous moments, one of the things I enjoyed with Pipo was walking across the two-hundred-foot front yard to wait for the mailman to deliver the mail. This was like a ritual every afternoon; at approximately one thirty we would stop whatever we were doing. We usually impatiently waited inside next to the gated and high steel fence. These were important regular letters, because they contained the vital remittances from our family and friends in America to pay for our expenses. Knowing their importance, I would run out of the gate and meet the mailman before he came to our home to get the letters first. Or, I would snatch them away from his hand as he chased all over the grounds and sidewalk to get them back. These acts of silliness were just benign expressions of my love for my father. And he knew it quite well, going along fully with these pranks to please me. But after ten minutes of fun, I said, "Okay, Pipo, here are the letters…" and as soon as he approached me, I would run away with the letters again.

He would say, "Miguel, enough with the playing, come back here now and give me the letters at once, before you lose them!"

One time I went too far with my playfulness and made Pipo upset with a very stupid stunt that I tried to pull off that backfired on me. It happened when I threw the letters in the air toward him and they got caught in a strong wind current that made them go airborne and over the fence. This one envelope in particular was flying better than any of our wooden mini airplane gliders that we often competed with, and surely an upgrade from the aborted no-lift second attempt of our Cubana De Aviacion flight to Mexico City. I could see vividly Pipo running underneath this white seemingly flying paper in the blue sky. It was as if there was a pilot on board, maneuvering to avoid the tall trees and the electrical street wires. We even saw a flock of birds flying too close to comfort. In the real world of aviation it is called a near miss. Wouldn't that be something if they had collided with each other? It would've been one in a million and we would be out of needed supplies to purchase foods. Luckily for us it did not occur, or, better yet, I should've said luckily for me…I could see Pipo's belt coming out for a much-deserved butt spanking. Remarkably, the letter flew back to our property unscathed, avoiding the twelve-foot fence and missing the trees and light poles as it descended slowly to a smooth landing in Pipo's open hand. This was an incredible sight, one for the ages, never to be forgotten. I then asked Pipo to open this long-traveled letter that he had just put inside his front pants pockets. I was very curious to get a closer look at this letter and its valuable cargo that it contained. However, Pipo made me wait, to get even with me for my stunt, knowing quite well how anxious I was to get hold of it. Then, while he caught his breath, he took other letters that he had placed in his shirt pocket and started to look through them, taking out the money orders and transferring them to his wallet for safekeeping. In the midst of all this, Pipo said, "Miguel, you know we almost lost this valuable letter that we depend so much?

Don't do that again! These letters contain funds that we must safeguard! Okay?"

After this speech he finally opened it up and I asked him, "How much money?"

At first, he said absolutely nothing, not a word. But after much poking by me, he said, "Let's go inside the house to get a Pepsi to drink and some snacks;" But I was determined to get hold of this letter, no matter what it took. So I pullED a so-called rabbit out of my pants. I showed him three more letters I was hiding that the mailman had given me. He was shockingly surprised by what he saw and eagerly wanted them immediately. He said, "Son, return those letters to me and I promise to take you tomorrow to Chapultepec Park, and I will take you today to the store and buy you some Chiclets and Lifesavers candy." He looked at me, smiling, knowing I had upended him with my smarts one more time. But it was all in love, just teasing, even if it was only for a fleeting moment in time and in space. I couldn't refuse this great deal—well, maybe! What I did was to make believe I was ready to hand him all the letters. As I got closer to him I snatched them from his hand, similar to when an eagle locks on its prey. In my case, it was the elusive flying envelope that I finally had in my possession. To appease Pipo's sentiments somewhat for my latest episode, I placed the three letters in front of him in the green grass. In the meantime, we were both busy looking through the contents of each letter. Shortly afterward, I ask Pipo about a letter containing a check with the number five and a zero on it. He said, "smiling, "Yes, son, it's a check for fifty dollars sent by your brother in America." Wow, what a revelation! These daily occurrences of waiting for the mailman to deliver good news in the form of remittance were so rewarding and highly anticipated by me because of being in concert with my ultimate hero. In these give-and-take routines that brought much joy to me, I also learned the value of having a big-picture mentality to keep things in perspective, even the minutest things. My father had the foresight to understand how to incorporate quality time with me no matter how many difficulties he was facing. This quality is often absent today with the old adage of not having enough time. My father was a wise, natural leader who was able to reflect on many things that had a positive impact, and in my case it is self-evident.

Life in the refugee home was magical in its essence. Everybody genuinely cared and looked after each other in just about everything we did or were facing. This attitude manifested itself in our daily activities, whether it was money, food, or being lonely or homesick; we were front and center to quickly stamp out these woes.

This unity was in full swing during our Christmas and New Year holiday of 1967–1968, our only holiday spent together in this refugee mansion and our first away from Cuba. Since we were conditioned to be very creative and make do with little, we all worked together for a common goal of making this the best holiday ever. We handmade all the decorations, cutting, taping, coloring, sewing, and folding cardboard to be painted from our many empty boxes that we saved from our supplies to serve as the background for our natural Christmas tree that we placed in the communal living room. I was one of many who had the responsibility of helping the ladies paint this cardboard white to create the illusion of a snow blizzard. We also used cotton all around the bottom of the tree to enhance these illusions further and create snow banks. We also hand made the Nativity scene. The men took care of all the ceiling decorations and the colorful lighting; these were donated to us by the Catholic Church. It was really a family affair in the truest sense of the word among the twenty-five loving people who lived there.

I remember our Noche Buena, a spectacular Christmas Eve party. This one exceeded all expectations by those who attended. We had invited the many Cuban friends that were staying at the Pal Hotel. Our mansion was packed with this amazing spirit of celebration, Cuban style, with a dose of Mexicana to go along with it. As the music and the dancing were full swing, it did not end until almost midday the next day. In the middle of all this was Pipo preparing two of the tastiest Cuban-style roasted pigs ever, as only he could. He had his own special seasoning recipe. He mixed it with his hands and rubbed it all over the pigs, working this unique magic for an out-of-this-world eating experienced.

It literally made the skin much crunchier and tastier. He looked like a professional masseur, attracting a crowd of onlookers fixated on his stylistic hand movement. By the end of the evening, these delicious garlic and olive oil seasoned pigs were simply history. Nothing remained but the music and the spectacular dancing that enthralled everyone and kept us on our feet, with the exception of a short toast and eating the traditional twelve grapes at midnight and taking a short drive to attend Misa Del Gallo (midnight mass) at the cathedral. We also had a feast of Cuban food, such as *arroz con pollo* (chicken with rice), *pan con bistec* (steak sandwich), *platanos maduros* (sweet plantains), *yucca con mojo* (cassava root with olive oil and garlic), flan, black bean soup, *batido de mamey* (mamey milkshake), *picadillo* (ground beef that has been sautéed with tomato sauce, garlic, and other spices), and guava paste. And let's not forget the great traditional Cuban coffee; it's specially served in a small cup called a *cafecito* (or a *colado*), a must to have in any social gathering. This is not to be confused with *café con leche* (coffee with milk), my favorite, for a larger cup serving.

But lurking in the winds a week away was New Year's Eve 1968. This was the party to end all parties in Mexico City and this home, before and after. At this big feast, Pipo gave another great encore presentation with his hallmark, signature dish of delicious, slow, open-flame-roasted pig in the ground. He said, "The secret is not really a secret; it is how well you develop its seasonings. Once you master it, you'll have them coming back for more." And, gee, did they ever return for more! At this New Year's Eve party, my father was once again responsible for getting the beer and spirits for this most monumental party, marking a new beginning for us and for our new Cuban friends. So this was an extra-special occasion and somehow we had to make sure not to run out before the party had crested. Since my father was well liked by the many vendors in the area, he was able to establish many connections. This led to an incredible encounter with the owner of a small start-up beer company called Cerveza (Beer) Corona. Yes, can you believe it? The now-renowned company is a household word in the world of beers. Well, Pipo did it again.

What was really so amazing was who this owner was. He was one of Pipo's friends growing up in Spain who had immigrated to Mexico years earlier. Upon knowing this, the owner offered my father a job as the president for distributions for Mexico City. But the Mexican government had the stickiest laws against granting permanent residency or working visas to Cubans. No matter how much they tried, they were not able to resolve this big hurdle. This outcome was a major disappointment for my father, because he preferred to stay in a Spanish-speaking country. This setback was short lived, as our mansion was inundated with plenty of Corona beer and other adult drinks. He also gave out crystal sets of beer drinking glasses containing different shields of Corona to go with beautiful hard aluminum trays, featuring a beautiful young woman hostess dressed in traditional Mexican garments. I am happy to have still one of these relics hanging on my wall today.

What I was looking forward to the most were the games. My favorite was pinning the tail on the donkey and smacking the piñata with a bat. This party was controlled mayhem with Pipo in the forefront of guiding this remarkable incubation of fun. The dancing was intense, as everyone was engrossed in the Latin rhythms of Cuban and Mexican music; our own guests, who took turns singing and playing different instruments, gave it the ultimate bolt of energy. The five hundred people that jammed our front yard really rocked this mansion's front yard and inside as well. Six days later, the holidays continued with the Celebration of Los Tress Reyes Magos (the Three Kings) on January 6, 1968. This was the happiest and most glorious day for everyone, none greater than for the kids. It was an amazing day of receiving gifts. The owner of the mansion donated large quantities of toys. In addition, other organizations like the Catholic Church were steadfast in making sure no child was left out from receiving at least two toys each. After all, the sanctity of a child's innocence was paramount, and I'm glad they did this, because I was one of those kids on the receiving line, waiting impatiently for mine. It was the responsibility of the mansion caretakers and my parents to distribute all the toys in house and to the many invited poor kids from the nearby *barrios* (poor areas). Since my parents were in control, I had a chance to get what I wanted. However, they instituted an alphabetical sequence to make it fairer and to take away any bias, so I thought I had lost out big time. But my mother was able to set aside the toy I desired without Pipo's knowledge. It was, of course, a used plastic cargo plane, and I couldn't take my eyes off it. My father did not approve of any unfair practices, no matter what, even for me obtaining that model airplane. I was very happy that when it was my turn, I got it, which later perplexed my father when he saw me playing with it and wondered how in the world I got the best toy of the bunch. When he was about to inquire, he was called away and never approached me again about the subject. I guess he had talked to my mom about it somehow.

On March 1, two days before Pipo's departure for Miami, Florida, we celebrated my ninth birthday party at the refugee mansion. It was a bittersweet event, because our sojourn time was winding down. All the great people that we had shared great moments with in trying times were beginning to leave, and my hero, Pipo, was next to go. In addition, we were also informed that my mother and I were approved to leave Mexico with an entry visa to Miami. However, my poor aunt Genoveva had to endure a nonconventional exit out of Mexico in the trunk of a car to cross the border. Earlier she had been giving a legal entrance to America, a month after our arrival in Mexico, but she had declined in order to stay with us and leave together. But a most unfortunate turn of events unexpectedly transpired: the government official who was handling her exit visa was killed. This incident had a severe ripple effect, displacing my aunt's paperwork And pushing back by one year her entry visa to the United States, causing my father to react to my mother's suggestions to take action to get her out of the country and into America. This subliminal idea that she implied did not sit well with Pipo; he did not wanted anything to do with it. He blamed my aunt for being too stubborn and not leaving when she had the chance to do so. Desperately she pleaded with my father, crying out loud, with my mother's strong arm twisting. I remember clearly the two men who had come inside the mansion to discuss the plan and all the minute details with both my parents and my aunt. Clearly Pipo was distraught with this proposition of sneaking my aunt through the border to reach Texas. At one time, I saw Pipo come out in disgust from this closed-door meeting, to calm himself down, while my mother followed him to calm him down so he could return with her to seal the deal. My father was very apprehensive about this plan, because of so many negative factors. The major questions he raised with them were the illegality and my aunt Genoveva's age, health, and well-being. These were paramount; he always stressed the possible ramifications of what could go wrong if we proceeded with this plan. My father always stressed to me to know your environment before making decisions. This was a watershed moment that he wanted to explore fully with all parties.

In the final analysis, the decision rested with my aunt, who clearly would not take no for an answer. The next task was to come up with the money. No easy undertaking, especially if you don't have the means for it. After we made several pleas to family and friends to increase the remittance to meet the hefty price tag in 1968 of three hundred America dollars that we had to raise, they responded accordingly for this dangerous undertaking. My aunt promised to pay back every penny herself once settled in America. The trip itself was a great ordeal, because, as my father had said, "she was elderly, heavy, with numerous physical problems." On numerous occasions she lamented to me how she tried to cope with the heat and the long hours of confinement of being locked up in a dark trunk. She also told me what kept her sanity was how much she loved my brother, Gerardo, and me, and the thought of reuniting with the family. All this time she was continuously talking to God to guide her through this terrible ordeal. My aunt Genoveva was well liked and loved for her generosity, always going out of her way to help others. She had a reputation of feeding people for free in her restaurant in Jobabo, Cuba, helping those who were hungry with no means to feed themselves.

At Miami International Airport, she was smothered with many hugs and kisses to her heart's delight. I was the first one to spot her coming out the doors of the long concourse terminal in a wheelchair. As soon as I saw her, I yelled, "Tia! Tia!" (Aunt! Aunt!). But she could not hear me, so I ran as fast as I could to be with her. When I saw her, I jumped on top of her legs while she as still in the wheelchair. She was so happy that she was able to get up and walk the rest of the way with me, holding hands, to the passenger arrival waiting area. My aunt's tears were gushing out of her eyes. But she was not alone; my mother and I wept together, embracing her. My aunt said, "I almost died! I'm so glad to be here. Los quieros muchos (I love you all very much). Thanks to God the Almighty himself for getting me here, alive and in one piece." She than kneeled and kissed the cement lobby floor and said the following short words: "Lo ice!" (I've made it!). Her watery eyes displayed so much joy and relief all at the same time. In the end Pipo was correct in his well-warranted concerns for her well-being when this journey was first proposed. This same sentiment was reinforced years later by my aunt when she confided that if she knew how perilous the trip was going to be, she would've never contemplated such an attempt.

CHAPTER 14

Chapultepec Park

One of my favorite places to go in Mexico City with Pipo was Chapultepec Park in the heart of the city at the end of Paseo De la Reforma. It's one of the biggest city parks in the world, and my favorite along with Maceo Park in Las Tunas, in my beloved Cuba. It covers about sixteen hundred acres; it's a grandiose place with many sights and sounds, not to be missed by anyone who travels to this historic city. For starters, it has a castle on the hill's apex that can be seen from afar, a very striking view that will leave you breathless. It contained, just to name a few attractions, an amusement park, lakes, museums, zoo, gardens, and even a house, the home of the president of Mexico. In the intervening five and a half months that we spent in Mexico City, countless hours were spent together in this park, enjoying the Mexico heat underneath centuries-old, tall trees, having many great picnics, as well as taking canoe rides alongside of Pipo, paddling our tiny vessel through beautiful scenery without colliding with the other boats in a heavy congested lake. It was lots of fun for me, but

I suspected it was very worrisome at times for my Pipo with so many boats navigating in the water.

When I had exhausted this adventure, I immediately wanted to go to the next one, as any normal child would, to quench my infantile curiosity. However, my search was really over for good quite quickly, because when I first looked up from the canoe, I saw the famous and heralded miniature train, full of kids with their parents, riding the rails above us by the lake. I was flabbergasted, with an insatiable desire to give it a try as soon as possible. I was hooked, just like a fish. This was by far the most memorable and meaningful activity to me, highlighting our many excursions every time we went to this park. But at first, I had to convince Pipo to take me on this train ride with him. This took some arm twisting in the beginning. This little magic train and crowd pleaser encircled the entire park and it took roughly an hour to fully complete. So Pipo was not very keen to spend so much time there after a hectic day of sightseeing. Well, after a couple of snacks and some cold Pepsi, Pipo finally took the plunge and agreed to take me with him on the miniature train. This set a precedent that never wavered on my end, one that he would repeat often in keeping the status quo of pleasing me to the very end of our stay in Mexico City. He knew that once I got on the train, I would never want to leave.

Once aboard it was a real pleasure as we choo-chooed above the people and saw all the exotic animals in the zoo, passed through the forest, returned to the center square, and saw a bunch of jugglers showing their amazing skills to large audiences in the middle of many vendors, pedaling all kinds of souvenirs and food. While riding by on our first trip, Pipo was able to snatch a loose floating balloon that had somehow gotten away from a vendor; I narrowly missed it a second before, jumping out of my seat unsuccessfully to grab it myself. At times, I would get so excited that my father had to hold me down because he was concerned I might fall overboard since the train was an open train with no cab to speak of. The most hilarious part was when I was able to convince Pipo for a second ride to avoid mom's boring and mundane activity. This made my mother go insanely ballistic. All she ever wanted was to walk around and look for bargains that the locals were selling. To me this activity was excruciating and I hated it so much, because it felt like we were always doing this everywhere we went and could use a well-deserved break, at least in the park. Well, my mother did not take it too kindly and made sure that everyone in our circle of friends and those people close by heard her loud tone of voice, dispatched fervently against Pipo and me in unbenign disapproval of our inconsiderate mind-set. However, this second ride did not take place right away. Pipo told me, "Son, your mother, aunt Genoveva, and the others are waiting for us to eat. We will come back here after we eat, I promise, so just be a little more patient and don't misbehave."

After he said those words, he placed his hand on the back of my head, then we walked together to get some snacks and drinks. An hour later, we returned to the train, as he promised, for another go-round of fun and adventurous riding. I think Pipo liked this journey big time, because he was waving and talking to many people, and, I might add, some animals, too, as we whizzed by about six feet above the ground at our highest point. We were for the majority of the trip at ground level or four feet high, especially around the lake.

In this park, I came full circle in more ways than one with my father. I was also able to think and reflect more deeply about this self-exposed revelation, uncovering my hidden goal once again in these little moments of truth—to help Pipo in the future, no matter where circumstances may take me. In other words, I would do everything in my power to repay him with unfiltered love, time, and, above all, help with all future financial burdens that he would be facing head on, in return for what he did for me.

In looking back to this period, I'm so grateful and endebted to Pipo for never, ever, complaining or making any excuses not to spend quality time with me, which he could've based on our dire situations. This early invaluable upbringing and disposition have made me today, unequivocally, a more sympathetic person.

CHAPTER 15

Exploring Mexico City

Besides going to Chapultepec Park, we also visited many ancient attractions and ruins that made a traveler's mouth water with eagerness to visit, similar to Pavlov's dog in his world-renowned experiment of classical conditioning, in which he rang a bell to condition the dog to expect food shortly and, after hearing it, the dog waited, salivating, for its reward.

Mexico City is built on the ruins of Tenochtitlan, which was the capital of the Aztec empire. This mega city is extremely large; it covers 571 square miles, contrasted with twenty-two square miles of Newark, the biggest city in New Jersey (where we all settled in America), and you really get the immensity of it all. Among the many, the Zocalo, Guadalupe Shrine, and the Pyramids really stand out.

The Zocalo is the main public square site for major public ceremonies and military display. It is known officially as the Plaza of the Constitution. Since the Aztecs' time, it has often been tagged the hub of Mexico City because it houses the National

Palace, the present seat of the Mexican government, as well as the National Cathedral. At this location, Pipo and I would often spend hours mingling with the locals as only my father could. He loved to participate with the natives in their many different ritual dances with costumes that they provided for him. He loved all this high-energy folklore at the square. I was amazed watching my father having a swell time during our visits. He became well known and liked, because whenever we got close to people, they would call his name to come to their area. My father always enjoyed these main squares, because they reminded him of his birth country of Spain. Mexico at one time was called New Spain because of the Spanish occupation after defeating the Aztecs. Walking with Pipo in this huge square always made me hungry and thirsty, exposed in the hot sun. I was a really happy kid once my father brought me a big bottle of Pepsi and my favorite snack, a bag of potato chips. These chips were delicious at first bite, and I became hooked. Everywhere we went in Mexico and then in America I had a bag of potato chips with me, since in Cuba we had none of this new novelty. I loved the taste of them.

In this square and wherever we went, I held on to Pipo's hand or I made sure I was always in front of him, a couple of feet at the most away from him, so he could keep an eye on me. He was concerned for my safety, because this city had a vexing kidnapping problem of young children being taken for ransom. This was an acute problem that was plastered all over the news and much talked about. Thanks to God I was never approached or anything like that. But there were kids from the affluent Polanco area, where we lived, that were unfortunately snatched. We enjoyed so many ceremonies, especially the native dances and the countless other spectacles. It was the epicenter for tourists from all over the world to join in on all the festivities. Pipo was like a magnet; we were constantly being approach by so many of his new friends, and it was so swell, seeing that electricity in his demeanor as people congregating around him as he told unique, funny stories to them. In the center of the square, you couldn't help, but notice a giant cross wrapped up often in a Mexican flag. These great outdoor festivals did not deter the large crowds one bit from the daily hot sun.

Another attraction was La Villa De Guadalupe (Guadalupe Shrine). This sanctuary is known for the Manifestation of the Virgin Mary to an Indian saint named Diego, whose vision started the conversion of Indians to Catholicism and became a rich and enduring symbol of Mexican people around the world. This holy place brings out some great recollections with our entire family. I recall crystal clear walking the grounds and then entering this old basilica (a new basilica opened in 1976). I was awestruck by the large amounts of construction equipment and supplies spread everywhere. My mother, as soon as we walked in, was told to be extra careful not to touch or hit anything because of safety concerns and priceless works of art that could be damaged or destroyed forever. This included one-of-a-kind items, such as altars, paintings, sculptures, and gold-trimmed frames. This transformation from the old to the new was very slow and delicate, naturally, to protect and preserve these treasures. However, what captured my attention rather quickly was the serenity and inner peace that I found in this holy shrine, shoulder to shoulder with my parents and aunt Genoveva. This incredible life-changing moment that I experienced inside this enormous structure, with the high ceiling and colorful religious paintings, touched as all like no other thing has, before or after. During our daylong stay at this shrine, we covered everything that there was to cover, leaving nothing unvisited by all of us. We visited the built-in museum and chapels such as El Cerrito (Hill Chapel) and El Posito (Water and Well Chapel). At El Posito I stopped and put my head inside the well while Pipo and my mom held my two legs. While looking down, I told them, "I can't see anything...it's all dark!"

My mother said, "You are right, you can't see anything." That was the whole point: there was really nothing to see, but I was too stubborn to listen to them. After my mother made that comment, people around us burst out with laughter. I was not amused, nor did I like one bit that I was made fun of.

I told Pipo, "I don't want to walk with mother anymore."

He said, "Son, do not worry too much about it. It was a fun joke, okay? I'll tell you what, come here next to me and we will look down together to see if we can see anything in there. And, whether we see something or not, it won't matter, because it will be our own little secret." Those words and actions by Pipo prompted me to take him up on his offer one more time. We both dived into this miraculous well in this holy shrine, and whatever we encountered, it remained with us, no matter how many people hounded us to reveal our secret. We then took a short stroll along the garden to purchase some artifact souvenirs. However, my father was not to keen on buying anything, since our budget was extremely limited. But he relented to my mother's request and bought me a tiny, golden-colored photo frame that featured, on opposite sides, Saint Anthony and the Virgin Mary. Saint Anthony was aunt Genoveva's favorite saint, as well as mine. Growing up in America, I always had this highly prized little shrine next to me, on my bedroom night table. Before I went to sleep, I would pray, looking to God and them. My mother was very active with me in the Catholic Church. While my father was a Catholic, he was not a churchgoing person prior to marrying my mother. However, he was a firm and true believer in God, somewhat lukewarm about organized religion. I kept this tiny shrine for seventeen years, until it broke apart. I still conserved those images in my wallet wherever I went. I finally gave the frame back to my hero at the Galante Funeral Home in 1985; while he lay in the open casket, I put it in the inside pocket of his suit jacket and thanked God and him for giving me those wonderful memories with him in Mexico City. This was an intense and emotionally charged few minutes, as my tears were rolling down my face. I was telling Pipo how much I loved him and to keep the frame safe in heaven for me until I see him again. It was only right that my father took it with him to the next world to complete the cycle of returning back to me and I will look forward with anticipation to seeing him holding the frame in his hands as I break through to the other side.

At the end of our visit to the shrine Pipo took me to a fair for kids. In this place, I took a photo dressed as a Mexican cowboy, mounted on a fake little pony with the image of Guadalupe in the background with inscription, "Recuerdo De La Guadalupe" (Remembrance of Guadalupe). This photo is very special to me and I treasure it dearly, because it brings to light again that day with my parents, family and friends. In addition, it is one of two known photos that we have left from this time period.

The last of the major sites that we explored was Teqtihuacan Pyramids, approximately twenty-five miles northeast of Mexico City. These are two megastructures, one representing the sun and the other the moon. This incredible site is called the City of God because of the pyramids' deep-rooted religious connections. It also has two main axes, the north and the south, and is notoriously known by the ominous name of The Avenue of the Dead. This entire area contains plazas, tomb buildings, palaces, and altars and is quite an impressive site that will leave you gasping for air as soon as you step in and see it with your very eyes. It is also considered one of the world's most important archaeological sites, because it contains one of the greatest mysteries ever contemplated by experts. They were dumbfounded by how the entire Teotihuacán populations vanished without a clue. This was also a place where many sacrifices were believed to be performed to the gods.

On our inaugural journey to the pyramids, we left our refugee mansion early in the morning for this much-anticipated trip. This unfortunately was our only visit to these historical grounds, except for a couple of fast dry runs on a taxi for a last look, if you will. We had nine people traveling in our party; among them were my mother, Maria, aunt Genoveva, uncle Marcelino, Pipo, two couples, and I. This trip was very amusing and fun because of Pipo and his brother, uncle Marcelino. We boarded this medium-size autobus at the Central North Bus Terminal in Mexico City to commute to the relatively short thirty-mile trip, or so we thought. At the bus terminal, we hopped on a local bus, instead of an express or tourist one, to cut down on our expenses. To our delight, the bus we took still had plenty of empty seats left, which made for a more comfortable ride for the approximately one-hour trip, at the most, since the bus had no air conditioning to speak of. According to the weather report, it was going to be a sizzling day. Man, were we ever wrong in our arrival estimation. The first thing I remember at the station was Uncle Marcelino looking so dapper in his double-breasted blue suit. (He loved to wear suits.) He was turning heads in the bus terminal and on the bus. Even my father, who was a fine dresser in his own right, was impressed. But, like my father always pointed out to me, "Know your environment." Well in this case he was correct, because he had listened the previous night to the weather report, like he always does, warning the ambient temperature was going to be in the upper nineties and to dress properly. So on this trip everyone was dressed casual and very light to cope with the heat. My father knew better and had tried to convince his brother, but he refused.

In transit to our destination, we quickly realized how often the bus stopped for pick-ups. The frequency was becoming a nuisance and very irritating to all us in the intense heat inside the bus. I recalled my father saying to Marcelino to start unbuttoning his jacket before he started to cook in the over-one-hundred-degree temperature. At this time, our collective patience began to decrease very rapidly in this ongoing ordeal. We just wanted to jump off the bus and go underneath a tree or inside a building for some cooler air. After an hour of traveling, the bus was becoming extremely overcrowded with the many locals. It reminded me of Japan, when they have to literally push people inside the train to close the doors. This was a developing scenario that was becoming very scary and dangerous. I said to Pipo, sitting next to me, "It's too hot! I'm sweating and I'm not able to breathe. There are too many people squashing me, making me sick."

He said, shouting, even though he was right next to me, because it was too noisy, "Yes, son, you are right! We will have to get out of here soon, before we squeeze anymore." While my poor mother and aunt Genoveva were sounding the alarm, buried with people on top of them, I could hardly see them. I just heard their outcry. The other couples were screaming, but I could not make out what they were saying one bit. I just remember Ramon and his wife, Gallega (we became very good friends in America), saying how inhuman these conditions were and that they would not be able to tolerate it much longer. My father, who had the aisle seat, was getting stepped on all over. He was baffled, shaking his head, wondering how in the world the bus driver allowed so many people to ride inside at one time. This was a real threat to the older people in the bus, like aunt Genoveva, Ramon, and uncle Marcelino. To make things even worse, three quarters of the way on our trip, the locals were bringing with them livestock, such as goats, pigs, and chickens. I tell you, the temperature inside this metal contraption had to be in the 120-degree range.

My mother started to call out for my father, yelling, "Gerardo!" Gerardo! Gerardo! I can't breathe anymore; get me out of here before I pass out!"

I was also feeling woozy as well. My aunt said to my mother, "There is no air and I feel so sick I'm ready to puke and then pass out. Please, please, let's get out, now!" In the middle of this fiasco, I began to sneeze repeatedly, which was insane; never before or after did I ever suffer that badly, even with my severe affliction with allergies. This condition quickly spread in the bus, as Pipo could not finish a sentence himself because of this terrible sneezing germ that was prevalent. We were constantly being spread with all the airborne mist that could not be avoided in this packed bus of roughly a hundred people and animals meshed together. If the mist was not bad enough, the dripping sweat of others on us was the most disgusting part of this ordeal. Finally, Pipo grabbed my hand and said, "No mas (No more)! Come with me we are jumping out on the next stop, no matter what, son!" True enough, we all literally evacuated this vessel by the rear exit door of the autobus, because the other two side doors were impenetrable. When we were finally in fresh air, everyone was relieve and happy that this torture was history. The aftermath was not pretty; my poor uncle Marcelino was the worst of the bunch. He and his sharp suit appeared to have been hit by a tsunami. Man, he was drenched! But that did not discourage us from moving forward looking like a fire hose was just unleashed on us.

We were walking alongside the unpaved road, where we found a good location to settle down, rest, and change our wet, smelly clothes. We made this settlement our temporary head-quarters to recharge our dead batteries. This turn out to be a good strategic move, because nearby we had many merchants selling and peddling greatly needed garments. It was great to see uncle Marcelino come out from the bushes, wearing a T-shirt and shorts and seeing those skinny white legs. He looked so funny and so different, because it was uncharacteristic of him to be caught in anything but a suit. This new fertile ground was what the doctor ordered. This gave us a shaded area to enjoy fine food that my mom and aunt prepared for our trip. This was a family tradition to always bring home-cooked meals with us wherever we went. After a couple of hours of relaxation and a full stomach, we decided to catch the next bus that had the fewest people on board. But not before a little drama: unexpectedly, a large, thick snake came out and chased us away, making us leave behind some finger-licking good Spanish tortillas.

It took nearly five hours to travel the remaining twenty-five miles to finally reach the pyramids. Everyone was astonished by this development. It took us less time to travel from Cuba to Mexico City.

Except for my aunt and Ramon, we all reached the base of the massive ancient structure. However, my father was determined to go to the very apex. This was very challenging, because when climbing, one had to endure the twenty-inch-high step-stones, with no railing to hold, one at a time when the sun was in full power. I decided to proudly go with Pipo, but soon enough, I became lightheaded and had to go down immediately with Pipo to stay with my mother. It was impossible to miss her, even from the middle of the pyramid; she was sitting on a bench, wearing an sun-attracting orange dress with a straw sombrero that Pipo had given her to cover herself.

While I was coming down, I was having a terrible time keep-ing my balance. I think it was more of a challenge to come down then to go up. I remember Pipo saying to me to try to focus on my mother only on the way down to avoid getting more dizzy and dehydrated. His advice paid off, and after he went to get water for us, he made make sure we were okay and said, "Stay here, son, with your mother, and I will be back soon, after I climb the pyramids, okay?"

I said, "Okay, Pipo, but I really wanted to go with you!"

He said, "It's too hot, plus you already went half way. That's more than enough! Just look at me going up, okay?"

In a somber voice I said, "Sure, Pipo, I will be looking up until you reach the top."

My father, at the age of fifty-seven, was in great shape; he looked like Spiderman climbing these imposing stones, one step at a time. Many times during the climb, he'd turn around and wave to us. I was so excited whenever he did that, that I started to jump up and down, waving back, until he disappeared from my sight in the blinding hot sun rays. About an hour later or so, he came down and told us all about the spectacular panoramic view which he just witnessed. He also commented on the tranquility and serenity he felt standing on top and thinking about how he lamented that this once mighty ancient civilization was here no more, and how the manifestation of time itself is our biggest nemesis, and we can never even attempt to suppress it, just like many previous civilizations, because in the end, it will always be victorious. He reflected and pondered this sentiment of renewal thinking before he descended from the pyramids. He was able to get more than just the thrill of reaching the top of the pyramids from this experience. He was able to transfer a deeper sense of looking at the big picture, which was to keep providing for us the same love and hard work that he has always employed before, and which he provided again in America in the coming weeks.

I asked Pipo, "What was on top of the pyramids?" For a young, impressionable kid like me, it was like seeing in front of your very eyes the gods who were, to my thinking, the legitimate authors of these incredible structures.

He said, "Well, son, before I do anything else, come here and let me give you a big hug." So I did, then all three of us sat on the bench for a few minutes, enjoying each other's company, talking, contemplating about what my father had experienced, and answering my many questions. Briefly he said, "Son, what I saw was many peddlers selling souvenirs and a couple of food stands providing needed refreshments." He also said that going up was very tiresome because of the high steps, which took a lot of energy; couple that with that extreme heat and it was definitely a worthy challenge. However, coming down was even more of an adventure because of the problem of balance; as you came down, you had nothing to hold on to. It was almost like a free-fall feeling. This made you quite dizzy, so you had to crawl backward to avoid this sensation and perhaps falling and getting hurt. This was a very dangerous situation in the making and I'm sure many people have gotten injured. We then accompanied my mother down to the ground level, with Pipo and me holding her on each side, to reconnect with the others.

In retrospect, my most lasting memories of this event were flying out of the smelly and congested autobus together with Pipo to the endless delight of a much-needed infusion of fresh air, and being privy to his heroic climb of the Pyramid of the Sun at his ripe age. It was simply amazing! Just like my amazing Mets a year later, in 1969, captured the World Series against the mammoth Baltimore Orioles. But this, by my own estimation, falls quite short of my father's accomplishment; he was the true champion on that day and the many days to follow.

CHAPTER 16

Hanging Out with Pipo

Besides going to all the great sites in Mexico City, Pipo and I were inseparable in the amount of time we spent together doing various activities. As a matter of fact, this time period was extra special, because we were able to be together due to my father's not working and my not being enrolled in school, because of strict Mexican laws. We took full advantage of all this free time and did many things together, more so than ever before and quite frankly never equalled again. Some I loved and some not so much, but nevertheless, one constant remained: looking forward every day to tagging along with my hero. These daily excursions consisted of going to the supermarkets and to the bank to get our wired remittance. He would also explain in detail the importance of the currency exchange rates between American dollars and Mexican pesos, which fluctuated at various times. He was very meticulous in making sure that he knew the exact rate was not shortchanged whenever we went to the bank or dealt with unscrupulous vendors who prefered dollars to pesos in exchange for purchased discounts for goods. My father would often give me quick lessons to bring me up to date with the new rates. He also played games with me in making sure I understood what he had just told me. He figured correctly that it was not only more fun for me, but also helped me to retain and comprehend it. This new learned information was quickly turned to action whenever we went to local bodegas to pay for groceries. If I was accurate, I would get a prize of my own choice. Normally I would pick an airplane model, or, if I was hungry, some Lifesavers candy and Chiclets. And if I was well behaved, I would get a second reward. Well, the second reward was really a bag of potato chips and a Pepsi, which he knew I liked and would normally get for me anyway. But he wanted to instill in me a work ethic posture that would guide me the rest of my life.

In one of these early sessions—well, mostly learning talks— he picked up a newspaper and showed me where to find the exchange rate information. At that time (1968 rates) the official exchange rate, as I recalled him telling me, was this: "Miguel, por cada dolar Americano tu coge doce pesos y cincuenta centavos (Miguel, for every American dollar, you get twelve pesos and fifty cents)." In addition, he taught me the difficult tasks of the mercurial exchange rates, not to mention the fun wonders of coin collecting, by giving me a Mexican one peso coin which had an eagle with a snake in its beak (the official Mexican coat of arms) on the front side. My collection rapidly grew to over two hundred coins, and I became glued to this hobby. I'm happy to say that I still have in my possession those very coins that my father gave me in those exciting, eclectic days. I tell you, everywhere we went, I had a bag of those addicting potato chips, munching away. Man, did I love those tasty chips; my taste buds could not get enough to squander my appetite.

I remember the time walking in the Paseo De La Reforma, an elegant, tree-lined boulevard that was about two hundred feet wide. This main avenue featured seven beautiful water fountain circles that made for beautiful landscaping. The reason I knew there were seven was because I used to count them as we drove past them on our many taxi rides, going with my family and friends to different places. These trips were mostly associated with getting our paperwork completed for different governmental agencies and for the American Consulate in order to secure proper entrance to America. I used to ask Pipo, why were there so many of these fountains? He would say, "Son, these monuments are to honor Mexico's great heritage, just like we honor Jose Marti in Cuba." I remember three of them in particular that left a lasting impression on me because of the sheer beauty and extravagance. These were the fountains for Christopher Columbus, the great former Mexican President Benito Juarez, and the Angel of the Independence, a symbol of Mexico national identity.

This boulevard was about six miles (twelve kilometers) in length. Sometimes I would get too tired to walk its entirety, so Pipo had to flag down a taxi or we would take the bus to return to the refugee mansion after a hectic day. My mother and aunt Genoveva were always in awe of these eye-catching works of art. They couldn't stop talking about them, giving my father and me a big headache with all the back and forth chattering. We also spent time visiting the Zona Rosada (Pink District), an upscale area featuring many hotels, restaurants, boutiques, cafés, etc.

We also were inundated with the high fever pitch of the 1968 Summer Olympics. Everywhere we went in the city, you could not avoid the full blitz campaign of this spectacle. The whole city was covered by these giant posters on bulletin boards promoting the games. I was puzzled. For the life of me, I couldn't understand what all the fuss was about. Olympics this, Olympics that; it was electrifying. Even the taxis, buses, trains, and main avenues were plastered with this five-colored-rings logo. I even saw dogs and their owners wearing flag paraphernalia together on their torso as they walked by. It was head-twisting time for my father and me whenever we encountered the weirdest of the weird in the propagation of these games in our daily outings. My father did the best he could, since he was not really a big sports fan, to explain the Olympics and put into an understandable context the aura surrounding this event. I remember him saying something like this: "The Olympics is a once-in-a-lifetime experience when all the best athletes in the world come together to compete, representing their proud nations. The epitome is to win and to be awarded the gold medal. But the highlight is really the ceremony and hearing the national anthem of your country being played, along with the raising of the flag as you stand proudly on the platform honoring your beloved country. It's a moment you can't put into words. You have to watch it to know what I mean. It is a shame we can't be here in person to experience this wonderful event. We will have to wait about five months to see the games on television in America."

The most rewarding part of viewing the games was the broadcast images of Mexico City, because it brought back those fond memories I had with my father in those same places. Plus, his detailed explanation of what the Olympic spirit was all about and visiting the Olympic stadium have made me a lifelong fan of this ancient Greek event that transcends sports.

My mother Maria and my aunt Genoveva naturally loved to go shopping, while my father and I preferred to go to Aztec Stadium for a soccer game or to see our favorite sport—bullfighting at the Plaza Mexico ring (the world's largest bullfighting arena). But we always lost out to their strong wishes for us to go with them. My father did his best to maintain the peace with the ladies and me. The only thing Pipo had to do to allay my disappointment was buy me my favorites goodies, like potato chips and Pepsi, to keep me in line and make me behave. I tell you, the two were professional shoppers. They went everywhere to get the best bargains. I remember two such stores; one was called "Gigante" (The Giant), and it was a huge store. You could practically spend a whole day and still not get done. Similar to a Super Walmart store today, "everything under one roof" was their selling point in those days. In order to maintain my calm disposition after a long day, my parents would at times bend a little bit to keep me distracted and happy and would buy me a toy or needed clothes. On one particular occasion, I was obsessed with a small domino set and this beautiful blue corduroy sweater. Thanks to Pipo, I was able to get the domino set. But, on the other hand, it took several more visits to convince my parents to dish out one hundred pesos for it. My parents did everything possible to change my mind; they even pointed out that it was used and it had a slight run, but in the end I won out. I guess they came to the right conclusion on how much I wanted it. Soon after they brought it for me, I put it on and wore it daily, happily. I wore it so often in Mexico that in America it quickly started to fall apart and my mother got rid of it, but not before I went on a temper tantrum for her actions and not telling me about my favorite garment. Well, my mother always had a proclivity to throw away clothes without telling anyone about it, which created many testy confrontations with the family over the years.

The other store was really a popular large indoor flea market that was known for the best bargains in the city. This place was always overcrowded with people looking for great deals, and my mother was front and center while Pipo and I follow blindly behind her to her many stops. This place was incredible; it had the latest technologies that captured the attention of the masses who shopped there. It also had a large indigent clientele that bargained hard for great prices, which caused long delays in getting salespeople to come to help you with your pertinent questions. Plus, there were long checkout lines. Due to these long lines, we all took turns in line to pay for our purchases; it also gave me time to wander with Pipo around this store. On one of these stops I was in awe at this amazing new hot gadget that had a large captive audience in a trance watching it. This new futuristic gadget was my first introduction to portable color television. I was glued, just like the many other spectators on the floor. I even suggested to my mom that from this point on, I would be very happy to come back here shopping with her as much as she liked. I was fascinated with the bright, picturesque, scenic color of this television adventure program called *Tarzan*, with Ron Ely. (Years later, this program became one of my favorite shows in America, along with my aunt Genoveva, who watched it with me with much anticipation every week. And, yes, Pipo would often sit for the duration of the program with us whenever it was on.)

My father, Pipo, at the flea market would stay with me until the show was over, standing, marveling as well, by the experience of watching color television. I remember a couple of times when it was simply impossible not to be in awe of the color variations of the show. For us, back then, it was like going today from a black and white to a spectacular LED HD television. The best scene that captured this transformation was Tarzan diving from a cliff and making a large splash in the water; and the one of him jumping from tree to tree by a connecting vine and seeing the vivid greenish jungle backdrop. Plus, who could forget riding on top of elephants, along with Cheeetah and the boy? Pipo and I would sometimes get a snack during these shows as we waited for Mom to finished shopping, just as if we were in the movies, which was another special activity that my father took me to whenever he had the time. These first experiences were unique and I'm so glad that I was able to share them with my hero.

However, there was one that I preferred to forget altogether. It occurred at one of those afternoon walking outings around the city, when he took me to Lincoln Park for some fun and recreational activities about three blocks away from our refugee mansion in the Polanco District, the most affluent part in Mexico City. (This area is very diverse, with a high population of descendants of Jews, Lebanese, Germans, and Spaniards. It also known for having the priciest street in all of Latin America, called Avenue of Tomas Masaryk, named after the first president of Czechoslovakia.) Being full of adventurous energy, I stepped inside a two-foot deep pond and slipped on the slippery algae, hitting my head very hard on the bottom surface. This shook me up and disoriented me. Every time, I tried to get up, I would slip and fall right back down again. I then began to panic and started crying out loud for Pipo, because I was swallowing lots of dirty water and felt like I was drowning in less than three feet of water. If it wasn't for Pipo's quick response, I would've definitely drowned. When my father pulled me out of the water, I was bleeding from both my head and knees and had a big bump on top of my head as well. I had taken in a lot of unsanitary water and felt sick to my stomach, and half way home I begun to puke my guts out. This incident left me shaken for the remainder of the day, as I withdrew myself to our favorite getaway spot inside fortresslike tree branches near the corner fence of our courtyard. I did not wanted to be bothered by any of my house friends, who begun to make fun of me. In addition, my mother got on my case and on Pipo's as well for not being careful enough. For those of you who have experienced the feeling of drowning, you know had debilitating it is. For those who haven't, I can't even begin to put into words what an awful experience it was for me. I remember my father, Pipo, coming to my tree hideout and sneaking through the thick branches to check on how I was doing. He told me, "You had a very bad moment, but that's over now. We all have those bad times; now go and play with your friends. Don't think about too much what happened today. It's no more. You will be okay! You are a big boy now. Let me see you smile."

I said, "I know I'm a big boy, but, Pipo, it still hurts!" Then he grabbed my head and took another look at my bump and said, "It's nothing too big; just put this ice bag on your head so the bump will go down quicker and not hurt." He then left, crawling out of the bushes, but not before I promised to him to be a man and to go back and play with my friends.

"But for now, come back inside the home to eat, before the food gets cold to please mom and aunt Genoveva," he said. One thing about Pipo, he always seemed to pull a rabbit out of a hat. And for me, when I needed him the most, he came through again, with flying colors. It was so comforting to have him around on that fateful day, which is impossible for me to ever try o decipher. I'm just glad he was there. There is no better man to be in a foxhole with than my father.

CHAPTER 17

Newark, New Jersey, America, 1968

On March 24 of 1968, my mother and I left Mexico City by ourselves (since my father, Pipo, had already left on March 3, 1968, three weeks earlier than we did). We flew out of Mexico City International Airport after spending a long, exhausting day in the terminal keeping busy and resting before departing to Miami, Florida.

After a relatively short sojourn in Miami for four days, we boarded an Eastern Airlines plane along with aunt Genoveva to Newark, New Jersey, arriving on March 28, 1968, with much anticipation of reuniting with our loved ones, especially my brother, Gerardo Jr., who we haven't seen in a year or so. Plus, not having my father, Pipo, around for three weeks was hard to take. As well, we missed the rest of the large Garcia family, who were the first to leave Cuba. One of the happiest occasions I ever remember was my mom telling me as we were descending for our landing over the city of Newark, "Look, Miguel, out to the right side of the window, and you will see all the lights below. That's where our new home in America is going to be!" I kept looking down intensely until we finally landed at Newark Airport at the Old North Terminal (this terminal was torn down in the late 1990s) as my ears became clogged up and I could not hear my mother talk anymore until they popped.

Newark Airport has quite a rich, long history. It was the first major airport in the New York area when it opened in October 1, 1928, as well as the busiest in the world until LaGuardia Airport opened in 1939. Not to mention, it has the distinction being the first commercial airline terminal. Amelia Earhart dedicated the Newark administration building in a big ceremony. (This building today has been renovated to the original condition and moved about a quarter of a mile away from where it once stood, and it now houses the current Port Authority of New York and New Jersey administration office. It is a must see for any aviation enthusiast and anyone who has a sense of history. I highly recommend a visit to this working crown jewel of a building, which also has a small museum as soon as you walk inside the lobby.) Today, this Newark Airport has become Newark Liberty International Airport, a place that I enjoy working very much as a Continental/United Airlines customer service agent, because of those close ties I experienced there with family when we arrived. However, I do miss the observation deck at the North Terminal and at JFK. Hopefully they will bring them back some day in the near future In addition, I had the privilege to meet several times the Continental/United Airlines chief executive officer, Jeff Smizek, who is a terrific and kind person who happened to be a Princeton University alumnus; I'm also so fortunate and proud to be employed by Princeton.)

At the airport we were met by my Pipo and my brother and many family members in an earth-shattering tearjerker of pandemonium. Upon seeing each other, we embraced for a solid ten minutes as we enjoyed this long-time-coming moment where we were united for the first time in one year, the five of us. It was really the core five, taking after the New York Yankees' core four bringing home a World Series championship in 2009. Well, to us this was our winning moment at the airport past midnight. This outburst superseded any of those emotions by greater than any of the "half-life" lengths of time that it takes to decay radioactive nuclear waste. After this happy moment we took a short ride that I still remembered so vividly and with so much joy inside the car. We went on US Routes 1 and 9 North to Delancy Street, where we exited and made a quick left, then another quick left onto South Street, and then over the Routes 1 and 9 overpass until we reached the intersection of Pacific Street. There, we made a right, drove another six blocks, and finally came to our new home at 41 Pacific Street, a six-family apartment building in the Ironbound section of Newark, New Jersey. This area of Newark is called the Ironbound because the city was surrounded by train tracks. No one could enter or exit without going over or underneath these tracks. It is also known by the locals as simply "Down Neck."

It was a small community, mostly composed of Italians and Poles. However, in the 1960s a large influx of new Spaniards, Cubans, and Portuguese begin to settle in this section of Newark. The city of Newark overall was heavily populated by blacks and, to a lesser extent, Puerto Ricans. This city was front and center during the outbreaks of the riots in 1967, which my brother witnessed within a short time upon arriving in Newark. These riots, as violent as they were, were smaller than the others occurring in cities across America. I think that today there is a clear consensus that the mass media's nonstop coverage of the riots contributed in large part to why the middle class and corporations fled Newark. This impacted the city for many years to come. It is now, after four decades of hard times, that the city has begun to really turn itself around. Today the city could boast of many improvements, beginning with Newark Liberty International Airport, that have served as the driving engine for this recovery, along with the Port of Newark, one of the largest container ship ports in the nation. It also houses Anheuser-Busch, one of the biggest beer plants in the world, known for its famous Budweiser beer. But what makes Newark a wonderful place to live is the diversity of many cultures coming together. Whether it is going to the new Prudential Center to catch a Devils hockey game or going to the New Jersey Performance Arts Center to watch a show and stopping before to enjoy world-class cuisine from fine Spanish, Portuguese, Italian, and Brazilian restaurants, just to name a few. Plus, the many parades and festivals highlight this diversity to its fullest, climaxing with the annual Portuguese Parade bash in the middle of June. The city also can boast of many arts and crafts fairs highlighting African cultures that bring so much richness to our cities. We also have minor league baseball at the Newark and Eagle Stadium. Not to mentioned the intellectual capital of its five universities and colleges. It also has one of the most beautiful cathedrals in the country, even though it often gets overshadowed and ignored by those who visit St. Patrick's Cathedral in New York City. I encourage everyone reading this book to drop by for a visit and appreciate the marvelous architecture. This jewel of a structure was where my niece Barbara got married in June of 2010. The city has also a great transit system, with easy access and connection to just about anywhere on the planet. It's been acclaimed as a world premiere transportation hub, culminating with the historic Pennsylvania Rail and Bus Station. And this is just the tip of the iceberg for making Newark a major player in the world. The enthusiasm of this city has spread to nearby communities like Harrison, which is just across the Passaic River and home to a new world-class soccer stadium and is the new home of the major league soccer team the Red Bulls. This sprung up in 2010 to bring the world a little closer to us and to let the world experience what we cherish so much every day.

CHAPTER 18

The North Pole Apartment, Our First

After our short three-mile taxi ride from the airport, we arrived at our new home in America. It was a six-apartment building complex located at 41 Pacific Street, on the right side of the first floor. The building itself was quite old, probably constructed before the turn of the twentieth century, with many needed repairs. However, the exterior was recently refurbished with light greenish aluminum tiles that gave it a much newer appearance. Our apartment had two bedrooms in the front, a living room, a small kitchen with a dining room, and a storage area in the back that led to the back cement yard, which consisted of an old, abandoned, dark shed that we often played inside and a big red brick garage for seven lunch trucks that rented this space. To get in, they had to squeeze by tightly through a long middle driveway without hitting our house and the other one, on the other side, and avoid running over us while we played stickball and catch. Not much fun, especially after a long day of work. Plus, after a truck struck one of my friends, slightly injuring him, in the backyard, our parents complained to the house superintendent about the danger, and he notified the owner and the trucks were eliminated from renting anymore. This was great news to me and the many kids who played so many sports and games in this area.

My father and brother worked very hard cleaning and furnishing our apartment as best they could. They scrounged up beds, a living room, tables, pots, blankets, and everything you could possibly think of to have it ready for us in about a three-week time frame. With very little money to spend, they had to be very creative, so what they did was to ask family and friends to chip in as much they could, promising to pay them back every week until they were paid in full. To save money, they would often carry all the furniture in tandem from many blocks away to our apartment after work. They often would stay past midnight to try to get things ready for us. This can-do attitude that my father has always displayed was a godsend for my brother's attitude in coping with life's difficult events, especially during this time when my brother was asserting himself as a responsible man, in a way passing the baton, if you will. I was still too young to do anything worthwhile, but in my own mind, I was eagerly waiting in the wings for my turn, with my secret plan to help my hero, as soon as I was old enough. God bless their hearts for their love and for what that place minutest piece.

But given all that, I still remember that black-and-white television console in our living room that was more antiquated than the one we had in Cuba. And as always I gave it to them with an earful of innuendos and jokes that never stopped for what they had brought to the house. This television set had to be from the midfifties, because it had that same look that you could find in the app or YouTube widget on the main screen of your iPhone. For starters, you had to use pliers to change channels, because the knob was worn out. In addition, the reception was so bad that you had to practically stand next to the small portable rabbit antenna and constantly move it every way you could to watch your favorite programs. We would have to rotate among each other to alleviate this most annoying and tiring task. Since we only had one television set, and were lucky to hae that, it was often challenging to accommodate everyone's viewing habits, so we developed a schedule to keep the peace that, at times, was a little testy. My hours were from after school to six thirty in the evening. This was great, because I was able to watch all my favorite cartoons and shows. My favorite were *Speed Racer, Gigantor, Hercules, The Flintstones,* and I really loved *The Little Rascals* and *The Three Stooges,* which I regularly watched with Aunt Genoveva, who stayed home making dinner for us while my parents worked. In addition, since my mom worked for Remco toy factory in Harrison, New Jersey (near the new Red Bull stadium), it gave me a chance to look at the many toy commercials that flooded this time period so my mom could bring them to me. I always couldn't wait till she got home to look inside her big pocketbooks to see what she had inside. On most occasions she brought the same toys I saw on those classic television commercials, a few of which I still have today in my recreation room on display. These included a few planes and some soldiers.

Well, after my time slot, Pipo watched the evening news. I often sat quietly next to him as he listen intently to world news. My father had a huge influence on me. Today I have become a so-called news junkie in large part because of those telecasts. Then my mother and my aunt watched the Spanish *novelas* (soap operas). I often crashed with my mother and aunt Genoveva because I wanted to watch *I Dream of Jeannie,* which was at the same time slot. Then came my brother, Gerardo Jr., who loved to tune in to shows like *Tom Jones* and lots of movies, especially war movies. The good thing about my brother's viewing schedule was that he was out often with his friends in Club España on New York Avenue about two blocks away. This gave me additional time to watch my favorite sports teams, like the Mets in baseball and the Rangers in hockey. I was a big New York Rangers fan growing up because of one player. His name was Jean Ratelle, and he became my idol. After he retired, I switched allegiances and started to root for the hapless New York Islanders, who to my surprise won four straight Stanley Cups from 1980 to 1983. In retrospect, those times clamoring with each other to watch television brought us very close and are dearly missed. Years later in our home, when we had five television sets, we became more distant, because we were watching too much television and not spending those precious moments with the family. And today, with HD television, video games, and the Internet, the family has taken a permanent back seat to these unworthy substitutes. This reality has caused many root problems that are making havoc in our current state of affairs. For all practical purposes, taking too much time away from the family unit has really come back to bite us in the butt, big time. This unnatural omission has contributed to the lack of respect people have for one another, which we unfortunately see the aftermath of all around us in our daily life, even within families themselves.

In this building there were four Cuban families, ours included, an Italian American family, and a Spanish one. Everyone was so nice and courteous to us and to each other. The best thing was that they all had about four kids each, which gave me many friends to play with. I remember the Italian family that lived on the left side of the second-floor apartment whom I became very good friends with. I used to spend so much time with them, having a great time doing giant puzzles on the kitchen table and setting up their traditional large Christmas train set that took up nearly half of the apartment with them and their son Michael, who was my playmate, plus his sisters and an older brother, plus some regular friends who always visited them. This family was cool to be with, very modern, and less strict than my own. I also learned English with them by playing with the four kids. I remember my first time I met Ann Marie (two years younger than me). She was the youngest of the four kids. We met in the back stairs the very next day after we arrived. I couldn't understand what she was saying to me and I quickly ran home to tell my parents all about it. I was dumbfounded, because no one had ever spoken to me in any other language than Spanish.

However, I learned quickly that when it came time to watch *The Ed Sullivan Show*, all activities came to a complete halt. The entire family gathered all around the living room on the couches while we sat on the carpeted floor with seat cushions for an hour of laughter and great music. My mom would often come up and call for me from halfway up the stairs to come back home, that it was getting late for school and all of that. I would resist as much as possible, because they had a new color television set that was incredible to watch. Plus, Michael's father would often side with me in having his son give me a couple of baseball cards that he had duplicates of to share with me.

But the overall most striking and memorable feature of this apartment was how cold it was inside. Poor Pipo and my brother, who ran around like chickens without heads in trying to get everything ready in time for us, but by not living there until we actually came, they did not know how inherently severe the heat problem of the apartment was, or, better yet, how bad the lack of heat was. Since I slept in the same room with my parents and my brother slept in the other room with aunt Genoveva, I was able to see Pipo clearly from my bed on the opposite side corner about ten feet away. And what I saw often was so funny I started to laugh out loud and could not hold back for the life of me, no matter how hard I tried covering my mouth so I wouldn't disrupt his sleep. During his bedtime preparations, my father would put on one of those recognizable Russian hats with large ear flaps, followed by a black wool knit hat that covered his entire face and three sets of long johns and three pairs of socks, plus a long, heavy, wool coat. In addition, after six layers of blankets, he had coats spread out near his feet for added protection. This house so frigid we had to buy two electric heaters for each room to stay away from freezing to death. Because the regular wall units were for some unknown reason inoperable, we contacted the super of the building, who called several different maintenance person- nel to get it repaired, but no luck. We were told by the landlord, who finally showed up after big fuss erupted, that he promised it would be taken care of ASAP. But unfortunately the repairs were major and required a complete overhaul to all electrical wires and outlets in the building. So it was going to take longer than expected. We endured these unbelievable conditions for three years, because we had no money to go to a more expensive place. In addition, Pipo was reluctant of going overboard with too many grievances and so forth. It was just not in his nature to complain about anything, especially in a new country. But not my mom, who did not leave any stone unturned in her justified rage against these inhumane conditions that we were exposed to. Her many loud outbursts were legendary whenever these cold winters came. We had to linger and live through three years of these harsh, low temperatures before we finally had enough. I recall one evening in particular that the outdoor temperature drop to fifty below zero with the wind chill factor. It seems like our apartment had no walls at all. You could feel a breeze inside the apartment with no place to hide, no matter how much insulation we put on the windows and doors. Well, as always, I tried not to laugh at Pipo, but when he put a trench coat on top of ten layers of clothing underneath, everything was fair game. I had a contagious bout with an uncontrollable laugh that lasted for twenty minutes at least, to my father's guarded chagrin. He was walking around the house continuously to keep warm. But with so many layers on, it was becoming obvious that he was having a hard time maneuvering. He looked more robotic than most robots.

Our biggest roadblock was going to the bathroom and taking a shower with nothing but our bare skins for protection. This most unlikely meeting with Mr. Freeze was one that we wanted to avoid permanently. But the alternative of not showering was not an option as far as we were concerned, even though it had an unusual appeal to it. So what we did to battle the elements was that instead of settling for the latter, we opened the hot water faucet for ten minutes to warm up the entire bathroom. We even had a big old clock on the kitchen wall, next to the bathroom, to keep watch of the time, because we did not want to run completely out of hot water. Every time we showered, it was basically hit and run to avoid becoming an ice sculpture figure. Our actual shower time was less than ten minutes in duration, including dressing super fast, before starting to get those annoying chills that you couldn't stop from shaking. However, by leaving the hot water running you created this incredible, heavy, dense fog, due to the mixing cold and hot temperatures in the apartment.

These fronts created the perfect storm that prevented anyone from seeing much more than two feet at any time in front of you. We had to use flashlights or candles to move around the house to avoid bumping or running into one another.

It was always quite hilarious whenever we had visitors stop by. Upon hearing the door bell ring, I naturally coalesced right behind Pipo as he opened the front door of our living room that connected to a small lobby (between the building's main front entrance door and our front door). I could see their disbelief briefly on their faces, just before the fog started to spread into the lobby from behind us and cover the entire lobby room as well. This scene often drove many visitors away (it reminded me of one of those frantic scenes from a Hitchcock film), and for those who were brave enough to come in, I'm happy to report that they did not overstay their welcome. Another insane sight after which I couldn't hold back my silliness was seeing Pipo at night sleeping with white smoke constantly coming from his mouth. He looked like one of those sugarcane towers in Cuba that I often saw. During this time, I was often also a really sneaky and bad little boy. I would sometimes get up in the middle of the night and tippy toe my way to the portable little electric heater and, without him seeing me, I would turn it off for fun. After the blazing hot orange and red coils went off, my father, not knowing what was going on, would put on the night table lights or the flashlight to investigate what the problem was with these portable heaters. I would make believe that I was sleeping, holding back my laughter, covering my mouth with two hands as hard as I could to prevent myself from being discovered. But like everything in life, I became very cocky and needed a daily fix of fun at Pipo's expense. Before I broke my armor by breaking into loud laughter just two feet away from his side of the bed, I got caught red handed, with no place to go and no excuses to honestly resort to, so I thought. When I heard him say something, I just froze in place and didn't move an inch until five minutes later, when I climbed back in my bed. Apparently what happened was my father was half asleep, scaring the daylights out of me. As far as I was concerned, it was business as usual for me. I did these acts several more times, even in my aunt and brother's room, to make the apartment even colder, just to have fun. I really enjoyed these infantile tactics, even thought I know now as an adult were very stupid, but I just loved playing games with my hero. How could I ever forget Pipo getting out of bed in the middle of the night with a flashlight, looking like Sherlock Holmes in London with his trench coat and hat in the midst of all the fog around as he investigated the source of the problem, half asleep and frozen? I always made believe I was sleeping, because if I wasn't it, he'd figure I did it and spoil the good times, or, worse yet, I'd get an awful, well deserved spanking.

Many times during these excruciatingly cold evenings, my mother berated my father to do something about the lack of heat in the apartment. My father often fired back by saying, "What do you want me to do? You tell me. This record, you know, is getting a bit old, so stop your constant complaining and yelling before you make everyone in the house crazy, because you are keeping all of us awake, including our next door neighbors."

She'd again take the offense and say, "We can't continue to live under these conditions anymore. We are all going to get sick, probably wind up with bronchitis or pneumonia. Don't wait until there is a disaster! Just look at all the electric heaters around the house. These are not safe! They could ignite a fire very quickly. We have rugs, bed sheets, and furniture that are susceptible to burn at anytime and kill us all."

Pipo said, "As you know yourself, the superintendent of this building told us that the problem is systemic, because the house is too old and needs a complete electrical overhaul. Plus, the owner has disappeared since the last time he came down here and promised to repair it very soon. It was probably after he heard the shocking price tag to take care of the problems. I think he is stalling for time to put the building up for sale to cut his losses. That's what the building superintendent confided in me a few weeks ago. So you see where we are? We are just waiting for word from the owner, whenever he shows up." Well, this deceptive strategy by the owner was a smoke screen to hide his real intentions of selling the building fully rented to get a higher asking price. He never really intended to repair anything. He just simply placated us as long as he could to synthetically appear to appease us by appearing to be sincere in his concern for our well-being.

But besides this most unfortunate situation that lasted for about four month each winter in this apartment that my mother called "the North Pole," we were, for the most part under this severe economic condition, a very happy family, enjoying and living life to the fullest and being very resilient, similar to our *modus operandi* in Cuba. This home also became like a factory because of the papellitos. The Loving Care Company made home-based hair coloring treatments that we had to put together, and this work helped out with some extra monies to pay for the remittance that we received while we were in Mexico City. (*Papellitos* means small papers in Spanish, but in our context it described the type of work we produced to make ends meet after our day's work, and in my case school, was over. What we had to do basically was to take a small instruction booklet, slightly bigger than a credit card, the insert a plastic clear bag that you had to fold numerous times to fit inside the book. Then the last item was a packet of liquid for hair treatment, similar to a ketchup packet that you find at McDonald's. After all these items were inside, you sealed the booklet in the middle with some Scotch tape. Then you put one hundred in each of ten cardboard trays, fifty on each side of the tray, to complete a case. (A case contained one thousand completed papellitos of Loving Care.) Once a case was completed, we would go on to work on the next one until we met our weekly quotas of roughly twenty-five boxes. We were paid three dollars and fifty cents per box, about ninety to one hundred dollars per week. This extra income supplemented my parents' low-paying jobs nicely.

Shortly after arriving in America, Pipo found work at Magnus Organs in Linden, New Jersey, on Routes 1 and 9 south, nine miles away from Newark Airport. My mother found work at Remco toy factory in Harrison, New Jersey, two miles away from our North Pole apartment. At Magnus, Pipo was a well-touted laborer who worked very hard. I recall several visits to the plant, where I saw my father, soaked in sweat, carrying and moving heavy boxes in areas without much ventilation. Even though I loved visiting Pipo at work, I couldn't stand the high temperatures in the place during the summer months, so I decided to go when the weather was much cooler. This gave me a more comfortable opportunity to explore the entire plant to see how those organs were made and speak to his co-workers. I was told by many of his friends that my father was beloved and respected by everyone, including the bosses. They told me his work ethic was impeccable, plus his simple, good-humored persona was contagious, which was very indispensable and most needed to reduce tensions that sometimes were at a high level. This sentiment was prevalent everywhere on the floor of this plant, wherever I was introduced as Gerardo's son.

What impressed me the most was seeing my father in action, assembling and packaging the organs (they looked like small versions of a piano). He even played a few tunes for me while he was working, and then I took over at his insistence for a couple of minutes as he stood by ten feet away, encouraging me (with his patient smile and thumbs up) to continue playing in front of his many colleagues. Some of his friends came in intermittently and sat by me with music books and played famous Cuban and Spanish songs. These trips to the plant were great fun for me, spending quality time with my hero. Because of stringent production quotas, my stays were about an hour only. My father so much valued these very infrequent visits by me because they helped me stay the course of seeing the benefit of hard work that he instilled in me in Cuba, reinforcing the planted seed once again, however in a much faster society in which time is eaten alive, rather quickly, at the expense of the helpless family that always seems to be working.

One day after he came from work, he surprised me by bringing me an organ, which he purchased at a substantial employee discount. After two months of driving everyone crazy with loud noises, I began to improve and learn many fine tunes from the many song booklets that Pipo gave me. Among them, I clearly recalled "Jingle Bells," "Frosty the Snowman," "Rudolph the

Red-Nosed Reindeer," and many other great Christmas classics. Within three months, we had all our neighbors and their family and friends of their family and so forth. It was mayhem, practically at our doorstep, asking to purchase one of these for their homes. It was a real craze, similar to today with the personal computer. It made for great theater. He was constantly pursued for six years, until he retired. It was the hot gadget that people most wanted for their home at the time, with some family purchasing more than one. And I was very lucky that Pipo, mom, and my brother all worked there at one time. This frenzy was fueled by the heavy marketing on television.

My mom worked at Remco toy factory, also as a laborer. She would bring me whenever she could a new toy for me to play with. I, as a young boy growing up, had it made, because my parents were working at the most known and talked-about companies in the country, but for little money. I always made a point to be home at 4:45 p.m. to wait impatiently for my mother to arrive and hope that she had brought me a toy, which she often did. My favorite toys from Remco that she brought me were the classic two-foot-tall walking Rudy the Robot and Voice Control Kennedy Airport set. As I did with the organ, I began to share them with my cronies and created, without knowing it, a monster. The word quickly spread that my mom worked for a toy company. And within the same time span, my mother was in the same predicament with toys that my father faced with organs, but tenfold higher. Our house was bedlam between the Loving Care (*papellitos*), Magnus Organs, and Remco Toys. It was overwhelming. Our apartment turned into a warehouse and assembly plant. We had no room at all; we had to use a storage space in the creepy basement that my mother was terrified to walk down to with a flashlight unaccompanied. We encountered many rotten spiders, and sometimes even drunks and homeless would sneak in and hide for shelter. But even this extra space was not sufficient for our storage space, and we would ask our apartment neighbors for extra space in their basement in exchange for free toys. The toy part lasted three years, the Magnus part was six years in length, and the *papellitos* lasted for the longest, an amazing twenty years.

This fighting spirit of never giving up and looking for alternatives to survive was our trademark spirit, as it was for many Cuban immigrants who came before and after us. Years later, in 1987, I worked for Welsh Farms Ice Cream Company in West Caldwell, New Jersey, and followed the same precedent with delicious ice cream. And finally, in 1994, I became employed at Apex One Sports Apparel. It was one of my favorite places I've ever worked. It was located in Piscataway, New Jersey. I met many great athletes, like baseball player Dennis Martinez and NFL pro quarterback Boomer Esiason, just to name a few. This company, along with Starter, dominated the sports industry with licensed merchandise. I literally could not keep up with demand and had to incorporate friends and family to help me with orders. After my mom lost her job at Remco, she was able to secure employment with Magnus because of Pipo's stellar reputation, joining my brother as well.

Meanwhile, I, after close to a year without attending school, enrolled at Lafayette Street Elementary School, five blocks away from our North Pole apartment, where my brother was in eighth grade. I was scaled back one year to second grade, because I was a foreign student and spoke no English. This was a really good public school, where the teachers actually cared about espousing a quality education. I was very fortunate, because my parents gave them Uncle Manuel's address instead of ours. This quick-thinking action prevented me from attending Oliver Street Elementary School, which had a bad educational reputation and ominous fighting. I was mandated by state law to attend Oliver, because it was only two blocks away, instead of five for Lafayette. However, my very first day in this wonderful school was not so wonderful because of what transpired while waiting for the early morning bell to ring on Union Street on the sidewalk. While my brother stood with his friends around the corner, during this time a fight abruptly broke out, and this ten-year-old boy was taking a real beating from at least two other kids. Watching this butt kicking, I was dumbfounded that no one was jumping in to help out with this massacre. I was always a person, even at this age of nine, who did not approve of injustice in any form or school bullies. So I did what came naturally for me. I immediately decided to intervene and help out this little boy, who was crying and bleeding from his nose.

While I was in the middle of this brawl, my brother, Gerardo Jr., and his friends spotted me and quickly came over to me and intervened by literally picking me up in the air. They hurriedly moved me away from the brawl to the front of the school's main entrance on Lafayette Street, facing the Church of Saint Mary of Immaculate Heart, our local church where we attended family Sunday services. Here, my brother berated me, telling me, "How could you, on your very first day of school in a new country, get involved in a fight? Are you crazy? You can't do this wild behavior in here. Newark is a tough place to be, unlike Cuba. These kids you were fighting against belong to gangs who carry knives and won't think twice of stabbing you. It was very dangerous to ever get involved with them, because you will get beat up by them. Don't ever do that again. Just mind your business if you want to stay in one piece. Do you hear?"

I shook my head in semiagreement to get him off my back, and I then said to him, brother, okay, I hear you, but I did the right thing. I was not going to let this kid get beat up and not do anything about it. That is not me and I would never tolerate it, even if I get beat up myself."

Then he grabbed me by the shoulder to escort me inside the school in one piece as the sound of the bell rang. He said, "You know they could throw you out of the school. I hope they don't notify mom and dad and cause trouble for them." This last sentence from my brother really hit home for me. This was the last thing I wanted to happen to my parents. They had their plates full, and I did not want to do anything that would create an extra burden for them. I immediately said to my brother, "When on in school today or what I did." I promised never to fight again or do any stupid thing that would get back to Pipo. My brother knew firsthand how much of a disciplinarian our father was, and he said, "Don't worry about it! It's our secret, brother!" As he patted me on the head, he said with a big smile,

"You did well in the fight. Where did you learn to fight like that?"

I said, "Have you forgotten already? I learned it from you in your legendary fight with our cousin Fidelito in the street in Victoria De Las Tunas, two years earlier," to his chagrin. After this fight, I became well known and started to befriend many kids in school that are today still my best friends. These included Gonzalo a Cuban, who became my first friend in America and whose father owned a Laundromat and lived at 63 Pacific Street, only a block away from our North Pole apartment; the Vidal brothers, Robert and John; as well as Efren (Freddy) and David, just to name a few. During my first day of class, I couldn't think of anything but the incident and what it would mean if word ever leaked to my parents. As you recall, my hidden agenda and decision in Mexico City were to do everything in my power to make life easier, not more difficult, for my hero in America. I did not want any unwarranted behavior by me to ever impact this stern goal of mine. My first day of school did not lend itself very well to that objective and almost derailed my plans and caused undue harm to my father's psyche. Luckily for me I was able to conceal it for a few weeks, and by that time the impact was negligible and no harm was done.

During our first year in this apartment, one event stands out among the rest. It was watching on television the returns late into the early morning hours of the November 1968 presidential election of candidates between Republican Richard Nixon and Hubert Humphrey, the Democrat. It was just a short six months after we arrived in America. It was my initial introduction to the world of politics, American style, which has hooked me ever since and has served as a platform to get involved in trying to influence the public policy debate. My parents were for Nixon; not surprising, because his secret plan to end the war in Vietnam prevented my brother from getting drafted and sent to Vietnam to fight and winding up getting killed and coming home in a body bag. This was a common scene being broadcast every day in the evening news. In addition, the reality of watching actual war combat footage was hard to avoid. It was called "the television war" because many well-known reporters like Walter Cronkite and Dan Rather and many others were embedded on the front line with the American troops, reporting as the sound of gunfire was all around. These reports were often very gory and hard to watch, especially if loved one were identified in these newsreels or if they were about to be drafted in a conflict that was never declared a war by Congress. And this was after we just had left Cuba to avoid this very same predicament.

I remember clearly seeing my father, Pipo, glued to the TV, viewing the Spanish evening news and at times switching to the big three national networks (ABC, NBC, CBS) and catching a violent image in front of our eyes. My mother would often complain to my father to knock it off and stop watching this madness. Since my father saw fighting firsthand during the Spanish Civil War, he knew the ugliness of what it was to be in a real-life combat situation, and you couldn't get any closer than those reporters who were risking their life to bring the war into our living room. However, my father would often cover my eyes to keep me from watching segments that were not suitable for me. There was pandemonium in our home when Richard Nixon became president elect and then president of the United States, mostly due to the Democratic Party's inability to handle the war and those massive antiwar rallies that broke into riots. None was more damaging than the one that occurred in Chicago during their national convention and split the party in half. As a result, Nixon had one of the biggest political comebacks in history, after losing six years earlier to Pat Brown in his unsuccessful bid to become governor of California in 1962 and, in 1960, losing the presidency to JFK.

Well, my brother did get a draft card, but his designated lottery number was high and luckily he was never drafted. As a result of being next to my father watching a PG (Parental Guidance) version of the horrors of war and news, I caught the news and political bugs, reinforcing my love for radio listening as well, which grew out of Hurricane Flora in 1964 in Jobabo, Cuba, with my father. This proclivity was very indicative from the very beginning at Lafayette Street Elementary School when I began to be an avid reader of the Newark *Star Ledger* newspaper.

Since, I had no money to pay the ten cents that it coat to buy the paper each day (in 2010, the price is one dollar), I relied on fellow students to give me different sections of the paper when they finished reading it, until I had the entire paper. The only section I kept was the sports section, rolled up in my back pocket to check the standings, schedules, statistics, and box scores of my favorite teams. Over the years it quickly expanded intermittently to the *New York Times, Wall Street Journal, New York Daily News, New York Post, USA Today, Reader's Digest, Time* magazine, *Newsweek, US News & World Report, Life* magazine, talk radio, C-SPAN (Cable Satellite Public Network), and finally many classic books on public policy and theory that grew out from school. In addition, I was on cloud nine when Pipo purchased me a new transistor radio that I proudly took everywhere to stay informed and to be entertained by hearing my beloved New York Mets baseball team.

I became involved in local campaigns without really knowing much about them. I was attracted by the fanfare and so-called glitter of it all, which I could not resist from sitting outside on my door steps of our building, watching these intriguing spectacles each day. So, after I exhausted my insatiable curiosity to find out what all the fuss was about, I finally got enough courage and walked into the local political campaign operation that housed its many candidates from the East Ward of Newark, New Jersey, only four buildings away from my own North Pole apartment. What caught my initial interests were the colorful hats and souvenirs people were strutting about wearing as they came and went. They looked like they were having so much fun that I wanted to be part of this same festive mood that encompassed the entire activities. I really wanted a hat badly, and the only way to get one was to help out with the mass distribution of pamphlets, signs, and internal work, so as the good soldier that I was, they finally gave me my desired hat and T-shirt with the candidate's name on it and some refreshments and food. This experience catapulted me into the arena of local, state, and national politics for both the Democrats and Republicans. However, one of my biggest thrills was my first presidential vote. I voted for California Governor Ronald Reagan just like many Americans did, giving him a landslide victory over President Carter in 1980, because of the 444-day ordeal of the Americans held hostage in Iran and the severe economic climate that was affecting the fabric of the American spirit. This lack of leadership was apparent to the voters, who made their point quite clear ar the ballot box, where it counts. The "Miracle on Ice" at the 1980 Winter Olympics in Lake Placid, New York, when the men's ice hockey team captured the gold medal against all odds, lifted the nation's spirits once again, but not enough to reelect President Carter. During the intervening years I volunteered for many candidates, but one was extra special and personal, even though he did not do well. His name was Anthony Santana, and he was a devoted husband, father, and public servant who often would get up in the middle of the night to help people who were displaced from their home by fire or by other circumstances. The reason I know this was because I dated his beautiful daughter, Josie, and would watch him often leave the house in the middle of the night (cheerfully, no matter how tired he was or what the weather was), while we comfortably watched television, shaking our head in awe) to provide temporarily shelter in his capacity as house inspector for the City of Perth Amboy, New Jersey. But he did not stop there; he'd constantly spend time apart from his offi-cial role. He would take extra work upon himself to streamline much government red tape that hinderd many fellow citizens in the city. He was a man of uncompromising integrity, humble-ness, and a second father to me, especially after my hero passed away. So when he asked me to come aboard, too, I was delighted to contribute to his mayoral election campaign in the early 1990s for his beloved city of Perth Amboy, with his lovely wife, Josephine, and his talented son, Anthony Santana Jr. I learned a lot from this grassroots campaign and the importance of having a big war chest of funds. This was his biggest Achilles' heel, and Mr. Santana could not overcome it. Years later the victorious can-didate and mayor, Mr. Vas, was convicted of corruption. Needless to say, the best candidate does not necessarily always win. In the case of Mr. Santana, it was so unfortunate the city of Perth Amboy did not choose the better person.

My father, Pipo, gave me the fundamental building blocks to be an informed citizen by instilling the importance of reading, listening, watching, and sharing uncompromising fellowship and whatever means we have at our disposal to enrich the life of others. It's as simple as that, my friends. In the case of Mr. Santana and those who have given the ultimate sacrifice and shed much blood to protect our way of life, I say, "We can never repay you for what you bravely did, but we can try to encourage everyone to partake fully and not be on the sidelines in this representative democratic republic that we all love and call home sweet home as a nation uniquely made of immigrants."

This work ethic of doing your best is a lesson Pipo taught me well, and it has flourished in my life. However, in this lifelong refinement, it has been a work in progress at times for me to deal with, causing many unintended headaches that I tried to avoid as much as possible and culminating in one of those big mistake that took place with a baseball bat that could've been prevented if it wasn't for my own sheer stupidity. I will get into it in the next chapter.

CHAPTER 19

The Baseball Bat

A round our neighborhoods we played all types of sports on whatever terrain or lots we could find. Often we would play a quick game on virtually the spur of the moment without going too far from home. Within this close confinement, most of these scrimmages were played in the streets (a half a block away from our house) on New York Avenue. We also played there because we could switch on a moment's notice to its wide sidewalk, which was near the intersection of Pacific Street, to avoid getting constantly interrupted or having the games stopped by traffic. We also played on Nichols Street and around the corner on Garden Street; we would eventually move in 1971 to 94 Garden Street. We also played at my Lafayette Street Elementary School playground and as well at the closer proximity school on Oliver Street. The most popular games with us were football, basketball, handball, stickball, softball, Wiffle ball, street hockey, and, my very favorite growing up, baseball. Often we played at Riverbank Park near the Passaic River, only three blocks away from the

Newark Pennsylvania Train and Bus Terminal. It was the home field of the East Side High School baseball team and track team. This was also my beloved old high school, home of the Red Raiders, where I graduated in 1978. The other park was called Independence, a.k.a. "mosquito park" by the locals, for the obvious reasons. It was just a couple of long blocks away from our North Pole apartment (at 41 Pacific Street). These games were often very competitive, putting local street pride on the line for bragging rights on who was the top dog when it came to having the best sports teams on each block. We all wanted to imitate our favorite players; mine were Tommie Agee, Tom Seaver, and Johnny Bench in baseball, while in hockey I made believe I was Jean Ratelle of the New York Rangers. And in basketball, I was naturally Walt "Clyde" Frazier, the coolest guy in town, flaunting proudly my new blue and white suede Pumas, Clyde's sneakers, just like he wore on the court of Madison Square Garden. My good friends Mario (John) and Gonzalo were firmly aligned with Jerry West and Bobby Murcer. This was the typical scene in our area from 1968 to 1973. We were very much entrenched in this most feverish pitch when it came to practicing our craft. I even had a very good friend of mine that would not go to sleep without carrying his baseball bat to bed.

And speaking about baseball bats, there was a most unfortunate incident that I wish I could take back, even today, so I wouldn't have to talk about it and wish it never have occurred— that it was just a figment of my imagination. It was so horrific and gory. It happened when we decided to play in this vacant dirt and grass lot on Garden Street, around the corner from the Costra Brava Spanish Bar and Restaurant. This lot was also accessible by jumping over the high-wired fence of our backyard driveway from our North Pole apartment. The irony of this lot was that it lay across the street directly in front of our second apartment in America, at 94 Garden Street, which we would soon relocate to after this event. This isolated ground was converted by all of us neighborhood kids in a slow, painstaking process into a decent baseball playing field. We played many games here in this gated and lock-secured area where our parents would keep a close eye on us, because they were rightfully concerned about our safety in a city with a large problem of gang violence that was running too rampant and too close for comfort. In addition, I was also very happy that they were there nearby watching me, especially my father, who I wanted to see me in action doing well. I would often scream to Pipo to stay a little longer and watch me play. Many times he would stay for an hour or so, looking through the wire fence and waving. But since the games took too long to finish, he would yell back to let me know that he had enough and was going inside the apartment to eat and rest. Even though these games here were competitive, they were much less so than the street games, which pit streets against streets for genuine street pride and unruly dominance. We also played some of these games for money, especially when no one had too much of it to begin with. This was the harsh reality, and none of us wanted to lose and pay out what little we did make by scrunching and hustling whatever we could, cleaning shoes, selling lemonade, and helping carrying groceries at Food Fair Supermarkets on Lafayette Street (they became Pantry Pride, Food Town, and today it is Seabra's Group, a local giant food chain that came out organically within the community).

During one of these fun games, we were abruptly interrupted by a guy named Tony, a Portuguese boy who was about my age and someone who lived in the same block that I did and whom I knew very well, along with the many kids who were with me playing baseball that afternoon. I even had purchased a bike from him two months earlier, one which he had built, paying him thirty dollars for it. So as far as I was concerned, he and I were cool, no past problems or altercation of any kind. I even admired his strong work ethic and his mechanical skills. The first thing I remember about him was his consistent yelling at all of us in the lot from behind the fence in his backyard. He was in full rage, ready to pounce at us if we did not do as we were told by him. His verbal assault of insane and threatening language was difficult to ignore while we tried to play on with our baseball game. With an intimidating demeanor, he lashed out at us and said, "You guys are not allowed to play here anymore! This is not yours, so get the hell out of here, before I jump over the fence and beat the crap out of all of you right now. I give you to the count of ten to leave or get beat up. I am in charge of this place and I'm kicking everybody out."

I replied (from the home plate area), "Why are you doing this to us? We have known each other for such a long time and now you want to throw us out when we are not bothering anyone, just because you want us out! Why, Tony? Plus, this lot does not belong to you or your parents! Until the owners show up and tell us to leave, we are not going anywhere, do you hear?"

He said, "If you don't leave immediately, I'm going to personally come down and kick you out, you got that? Punk bastard!"

I said, "Tony, listen, we are not bothering anybody, just let us play.

But he kept on harassing us and wouldn't stop using insults, mostly the F word, until he came charging down on us, having just jumped over the wire fence with a long broomstick in his hand. He once again said, "This is your last chance to get out of here in one piece before I give you a lesson in front of your buddies!"

I told him clearly that we were not leaving and that's that Even though some of the guys were telling me to just drop it and get out and go play somewhere else, I refused their sentiment and decided to stand my ground and fight back if that's what it took. First of all, I never liked bullies and never will. And second, I wasn't going to let anyone boss me around and intimidate me. No way, no how! Least of all, try to impose his will on me or on my good playing friends for no apparent reason. This mindset of mine was and is today nonnegotiable for those who try to come at me physically or mentally, whether it is at work, in the streets, or in any other setting.

I said, "I'm not afraid, and I'm not going."

He quickly replied, as he held his stick firmly in his hands, "Come on now…punk," swinging his stick lightning fast at my friends first to push them back farther and get to me. I saw an opening and grabbed the baseball bat to defend myself, since I had no other recourse at my disposal. As the adrenalin rushed in, I tried to hit his stick to disarm him and fight *mano a mano* (hand to hand), if you will, but I narrowly missed. Then he started to swing his stick toward me so fast I could not see it at all. You could hear the whipping sound in front of me as I held my bat in front of me to intercept the blow somehow and break the broomstick, because if it connected, I would be in a big hurt, most likely a fractured bone at the very least. This confrontation went on for a solid ten minutes with an ever-increasing crowd as the word quickly spread in the neighborhood. My strategy was to avoid getting hit too hard and to knock the stick from Tony's hand without a severe injury, if possible, to both of us. I had no other intentions than that.

My ultimate goal was simply defensive in nature and I certainly did not want to kill anybody. However, an unexpected twist and turn by Tony caught me by surprise and almost resulted in the unthinkable. In one of those stick-versus-bat exchanges, I tried my very best to keep my swings low, from the waist down. I was mostly focused on the thighs and nothing more to avoid striking the head at all cost, even if it backfired later on in the fight with a greater chance of getting more severely injured as a direct result of this ongoing battletime decision. On one of those low swings by me, Tony faked me to his right thigh and criss-crossed back to the left, ducking down to launch at me to take me down, when he ran into the force of my swing, catching him on top of his head solidly. The impact was so loud it sounded similar to a hitter connecting in the sweet spot of the bat and hitting a home run.

The first thing I heard after that was the incredible loud screaming by Tony as the blood gushed out of his head. My initial impression was that I had killed him or he was going to die shortly and I was going to go to prison and destroy my parents' lives—no greater pain than for my hero, who left everything behind in Cuba to gives us a better a life in America. When I saw all the reddish blood on the dirt, I quickly panicked and ran home. In my sprint home near the Costa Brava Bar and Restaurants, I noticed that my best friends, Robert and John, cousin Ralphy, and his own best friend, Nandito, who were in their twenties, where standing

outside when the incident occurred and heard the loud screaming. I quickly and nervously stopped and explained to them for
fifteen seconds or so that it was an accident and that Tony was
bleeding to death. Over the years, every time I crossed paths with
Ralphy (who had and still has a strong passion for baseball, having played and financed local teams in the Ironbound section
of Newark), he reminds me of the most eventful day in my life,
when I thought for sure it was a matter of time before the police
came looking for me to take me away permanently. He often
would say, smiling and kidding around with me, "Man, that was
some hit."

My reply to him was, "It was really a fluke, and I regret that
ever happened!"

"Sure it was…"

I don't think he'll ever believe me. But it was the truth! And
like they say, the truth will set you free. Well, in my case I am free.
End of story.

When I got home I feared the confrontation with my father,
Pipo. The first person I saw was my mother and Aunt Genoveva,
and I told them what just had transpired in the back lot. I said,
"Mima (an endearing name for mother in Cuban, just like Pipo
is for father), I didn't do it on purpose, it was an awful accident."

My mother started to flip out and really get upset even more
as I explained further. I had told her about all the blood covering Tony's face as he lay down on the ground. She then said,
"What is the condition of Tony?"

I said, "Mima, I'm afraid that he is going to die…there is so
much blood…that I ran, I couldn't take his loud screaming and
the blood pouring from his head."

My mom then said, "I'm going to the backyard to see Tony
and check on his condition," and I accompanied her. But when
she looked from our backyard, the lot was completely empty.
Tony had been immediately taken by someone who knew him to
the emergency room for treatment at Saint James Hospital.

When we returned to our apartment, Pipo walked in from
the bedroom to the living room to ascertain what all the commotion was about. He had come from work forty minutes earlier

and had taken a small nap just before having our family dinner together. My mom explained to Pipo that I was involved in a fight where I had caused a substantial injury to Tony, the Portuguese boy from the neighborhood, who lives just four houses from us and who had sold me his bike two months ago. The worst part, she said, was that I had hit him with a baseball bat and cracked his head wide open, and nobody knew his condition.

My father said to me, "How in the world do you always get in trouble? You've got to stop all these stupid things you do! Think for a change! Know your environment; never, ever put yourself in these types of predicaments again! Walk away, and diffuse it. Do you hear me, Miguel?"

"Yes, Pipo, but it was in self-defense this time. He had a broomstick and I grabbed a baseball bat to block him from hitting me. It was an accident. I was trying to hit him in the legs, not the head, but he ducked low to jump on me and my bat struck him in the head."

My father was getting really desperate and concerned about Tony's medical condition. He said, "Son, if something permanent were to happen to Tony, we would be forever ruined in America. All our plans for your brother and you for a better life would be no more. Everything we did to come here would've been for nothing!" During this time, he had my brother called Saint James Hospital several times to find any news about Tony, but we were unable to get any information. The only thing I had in my mind was waiting for the police to knock on the front door and take me away from my parents for good to go to prison. This unavoidable knock I hoped would never come, but I knew it was simply a matter of time, not only for me, but for my nervous parents, aunt Genoveva, and my brother as well. It was really the worst of times in this household, full of tension.

After a couple of hours had elapsed following the incident, waiting for official word as we comforted each other, we heard a hard knock on the door followed by the doorbell ringing. I said, "That's the police! They are going to take me away!" So I ran to the very back of the exit door where we kept all our junk in this small storage room to wait it out, hiding behind the many items (however, with enough space in between to peek through and to listen intently to what they were saying about the situation in the living room). This distance behind the kitchen provided a strategic advantage that gave me the potential to make a run if needed from my incognito location. My mother could not bear the suspense of opening the door, or anyone else, for that matter. So she said in an uneven keel to my father, "Gerardo, are you going to open the door?" while everybody looked at each other with a weird, puzzled demeanor of knowing this was it. The moment of truth had arrived. Who would be on the other side, waiting to disclose the uncertain news that we feared, but did not look forward to confronting?

As my father opened the door, he was met by Tony's father, an elderly man, who informed Pipo that his son was taken to the emergency room at Saint James Hospital in Newark (which is roughly six blocks away from my North Pole apartment). My father instantly asked him what the condition of his son was. Tony replied, "Luckily, the impact was on top of the head, not the side on the temple. It would've killed him for sure. The wound was cleaned up and they put in twenty stitches."

My father was so apologetic and lamenting deeply how sorry he was about the injury to his son, and that no words he would be able to express to him could truly convey how badly he was feeling. Then Tony's father said, to ease my father's frame of mind, "Kids are kids and sometimes they do stupid things."

My father said, "You are absolutely right, but this is a very serious injury, and a few more inches closer to the temple would've been deadly."

Tony's father was a proud, hardworking man just like my father, old school, if you will, and did not like anything to do with lawsuits or payouts of any kind. "The only thing I want is to cover the emergency cost of $188 that I had to pay, because I lack insurance," he said.

My father, Pipo, said, "Of course, I will get it for you right this minute," shaking his hand as he went to his bedroom closet and took the money that he was putting away to pay for the remittance from Mexico City, which was in full progress. In 1970 that was a significant amount of dollars, equaling two weeks of hard work for my father and four weeks for my mom. No small change. This event was certainly not over for me. After coming out of hiding at my father's calling to apologize to Tony's father and allaying my wild fears of going to prison from my untimely deed, my father gave me the biggest belt whacking ever, to last a lifetime. Plus, I was banned from watching television or playing baseball for a month. He also made a point crystal clear: to swing the bat only at baseball games or else. He had a stern look on his face that I had never witnessed in him before.

A day later my father told me to look for Tony and shake his hand and say that I was sorry and ask him to forgive me for my stupid act. Tony was nothing but a class act; he gave me his hand unsolicited and accepted my sincere apology, and I never had any confrontations again with him. We became very good friend for a long time afterward. Over the years, when we have crossed paths, we often talk about the day that will live with us forever as he showed me the remnants of his scars, laughing. He turned out to be a fine man that his father would be very proud of, looking down from heaven.

In retrospect, I am often reminded by my inner voice how fortunate I was that this event ended with so many positives lessons. I was more determined than ever to try to repay my father, my true hero, every penny for my errors for causing so much distress to him at a time when he was barely keeping his head above water. I implemented my plan by doing more after-school odds-and-ends jobs, whatever it took, even if it meant not playing sports or hanging out with friends, which was fine with me. I became enthralled with selling and carrying just about anything can you think of. Whether it was looking for recycled bottles that paid a good five cents each or carrying groceries, I was there for hire. This was on top of my regular shoeshine and lemonade businesses. In life, the biggest obstacles are not making mistakes, as in my case with the bat, but in not learning from those fertile seeds that my father planted in me to make better judgment given the ever-present stimuli in our everyday life. This is a sort of coping mechanism which we have lacked profusely from the beginning of creation. Gracias, Padre! (Thank you, Father.)

CHAPTER 20

Paying the Debt

In our first few years in America, my parents were mostly preoccupied with paying down our debt from the remittance we incurred in Mexico City. This period was very difficult for them, because they were starting from scratch and having this giant elephant put in front of them, directly in their face, with no place left to go around. This was the hard reality they were facing in their everyday struggles to put food on the table and pay the loans back to family and friends. The most difficult times were from the very beginning in 1968 to late 1970. This time period was also a very challenging time simultaneously for America that you could not avoid even in your living room watching the news that was shaping our nation. These events were memorable for me because of watching the news with Pipo and my mother while they were talking with each other on who to pay first and how much could we afford. Discussions like these often took place, and I remember them so well with what was occurring intertwined in front of our eyes in disbelief.

It begun roughly with the first days of the Tet Offensive, when South Vietnamese General Nguyen Ngoc Loan raised his sidearm and shot a Vietcong prisoner in the streets and it was captured by NBC TV cameras and by AP Photographer Eddie Adams and quickly plastered around the world, frozen in time forever. These snapshots became the rallying point for the antiwar movement, which was becoming massive in scale, questioning everything about America and its allies, the South Vietnamese, despite later claims that the prisoner had been accused of murdering a Saigon police officer and his family. Shortly after, President Lyndon Johnson decided not to seek reelection, and then came the shocking news of civil rights leader Martin Luther King Jr. being assassinated outside a Memphis hotel, and, two months later, Democratic presidential front runner Robert Kennedy, brother of President John F. Kennedy, was gunned down in San Francisco, California. Next, the Youth International Party (Yuppies), led by Abbie Hoffman, disrupted the Democratic National Convention in Chicago. These massive riots helped elect Richard Nixon president in a very close election that went back and forth. I remember the entire melodrama, because of all the commotion with the election returns, which were always changing through early dawn. It was a circus environment; I kept hearing, "Humphrey is ahead now!" A few moments later the chanting was, "It is Nixon! Nixon! He has taken the lead," and so forth.

As a youngster, I was more concerned with staying up playing with my many friends through the entire six-apartment building whose families were glued as well to their television sets. Needless to say, I was excused by my family to stay home the following day from school so I could be part of this historic occasion. In our building the majority of the families were for Nixon because of the plan to exit from Vietnam and the disarray within the Democratic Party And I'm glad that they used good judgment in making that decision, which eventually became the genesis of my love affair for politics and watching presidential elections returns ever since, and thinking about that particular night with Pipo's vibrant energy pulling strongly for Nixon, along with the rest of the family. There were also other shaping events, but the shooting by some National Guard members at some universities caught the attention of everyone in our home and impacted the nation, none more so than the killing of four students at Kent State University. It was a horrific event that is best known for the photo of a horror-stricken teenager on her knees, next to one of the shooting's innocent victims. It became a symbol of carnage and how divided the nation had become.

But there were some remarkable stories that not only united our country but the world as well. It was the landing of men on the moon, with Neil Armstrong setting foot on lunar soil for the first time. My father and I shared many of those memorable moments with an amazing feeling of witnessing such an achievement. He also pleased me by fueling his car at the Sunoco gas station, because they had a bunch of promotions featuring man-on-the-moon souvenirs with capsules and rockets that I wanted to collect. It was also a godsend, because it distracted him from the reality that he was facing during those days. Since we lived in New Jersey, in the metropolitan area the home sports teams were celebrating championships, beginning with the Jets, who won the Super Bowl after the flamboyant quarterback "Broadway" Joe Namath guaranteed a win over the heavily favored Colts and the New York Knicks captured a title as well. Not to be outdone were the amazing Mets, who won the World Series. This time period concluded with the spectacle of Woodstock in upstate New York celebrating "give peace a chance" with great music.

In the midst of all these events, my hero was facing his biggest challenges, heavy debt and age. He was closing in on his sixtieth birthday and time was going by too fast, which gave him less time to repay his obligations. Often some of these folks were impatient with Pipo and would ask him often when they would get their money. Their attitude was shortsighted, because Pipo was doing everything in his power to accomplish this very goal as soon as possible. This constant pressure was taking its toll on my father, giving him massive headaches; he had to tie a handkerchief around his entire head for relief, due to lack of sleep. He was working sixteen hours a day, with no days off to relax and rest.

At times my father confided to my mom how much people has changed in America. "There is too much emphasis on money; I don't know what it is," he said. "But whatever is driving this kind thinking or attitude, I want to remove this deep cloud that's hanging over my head. It seems like whenever I come across the people to whom I'm endebted, they act very strange and fidget, like they want to know when are they going to get paid back, without really asking for it directly. It's very disheartening to me and I want to eliminate this from happening too much longer. In Cuba, we just all lived to help each other with the little we had, no matter what. In America, this mentality is not practiced, and this leads to division within family and friends. So, even if it kills me, I will pay everyone back in full whether they want the money or not. This is the new mind-set culture we face in America, and we will learn to adapt to it, because money rules and is expected."

My mother had a different view; she wanted to take a much slower path to pay these people back. She would say to Pipo, "Let them get all worked up. Have they forgotten what you did for them in Cuba, always going out of your way, even going against my wishes numerous tines to help them when they needed you? And this how they pay you back now, by aggravating you whenever they see you? I am not going give them the satisfaction to make my life miserable. I'm going to save to go on vacation in Spain, go to the Jersey shores, have our regular picnics, throw parties, and enjoy life. But I'm not going to let you superstreamline the payments and have no life, to the detriment of our family. I am not going to let that happen. They will get their money at the proper time and no sooner."

My mother was the type of women who never backed off from a fight, and those who knew her would surely attest to her strong, unyielding persona. While Pipo was from a different world altogether, he was admired and well respected and never raised his voice at anyone. But he sensed the immediacy of paying the remittance, because he took the position that it was this new culture that had changed the attitudes of our family and friends and that they were in the same predicament that we were facing in controlling debt. This position was not shared by my mother one bit, and she would often battle my father in firestorm ways to change his thinking and ask him to wake up and face reality because they were in a much better economic condition than we were. Whether this was true or not, it did not resonate with my father one bit. His overriding concern was to be debt free as quickly as possible, and he was going to see that he never derailed from the goal, because he felt it was the right thing to do, at the cost of making my mother upset.

One of my paramount goals was to earn some money to give to Pipo for the liquidation of the debt. I was nine years old when I started after catechism classes at Immaculate Heart of Mary Church right in front of my Lafayette Street Elementary School. I walked three blocks nearly every day to carry groceries from Food Fair Supermarket to customers' cars or their houses, the latter of which was kind of dangerous, but I never mentioned to anyone that I was doing that or else my parents would've stopped me. Some weeks I would make nearly thirty dollars, almost as much as my mother in her full-time job at Remco toy factory. Man, I was so happy and eager to take it home and give all of it to my father. Other weeks I made much less, but neverthe-less, I was able to compensate by shining shoes. I was very for-tunate because of the great logistics in the area. I would cruise the entire Ferry Street strip, the main avenue in the Ironbound section of Newark, which was full of bars and restaurants, and I would hop in and out every weekend and make thirty dollars for about eight hours of work with tips. (Today this area is famous for its great Spanish, Portuguese and Brazilian cuisine.) Not too bad in the late sixties or early seventies for a young kid like me. I was a hustler who knew what it took to make money. This inher-ited attitude grew in Cuba, where we had to be creative in every facet in our lives to survive. These skills were put to good use in America to produce additional income to pay down the debt and help my parents.

To me it was a piece of cake, much easier than I thought. I would often be attacked by friends who did not understand my ways. Some of them were Cubans whose parents were facing some of the same realities that we were facing, but they did not scrounge up enough time from playing to earn some money like me to help their parents. The Americans kids had no reason to relate to our condition and were oblivious as to why I was doing what I was doing. They would often ask me, "Why are you working so much?" I would simply say, "I like to work, not simply play. Plus, work is not simply work; it's also lots of fun." Often they would help me in selling lemonade from outside my house in exchange for a free glass. This enterprise was very popular with the many locals in the neighborhood, because it tasted good and was cheap. Within a couple of weeks these outdoor table stands spread out quickly as other kids open theirs and competed with one another. But to stay one step ahead of them, I would give a half off on a second drink or a discount on a shoe shine. Whatever it took to keep my clientele and recruit new costumers. In all my endeavors, I was very persistent and never lost focus on what my objective was because of the high stakes that were driving me: generating enough disposable income for Pipo. It was the best feeling in the world, every time I had a successful week, to give Pipo the money I earned and watch his golden smile as I handed him the cash. These were priceless moments that I will cherish forever, and they were nothing compared to what he did for me in my development. However, there were times I did keep a small portion for my expenses and to purchase supplies for my enterprises. Sometimes I felt kind of guilty, because I used some of the money to purchase firecrackers and other stupid things like that. The firecrackers and many other fireworks were very popular in my neighborhood, and before I began earning money I would sneak in my mom's purse and take change to supply my affinity for these dangerous pyrotechnical games without her knowing. But, as with all good things, I got greedy, and she caught on quickly and hid her pocketbook, and I was permanently cut off. On the other hand, for the record, I never went into my father's pants to take any money or anything like that from him. I never even contemplated for a second such an undertaking, because it would've been against what I was trying to achieve in the first place—to give, not take, from my hero. That was really my only goal in my early life, and it never left me, thanks to God!

CHAPTER 21

Starting Over

After my father had passed away on July 24, 1985, I often wondered how difficult it was for him and my mom to start a new life again in a strange, new land. This enormous transition was a daunting task for them. However, they were full of optimism and courage. They welcomed this challenge with a strong hunger to adjust and succeed in this new environment we called America, the last great hope for mankind, as the old saying goes, and they knew it would not be easy.

Today is September 8, 2003, and I'm writing this chapter from Roosevelt Park in Edison, New Jersey, formerly known as Menlo Park, because it was here where inventor Thomas Edison had a factory where he worked on his many inventions. This park site was chosen for me because of many happy times with Pipo, family, and great friends sharing great company and delicious Spanish and Cuban food. The park brings up many childhood memories as I look all around me while sitting on a wooden picnic bench that has a combined table. As I look slightly to my left,

I see clusters of picnic tables and barbecue grills about 150 feet away. This area was extra special for me, because it was where we all flocked for Sunday afternoon picnics, as well as the last time we were all united in this very park. As I keep looking toward that area, I also see nearly two hundred tall trees that enrich this natural beauty and that kept us shaded from the hot sun during our many visits here. As I write further in my notebook, I keep getting an unexplained, vibrant urge to walk over there and just sit quietly on one of those very picnic benches where I sat often with my father, Pipo. After giving it one last look, I decided to go with my instincts and just keep writing this chapter from this location for now, because it will give me a better view from afar to reminisce, if you will; on top of that, for some unknown reason, I can see instant flashes of those great family outings coming alive in front of my eyes, similar to an actual videotape coming and going. But it's only in my subconscious mind, where Pipo and I and the rest of the family are having a swell of a time. It was exactly like the good old days when I was a child, but this time it was more of a very spiritual experience, because this go around I am not a child; I'm an adult and I've learned the true value of my special teacher, who taught me everything I need to survive in this world.

I get the feeling he wants me to tell me much more—what else could've brought me to this park in the first place, if it wasn't him? I guess he wanted a place that I knew quite well and was very quiet and peaceful in nature, so I would not be distracted. Having said that, I march to my beckoning spiritual calling to be near him as he pulls me ever closer to him. Once there I'm in the middle of the clusters of picnic tables, luckily alone, with the sole exception of some squirrels, bees, mosquitoes, and birds. There are many different worlds and dimensions that we are not privy to fully understand, but let me tell you, unequivocally they do exist. My father, my hero, has guided me here to this serene landscape for one more lesson as a grown-up that he wanted to shared for my well-being. In this spiritual world, my hero is very much alive, living life to the fullest, with no pain due to any earthly things or concerns that evoke so much stress. This clear consciousness is not easy to obtain in the carnal world, only in the next one. However, this division does not prevent my hero from communicating with me, because of my genuine love for him. He tells me, "Son, just relax and enjoy the moment, and every moment after that! Don't forget it! The most important thing you can do is to keep going forward. I know it is tough, but, son, you can do it. Never give up on anything in life. Listen, son, to my words. I am in the kingdom of heaven, at peace with the Creator, and he has sent me like an angel to help you in difficult moments."

I kept hearing this constant message from my father, Pipo. This was his way of opening my mind in a time when I was feeling somewhat down and needed his voice to lift myself from a nagging, defeatist attitude that was trying to get a stranglehold on me.

During this same episode, I was getting flashes of my father playing Frisbee with me in the grass to the left of our picnic tables, near the brook where I went to blow up firecrackers in the water to make a huge splash. One thing about Pipo, even though he was in his sixties, he always tried his best to keep up with me, no matter how tired he was. My father would often spend quality with me in some fashion, whether it was by the manmade lake fishing or just taking a walk. It was a most welcome pleasure to be next to my hero, doing things together. When I got older, in my late teens, he would share beers, mostly Lowenbrau's and Millers, with me and shoot the breeze. We would talk about everything under the sun, from politics to cars. But what I remember the most was his patience and his love for everything he so eloquently spoke about, never criticizing anyone or thinking negatively about life's difficult circumstances. One thing about life was, he told me to acknowledge that life is very difficult and to get past it and move on as quickly as you can to be completely free of this potential handicap that traps people all the time. He said, "It was a prerequisite for a better life that I picked myself up during my early years in my birth home in Valle De Las Casas, helping my parents and nine siblings in the hot country fields and later on in the military."

I made a promise to Pipo in this natural cluster of trees that I would listen and take his message to heart with all my strength and never deviate from it, no matter what I have to face in my life. Every time I need to energize my mental battery due to the heavy negative drainage caused by just living, I know for sure that my father will be on the end of the regeneration plan, if you will, to provide me with the necessary fuel to keep me fully fueled and ready to dispense with whatever comes my way, just as he was able to do whenever he faced obstacles in his own life that tried to block him from going forward. This constant reinforcement is within me at my beck and call whenever I call upon him for advice to move forward, and it has not been higher than at this present time, as I write this chapter. It's like this location is serving as a conduit directly to my father, in this a place where he is so much spiritually alive.

As I wrote the last sentence above, I couldn't help but shed one large tear, which landed on the word "moment" on the left side of my notebook and literally soaked through the page behind. This natural response by my senses indicates to me my how deep my love is for my father and how much I miss him. I have come to the realization that my father is very aware of my sometimes stubborn nature, which causes me much turmoil, whether it is with family, friends, colleagues, acquaintances, or any economic or other issues that arise. That is why he has followed up from a previous occasion and brought me here—to reassure me that he is next to me and to just relax. In all of this, as I continued to write, I couldn't help but wish that I was able to share a few minutes with Pipo with a big hug and a kiss and say, from the deepest part of my heart and soul, "Pipo, I love you very much! Just come down here for fifteen minutes and walk with me alongside the pond, admiring the many ducks and fishes like we used to do. And after, we could shoot some hoops on the basketball courts and ride the bike one last time before calling it a day with mom's and aunt Genoveva's fabulous Spanish tortillas that were out of this world. You could give me a few small Lowenbrau beers without telling Mom, and then we would fall asleep together in the green grass underneath the tall trees for a little afternoon siesta to recuperate from the long day of activities." This was what I wanted to occur, but I knew it was not realistic or practical and would never come to fruitionbut I did not care one bit. It was my dream and mine only, and I couldn't care less what anyone would think. It was my desire, especially after what had happened to me in this time frame, which was about five hours in duration in this sacred environment.

I think coming to this park, which is like a sanctuary for me, was an awesome revelation. It gave me maps of Pipo's internal views of the world and all his permutations and processes that helped him cope whenever he was in troubled waters, so to speak. This was never more true than on my way home during my forty-five minutes' drive to my house at 429 William Street in Harrison, New Jersey, via Routes 1 and 9 north, the long way, instead of taking the New Jersey Turnpike. I chose this route because I wanted to extend my ride home to give me more time to fully grasp and discern completely what had just taken place with my hero and to put it in perspective. My findings were crystal clear, revealing life's mysteries in the simplest terms imaginable. You don't have to be a scholar or anything of the sort; the only prerequisite that you need is to move closer to the Almighty and ask for divine help. My father's good humor and humility were virtues given by God to him to export, which he did with flying colors. Without having God so close by my father's heart, my father would've thrown in the white towel and surely surrendered.

Starting over for my father was not really starting in any materialistic sense. It was one of living moment to moment solely, and not living one second beyond it. Whether it was coming to America or staying in Cuba, my father's magic formula remained intact. Since he was always living in the present, my father never succumbed or became too flustered to move forward. He was fully armored to withstand any invading force that tried to negatively affect his spirits. My father, by following this path, never became a slave to things that we have very little control over. How often have we, including myself, indulged in this destructive attitude and behavior? My many mistakes have proven costly has and have led to all sorts of problems, none greater than economic, marriage, and feisty attitude problems that have led me astray for many years; over the years, I have met people, who have been institutionalized or even committed suicide for not staying focus on the present.

In closing this chapter, I want to reiterate the most important question that I proposed at the beginning; how did my hero start over? For me to answer this question was simply too difficult, but for my father it was as simple as riding a bike. Once you know, it becomes second nature…right? My father was able to share twice this reservoir of advice in his own good-natured way with me at Roosevelt Park to finally awaken me, first spiritually and then in his entire earthly life. The answer was for me to seek always the Divine with a relentless submission of adoration and faith so he can give me all the wisdom that I'll ever need to confront life's many uncertainties just like my father did, "one moment at a time." That was the most important lesson that I've learned, and I will treasure it forever as the crucible in my life. Gracias, Pipo! (Thank you, Pipo!)

CHAPTER 22

Snow

Coming from Cuba, where it never snows, I was looking forward with much anticipation to my first glimpse of snow. My father, Pipo, on the other hand, as well as my mother and Aunt Genoveva, were not so enthusiastic, not to mention my brother, who had experienced it in Spain and in America. I remember constantly asking and pestering my father with this broken-record question: "When are we getting snow, Pipo? I want it to snow so I can go and play in it. Please, let it snow soon! I can't wait for it." My father knew quite well the difficulties that snow brought with it. But for a young child like me, it was all positive, no down side. This snow craze thing was not limited to me only, because one of his work colleagues, named Cruz, at Magnus Organs camped out at our North Pole apartment all night, waiting it out for the first signs of flakes to come down, along with his three-year-old son and his wife. Acting like little kids trapped in a toy store, this enthusiasm they espoused quickly spread in our home and our building. Often we would go outside in front of building and congregate with the many neighbors who were swept away talking with Cruz. My father at times would join us and stay with us for a while, looking up to the night sky, and would start kidding around with all the hopefuls with his good humor, telling many interesting stories about everything you could think of in the very dark night sky. On this particular night when it began to finally snow, we all began to dance around each other, led by Cruz, as the flakes hit our faces. This great occasion was a landmark for me and those who were there. It was a full-blown winter fest, Cuban style, of living for the moment and not beyond. This amazing evening was incredibly fun; even our American neighbors got into the act and joined us.

Our first big snowstorms did not occur till two years later, in 1970, and then eight years later, in 1978, in late January and early February in back-to-back blizzards. These storms were most memorable for various reasons. First, it was great fun to play with all my schoolmates in this wonderful, frigid winter wonderland that most adults would shy away from. We loved to have snow fights with each other in a barrage of fierce exchanges that left very little visibility in the area. Most of these games were held at my Lafayette Street Elementary School playground, but they continued all the way home, even hitting some buses and cars that got caught up in the crossfire as they went by. That was not a smart or a good thing, because a few times we had to run for our lives from these upset people, who chased us throughout the neighborhood, jumping from yard to yard. We were lucky to escape without being getting our butts kicked. Some of these storms left in excess of twenty inches of snow on the ground, which made it fun climbing many streets full of snow mountains about twenty feet high. This natural gift from Mother Nature did not sit well with Pipo. It meant a big pain in the rear, with a lot of upcoming hard work shoveling the dreaded snow. But since I loved snow so much, I gladly volunteered to help my father dig out my brother's 1970 Ford Torino that was buried in the snow so deep that the only visible sign that a car was underneath was the front antenna. (This auto was given to my father after my brother married in 1972. Subsequently, when I turned seventeen,

I purchased the car for $2,200, even though my father would've given it to me cheaper or free. I declined, because I knew how much he needed the money and mostly because of my deep love and respect for him.)

Like my father said, shoveling heavy snow was not an easy task, as I found out very soon.After twenty minutes into my so-called fun activities, I started to sweat and get the chills from all the snow removal in front of our North Pole apartment at 41 Pacific Street; it certainly felt like the North Pole from the inside, and now the outside had caught up, resembling the real North Pole. The best and funniest part was getting prepared to go outside to meet Mr. Snow and shovel him away. I remember laughing so hard with my mother and aunt Genoveva, watching Pipo getting dressed up in the living room before stepping out of the apartment. He began this most entertaining odyssey with multiple layers of cotton and wool socks. Then, over his boxer underwear, he had two pairs of long johns, followed by two pairs of pants. On the upper torso, he had a sleeveless undershirt followed by a T-shirt, coupled with a flannel shirt. If this was not enough, he would go back to the bedroom and pick up two more sweaters before putting the final two pieces on to hold the coldness at bay. Then came the long black trench coat and the boots, which were those that you could put your shoes inside for extra protection. Oh, I almost forgot the very last item…if you were guessing hats, you were right! First was a ski mask with small openings for the eyes only. Then, the last hat that he put on reminded me of a Russian soldier. It had those large flaps on the side that snap on underneath the chin, with lots of wool on the forehead. It was so comical watching Pipo doing this routine that it never got old or stale for those witnessing it.

During the late sixties and early seventies, the weather in Newark, New Jersey, was extremely cold, much more frigid than what it was in later years. These temperatures were normally around the ten-below-zero to single-digits-above Fahrenheit range. On the other hand, my ritual to go outside was unlike Pipo's; I just put on my hooded sweatshirt and my only jacket that I had, and off I went. This blue leather jacket was given to us by the Catholic charities, and I treasured it very much, since it was the first one I ever wore. However, for some reason the leather was extremely hard to move around. I felt like a robot, similar to Pipo's demeanor with all his layers of clothing. That rigidity of my movements made me perspire almost immediately, just by moving my torso, without much effort. This would create a problem once I began shoveling, and I had no choice but to unzip it and ultimately remove it, because it was impossible to get any rhythm in helping Pipo dig out. Luckily it had stopped snowing, so I only had to deal with blowing snow, which was not too bad to take.

Well, back to Pipo, and you might be wandering about his hands. Yes, he did wear two pair of gloves. The inside one was made out of soft wool, while the outer was from solid leather. But before we marched in tandem to go outside to meet the elements, I couldn't help but sneak away and hide the shovels from our little storage area, behind the kitchen, to play a trick on Pipo. He would go in a tailspin wondering why the shovels were not where they supposed to be and who moved them. My father was very meticulous about tools and always made sure that they were organized properly. I remember his forceful voice addressing this issue of the missing shovel, thinking that they were loaned to neighbors by someone in the house and never returned. He said to my mom, "What became of all the shovels we had in the storage room?" as I played stupid nearby, while my mother was also puzzled to the whereabouts with no satisfactory answers to this mystery. My father continued to hide his dejection, searching the entire house and looking out the windows to see if anyone outside was shoveling with our missing shovels. He said, "How could this happen? We have the biggest storm to dig our cars from, and like magic the shovels have all disappeared and are nowhere to be found?" My mother did her best to calm him down before he really went on the warpath. I began to giggle, and before bursting out in a loud laugh, I went near the faucet and turned the water on to mask my laughter, because I knew my childish prank would soon be blown with a harsh tongue lashing by my father, who was getting hot underneath his many clothes.

And, sure enough, after fifteen minutes of searching, he became flustered and started to unbutton his trench coat and took both of his hats off. You could see his forehead dripping with sweat, poor Pipo, while I was behaving like a bad boy to have some fun with my hero. But to me it was never malicious or anything so grievous as that. It was, from my point of view, good natured in origin, something that I would keep on doing with Pipo for years to come.

Shortly after a last-ditch-effort search by everyone in the house, except me, of a course, without any success in locating these missing shovels, I decided to finally stop the bleeding and retrieve them from my secret hiding spot before it got uglier. It was the only area that they did not think about looking in, which I thought that they will surely do, but they had skipped it. It was our old cement shed in the corner of our paved backyard. It was the size of a typical bathroom; however, it was extremely filthy, full of junk, and had no lights. The only way to see what you were doing without getting bitten by one of the mammoth rodents that called this place "home sweet home" was to bring a flashlight with you at all times, entering this very ominous terrain at your own peril. So I took a very stupid risk in my hurriedness to hide the shovel blindly. So, in retrospect, it was indeed the perfect place to hide the shovels.

Now I had to figure a way to redeem myself in the eyes of my hero without him or anyone else suspecting my involvement. I came up with this scheme: I said, "Pipo, we have gone through the entire four-room apartment, including the basement, and found nothing. The only places we have not looked are the backyard and the dark shed."

He replied, "Go into my bedroom to the night table and get the flashlight and give it to me. I will be waiting for you on the back doorsteps, okay?"

"Si, Pipo (Yes, Pipo)," I said. However, by the time I came back he was near the shed, waiting for me. I said, "Pipo, aqui esta, la linterna (here it is, the flashlight)." He then pointed the flashlight, standing at the shed door, and clicked and clicked and got no illumination at all. He said, shaking his head in disbelief, hijo "Hypo (son), go back inside the apartment and get new batteries."

I said, "Pipo, a donde estan las baterias (where are the batteries)?"

"They are inside one of those cabinets in the kitchen. Ask your mom if you can't find them!" he said.

"Si, si (yes, yes), Pipo, I will find them!" After a lengthy search looking for batteries with my mother, it seemed we were out of batteries. I ran back to my father and informed him of the bad news. Upon hearing this news, he quickly went back inside the apartment, while I stood in the backyard, buried knee high in snow, waiting for my father to return. A few minutes later, he came back holding our kitchen lantern, illuminated, and went inside the scary pitch-dark shed as a couple of black cats ran out. When he finally came out, he was smiling and holding the three shovels, two metal and one plastic, that I had hidden in his right hand; the lantern was in his left. He was ready for the digging phase of clearing up the snow from our car and building. Even my father did not question me, or anybody else, for the matter; it did not mean he did not suspect any foul play by me or wonder about the reasons why the shovels were placed in there. He was more concerned with the practical task at hand than finding out who did what and why. As we left the shed, he put back the lantern on a shelf in the storage room and then proceeded walking on top of two feet of snow on the long, narrow, one-hundred-foot driveway of our building to reach the street. In the midst he said, "It's work time; be prepared, son!" It was a wonderful experience looking at my father jumping and hopping like a young paratrooper cadet in front of me, making twenty-inch-deep footprints in the virgin white snow while star-shaped flakes came down, adorning him. It was like one of those beautiful Hallmark Christmas cards or commercials on television, so surreal and impossible to ever forget. It was such a captivating moment that every time I pass by this building, I see my hero walking in front of me again, marching with the innate, God-given, great attitude of living each moment to the fullest, as if it were his last. Man, he had something very special that very few people possess, and I was thrilled that he was my father.

Well, like Pipo said, "It's time to go to work," but for me it was a duality of pleasure and work, and I couldn't wait to begin. My principal goal was to remove the snow with him, as well as to pull another capricious stunt at my father's expense, which was always an option that I could not resist, especially with my first experience with snow. My father was very organized in knowing where to place all the snow that we removed. He told me, "Son, try to put the snow that is on both the front and back of the car as close as possible to the curb, leaving three feet from the car, so we have enough space to drive off, okay?" Not that we were leaving from that prime location in front of our apartment building anytime soon. My father was always very cognizant of keeping an eye for this parking spot, and whenever it was vacant, he would immediately run to where my brother's car was parked and bring it over, since he did not have his own car just yet in the beginning. At times, I would just stand there in that spot at his urging, so no one would park there and take it before he arrived. Once strategically parked there, the car sat in front of his bedroom window, where he could keep an eye on it and sleep peacefully. This action was his trademark, which never abated, juggling three cars at once in the future, including, years later, my new 1978 Thunderbird, which he guarded even more personally. During this sort of excavation, when Pipo was not looking, I would stop and quickly make a snow ball and put it in my pockets and continue shoveling. When I saw a good opportunity, I would throw the snowballs up in the air to land in front of him, or I would hit him in the back of his coat. I would deflect the culprits to the many people around us, who were entrenched with their own diggings. However, my father was no fool. While he looked at the mass of people shoveling away, he would say, "Son, keep an eye where all these snowballs are coming from, because sooner or later someone here is going to spot who is responsible for this act and guess what is going to happen to these people?"

I said, "I don't know!"

"Well, he'll either be bombarded with snowballs or, better yet, beat up…"

I said, "Pipo, you think that will happen?"

"Si y si (yes and yes), it sure will, son! But don't worry about that too much! You don't have much to fear from that because you are busy working with me, right, son?" In retrospect, my father knew I was the real culprit, but he took the high road and got the message across crystal clear, similar to the great television show from the 1950s called *Father Knows Best*. He taught me a good lesson: never try to outfox experience. He was always a step ahead, always aware of his near surroundings, a philosophy which he promulgated continuously to me from my earliest recollections, but never forcing it.

During these hours in the street, I could not get over how many people would congregate with us. They loved to hear my father tell stories and jokes, even in this cold climate. It also gave everyone a few minutes to catch his or her breath. Our neighborhood on Pacific Street was really like family, so it was natural that people would bring us coffee and hot chocolate to warm up. I had many friends, such as Robertico, who lived right next to us, and Julito and Albertico, who lived at 43 and 45 Pacific and were also my best friends, and my family would often let me go with their parents to parks. So this closeness was a welcome asset in these massive storms as we worked in unison diligently together to clean up our sidewalks and cars. My biggest satisfaction was noticing the glow on Pipo's face when we cleaned and pick up all the snow, especially looking at my brother's 1970 green Torino not being submerged under the snow anymore. It was a great accomplishment and we felt very proud of the good work we did. We then looked forward of going back in the apartment to dry off and have a delicious Spanish tortilla omelet with *café con leche* (coffee with milk) that my mom and aunt Genoveva prepared for us. There was a sense of family unity in those early days that has, for some reason, never been duplicated. This has been most troublesome for me over the years, because I know what went wrong. It was simply spending, at times, more than we should have, and spending more hours at work than at home. Under this scenario, something had to give. For this reason, I hope who-ever reads this book will pay close attention to a simple concept that has been part of philosophy and psychology worldwide: bal-ance. Any time you depart from it for a long time, you create a vacuum that is difficult to refill. Creating all types of problems for the psychic and the spiritual well-being of our organisms, this ultimately leads to the breakup of the family, snowballing, if you will, to the demise of the body with undue stress and causing our modern society to break down.

In the snowstorms of 1978 in late January, I was much older, in my late teens, while my father was nearly seventy years old. However, I will tell you age did not slow down Pipo one bit. He was the same as he always had been. Quite frankly, he was not afraid of work, and these particularly wicked storms, courtesy of Mother Nature, were not going to detract from digging out his beloved cars. Well, this time we were living at 362 Lafayette Street in Newark, New Jersey, at the apartment we called "the landfill" at the corner of Pulaski Street on top of the well-known Dugout Pizzeria, where I worked. During this one-week period we had two storms, leaving forty-five inches of snow on the ground. It was a one/two combination for the ages, record breaking totals. The only storm that had come close to matching this total was the granddaddy of all, which gave us in one sitting thirty-two inches of this white powder that now, as an adult, was beginning to be a pest. There is nothing purer than being a young kid and looking forward to the real innocence of playing in the snow with your friends without any regards for anything else but a fun time entering your mind.

These storms also awakened me to fine tune my pranks with Pipo once again. But this time I just wanted to get the snow removed as soon as possible to go and hang out with my friends, and I did not pursue it. However, during this time frame, my very best friend, Robert (author of *Bloodcaine*), was in the Navy and stationed in Seattle, Washington, and wanted a photo of the big snowstorms, so I took a couple of our street full of snow and sent them to him for him to get a glimpse of the whiteout in his home-town. While I was taking these photos, my father was calling me to go to his Elm Street garage to dig out his car. This multiple-car garage was two blocks away from our apartment. When we got there we could hardly even approach our garage, because our car was the last one and it sat in the very corner. This was not good news for Pipo and my mom; we had no place to put the snow without blocking the other people's garages. This created a real dilemma for Pipo. I told Pipo, "Let's put the snow to the left side," but he wouldn't do that, because by placing the snow there it would block the front door of the next-door garage. My father would not accept my proposal under any circumstances, even though some of the people had thrown snow in front of his garage to get out. He would not do as they did to him. End of story, as far as he was concerned.

My father came up with the plan to carry the snow on our shovel to the front corner entrance of the garage, about seventy feet away, and set up a giant pile that would not interfere with anyone. This task was very tedious and tiresome. It took us three days to complete this ordeal that I hated so much. What I remember best was the copying of my father's good deeds as everyone chipped in, even those who had thrown their snow earlier in front of my father's garage, and worked together to clean up a real pain-in-the-butt snow that my father had told me so much about in the past upon arriving in America. This large amount of snow removal went without an incident, and sharing much food and drink became the norm in this undertaking. We got to know each and every person who parked his or her car there and his or her family, and we became good friends with people we never knew before the snowstorms. I give a lot of kudos to my father for taking the initiative himself and preventing a possible riot in this multiple garage facility; for doing what he did and not taking my ill-conceived, shortcut, narrow-minded advice.

Well, back to our apartment. My 1970 Ford gold Torino (repainted from dark green after my brother had an accident) that my father previously own was perfectly clean and was clear of any snow. I couldn't believe that my father had done that. I felt very bad about it, having overslept. My mom, feeling like I was down, later on told me that Pipo had discussed with her not to wake me, that he would take care of it, even going against my mother's wishes that I should help with digging out my own car. The only thing left to do was to help my brother dig out his big 1974 Ford LTD car, buried on the opposite side of the street, just below from our third-floor kitchen window, which my father normally sits next to, keeping an ever-present eye on our cars and everything that went on below, as well as listening to the radio and tuning to Spanish channel 41 and watching Rafael Pineda delivering the news.

My father was always hands on with everything he did. These manifestations of kindness that he seamlessly imparted by helping others were a cornerstone of his entire life. It did not matter if it was something so horrific as a snowstorm or hurricanes, a war, or just any of the most innocuous events; my father, Pipo, was a once-in-a-lifetime man who came to his natural calling of helping his brothers and sisters without any hesitation whatsoever, whenever people were in need.

I am very lucky that my father was given to me by Almighty God as the most special gift a son could ever have in this temporary world.

CHAPTER 23

Getting a Driver's License

O
ne thing Pipo did upon arriving in America was to obtain a
driver's license from the Division of Motor Vehicles in New
Jersey. This was in 1968 and 1969, and back then it was not an easy
process. It was torture if you did not understand or speak English,
because there were no bilingual people who would instruct my
father on what to do during the road test. He was so frustrated
and demoralized after four failures to pass that he was going to
give up his quest. Keep in mind my father was a very proud man
who served his native country of Spain in the military and had
several established, successful businesses of his own. He owned
a mass distributor of wine and spirits in Cuba and a famous bar
in Spain where he catered to mostly a military crowd. But he
knew quite well the importance of being able to drive, so he tried
one more time to take the road test. This time I accompanied
Pipo and hoped that it would turn out to be a celebration and
that I would see him with a new spirit of confidence, which had
been obscured due to his failings and the teasing by family and

friends and the arguments with my mother about his inability to pass this stupid test. I too was guilty of making dumb jokes about this situation, which I thought at the time was very funny. My father, Pipo, was not having any of that, scolding me and telling me the importance of providing for the family and that if he didn't get this license, it would affect everything we did—so to stop teasing him *now*. This was a real wake-up call for me because I realized the consequences of not having money to pay for our apartment and food, but to me the most important consequence would have been to not be able to go the famous Palisades Park Amusement Park with family and friends.

Palisades Park was probably the most visited and is still the most talked-about family destination of a bygone era when life was much slower. The view of the New York City skyline, along with the George Washington Bridge on its left, while you rode the thrilling roller coaster and Ferris wheel was mesmerizing. It was quite unique and unmatched—without having to paint a word picture of the beauty of nature. I just loved going there and meeting all my comic and TV superheroes like Batman, Superman, Spiderman, and others; it was like heaven to me as a young, impressionable child.

Well, we arrived at the test site, somewhere in northern New Jersey at that time, for his road test. Pipo was extremely uptight during our trip there with a member of the family. As we got there I looked at all the road test examiners, preferring to have someone who would be more empathetic to Pipo's chance of passing the test. After a two-hour wait I had enough time to find out enough who was the best examiner for my father to succeed, based on my perception of their respective demeanors. I was hoping for this black, middle-aged woman who seemed very nice with so much patience for the examinee. I watch her put these nervous student drivers one after the other at ease by taking the time to reinforce in them that she was there to help them, not to fail them. As I got close to her, I heard her saying, "Just imagine we are going for a Sunday afternoon ride with family." Wow, if only my father could get lucky and have her administer the test—he would be less nervous and more focused instead of being in a fog with a cloudy mind. Well, I had a very bad feeling that she was not going to be the examiner for his road test. I was hoping to be proven wrong, which I never am when it comes to feelings and thoughts in predicting events. I don't know why, but I have had this gift from birth and it is unshakeable when it comes to crunch time in getting a glimpse at the future in the present.

My father's name was called—"Gerardo Garcia, come to the front for your road test." He hurried there and was told to wait until the black women that I wanted for my Pipo was ready to begin. As she approached us in our car, she was called away just before we came out of our car. I was shocked and disappointed for Pipo. She was replaced by this tall, white male who I had observed earlier being insensitive and extremely loud with students. Poor Pipo, he could not get a break at all. As he returned from the road test, I noticed the examiner with his clipboard going over his notes, thinking and looking at Pipo's sad face without any joy in it. Pipo looked at me, shaking his head and saying, "What am I going to do without a license?" As the big guy approached us, he read the results to me to interpret for my father. He made a right turn without using signals. He failed to make a proper U-turn. He failed to keep both hands on the steering wheel when driving in reverse. He failed to understand the examiner's instructions. Final result:*Did not pass!*

(Just a note on the examiner: I heard from others on line that he had highest failing rate of anyone there, and his tolerance for Spanish people who knew little English was zero.)

I explained the negative outcome to Pipo and his eyes started to turn watery, and the sound of his voice was somewhat hoarse as he spoke to me. On the way home he kept talking about how my mother, Maruga(Maria), was going to react when she found out the result.

When we got home, my mother, who is normally combative on everything, was able to hold back her unnatural first instinct of unending rampage and criticism and disappointment with Pipo; instead she encouraged him to go to a driving school and explain his situation. He found out that it would cost him three hundred dollars to pass the test with a firm guarantee or get his money back, Three hundred dollars was a lot of money in 1968 which my parents did not have. My father's salary was about seventy dollars and my mother's was only forty-five. A week later they borrowed the money from friends and family and took the road test again, this time with a Spanish-speaking examiner, and he finally got the monkey off his back and passed with flying colors. We celebrated by having a party at our home with friends and family, but not before we went for a ride in a 1964 black convertible Buick that was given to us by a family member four months earlier and had remained parked on the street of Newark, New Jersey, until that day—even though I suspected my brother, Gerardo Jr., had used it many times with friends and girlfriends without the permission of Pipo and my mother Maruja (Maria). It was the best feeling to see Pipo just like he had been in Cuba: happy and full of life, with a concrete purpose to provide a better life for all of us. I truly understand now fully what it meant to him back then getting his license. I often imagine myself now in my father's shoes, leaving everything behind and going to some strange land like China and repeating what Pipo did in America at that age of fifty-seven with two young kids to go along.

Man…that's what I called a true hero, my Pipo.

CHAPTER 24

Gang Fighting
Outside Our Apartment

In the late '60s and early '70s, gang violence was a major problem in Newark, New Jersey, on the heels of the riots of 1967. It was a torn city, and if you were out in the streets, you were in deep trouble for your safety. The Ironbound section Newark, a small community of Polish, Italian, Spanish, Portuguese, and Cubans, was very close knit and definitely a lot safer. However, even within this community there were strong ethnic divisions within the younger generation. Everyone had be careful of trespassing on their so-called turf. There were street demarcation lines and we were allowed in some areas only to compete in sports and recreational tournaments, These included street stickball, street hockey, street football, playground basketball, playground softball, and baseball at Riverbank and Independence parks (the latter was also called Mosquito Park and was located in front of East Side High School). It was literally streets against streets.

These tournaments sometime turned nasty, and much fighting took place, but the violence was limited in most cases to individual, *mano a mano* battles of machismo in the streets, which drew large crowds of people in circles to watch these fights. Most of the time they were planned, but other times they were spontaneous uprisings. These everyday events were the norm around our neighborhood in those days. My streets were Pacific Street, Garden Street, and Nichols Street. I normally hung out no more than about two blocks away from our apartment, the North Pole, at 41 Pacific Street and later on at 94 Garden Street, just around the corner about a half a block way. It was the area where I rode my bike, played catch, played hide and seek, sold lemonade, played with my friends, and waited for the Mr. Frosty truck to buy and eat delicious ice cream with family and friends right outside our apartment doorsteps. And in my wicked time, we threw eggs and snowballs at passing buses, trucks, and sometimes cars. It was lots of fun until someone got out of their vehicle and chased us through the neighborhood, with us climbing through people's backyards and trying to avoid getting bitten by barking dogs. It was exciting and scary being chased by irate individuals who wanted to beat us up after what we did to them. It was stupid thing to do, but since it was the thing to do, I just blindly followed my friends' dares and behaviors. The pressure to be tough was paramount in our circle. This peer pressure was so strong that it could not be avoided; if you did not act, you were called a girl and a sissy.

My biggest concern was to remain with my friends and back them 100 percent without getting in trouble with the police, because I did not want to disappoint my parents. I was given orders by my mother as well Pipo not to ever leave the area or else I would be punished and not allowed to watch my favorite cartoons and TV shows. Pipo told me, "If you leave this area, you know what's coming your way…"

I said, "Si (yes), el cinto (the belt)." I was terrified of Pipo using the belt because it really hurt so much that my skin would turn red with marks and furiously vibrate with agonizing pain. So I listened to my parents fervently.

On this particular evening in our Garden Street apartment, I was playing in our driveway when I saw Pipo open the gate of our side driveway and immediately yell at me, "Adentro, rapido (inside, quickly)." I flew inside the house with Pipo right behind me. He told my mother to shut off all the lights in house and stay away from the windows facing the street.

My mother said, "What is going on outside in the street?"

Pipo responded by telling her that over one thousand kids on our street and on Pacific were ready for a gang war. They were heavily armed with baseball bats, chains, machetes, butcher knives, swords, pipes, etc.

Pipo and the owner of the house got together quickly and were able to get hold of several homemade weapons to defend both families if needed. They remained on guard, pacing back and forth with several long metal pipes, ready to put a hurting on any intruder that decided to break into our home. I ran quickly to the window and was able to get a sneak view from my parents' bedroom without Pipo finding out. What I saw was an army of gang members converging on the corner of Pacific Street for a battle. They were making lots of noise by using the metal covers of garbage cans like cymbals. As they passed by my house, you could here a strong stomp, like a marching formation. I witnessed their wild behavior of flipping cars and breaking their windows with bats, and I constantly heard a chant of "we are going to kill those fags now." One time a rock was thrown through our windows, and it got Pipo's attention. He ran to us, screaming at my mother and to get out of the window at the same time. He kept saying in Spanish over and over, "Me cago en la leche...me cago en la leche...me cago en la gran leche (I shit in the milk)."

Seconds later a gang member stopped next to our window and put his ugly face on it and motioned with his fingers, "I'm coming in." Pipo ran toward the window with his pipe in his hand, ready to unload all his strength at this gang member, but was intercepted by my mother, aunt Genoveva, and the owner of the house, who pleaded with Pipo to hold off his natural instinct of protecting the family. Well, Pipo would not budge;

he put his face near the windows and motioned to indicate, "If you come into our home, you will not leave…" (in an imposing, loud voice). This went on for about two minutes, but it seemed like a lifetime, and Pipo did not back down. It is fair to say that without Pipo taking the strong, aggressive posture with this gang member, he surely would have broken in and hurt us or killed us. Pipo's stubbornness proved to be right. Looking back now, I think he was correct to take that stand in a very dangerous and temper-filled atmosphere on that evening. His prudent course of action is part of his Spaniard DNA heritage, which is defending and fighting for family at all cost.

Moments later we heard police sirens going off, and we ran back to the window and saw hundreds of policemen in riot gear and wearing masks, dispersing what looked like tear gas bombs and polluting the entire street with white smoke. We saw gang members rapidly fleeing the streets and returning the streets back to us.

An hour later we all came back outside, along with the neighbors, and started the cleanup of our streets. There were many busted car windows that we picked up and piled up in a corner until the sanitation trucks came in and hauled all the debris away an hour later. Except for some broken windows on houses, scratched cars, and flat tires, the area was once again vibrant—especially when you were able to see the kids from the neighborhood playing and having a good time, including myself!

Pipo asked my mother, Maria, on that particular night, as well as other times, "Did we make the right decision coming to America? We all could've been killed tonight. We left Castro's Cuba and we are not doing much better."

My mother replied, "Just think about the kids, all right?"

Nodding his head in agreement, he said, "Yes, the kids!"

Looking back, both were right, because my brother and I would be transported somewhere in South America or in Angola in the jungle, fighting in a proxy war against American imperialism supporting countries during the Cold War between the Soviet Union and United States.

Pipo's courage was heartfelt among all of us who lived through the nightmare tinderbox evening at 94 Garden Street.

CHAPTER 25

Going for a Picnic

Going on a picnic was a wonderful family tradition that began when I was a very young child in Cuba and continued in Mexico City and in America. The best part of these family outings for me was my kidding Pipo from the back seat, telling him that he was driving too slow. I would look back and would see all these cars and trucks tailgating us in our 1954 black Chevrolet sedan. In the back seat, I was sitting next to my brother, Gerardo Jr., and my aunt Genoveva (she raised my mother, my brother, and me) while my mother acted as co-pilot in the front seat. As I looked from the back window, I could never forget the spectacular cloud formations in the sky. I was mesmerized by their beauty. Sometimes I could see peoplelike figures up there. Other times I would mention to my aunt and brother in the back seat, "I see God up there! Look, look! Look! Up that way...you see it... it's God...Pipo, God is up there watching us." This curiosity of mine always came through when trekking to the picnic location as well as going to the beach. There was a remarkable scenic view throughout the countryside. You could see the sugarcane fields on both side of the road as we drove by. At times, Pipo would stop the car, grab a machete from the trunk, and go and cut some sugarcane from the roadside fields and bring it to us. As we savored its delicious and refreshing taste, I would never forget the sheer beauty of our surrounding. It was so green all around us, with so many palm trees, and the striking blue sky above; we could also see the changing of the sky's colors from blue to the stunning mix of oranges in this tropical paradise of an island. This transformation of weather resulted in multilayered rainbows on the horizon. Everyone really acknowledged the pure scope and beauty of these phenomena by observing them in some divine manner. All of their eyes were firmly locked on those sites, including Pipo's while he drove.

Inside the car my brother and I played a prank on Pipo and mother. This prank was to pinch them in the back of the neck. Most of the time it was my brother doing it while my aunt slept. No witness…just my brother and me. Now the question was, who was going to get the punishment? Since I was seven years younger than Gerardo Jr., I was given more rope to hang myself. Pipo and my mother (to a lesser degree) blamed my brother. This resulted in my getting pinched and punched by my brother, and as a result I started to cry loudly and tell Pipo what happened. These playful moments went back and forth on most trips. Pipo would get upset and threaten to use his big belt from his waist, and he did! We were bad—making lots of noise at times, giving Pipo a headache, and making him irritated as he drove us to the picnic site next to a river.

The river picnic area which was called Vijao, and it was our so-called home to spend a fun and restful day with our many family and friends who converged on this magic spot. Our car trunk was full of sodas, beer, water, and food. The food was incredibly good as we sat near the river and enjoyed Spanish tortillas, tamales, and steaks. But what I liked the most was the roasting of the pig. Watching Pipo and family and so many friends and strangers gather around this great treat and salivate at the aroma of the roasting pig…you cannot get any more Cuban than this ritual among family and friends. Pipo always made sure I got the pig's tail. He knew it was my favorite piece and he always made a point that before the roasting began, everyone was aware not to touch this part or else. When Pipo ripped apart the tail end from the pig and gave it to me, I was the happiest kid in the world. This habit of getting the tail became the norm for me for all holidays, including the granddaddy of all, Christmas Eve, when we had multiple pigs for the many who gathered, sometimes over thirty family and friends. In addition, we had many trips to the countryside, where family always roasted several pigs. Even in Fidel Castro's Cuba, we were still able to feast on fine food and drink.

This river was unique to many people because of the terrain of slight hills and very green grass away from the water. Speaking about the water, it had this twenty- to thirty-foot waterfall cliff where we all enjoyed going to rinse off. It was also the safest spot for me because it was no more than two feet deep.

Pipo was so animated in this environment. It seemed he always had the crowd with him, and who could blame them? He would tell a bunch of humorous stories, recite poetry, sing, and dance. He was a very charismatic and humble person, which, looking back now, did attract many beautiful ladies near him, which my mother was not very pleased with. She would call Pipo over or make faces to stop his amusing stories and get him to come over to her, where he would get verbally blasted for his amusing storytelling. The whole atmosphere was so charged with so much positive energy that it seemed like we had just arrived at the river when it was time to go back home. Time just flew by so quickly.

Another time when it started getting hard to get milk for us, Pipo was delivering beer through the small bodegas that were on the side of the road when he met this man and started talking to him. People were scared to death of the man because they said that he was a crazy man that wouldn't think a minute about killing anybody, but, like always, the more that my father talked to this man, the more he liked my father, so as they kept on talking, my father started telling him how hard it was to get milk. This man said to him, "Don't you worry about it. Every day when you pass by here, I will have a container of milk for you, and it will be free. You won't have to pay for it." So every day my father would bring fresh milk to the house, and a lot of people would wonder where he was getting this milk, but he never said a word; he just kept bringing the milk, which a lot of times we shared with our friends. Well, this went on my father, every once in a while, gave the man a bottle of Cuban rum, which he loved.

One day he was waiting for my father and said, "I would like to invite you and your family for a picnic at my house, and if you like hunting, I have plenty of rabbits on my property, so we will do a little hunting and then will eat."

My father said okay. The people that were around them were saying things like, "This man has never done this," and they looked at my father like he was crazy to go over to the man's house, but my father didn't care what the people thought about it. About two weeks later, we got up early and, with other family, we went to his house, which was in the middle of the woods. He had a big piece of property, so he came to meet us and introduced us to his very young wife and the two kids that he had. We went into his house and he offered us something to drink, and after a while he said, "Well, it's time to go hunting," so he, my father, the other family members, and my brother all went hunting. After a while you could hear the shots being fired And after a while longer, there they came with a few rabbits. Then the man said, "It's time to kill the pig and get it ready for roasting," so my father went out with him and they grabbed this nice-size pig, killed it, and got it ready for roasting. They all went to the back corner of his property and they dug a hole in the ground, got some wood, and started roasting this pig. I was amazed when he started covering it with some guava leaves, and he said, "That's to give it some flavor."

After a few hours the pig was ready, and his wife came out of the house with pots of white rice and black beans and yucca, and he cut some parts of the back of the palm trees' leaves and made a table on the ground. He put out this delicious pig and the rest of the food and had coolers with beer and soda and the like. We all sat down on the ground around this makeshift table, and we started eating. Boy, what a feast this was. After that we all sat around and had some Cuban coffee, and we just started talking. The man took my father to the back of the house, where he had a barn, and there we saw a bunch of fighting roosters all in cages. We were amazed by this, and the man said to my father, "Pick whichever you want and it's yours," but my father said no to him because he really wasn't into cockfighting. After that day, nobody who was on that road where my father was delivering the beer, sodas, and liquor would even dare say anything wrong to my father, because they all knew who that man was and they all knew my father was his friend. After that we went over a few more times for picnics, and the man and his wife came over to our house. That was the type of person my father was. He would make friends with anybody, and everybody liked him

In Mexico City we had no car, no money, and very little of anything else; we depended on our family and friends for financial support from America, including from my brother, Gerardo, who sent us whatever he had made in part-time jobs along with money from some charities from the Mexican Catholic community and other organizations. Specially, one superrich woman gave us shelter in one of her mansions, and many other Cubans lived in this house with us as well. She also provided a large quantity of dry foods such as cornflakes.

Since we had no car and nobody else had one, either, we took the bus full of goodies with our friends to some woodlands near the Great Pyramids for our getaway picnic. On the bus trip, we encountered many local people selling chains, necklaces, sombreros, scarves, pyramid figures, and all types of tribal clothes. Most of these people were Indians dressed in colorful native garments. My father, Pipo, wasted no time with some these people and invited them to come to our picnic to share great food. On the bus ride, Pipo was rambling with great stories for us, and the natives took a liking to him and gave him various artifacts as a show of their affection. These people told Pipo how much they depended on tourist pesos for their living. They made everything themselves and made this trip daily, hoping to make enough money to eat. Upon hearing this lament, Pipo made sure that they would come and join us for the picnic, and they accepted and joined our group, but with one caveat: that Pipo would join them in a spiritual dance of unity. It was real treat for my mother and me seeing Pipo in his natural element of enjoying life to the fullest. His performance was received with loud applause and many pats on the back. My uncle Marcelino, who was also with us, added an extra spark because he was with us in Mexico and was our only other family member there. He was suave and had a sense of style and elegance similar to Pipo's, with a striking personality, especially with the ladies. They made a dynamic twosome. However, since Pipo was married and uncle Marcelino was separated, he continued the party while Pipo stopped—for most of the time he was on his own.

What makes life really rewarding is the people who you love and adore, not the richness of material possessions that we are consumed with twenty-four hours a day, seven days a week. In Mexico City we had very little…but did we? But maybe Pipo and my mother gave us the ultimate lesson…and that is to never give up and to fight on with an unshattering faith in God and family; this strong bond among each of us helped cope in difficult times.

In America, we continued this family picnic tradition in three different parks within twenty miles of our home in Newark, New Jersey. Guarinango Park in Elizabeth was the closest to our home, about eight miles away. The other two were Roosevelt Park in Menlo Park, a town famous for Thomas Edison, who invented so many products. The other park was Branch Brook Park, known for its beautiful cherry blossom trees.

The ride was short, with none of the scenic views of going to the river park in Cuba or Mexico City. Our ride consisted of taking US Routes 1 and 9 south, a very industrial, concentrated area. But all things were not lost; my brother was again back with us after not being with the family in Mexico City. This made my mother and Pipo and aunt Gevoveva and me very, very happy. In those early days in America we were again very close to each other. We took the time and invited many family members and friends to picnics with all these fine Cuban and Spanish foods without missing a step. By this time my brother, Gerardo, did the driving in his 1970 Ford Torino until he got married in 1972. Then my father took over this car till 1976, when I brought it from Pipo for $2,200 when I turned seventeen and got my driver's license on my birthday. After my brother left, Pipo began to drive us again to these sites. I even started to kid with Pipo because of his slow driving tendencies. After not having a car in Mexico City, we were happy and thankful for the convenience of taking all our goodies for our picnic in a comfortable fashion.

Guarinango Park had a large Cuban ambiance in those early days. It seemed like I was in Cuba. I could smell that delicious food aroma all over the place, making everyone reminisce about Cuba. I could see so many pigs being roasted throughout the park as Pipo and I walked and mingled with our *compadres* (people). The music and the noise were just so enticing that we were sometimes away from our own gathering for a couple of hours. This made my mother furious and she would start to search for us until she found us in the other picnics. When she found us, I was playing with other children while Pipo was doing his normal storytelling and poetry while drinking a beer and eating *lechon* (roasted pig). Several minutes after my mother calmed down, she would succumb to our *compadres* in an unrelenting invitation to join them to share with them some fine typical Cuban food and drinks. This closeness was very solid in the Cuban community in the 1960s and 1970s.

As I got older I would drive Pipo and the family to this park, but I would have strange feelings because I remembered Pipo, so in charge and full of life, and now I was starting to realize that he was getting older and was not able to do the things he used to do with me and our family. So I decided to let Pipo drive to the picnics, just like the old days. I wanted to do this because I wanted him to feel young and with a strong sense of purpose. Many times, he would say to me, "You drive today, son, I'm tired…" I would just grab the keys and do what he said, Simultaneously, while I was driving with him in the car, I could not stop from thinking about those golden moments from the past with Pipo in the back seat of that black car. Now, I was the pilot and Pipo was my co-pilot in this thing we called life.

I made a commitment back in Mexico City to take care of my father, and that position had not wandered at all, even while I was hanging with my own friends and girlfriends and could not attend or didn't want to go. I felt so guilty that I would stop on my own and be with them just like the old days. This time I would drink many beers or a Cuba Libre mixed drink with Pipo and savor his wisdom in speaking to me. I no longer had slingshots to kills *lagartos* (small lizards) or other so-called distractions to take valuable moments away from Pipo. This gave me more time to lay in the grass next to him and feeling so at peace—resting next to him while he slept and pondering how much he had meant to me in my life. I treasure those father-and-son interactions immensely. I kept those feelings hidden from Pipo because I wanted to ensure that I was not letting him think that he was beginning to be a distraction to me living my own life. Guarinango Park was a place we spend an exorbitant amount of time in paddle boats peddling our way to a fine Cuban meal, full of *congri* (rice and beans), plaintains, yucca (cassava) with garlic, avocados, pig, and cold cerveza (beer). The list is too long to enumerate. Our favorite was barbecuing sausages, steak, chicken, hot dogs, and hamburger. These food choices were now the new norm in our new updated menu in our picnics in America as the years passed.

Branch Brook was the closest park to our home in those early days for picnicking. It was also a very dangerous place to go for to visit. You had to drive through downtown Newark and then up Bloomfield Avenue for four miles of a rock-throwing environment. Plus, there were dangerous situations when waiting on traffic lights to change. Knowing this, Pipo did not want to take unnecessary risks in getting robbed or kill. It was my mother who insisted on going and looking at the cherry blossom tress. It was said that there were more cherry blossom trees there than in Washington, D.C., on the famous mall.

On this trip which I knew Pipo was apprehensive about because of the arguments between him and my mother, I used give him the real big tease. I would say, "Pipo, Guarinango Park and Roosevelt Park are two parks with no problems associated with violence—a place where you could relax and go to sleep in the grass and experience much peace and tranquility. And you are coming here were you have to stay vigilant all day. I just don't get it, Pipo."

He would say, "You go ahead and ask your mother why."

"I asked her, Pipo, and she said, 'The cherry blossom trees,' Pipo...what else?"

"Well, if we continue to come here to see these trees, one day we are not going to have a car to go back home. She has decided that these trees are worth coming here to see at the expense of a punctured tire or a broken window. In the mean time," he said, "I will take my chances in the condensed bush with snakes and other animals about three hundred feet to the right, rather than in this open space by these tress."

I just loved to have some fun with Pipo every time we went out.

CHAPTER 26

The Landfill Apartment

The landfill apartment was our third home in Newark, New Jersey. It was located at 362 Lafayette Street at the corner of Pulaski and Lafayette Streets on top of Dugout Pizzeria. This establishment was well known in this community for many years for great Italian food. It was about ten blocks away from the previous Garden Street apartment. Our main entrance was through the Pulaski Street side because the owner, Checky, did not want to open the front door. He said doing so would affect his food preparation area. Anyhow, after looking at several other apartments, we decided to move into this roomy apartment with three bedrooms, a kitchen, and a living room. Sorry, only one bathroom. It was my brother, Gerardo Jr., and mother who took the lead in finding this location.

When Pipo and I accompanied my brother in his sporty Mercury Cougar car with my mother for the first time to see this apartment for ourselves, I recall vividly Pipo saying, "I have a bad feeling about your choice." Upon getting there, my brother, with the keys, got out of the car and said to us, "It needs some work, but don't worry, Pipo, I will come here every day after work and get this place fixed up real nice." Well, Pipo was skeptical, especially after my mother told him as we climbed up the stairs to keep going all the way to the top floor. He was shaking his head, lamenting that it was a third-floor apartment and had no front door. Pipo's concern was warranted, because we had the *papellitos* to do from home, and that consisted of carrying many boxes of raw and finished materials The papellitos were extra income under the table that we all did after work, and in my case it was reluctantly done after school. This extra cash provided a huge help for us during those early days in America, and beyond. This type of work from home was very prevalent in the Cuban community and furiously sought after. However, Pipo was very close to a fellow Cuban immigrant, named Moises, who was in charge of choosing the people for this work-from-home job. He had a very demanding German Jewish owner who had the last word on quantity allocation and pay. Years later, Pipo and I would work for him together at the Essex County warehouse in Newark at McCater Highway (also known as Route 21) along the Passaic River). At one time it was heralded as the most polluted river in the country. This old red factory, made out of bricks, was demolished in the late '80s and now is part of the renovation of the new New Jersey Performing Arts Center area that sits right across the street from the papellito factory. (The factory's appearance really did encapsulate Newark, New Jersey, as Brick City to a tee)

When my brother opened that first door to the apartment and we walked into the kitchen we were overcome with the worst intense smell; it was a combination of urine and poop. It made Pipo and me gag for air, and immediately we went running to the window and put our heads outside for fresh air as we closed the kitchen door behind us and stayed in this area between the steps and kitchen until we recovered. Ten minutes or so passed, and reluctantly we went back into the apartment and joined my mother and brother with our noses firmly closed as we walked and jumped over the debris while we looked around. What we saw inside was unlivable for most living creatures, with the possible exception of the large rodents and roaches that were very visible as we walked through the rooms.

I told my Pipo I was going back to our Garden Street apartment even if I had to walk the ten blocks' distance. I was going to leave this smelly landmine apartment. After much pleading by Pipo, I decided to stay. We made our way to all the rooms, and you could not help but ask yourself how in the world anybody could live like that. We inspected closely for what was causing the odor. My brother, Gerardo Jr., told Pipo that the owner of the building, Checky, had thrown the previous tenants out of the apartment because they had too many dogs and that the Polish family on the second floor had complaineds multiple times to Checky about the wicked smell.

This apartment was in lockdown mode for three months, so whatever was there just compounded the smell. The owner told us that he was aware of the garbage and trash in the apartment but had no time to clean it up. So he had offered a low rent to any prospective tenants if they would clean and fix the apartment. Since our apartment rent in Garden Street was being increased by a very strong-minded Spanish owner, my mother had to take action immediately to move out before this forthcoming increase came to fruition.

Our rent was going to be $125. The landfill apartment was about $75 less per month than the current apartment, and had two additional rooms. It was a no-brainer, providing we practically transformed this landfill to a livable home for years to come. Under this economic savings scenario, Pipo was finally on board to dig out of this mess. This mess was old and had very solid dog poop configurations that were plastered on all the floors of this apartment.

Our first day of beginning our cleaning detail included bringing scrapers and shovels and plastic bags and just filling them up until you could walk around the apartment without jumping over trash.

In the first week that was all we did. We must have filled over a hundred plastic bags. It was certainly a job for the ages—we sweated our way past midnights many nights. Aunt Genoveva's room was the worst, even after we had cleaned it—the smell was still profound. It was the only room with this problem still. We were baffled and couldn't understand why this was the case until my brother hit the corner with a hammer and went through the Sheetrock. He then called us to come and see what he meant. We all converged in this corner and began to knock it down while covering our noses with one hand as the smell became unbearable as we broke through. To our surprise, this wall was just a cover wall for all the poop from the dogs that was stacked over the years and was not cleaned up, because it was so solid that you had to use heavy tools to remove this mountain. The last tenants figured it was a lot easier to put a wall in front of the old wall than to clean up the stone-hard dog poop. It took us a couple of days just to get to the surface and to the real wall. Upon completion of cleaning this apartment and making it sanitary for the first time, we decided to begin to bring food and drinks in a cooler with lots of ice, while we worked on the restoration. We also brought in my black-and-white twelve-inch portable television that I got as a gift from my parents in 1972 for Christmas. We were on the way to moving in four weeks to our new home. The spirit and mood now were incredibly upbeat during the sprint to our move-in day. I noticed Pipo many times stopping painting or other things and turning on the television to the Spanish channel and watching wrestling alongside my brother, and I would follow along while my mother went on a rampage with them about not wasting time and getting back to work; it was mostly with Pipo, not my brother and me, Since wrestling was only showno on Saturday afternoons on channel 9 in the New York area in English and the other telecast was at night on channel 41 or 47, the Spanish channels, these two hours of being glued to the TV were not negotiable for him. I also became swept away in his enthusiasm as well, both during the cleanup and for many years after that, with Pipo alongside me.

In these six weeks of working together in this landfill apartment, we spent such valuable time together that was never as much in the future. Shortly after finishing the final touches of getting reading to move in, Lali, a longtime friend of the family from Cuba, suggested we use the same varnish finishing on the worn-out floor that she had used in her Brooklyn apartment, which we often visited for many family get-togethers. She told us it must be done in an empty apartment because it took a while to dry and the strong smell to dissipate. My mother took her advice and we purchase this expensive varnish and applied it to our lifeless wooden floors. We also shellacked the varnish coating, and two days later we came back and were flabbergasted at the beautiful finish. It gave the floor a glowing and elegant touch that resonated with family and friends that visited us.

We went downstairs after we moved in and contacted Checky, the owner of the building, to come with us and have a look at our new apartment. He agreed and walked upstairs with Pipo, my mother, and aunt Genoveva, and my brother and I tagging along behind them. Checky was shocked when he entered the apartment. He did not know what to say to us about this transformation. You could see it clearly displayed on his face. It was like he saw a ghost. He was not able to say much but "Gracias" in a mixed Spanish and Italian accent as we walked. He then made a joke about raising the rent to $300 because of how beautiful this apartment had become, and as he turned around and everyone broke into a loud laugh, he then promised not to raise the rent, and if he did, it would be marginal increases at best to offset any hike in property taxes. Which he did, honoring his firm pledge to all of us on that evening, until his high-maintenance wife and his spoiled son, who had lost his pizzeria in Toms River, New Jersey, needed more money to cover their lavish lifestyle. Fast forward twelve years later in 1985 and we get a handwritten note delivered to us from a young kid who worked at the pizzeria. That note stated very clearly that in two months this apartment of ours was going to go up to nearly $600 a month without counting the utilities, an increase of $350 in one swoop. This unexpected increase had a demoralizing ripple effect on all of us. Pipo was shocked and dismayed upon hearing this news (I was present that afternoon in the kitchen when the note was given to us) because he knew we could not afford this amount. He told me that the next afternoon about 4:30 p.m., as soon as the pizzeria opened up, he would go and talk to Checky. Pipo told me, "Make sure you are here so you can be my interpreter."

I said, "I will be here, Pipo."

Well, the next day came and we went downstairs to talk to Checky about this grievous situation. Pipo and I entered the pizzeria and called him over, and I explained to him that my father would like to speak in private. He said, "Sure, let's go right outside the store for privacy." One thing about Checky, he always liked and respected Pipo; that was very clear to me, because he always mentioned it to me over the years when I would hang out in the front of the store trying to pick up girls from East Side High School that gathered there and to be with friends with whoever was always around. in addition, I knew him personally because I worked for him at times as part timer in the pizzeria and also made deliveries.

Checky was a very likeable person with everyone in the store, a great person to be around. He would give you anything you asked, and I was a witness when many people asked for some cash or to borrow his car or to have a place to crash down at the hot Jersey shore. He was a stand-up person and I will always have great memories of him. Well, Pipo handed the letter to him, and he read it and said, "I did not write this letter, and I am very sorry for your trouble. This letter was written by my son without my approval. You will continue to pay your regular rent, and as soon as I get my new taxes, I will let you know how much it is. It should increase no more than $30 a month, not $400 like this crazy amount in this stupid letter."

My father, Pipo, was so relieved and happy with this account that he and Checky shook hands, and he left with a great sense of satisfaction. But this happiness was short lived; a week later the son came up to the apartment. I was there. He told my mother that the rent in the note would be enforced and that his mother was in charge of the building, not Checky. Well, lo and behold, the mother came and visited us in an expensive black mink coat. She also made sure all her gold chains and gold bracelets were visible to us. She told my mother directly that she was the new owner of this place and she expected this new monthly rent to be fully paid in two months or she would evict us. My mother, Maruga, who is a fighter, went back and forth in a shouting match that lasted for what seemed like forever, even while Checky's wife was going down the stairs. My mother told her she would not get a penny more than what Checky and Pipo had agreed. I said to myself, "Poor Checky for putting up with her demanding personality." I knew then, crystal clear, that we were moving again. One thing we noticed in the late evening when the pizzeria was closing was how loud and drunk Checky was becoming. His many outbursts of cursing and yelling were so uncharacteristic of him that it was difficult to see his demise hit so hard, especially in the last year or so before we left. Upon hearing that he was found dead a year later in an abandoned area, it was heartbreaking news for all of us. He was surely missed by all of those who knew him. It is fair enough to say he was having some severe family problems during those days.

Our first impression of this landfill apartment had been one of trepidation and challenge, with all of us trying to restore this waste dump. It was self-evident in our bewildered faces and comments to each other in 1973. However, this landfill apartment was also filled with so many priceless memories from 1973 to 1985—the ages of thirteen to twenty-five for me, the most formative years in my life with my family. There were so many interesting stories and permutations during this time in my memory lockbox that I would like to share some of them briefly.

One surprise came on our 1974 trip to Spain to Pipo's hometown of Valle De Las Casas . Pipo called me over as we visited his old friends and said, "I want you to me this man right over here. His name is Bedenito. He and I were childhood friends."

I said, nodding my head in approval, "Yes." As I went near him, I could not believe how scary he looked. He was about six feet seven inches tall and weighed easily over three hundred pounds, with a monster's forearms He was a person you did not want to make angry at any cost. I was very much intimidated standing next to him like a midget and listening to him attentively as he talked about how he was building this beautiful chalet around the corner and asked Pipo to come with him for a look, which we did. I was not crazy or stupid enough to say no or make any type of negative remarks that he might misconstrue and that might make him angry at me.

Well, shortly after he finished his tour of the chalet, he grabbed my father by the shoulder and hugged him and told me how great Pipo was as a wrestler in those days and how he used to beat some of the semipro wrestlers in the area. He clearly told me that he had all the natural abilities to be a great one if he'd had the time to train and develop, which he did not because of farming and the many chores of village life in an agrarian society like ours. Pipo then told me in front of Benedito, now in his late fifties, that he was considered the best wrestler in this province of Castille and was also heavily regarded as one of the best in all of Spain in his day. Man, was I proud of Pipo and all the great stories I heard as we traveled trough Spain.

Now, in America, my passion for wrestling went to another level of excitemen, knowing the history of Pipo's passion for this sport. Even though he knew this version of wrestling was not his, he still loved the maneuvers and the techniques involved in this spectacle. His favorite wrestler was Chief Jay Strongbow, just like me. He liked the way he danced before and during the matches and all the running around that he did. Pipo really got excited watching. He would make all types of noises and say, "Get him! Don't let him go! You got him now!" and so forth. Man, I was hooked totally because I knew Pipo's history and fascination with this sport and that he wanted to wrestle when he was young but could not due to family obligations. He was reliving his youth, and I was so glad that I was with Pipo for that ride for all those years.

This was also the time when my brother, Gerardo, had two kids—Barbara, born in 1974, and Gerry, in 1977. On many occasions my mother would get a call from my brother's wife, Maria Elena, to baby sit for the kids; normally it was for Barbara. My father, Pipo, used to go ballistic with my mother because it always happened in the evening, and in our area parking was very limited. Most of the time, Pipo, once they parked their car on the street, did not move it again. Well, Pipo made sure he got that best spot as viewed from our third-floor kitchen window looking down on Pulaski Street where he parked his auto. The funny thing is that these occurrences happened every week, just about, and it drove Pipo insane going to Harrison, New Jersey, in all types of weather. But it did not matter. My mother loved Barbara so much that she never said no to Maria Elena Maybe it was because she never had a daughter of her own. Barbara became her daughter, so to speak. I used to argue with my mother constantly and tell her to stop doing this to Pipo. "You know there is no parking in this area after seven o'clock at night," I would say, but she never took my advice. I told her many times, "You have to take care of Pipo's wishes more often, because when Barbara gets older, she will not take care of you. Just watch." I hated to see Pipo coming from picking Barbara up and dropping her and my mother at that house and then spending sometimes an hour driving around looking for parking and not finding anything. At times he left the car in the Pathmark parking lot blocks away and walked in the frigid cold, worrying about getting mugged. One time an attempt was made by someone with a knife, but Pipo was a proud and stubborn man and he was not going to surrender his wallet to this robber. He fought him off by using a small Swiss army knife that he would always carry to cut the home work supplies. At times I would go with Pipo to keep him safe. I was raised in Newark and I knew the dangerous areas well and did not want anything to happen him. But I loved chatting with Pipo in the car while driving and wasting gas together.

But in all honesty, I used to playfully kid with Pipo constantly about anything that came up, whether it was Barbara or not. Many years later Barbara told me how much she loved Pipo and the house where she was raised and all the great times and the close family ties that were always present during those years at the landfill. I told Barbara, "I bet you have passed through Pulaski Street, maybe going out of your way, and made an effort to return and swing by this apartment. Just look up and reminisce about Grandpa (Pipo) at the window and Grandma (Maruja) at that back window hanging clothes and Genoveva being Genoveva."

She said to me, "Tio (uncle), many times," with tears falling from her eyes as she looked at me. You could see sadness in her face.

One particular incident that occured in this apartment that left a sour taste in my mouth was a potentially explosive situation with my brother, Gerardo Jr., having a little too much to drink on Thanksgiving evening and challenging my father on his manhood. It happened about 10:45 p.m. when that second-floor tenant came up and spoke to my father and asked him to please stop the loud music because her elderly mother was not feeling well. It was the first and only time she ever came to complain (because Pipo always was very cognizant of loud noises or music that would interfere with our second-floor people). When my brother heard the news to stop and or lower the music playing, he went ballistic and told Pipo that he was a wimp and had no courage. It was a ferocious screaming match that poisoned the party.

I quickly came to see what the hell all the commotion was in the bedroom. It was a loud donnybrook affair between a son and a father that should never have developed into a tinderbox situation. I was very nervous and scared for Pipo, because he was in his late sixties and I did not want him getting hurt or something in not backing down to my brother's rapid-fire assault of profanities. (At that time my brother was twenty-eight years old and had recently split from his first wife, Maria Elena, and was living with us under my father's roof.) My father told him, "If you are not willing to follow my rules, you can leave right now." But my brother kept on calling him names and was ready to fight with Pipo when I came into his split bedroom that he shared with Aunt Genoveva.

I said, "What the heck are you doing, bro? He is our father—stop it! Stop it!" I was about twenty years old when this ugly situation arose, so I was strong enough to hold my brother at bay along with family and friends, who also intervened and got in between them with no chance of getting close again and reigniting the flame. Well, the next day my brother felt so bad and apologized to Pipo with a big, long-lasting hug and a kiss, and he promised this intolerable behavior would never repeat itself again. Thank God, it never did. Pipo's smile said it all in forgiving my brother.

Sitting next to the window in the kitchen was a normal ritual for Pipo. He loved to watch the Spanish evening news at 11:00 p.m. on the small black-and-white television sitting on top of the kitchen table. The anchorman was Cuban-born Rafael Pineda, whom Pipo loved to hear every night before going to bed. He also loved to hear the latest breaking news as well on the radio, which was located on top of the dinner table, where we also did the papellitos for extra income after the 11:00 p.m. broadcast TV news with Rafael all by himself. He also wanted to have a clear view of our all cars parked in the street just below our apartment from our third floor. He was preoccupied with the notion of having his car, and years later my brother's and my cars, stolen or vandalized. His concern was warranted, because in those twelve years our cars were stolen or broken into ten times. Most of the time it was for the eight tracks or cassette stereo sets that were very expensive and a hot item to possesses in those days. But it did not stop with these stereos. Another major problem was the random vandalizing of cars in the street by gang members. At times, blocks of cars were scratched by screwdrivers, destroying the paint on the cars. Other times the windows were blown up and splatter by BB gun assault, not to mention the 1974 and 1979 gas shortages due to the oil embargo of OPEC. During this time it was open season on siphoning gas from people's parked cars to fill the theives' cars or resell it for a big profit. This was a widespread phenomenon because of the high demand for gas.

In addition, my brand-new 1978 white and burgundy Thunderbird was vandalized by acid and the white paint was completely removed near the antenna. In addition, on one occasion I was standing outside our apartment talking to my good friend Albino and suddenly a red Corvette passed by and fired two gunshots at us, and we scrambled for cover by running as fast we could. When we came back to the shooting site, we then saw the two bullet holes in the garage door about seven feet high. We were running for our lives without looking back. It was a scary moment having people take shots at us for no apparent reason. But these were the streets in Brick City, fueled by the drug culture mentality, especially in the late '70s and early '80s when cocaine was the drug of the day. To maintain their strong addiction people in the street resorted to stealing to maintain their habits. That's why stealing cars or expansive hubcaps was quick money and so rampant in our streets. Pipo learned this lesson firsthand when he was taking my mother to work early in the morning to Sealand Company at Port Newark when his car just came to a hault. My mother told Pipo to check the gas gauge to see how much gas was left in the tank. Pipo then replied, "Are you crazy? I just filled the car last night before I parked." After my mother insisted that he check the gauge, which he did reluctantly, he became upset to learn that his tank was on empty; he had been robbed of his gas during the night, just like so many others.

When Pipo was sitting in the window, it was also a time to play jokes on him, especially when he fell asleep. I would sneak up on him and turn on the lights in the kitchen and turn up the volume real loud on the television set to see how long it took for him to notice. Sometimes I would go into my aunt Genoveva's room just behind the door curtain so I could see Pipo's reaction without him seeing me. It was a lot of fun to play this cat-and-mouse game with Pipo because it was the only time I had the opportunity be with him alone. Speaking about that window directly across the street, there was a parking lot for a company on the corner. This was the location where we played stickball with my many school friends. I remember one particular afternoon when I was playing with Robert and his brother John Vidal. Robert got hold of one of my pitches and hit it so high and hard that it struck that window over the tress and shattered it, and half of it fell to the ground. I immediately asked them to help me in replacing the window before Pipo noticed it. He had warned me many times not to play ball in this yard because of these possibilities, but I ignored it always due to my stubbornness or peer pressure from my friends. Anyhow, I did not want to face Pipo's belt when he got home. To my surprise, Robert, who was my best friend growing up in Newark, helped with some quick thinking about replacing it. (Robert has written a book called *Bloodcaine* on his life on the streets of Newark and is in final stages of having it come to life in a feature film in the theaters near you). Robert knew a friend who owned a window business company, so we went there after getting the measurements. When we got there, Robert's friend at the window company said, "We only do car windows."

I said, "Felipe (I always called Robert "Felipe" in those early days), what am I going to do now? I'm going to get my ass whipped with the belt, you know that."

He said, "Tell him that you will pay for the window."

I said, "With what money?"

He replied, "I'll get the money for you; trust me, Miguel" (he always called me by my Cuban name). Well, as my father got home, I saw him get out of his 1976 silver Ford Granada. He quickly crossed the street and went up to the apartment, and I quickly noticed him in his lookout post looking directly down and spotting me below. He called my name to come up and face the music. He said to me, "I've told and I've told you, so often, don't play stickball in the lot, and you disobeyed me, and look what happened…not only that, but you could've injured us in the house." I pleaded and pleaded, but to no avail. He took the belt and swung at me on my legs and back, but my mother, who got in the way to protect me, was caught in the crossfire of the belt. Pipo really loved me, but he was trying to teach me a lesson about responsibility back then by punishing me. He was following his Spanish roots of discipline, just like his father administered to his nine siblings growing up in Valle De Las Casas in Spain. As I got older I realized how well that discipline served me in my life on the streets of Newark. It served as the benchmark for me for turning down drugs when all of my friends were experimenting with them. It was tough to say no, but I did, even when a pretty girl offered drugs to me as a stepping-stone for having a good time with her in a car or motel. What Pipo gave me back then was the strong love between father and son that was in short supply yesterday, more so today, and hopefully it can return in the future to make better citizens. What an unfortunate time we live in today, when many kids are abandoned by their fathers, who are not willing to step to the plate as my Pipo did with me.

As I got older, I would pass by my house in my car with friends, and at times with my girlfriends, and I would look up and see Pipo's silhouette in the window late at night, knowing he was looking down and waiting for me to get home safe and sound. Many times I sped up to avoid getting spotted by him. Other times, I could not, because of the intersection's traffic light, where I would get stuck due to the red light, leaving me directly underneath the windows. Man, as a teenager you felt it was time to branch out and be your own man, not wanting to be controlled by your parents. Pipo's silhouette will always be with me in my many life's travels.

Growing up in this era was full of protests about the Vietnam War, women's movement, and getting high while listening to music in the hippie and free-love generation.

In this apartment building, the nephew of our second-floor-apartment family was living with them—a long-haired hippie by the name of Gregory, who was heavy into the drug scene. He would tell me the many trips he had taken with acid. At times these mind trips were pleasant; other times they were scary. He told me about this drug trip in his apartment in which he was lying down in his bed in his bedroom and saw blood gushing through the windows and rising and rising from the floor until it started to cover him up, and he stood up and ran across his room to the exit door to avoid getting drowned by the unrelenting blood chasing him. This culture was unavoidable in the apartment because of the many hippies, in excess of two hundred, who gathered with Gregory outside our windows and smoked pot, sang, took their clothes off, and had sex without missing a beat. The music was so loud and the pot smoking was so strong that Pipo had to close the windows to prevent the strong marijuana aroma from coming into our apartment. I kidded Pipo and my mother about getting a secondhand high from the pot.

These drug-influenced hippies would go to our building and sleep it off on the first floor outside the pizzeria's rear door, which was seldom open. This area had no light and no door

lock, so it was also very dangerous because you could not see anything or be secure until you stepped in or, worse yet, got mugged
by these hippies. I tripped over these bodies as I made my way
to the stairs a few times, landing on them. My brother, Gerardo,
told Pipo after he got blindsided by these friends of Gregory's
who smelled like skunks from living on drugs and alcohol that
he was not walking to the apartment without protection. He purchased a gun, and every time he got out of his car he took it out
and put it in his jacket pocket as he approached this darkened
area. I followd my brother's track and purchased my own gun,
which took a lot of convincing of Pipo and my mother. Pipo did
not like guns in the house, period. He was always used to having
guns around because of his military background and knew how
dangerous they could be, so he told me never, ever to have the
gun loaded in the house and to make sure it was open, which I
did. I had a .38 Colt Detective Special, so I guess he noticed how
dangerous the back entrance was to this Landfill apartment and
he conceded to our concerns.

Pipo and I went to Rays Sport Shop Gun Range to fire away
in a friendly competition of target shooting. He still was the
king among the two of us. He would outshoot me consistently
in those fabulous times. I told him every time I shot there was
a muzzle-loaded gun discharging and I couldn't see my target
because of all the smoke from the aftermath. This was not true
by any means; he was simply a much better shooter than I. It did
not matter that Pipo was in his late sixties.

CHAPTER 27

Learning to Drive at Port Newark

Every young kid's rite of passage is learning to drive and obtaining his or her driver's license and buying a car to have the freedom to anywhere with friends and show off his or her stuff. I was no exception, especially after returning from our 1974 vacation in Spain. My desire intensified because my cousin Jose Antonio let me drive his tractor and auto in the fields and dirt roads of GIA village in Galicia, about twenty miles from the city of Lugo. That city is famous for the prominent wall that circles the entire city; it was built by the Moors when they occupied Spain and the Iberian Peninsula for several centuries.

The assignment for me learning to drive fell to my father, Pipo, in 1975 and the beginning of 1976, when I came up with the idea. After he had taken a deep breath, he welcomed it with a little trepidation and agreed to teach me with one important caveat: Listen, listen, listen, and pay attention to all his instructions. I said, "No problema, Pipo." I was from the outset very impatient and wanted to start driving right away, while Pipo was in no hurry to reciprocate and did not share my youthful enthusiasm about driving. To get a kick start on my deep desire to drive as soon as possible, and without waiting for Pipo's slow deliberation, I proposed to him that he give me the key to his 1970 Ford Torino that was park on Pulaski Street below the landfill kitchen window. He said, "You know you can't drive the car, and I'm not going to let you operate the car without me inside. And forget about the keys for now. What I'll do is let you start the car by turning the ignition key so you can start the engine while I am sitting behind the wheel." I agreed to those terms because it gave me the aura of having a little input that turned out to be the genesis of my long-lasting dream of finally driving on my own. It worked out great because my father would go and pick up my mother at work in Port Newark, New Jersey, every afternoon about 3:45 p.m., so I took this as an open opportunity to travel with Pipo on the seven-mile trip and try to streamline my lessons.

After a month of turning the ignition key on while Pipo was behind the wheel, I wanted to progress much further in my development and to begin on my own to the start the car solo. Pipo was more confident by then, and he agreed to give me the key. He watched me from his favorite window, observing my every move. After doing this for a couple of weeks, I suggested that we leave our Landfill home earlier so we could have more time to practice in the large parking lot at the Sea Land Company, where my mother was employed. Well, one thing about Pipo was that he always liked to take a nap before he picked up my mother, so I had to go to his bed and jump on it or put on the television or radio to interrupt his sleep by waking him up a few minutes earlier. Plus, other times he would recite poetry sitting on the bed for five minutes after getting up. In the beginning, as I traveled this route with Pipo from the moment my mother was first employed, I could not help but realize how congested, noisy, and smoky this short travel was. It was very intimidating, even for the most seasoned driver, because it was tractor trailers galore. At times, we used to get caught in the middle lane with two tractor trailers on each side. This gave me ammunition to joke with Pipo from the passenger side to disclose to him how close they were to where we were and that they were getting closer to our car and to drive faster before we got crushed. He used to get a little nervous hearing those big tires whistling in his ears as we tried tio outrun them, but we could not, so he would slow down and fall back. But other times he was not able to take this option because of high-speed, tailgating trucks behind us, blowing their horns. It was a challenging and dangerous platform for any student driver. But it did not faze me one bit; I was determined to accelerate in the midst of this environment.

As we waited for mother to get out of work, my father would take his car to the far side of the Sea Land parking lot (which today is the main headquarters for US Customs). We would go to an area where there were no parked cars, and he would show me what to do while he drove. He said, "I want you to stay within the last two lanes and don't go to the others." I quickly opened the door while slipping out of the passenger side, and I finally got my chance to take control of the wheel. But before I did, I had to adjust the rear and side mirrors and bring the seat back a little bit before my first official drive. Pipo had the proclivity to drive with his hands on top of the wheel and using two hands, while I considered myself cool and always drove with one hand, not two, like fogies do. I used to tell Pipo all the time to drive with one hand, but he did not welcome my idea. Who could blame him? I was an inexperienced rookie driver and he was not going there with my silly request. Even years later, after driving for nine years myself, I used to get upset with Pipo driving with two hands because he looked old, and I did not want that. I wanted to preserve Pipo's youthful vitality just like in Cuba and Mexico City.

Well, my first maneuvers were to go north and south of the parking area in those two lanes and avoid any traffic for my first time driving. However, between these two lanes, near the end on each, there were two tall light poles with large concrete bases that I almost harpooned on the very first day. It was a close call that I fortunately avoided and did not wreck Pipo's car. After Pipo recovered from the big scare, he said, "Try doing this maneuver a few more times until you are able to calibrate the turning distance between objects." These words by Pipo reinforced and instilled much-needed confidence in me. This life lesson was proof that when you are down, you need to pick yourself up by your boot-straps right away and, without missing a beat, take charge of your life in any endeavors that are inhibiting your goals. In the many subsequent trips to this area, Pipo had me drive with two hands on the wheel and back up and go forward straight inside the white parking lines. I did this maneuver north and south for months. In addition, I had to do a U-turn and finally parking. We took with us a couple of cones in our trunk to learn how to park properly. In Pipo's car it was difficult to park because the back window was slanted and did not give you a good look at how far you were from any cars behind you. To park this 1970 gold Ford Torino, your head had to be touching the ceiling of the car with one hand on the steering wheel and the other grabbing the pas-senger seat's upper head rest. A funny thing happened the first time my father tried to park the car within the two cones I set up. Like always, I played a little joked with him. I set up the cones close together, leaving a smaller parking space to put this baby in there. I was breaking into an uncontrollable laugh at seeing Pipo knocking those cones constantly. He was getting hot under the collar, spending all his energy turning the steering wheel left, right, left, right, no, a little more to the right...no, stop, go for-ward...now back, turn the wheel more to the right. "Pipo, what's going on? You are hitting the cones. Forget it, you just knocked the cones down!"

"Wait; let me get out of the car to set them up again," Pipo said, shaking his head as the sweat drops were falling down his face. Remember, this car had no power steering whatsoever. It was all muscle and endurance in getting this car fitted into a parking space. Compounded by the fact that there was no vis-ibility out of the back window, it was a major problem for me to park this car in the real streets in the years to come. It was nerve wracking and exhausting for me because I took over this car from Pipo for almost three years. I had to deal with the frustration and sweat that Pipo did in that parking lot. Fast forward a few months later and I was the same guinea pig, just like Pipo. And I wasn't laughing this time. Well, Pipo was not laughing, either; he told me, "Make the parking space longer and you try now to park the car in this heat." Oh, by the way, we had no air conditioning in the car. It was boiling hot inside that car on that afternoon. I did my best and was finally able to park while my mother patiently waited for us outside the door in one-hundred-degree heat.

As I got better, I stared to drive in the entire parking lot and be very cognizant of cars pulling in and out of parking spots. I had a few close calls, but luckily no accidents, knock on wood. I did worry when the other drivers did not follow protocol properly and came too close to my side of the road and I had to get much closer to cars on the other side. I did blow the horn several times, but Pipo told me not to do it anymore because I did not have a driving permit yet. He was concerned, and rightly so, that we might get pulled over by the Port Authority Police and get a heavy fine. Needless to say, we had several close encounters with the police, but they just looked and did not put the red light on to stop and check us. After I got my permit I was able to drive to other parking lots and small streets at the port. With Pipo gaining confidence in my driving skills, I took it upon myself to go on the road in the right lane, the slow lane, and mingle alongside the big boys, the tractor trailers. I kept hearing from Pipo, "Watch it, slow down, you going too fast, slow down." It was my first time on the highway and I could not wait to tell Mother. It was only about a ten-minute drive, but I was so excited and proud to have taken this giant step. On the way back home I could not stop my driving to mother while Pipo heard and pay attention to the road.

In the coming months I would continue to practice in the lots, but I was pretty much driving everywhere at the port. I asked Pipo inside the Landfill apartment to let me drive the entire distance to the port and pick up mother and drive back. Before I left the apartment, he mentioned to me, "Be careful with the South Street entrance to the on-ramp and the traffic converging on Routes 1 and 9 south, and then stay all the way to right to bear to the right to get to the port. And also be careful with the small but deadly forty-degree ramp at the port...as you know, you and I have many times witnessed flipped tractor trailers, cars, and trucks in these spots."

I told him I would be extra careful and wouldn't disappoint him. Without saying a firm yes, he gave me the keys and off we went, driving all the way down Pulaski Street (I was hoping some of my schoolmates would be outside and could see me driving, but no such luck). We went to the intersection of South Street and made a left and went to the top of the bridge and made a right, then took the underneath ramp connecting to the very dangerous, high-speed traffic. We then waited on top to see an opportunity to jump on Routes 1 and 9 south and make a quick right about an eighth of a mile away. (My father really despised this part of the trip. Today they have replaced the underpass with a better one, but it is still dangerous.) So far, so good. As we got to the next bridge, Pipo said quickly, "You are going too fast! Slow down!" The speed limit on this bridge was fifteen miles an hour. I was going about thirty. Much too fast! Pipo was correct and I slowed down. I was going fast because I had a tailgater behind me and did not want him to blow the horn at me. He said, "Don't worry about who is behind you; just pay attention to what's in front of you."

I said, "Fine," and we continued safely for the next two miles to pick up my mother on time. When we got there we had about fifteen minutes to kill, and I kept asking to drive back because he was hinting that my mother would be too scared to get in the car if I was driving. I finally convinced my mother after a few minutes of her standing outside the car to come inside, which she did, but only after I promised her that I would drive in the slow lane. Well, we made home to the Landfill apartment unscathed. Months went by and I anxiously waited for Pipo to take this joyful ride with me again and again as I was practicing for my license test, which I passed on my first try—something that did not go unnoticed for me in fueling the fire with Pipo once again. As you recall, it took Pipo six tries to finally get his license. Man, did I have a field day with Pipo on that day when I showed him my license. (Believe it or not, I still have the first license saved in one of my photo albums.)

Even after I was driving my own car, I would accompany Pipo while he drove to pick my mother up because I wanted to be with him so much that I really looked forward to these forty-minute round trips. These were great times for me because they gave me so much valuable time with Pipo that I did not get at home or any other place. In the coming years he would ask me many times to drive while he became the passenger, but I always preferred for him to drive and I would try to talk him out of making me drive. I wanted him to always feel like he was in control, because it gave him a purpose, and I did not want to take that away from such a proud, loveable father who was my inspiration. Years later when Pipo was not around, I went solo many times to pick up my mother with really such an empty feeling of looking around as I drove and recalling those many magic years with Pipo, mother, and me.

Speaking about my mother, she somehow convinced my father in the same parking lot to teach her how to drive. Without gradually practicing like he did with me, Pipo and my mother switched sides and soon she was ready to duplicate me in achieving her longtime dream of driving. I was sitting in the back seat, but I moved up, holding on to the front seats to get a better view of her performance. My father put it in drive and explained to her not to touch the gas pedal at any time; just concentrate on the wheel for today only, he told her vividly. He moved near her with one foot on the brake to make sure nothing crazy happened, like putting her foot on the gas or something like that. I was in the back seat not believing my mother was actually driving. I just did not picture her being ready to drive. I had a really bad idea, but I still encouraged Pipo to give her a shot. While finish adjusting the seat and the mirrors and getting comfortable, Pipo asked her, "You want to do this?"

She said, "Vamos (let's go)."

Pipo put the car in neutral, and she was doing well until she saw a car coming her way and lost her composure and grabbed the wheel very hard. She did not listen to Pipo's command to turn the wheel all the way to the right to avoid the oncoming traffic. Pipo all of sudden grabbed the wheel himself and tried to turn to the right, but my mother was frozen at the wheel and pulled it to the left, so the wheel was in the middle position. At the same time my mother stepped on the gas pedal hard while my father pressed on the brake to stop the car while it was rolling along, jumping up and down and heading straight for the light pole less than two hundred feet away from a major impact. All hell broke loose in twenty seconds of pandemonium and confusion by both of them. I was thrown to the back seat and, with the car jumping like a rabbit, I was not able to hang on to the front seat back. My father quickly was able to get hold of the ignition and turn the car off about five feet from the light pole. His quick thinking saved the car and prevented injuries to all of us. Pipo and my mother continued this back-and-forth bickering the entire trip back home and beyond. Pipo told my mother after this episode that he would never teach anyone how to drive again. Many years after the death of Pipo, my mother always lamented to me that she should have gone to driving school from the beginning. I told her she should've. Looking back now on the incident, I think it would've made great theater in some kind of a satirical sketch performance on *Saturday Night Live* or Johnny Carson…but maybe it is never too late…

CHAPTER 28

Working with Pipo at the Factory

After my father retired from the Magnus Organ Company in Linden, New Jersey, in 1975, he then went on to work under the table (off the books) at the place we called the papellito factory. During this time my mother, Maruga (Maria), also lost her job and went to work at Port Newark for Sea Land Company. My brother, Gerardo Jr., who also worked with at Magnus, decided to leave the company and go to work at a new plant called Alcan Aluminum Siding in Woodbridge, New Jersey, before he got laid off. The writing was already on the wall. There was a significant downturn in the economy because of the oil embargo in 1974 from OPEC, and it affected the sales of these expensive organs. They were popular because they were still less costly than pianos at the time, plus their mass marketing campaign through television, newspapers, radio, and bulletin boards was very extensive. It was similar to today with the computer; just about everyone had one. These organs came in all sizes, and many families owned several of them to proudly display in their home. It was the chic thing to own.

My father already had a seven-year working relationship with the papelito boss, Jack, and Moises, the Cuban immigrant who was a working machine himself and in charge of the papelito operation, so he was quickly given work at the factory while we also continued the papelitos at home. (The owner was a very hard-working German Jewish man who would work his butt off, as would his two sons, and they demanded the same work ethic from their employees.)

The introduction to the papelito business begin with my brother, Gerardo Jr., who stayed in our uncle's home while were still in Cuba and Mexico City (my father's oldest brother, Manuel, and his wife, Marciana, lived in America). This gave my brother a little income to send to us in Mexico on a bi-weekly basis, and it was very much needed since the Government of Mexico did not permit Cubans to work in their country. We depended solely for our income on the many families and friends who sent us Money Grams from America.

I came to work at this old and rat-infected factory in the spring of 1977 in my junior year at East Side High School. I initially started as a part-timer working from 2:30 to 6:30 p.m., making $2.50 an hour just like Pipo and the rest of the workers. After working at High Seas Italian restaurant on River Road in North Arlington, New Jersey, for five months in 1976, I finally had the opportunity to work side by side with Pipo, but it was for one hour a day. At 3:30 he had to leave to pick my mother up from work at Port Newark. But as the summer approached and school was over for the summer, I was able to work a full schedule of forty hours a week, the same as Pipo. This was the first time I was able to work with Pipo and I was thrilled. My brother and my mother already had this experience at Magnus, and this was my time to share and observe from a different perspective. It was a rude awakening for me to work eight hours a day and wake up early and report on time to work, all in one fell swoop. And Pipo made sure I was not late to work in the morning. It was tough to get up after spending the evening hanging out with my friends outside Tony's Pizzeria on Pacific Street past midnight.

Even the days I stayed in the house, I just had to watch my favorite evening show. There was no other show in late-night television more popular in those days than *The Tonight Show*, starring Johnny Carson. I could not go to bed without seeing the whole show. Pipo, from his bedroom, would yell, "Come to bed now, because you have to get up to go to work." Man, the word again.... The show ended at 1:00 a.m. and I had to get up at 6:15 a.m. while Pipo took my mother to work after waking me up, and as he left the house I went back to sleep until aunt Genoveva came calling my name a couple of minutes later in a very loud voice: "Miguel...Miguel...Miguel...*levantate* (get up)." over and over, and moving me in the bed. She also did this routine during the school year at times. I would get so upset with her that I would rage at her with profanities for her to go away and leave me alone, but this time I could not be late and be confronted with Pipo and letting him down. I needed the money to help him pay all the mountains of bills that he owed to friends and family from the Mexico days. Now it was time to pay them back. And I was determined to earned this money for him just like I promised myself to do in Mexico City as I got older, and this never, ever waivered one bit. Pipo was my number one focus; nothing else mattered to me. Nothing! Even those terrible migraine headaches I had every morning due to lack of sleep were not going to stop me from achieving my goal. In addition, Pipo had vouched for me with Jack, the owner, and I did not want to disappoint him and not measure up to what was expected from me. With everything Pipo had gone through in his difficult permutations of experiences in America, no way, no how.

I started that summer of 1977 doing three different products right alongside Pipo as a helper. My job consisted of, for the first half of the summer, pulling apart seven-foot-high pallets that contained comic books and having them put in clear plastic in batches of five and ten for resale. While Pipo was responsible for what we called the giant oven sealer, his job was to take my setup work and run it through the oven to completely melt the plastic and seal it. After that he would put the sealed, finished product in boxes and tape them. He would then put the boxes on a pallet until it was full and take it to the designated finish area. It was a fine art working with this mercurial machine, and Pipo had the so-called right stuff to make sure the heat intensity was set perfectly or else you would burn the comic books or the machine would break down. You needed a fine balance to successfully operate this machine, which contained none of the gauges or digital panels that exist today. My father was fully in charge of this machine, and he ran it with much diligent care. Nobody touched this machine without the approval of Jack and Pipo. Before Pipo started to work on this machine, it had been a nightmare scenario. A few times the machine was engulfed with fire by the previous designees and delayed the production of the comics' and paperback books' repackaging operation.

I was fascinated not only by seeing Pipo take pride in putting out an outstanding product day in and day out, but by how much he was liked by the thirty people who worked with us. Nobody ever said anything negative about Pipo. Plus, he never engaged in water cooler gossiping like the others. He came to work with a strong work ethic that was welcome and noticed by his co-workers, including myself, and by the bosses. During our twenty-minute break in the morning, he would drink his *café con leche* (coffee with milk). I noticed that he was using the same Thermos that came with my second- and third-grade *Lost in Space* lunch box that I had used ten years ago. I still to this day have the lunch box. but not the Thermos container. It was and is still unique because it has the distinction of having an Apollo capsule and the rocket painted on the container and not anything associated with *Lost in Space* itself. It's a real collector's item. I still possess the lunch box today, and I keep it because of Pipo's usage. I have been offered four hundred dollars in the past but turned it down. The Thermos finally cracked after all these years at the papelito factory while he was getting ready to drink his favorite café con leche at break time. He always brought in a brown paper bag for his food and drinks; no fancy coolers or lunch boxes like we use today. I helped him separate his mushy food and offered my sandwich to him, but he told me that no food of his was going to waste. He even tried to drink his café con leche until he saw the broken glass come out of the Thermos. He was a tough cookie and had no time for things to go to waste; if he could prevent it, he certainly would! I know, because I saw it many times in my presence and have been told so by others as well. In retrospect, yes, I should've kept the broken Thermos for a souvenir and kept it with the lunch box so the set is complete, but I did not. The irony was I threw it in the waste basket because of the broken glass. During these breaks I noticed how many would come near Pipo just to listen to his stories, with a mix of poetry or small talk about currents events. It was like he was a magnet, pulling people into his circle without even consciously being aware of it. His presence was humbling and pure; no hidden agenda whatsoever. I did enjoy these times with Pipo and listening to co-workers comment about how much they like Pipo and so forth.

The area where Pipo and I worked was the darkest room on the entire first floor of the warehouse, and this made for scary situations for me; especially, you could hear the rats and you could see also the ugliest spiders hanging in webs and walking around the ceiling, floor, and walls. First, the entire floor structure was covered with old wooden boards about ten feet length, and every time anyone or anything took a step, you could hear the sound of the wood coming up. It was similar to one of those haunted-house scenes you see in the movies. But this time it was no movie; this was real life, and you were in Newark, the most dangerous city in America. Couple that with the Passaic River, the most polluted of all rivers in the country, on the back of the factory. It was known for an infestation of snakes and cat-sized rats, so you had a potential perfect storm of maximum uncertainty. I kid you not; I was very concerned for my safety on nights when I worked overtime and did not leave until 7:30 p.m. Those nights we only had three other people left in the building. So, we were pretty much dead meat to any gang member who was armed with weapons. We had many cars stolen from our parking lot, which stood only two feet from the front of our building during my time working there. We had to escort our female workers to their cars every day carrying a butcher knife and machete to ensure their safety. Our only security person was an elderly man who looked like the hunchback of Notre Dame. He lived in the factory and was invisible during the day. He looked very scary, with a very wrinkled face, big eyes, a big head, big eyebrows, and dirty clothes. I had spoken to Moises about this man, who gave me the creeps. He said, "Don't worry about him; he doesn't bother anyone and he rarely talks. But you won't believe what I'm about to tell you about him. He is a brilliant engineer who never went to those fancy colleges, but he has designed many engines that are so efficient that GM, Ford, Chrysler, and others are constantly sending their well-dressed representatives to buy his patents for millions of dollars, and he refuse to sell them those patents."

"I can't believe it; he looks like a bump."

"He does, but that's the way he is."

A couple of weeks went by and Moises called me and said, "Come with me." So I went with him, not knowing where I was going. He took me to the scary old man/night watchman's office, a very secluded area on the first floor. As I walked into the office with Moises, I saw paper all over the floor and a big table with many long sheets of white paper stacked about two feet high. The watchman called me closer and said, "I know your father and he is a good man, and Moises is also a good man, and for that reason I'm going to have you look at my drawings that I have spent my entire life working on." We spent about one hour together in that office and he came across as a man that became too involved in his work at the expense of his family. As I was leaving his office, he gave me a little smile and said, "You are a good kid; stay like that."

I said, "Muchas gracias pot tu tiempo (thank you so much for your time)."

The moral of the story is not only not to judge a book by its cover, but to constantly strive to learn and grow in any environment, which I firmly believe I did. I was able to internalize this enlightening encounter with this genius of a man, who gave me priceless advice in the papelito factory, of all places. He reinforced again my previous set-in-stone goal of putting Pipo and family first instead of any personal achievement or aspirations. Two years later, one of his sons came and asked his father to live with him, and he accepted and left the papellito factory after twenty years of isolation. Good for him!

The thing that really bothered me the most inside the factory was the heat. It was torture, especially for Pipo. I could see his sweat drops constantly falling to the floor from his forehead, even with portable fans in the rooms. So I went to his machine and asked him to teach me what to do. I wanted to learn so I could give him a chance to cool down. After all, he was sixty-eight years old. I was happy to be near Pipo, but I tried never to show any over-the-top emotion. I kept it at bay and to myself. In addition to our regular work, we had to sometimes unload many boxes from the many people who brought in their finished papellitos from home. One time I saw Pipo get into Moise's white company van and help him unload heavy boxes of papelitos. Sometimes it was Pipo and me unloading all these heavy boxes since there was no one to do it. My back bears witness that the pain was no joke at all. Pipo worked like a horse, going nuts to get the job done and then quickly going back inside and continuing to do our regular work. I would always tell Pipo to slow it down, but he did not listen to my calling. One thing about Jack—the demanding owner—every time he saw Pipo unloading anything, he stopped him and did it himself or called someone else. He had compassion for my father, and he would pay him for holidays, give him a Christmas bonus, and pay him when there was no work to complete a full week, which he was not obligated to do. He would pay him the full amount anyway. He made this gesture to only four other people in his factory.

I learned a crucial lesson at the papelito factory that has served me to this day. Jack told the supervisor to take me and another person to work on the *Animal House* (the movie) apparel on the third floor. We waited near the old freight elevator until the supervisor finished with some clients. As he took us to work on this important project that was two weeks behind schedule, I could not help but notice as we went up to the third floor how much shaking the elevator was going through. My co-worker on this project asked the supervisor along with me, "Is it safe to use this elevator?" The supervisor replied with a smile, "Well, I've been here using this elevator and never had any problems." We both looked at each other in disbelief and left it at that.

We were given the task of repackaging apparel from the popular 1978 movie *Animal House,* one of my favorites. After a few instructions and a couple of trial runs on this project, he left us on our own, and as he was leaving, he mentioned he would be back in two hours to check on how we were doing. Well, after a few minutes of exploring the entire rat-infested third floor, we began our work assignment on time. There was no quota, but the entire *Animal House* project was to be completed as soon as possible. It was our responsibility to move this work quickly and get ready for shipment. But my co-worker and I were caught up in all these 1960s chic clothes that it was very fashionable to wear in those days, especially for me as an eighteen-year-old teenager. I was in awe and wanted to browse all these items instead of working. My co-worker, after five minutes of browsing, went back to work and kept calling me for several minutes, or so I thought. But it was an hour that went by and we were far behind. We had to speed it up real fast before the supervisor came by. However, it was very damp and cold and it was affecting our work output. So we decided to take our jacket off and put on several layers of T-shirts, sweatshirts, and one black nylon jacket underneath our own coats. This took several more minutes from our work. Now we knew our production was lagging big time and were hoping the supervisor would be delayed somehow from coming back to check on us. But it was not to be, even though we were working at a lightning pace to be in line with what was expected from us. As we worked, we heard the squeaky and noisy elevator coming up, so we knew we were in trouble.

My colleague said, "Come here quickly so I can button your coat, because the *Animal House* clothes underneath are showing and we don't want them to think we stole them."

I said, "Yes," nervously. I did the same for him. As the door opened, it was not the supervisor; it was the owner, Jack, who walked out of the elevator and headed toward us. Man, we were shock! Jack walked around and looked at our work and asked, "Where are all the finished pallets? I only see one and a half."

We said, "That is what we've been able to do so far." He called me over and told me to come with him downstairs (while my co-worker stayed and was giving someone else directions to work with him later on). In a dejected mood, he quietly told me, "If it wasn't for your father, Pipo, whom I respect so much you would've been fired immediately. Go home now and come back tomorrow and begin anew, and I will give you another chance without informing your father."

Man, I was so relieved and happy that Jack, who was a very demanding person, gave me a real life lesson. That lesson has served me well and it has been with me ever since, and I have also shown the same compassion and reciprocity with my subordinates that Jack showed with me on that date in 1978. It was a very close call with disappointing my true hero, Pipo, not only by not performing my job well but by stealing those garments underneath my coat as well.

There was an incident that took place at the papellito warehouse that is very indicative of Pipos' hardworking philosophy. It took place at 12:30 p.m. on a Thursday. The previous day Jack had left assigned work to the forty-five or so people who worked there. As he came in he walk around the warehouse and, upon the workers seeing him, everybody look busted in their work area except for Pipo, Moises, his wife, Teresa, the supervisor, and a couple of others. I, like everyone else, was busy working. About twenty minutes later, from the loud speakers in his office, his secretary started calling names to come to the office one by one. As their names were called, we found out that all those people were let go for looking busy but not completing their work. Jack knew Pipo had done his work like he always did and never even bothered to glance at him at all during his walk around. This was an eye-opening experience for me. Pipo told me, "See what happens when you try to put things over on people? Sooner or later it catches up and bites you in the *culo* (butt)." I laughed a little bit as I looked him in the eye. His messages resonated with me crystal clear on that day and beyond. Working with Pipo was great, but at times he had to straighten me out because I had started to read the many comics and paperback books that we repackaged for redistribution. Even though I did not do well in school, especially in high school I was an avid reader. A year later that helped me immensely in getting my bachelor's degree in liberal arts. Pipo, in our time together, would always call me out and said, "A trabajar, a trabajo (work, work)," meaning to stop reading the books and get to work. I reluctantly did, but it was tough to put them down, especially the sports books on Wilt Chamberlain, the Steelers, and the Yankees. (Even though I am not a Yankee fan, I still read them. I never saw any on my Mets team during those losing years of the '70s. The Yankees were winning the World Series, but the Mets were awful, so no books on them. I'm lucky in a way because I would have been fired for sure (*big, big Mets fan!*).

The papelito factory will always be with me because of finally working with Pipo as well as the time we spent in our house making the papelitos while growing up. As a child and a teenager, I hated to do this work, because naturally I wanted to play with my friends more. There were at times confrontations with my mother, but when she threatened to tell Pipo about my not helping them, I would buckle to her demand and sit at the kitchen table and help out for one hour only.

The papelitos were heavy work, especially bringing supplies to the third floor at the Landfill apartment. Some of these boxes weighed over fifty pounds, so it was no picnic bringing them up and down on a daily basis. This extra income for us gave us the opportunity to pay off our family and friends who sent us the monies while we stayed in Mexico City waiting to come to America. This first real job for me was helpful in three important ways. It satisfied my insatiable thirst to help Pipo with additional income to alleviate some of the psychological and economical stressors facing him. It made me very happy to see my hero with resonating and renewed energy when I gave him the money. I did this in a fun-loving way, one bill at a time. He never knew how much I was going to give him. I handed him the money in his open hand as I counted it. I would say, "Pipo, abre la mano (open your hands)," as I dropped different denominations of bills into his hand. Sometimes I would pause and stop just to look at his face and see his reactions. At times I would avoid Pipo altogether for several days, and he would seek me out and rub his thumb and first fingers together, displaying that it was time to pay the piper, which I knew, but I wanted to play him a little longer and get him worked up for it; even my mother at times mentioned, "You haven't given Pipo money the last few weeks; what's going on?" When he did find me, I gave him so much more, but I would hold back and stop for a second or so and continue until he was happy! It was so much fun to play with Pipo in this father-and-son way that I came up with.

The second thing I did was to save up for a car, and when I had enough for a brand new Thunderbird (1978), which was my dream car, I purchased one in October of 1978 for $7,200, I borrowed $2,400 from my parents and paid them back in three months. It was my strong conviction to pay them back as quickly as possible because I knew their precarious economic position. Plus, Pipo was kind of nervous about the large amount of money I was on the hook for. In 1978, that was a huge amount of money.

Finally, I needed spending money to buy fancy clothes from boutiques (I bought mostly designer cashmere, wool, and cotton apparel). I was a big spender and wanted the best, so I never compromised on quality. I wanted to look good for the ladies, and I did my best to do so, but I never lost focus on Pipo's and my family needs.

I many time broke up with girlfriends because they were high maintenance and I was not going to allow them to them break my bank at the time. Even though I did well in controlling nature's urges for a beautiful woman, I too have overreached at times with them and have paid royally. I would like to believe all in all I've been better than most, but the jury is still out. I think it is in the DNA, because Pipo was a real sharp dresser in his days as well. He wore those stylish double-breasted suits in Spain that, according to some family and friends' stories and the photos I have of him, made him a quite attractive fellow with the ladies in his days.

Thanks, Pipo, for passing it on!

CHAPTER 29

Pipo Denting My New, Beloved 1978 Thunderbird

One thing that I wanted very much in my late teens was a new car so I could impress my friends and the ladies. Even more important than that, I wanted a car that I liked and that fit my personality to a T. When I saw those Thunderbirds for the first time at Riverside Ford on River Road in Kearny, I fell in love with them. This new Thunderbird, with a sleeker new model design for 1977, was the car for me. It was everything I wanted in a car. It was literally made especially for me. That vibrant attitude resonated with my thinking at the time, and I don't believe I have changed too much from that thinking even today. (I would love to buy one today if I could find one at a reasonable price.) This delightful encounter happened 1976 when I accompanied Pipo to pick up his new 1976 Ford Granada, which was my favorite car until I saw that T-Bird at that dealership. I was mesmerized by the sheer beauty of these Birds. Since I was not able to get a good view where I was standing behind a wire fence, I told a salesman that I wanted to get a closer look at these machines, because I would be buying one of them soon. He said, "Wait here and I'll get the keys to open the gate so you can get into this secure lot."

I said, "I will not move from this area until you come back." He looked at me with a slight smile as he hurriedly left to get the keys. Man, as an eighteen-year-old kid I was frozen, staring at all those beautiful Thunderbirds parked alongside each other while I waited impatiently for his return. As he opened the gate I ran toward the blue one, and then I noticed a darkish, shiny green olive color that stood out among the ten. I ask the salesman, "How much are these Birds going to cost?" since they had no final price tag on the stickers on the side windows.

He said, "We just got these two days ago and are not yet authorized for sale. We will be taking advance orders in the next few days for additional Thunderbirds because of the high demand for these cars. We have already committed these ten cars in our lot to our best and most loyal customers when we get the okay to sell them to them." I spent a good twenty minutes admiring the cars and imagining myself driving to the Jersey Shore, discotheques, and around my Ironbound neighborhood in the my new Thunderbird. I asked the salesman, as Pipo and my mother waited in the lobby of the dealership to have their new car brought out of the garage to take home, if he could open the door so I could get in and sit behind the wheel for a few seconds. He responded that only the big boss had access to the keys and he was not there that day, and nobody was allowed inside the cars without his approval. "However, the dark blue model's passenger door is open," he said, "and you are more than welcome to check it out if you like."

I quickly jumped at that opportunity, opened the door, and checked out the velour blue interior and the eye-catching eight-track FM radio player—and I was in love. This particular car was loaded with extra features; it had a moon roof so you could get closer to the stars, I guess, but I was already in heaven in my mind, surrounded by infinite numbers of these glowing stars. I wanted to share this experience with Pipo and my mother before we left to go home. A few minutes later the salesman knocked on the driver's side window and told me to get out because they were closing the dealership in thirty minutes. As I opened the door, he said, "Come back in a couple of weeks and I will let you try out one of these Birds on the road."

I said, "You read my mind, sir. I sure will." Before we left the parking lot, I asked him what color the olive one was. It was a color I had never seen before. He said, "You are right, that color on that T-Bird is unique, and is not olive, it is a champagne color with a special shine. It has captured the attention of everyone that works here, and everybody wants one for himself." It was my favorite color by far at the time, followed by the dark blue.

Before we left for home, I wanted Pipo and my mother to come and look at these cars. After a long, childish rant with Pipo, I was able to convince him, with my mother's insistence, to make me happy and go with me for five minutes and check out all these cars. I was like a young toddler in a candy store with my hero right next to me, taking part in an important father-and-son activity of looking at cars. But it was not only about cars; it was the back-and-forth special moments of sharing the rites of passage between the two of us. In the lot, I told Pipo, "This is going to be my next car after I graduate from high school and get a good, permanent job."

He said, "Miguel (he always called me by my name), you need to save *mucho dinero* (lots of money) and not waste it and maybe you will be able to afford one of these." I told him I would be on a mission to do just that. At the same time, I was not going to let anything, even this car that I wanted so badly, distract me or derail me from my number one goal of helping Pipo financially. During this time I was working at the papellito factory after school and then I would immediately go to work for an Italian restaurant called High Seas in North Arlington, New Jersey. I also work briefly at Port Newark in the Puerto Rican Marine Building, where my mother got me a job buffing the floor, and I also worked at UPS in Parsippany loading trucks. Finally, I had my permanent job at Alcan Ingot & Powders in Union, where I was making a good wage of $5.08 per hour. This job provided the financial engine to get my T-Bird and really help Pipo and my family big time during my seven years with them. Pipo's constant advice of being able to live within one's means was a true godsend for me because it provided the structure that I really needed growing up in our disposable society.

As I followed Pipo and my mother home in my 1970 Ford Torino, I was so happy to finally see them enjoying their new 1976 Ford Granada (four-door silver and red), even though it was a bittersweet pill for Pipo because our money was very limited. One thing that happened with Pipo's decision to purchase a new car was my mother's never-ending demand and complaints that drove my father crazy until he finally caved in. I told Pipo to get the Grenada because it was my favorite car, and additionally I did a lot of research on it through magazines such as *Motor Trend, Road and Track*, etc. However, a few days earlier my brother, Gerardo Jr., had convinced my Pipo and my mother to buy a Buick Skylark instead of the Grenada, so I went ranting to the Buick dealership with my brother and mother until Pipo changed his mind and decided to go with my choice based on my research and how poorly the Skylark was ranked compared to the Grenada.

Needless to say, when we arrived home I parked my car and joined Pipo, mother, and aunt Genoveva on a forty-five-minute cruise in our new car around Newark and the surrounding cities. Man, it was so enjoyable for me just sit back and see Pipo and everyone look so happy. It reminded me of the bygone era in Cuba in our black Chevy, going places. I was transported in time for those few minutes that I will treasure forever.

The first time I was in a Thunderbird was in 1977 after the brother of one my best friends, Frank, got married at his house on Ferry Street in Newark. After the wedding a friend suggested that we check out this movie by the name of *Saturday Night Fever*, starring John Travolta from the television show *Welcome Back, Kotter*. To everyone's surprise, this dude had just purchased a fully loaded 1978 Thunderbird landau with the sticker price of $12,500 (the sheet was still left on the backside window, glued there for everyone to see as he picked us up on the corner). You could smell the fresh new-car aroma inside the car as we drove to and back from the State Theater in Jersey City about ten miles away. I was in awe, asking the owner all types of question about the car and the cost. He was somewhat concerned that he was not going to be able to keep paying the monthly payments in the future. This lesson in Economics 101 was very helpful to me when I purchased my own car.

The most popular cars during my era, circa 1977, were the Lincoln Continental Mark V, Cadillac El Dorado, Corvette, Cutlass Supreme, Ford Grenada, and the Ford Thunderbird. It seems most of my friends owned one of these at one time or another. I could not help but notice many of my schoolmates driving around town and showing off their machines in our so-called little world. You could see them strutting their pride and joy nightly, cruising on Ferry Street, just like in the movie *American Graffiti*, until a city ordinance was passed which pro-hibited cruising and imposed a large fine. I was also guilty of cruising in this forbidden, heavy-traffic area. Luckily I never got caught.

It seems wherever I went, I encountered many friends and co-workers switching to the new T-Bird. Among the many, Robert (the author of *Bloodcaine*, soon to be released as a film) stood out because he had the best two-tone color (grey and dark blue) paint job in his 1977 Thunderbird in the business. It cost him a whopping $6,700. In 1978 that was unheard of for a paint job.

Fast forward to September 12, 1978. Pipo and my mother accompanied me to Watchung Ford in New Jersey to finally pur-chase a new car after my 1970 Torino started breaking down rapidly and I was spending a fortune on repairs. At the dealer-ship I was looking for a blue one, but they had none left at the time. The salesman told us, "We only have a few left because we are getting rid of inventory for the 1979 models coming in as we speak. So the remaining 1978s are being reduced in price to make room. Plus, you could get a substantial savings with these 1978 ones."

I told the salesman, "Let me look at these models and their sticker prices, and when I like one I will come and get you."

He said, "Okay, just come to the showroom."

I remember it was a hot afternoon and the sun was melting Pipo and me. After looking at all the models I decided to check out a white and burgundy model with a leather interior. Pipo looked intensely at the sticker price on the window, and it was listed at $8,200. Man, that was too much money for me to spend, and Pipo agreed. However, my mother fixated on me walking out of there with a new car no matter what. I, on the other hand, wanted this car even more so but did not want to spend beyond my means. So I called back the salesman and gave him an offer of $7,000 and went back and forth for a half hour with counterproposals until we came to an agreement of $7,200, not including the taxes and the other fees. The final cost was $7,781. I finally had my dream car. But before we signed the papers, I needed to take it for a road test with Pipo as my co-pilot right next to me, where he belonged. I would never have had it any other way. If the salesman had insisted on being in the front with me, there would have been no deal! But it never came to that point.

Now the financing was my responsibility, and I needed more money to close on this deal. I knew it was a great deal, again based on my research. But I needed more money to make this happen, so my request to my parents was to give me $2,200 as a loan. She stressed this was a loan, not a gift, and had to be paid back quickly. I did just that; it took me less than three months to pay them back in full. In addition, I gave them back $300 more for lending me the money. My mother, Maria, signed for my loan in her name for four years at $162.01 per month, which I never had any problems paying. The next day I picked the car up with the entire family and drove back home listening to my FM radio in style. The minute we arrived at home, everyone jumped in my new T-Bird and did the same as we had done with the Grenada, taking an afternoon cruise around Newark. This had become a new tradition for us. The best part was having Pipo with me in the car the very first day. We had a blast. I asked him to take the wheel but he refused on that day. He said, "This is your car and your day, so don't ask me today," because he knew I would not stop asking him to do so. I think he was also concerned of having an accident with this car of mine. I wanted to share my happiness with Pipo and have him take the wheel of my dream car while I sat next to him. This time, I would be the co-captain and he would be in the captain's chair. After cruising for almost two hours, we packed it in and went back to our Landfill apartment to called it a night. But not for me. I stayed inside the car, soaking it all in and listening to the music on the radio in the comfort of my leather seat pushed and reclined all the way back. It did not stop there. I was also in Pipo's window chair admiring my car just like Pipo. Guess the apple doesn't fall too far from the tree.

One thing Pipo did was to keep a keen eye on our cars, parking them near the window-view seat to make sure they were safe and not broken into or stolen. Since *Newark* had the highest auto theft rate in the country, he was uneasy about our cars, including my brother's. He was very fervent in parking the cars there, even staying up late into the evening and moving the cars like a parking lot attendant. It was hilarious to watch him in action do his thing. My mother always complained to Pipo about his compulsion with the parking of the cars. I must confess, his meticulous behavior also annoyed me at times. At times, when I had the perfect spot, I decided to leave and spend time with my girlfriend and friends. He would get so upset as I walked out the door, he continued to lecture me about how problematic the parking would be upon my return home. He was so right, but I would never 1 listen, and I surely paid dearly for it later when I rode around the neighborhood for an hour looking for a spot. Pipo would look for my car early in the morning and bring it to our designated street parking spot on Pulaski Street, and it would be right there for me. I felt bad that he did that, because he was approaching his seventieth birthday and was not as young as he used to be. So I wanted him to take it easy and not be bothered with all this trouble that I created. He lamented to my mother at times that I was very careless with the upkeep of my car, especially changing the oil and having plenty of gas in the tank. He also confided to her that he was not going to worry anymore about my irresponsibility in maintaining my car. But he never did stop worrying. He even filled my tank many times with gas in the morning when the gas needle was on empty.

In those early days I waited for Pipo often inside my Thunderbird till he came down from our apartment to drive off and pick up my mother from work. I believe it was the second day when I told Pipo to drive my car and that I would go along for the ride. I also wanted him to share the enjoyment of driving my new car. This was important for me because it was this area where he had taught me how to drive for the first time. So it was logical from my perspective that he and I would rotate the driving for a while. At first he was a little hesitant but he came around to my thinking. In the days ahead I insisted that he drive my car all over the place, and this included the daily mother pickup from work in the afternoon.

On one particular day while going to pick up my mother, Maria, a tractor trailer smacked my Thunderbird outside the Puertorico Marine Building at the Port of Newark as my mother entered the car around 4:00 p.m. My father, Pipo, saw the trailer coming toward my car and stepped on the gas to go forward as quickly as possible to avoid the impact but was not able to do so. The car was struck on the back of the fender, and this cracked the fiberglass tail on top of the back lights. My father was furious when this happened, screaming at this person in Spanish when he came out of the truck to take a look at what he had hit. Luckily for Pipo, his big boss saw the whole thing and put my father at ease, telling him that he would take care of all the damages and pay for all of it himself. My mother said this was a very good man that she knew very well who had witnessed the accident. He told Pipo to wait until he got the paperwork to fill out. "Do not leave," he told Pipo. In the meantime Pipo was thinking about me and how I was going to react to my damaged car.

CHAPTER 30

Preparing for Naturalization

Pipo could not, for the life of him, for some unknown reason, grasp and learn the English language, no matter how hard he tried. Poor Pipo! Even, at the most basic level of functionality, he was totally lost. It was both his Waterloo and his Achilles' heel, and again it compounded the potential problem of failing miserably—similar to his previous driver's license woes that almost broke him into pieces. With seven years under his belt in this country, he decided to apply for US citizenship with my mother, together with the hope of having better results. This would still be a challenging situation for Pipo, to say the least, but with my mother going through the process equally with him, she thought it would be a much less stressful path, or so we thought.

Pipo's universe in those early days in America was to work at Magnus Organ and with the papellitos at home to pay those family members and friends who sent us money when we were living in a transitory state in Mexico City. In those work environments, no one spoke English, so there was not a pressing need to learn the language. It was a double-edged sword for him; it reinforced his native Spanish tongue at the expense of his slowly picking up a few English words. My mother, on the other hand, benefited by learning English more quickly, because in her jobs after she left Magnus Organ, her colleagues for the vast majority were Americans who spoke English only.

Now the question for my mother was how to get Pipo to agree in joining her and becoming a US citizen. Her angle and argument was a simple one; it entailed no trickery or false pretenses. It was sprinkled with the very fact that it would streamline our trip to his home country of Spain and my mother's adopted country as well. Simple, right? Well, this was the key point of her argument to Pipo to come around in spite of the past license debacle. Even though there were so many other convincing points, she hit the nail on the head with this one in persuading Pipo to say yes.

I remember quite often going with Pipo to the Federal Building in our home town of Newark. We woke up at 2:45 a.m. and waited outside that building in line until it opened up at 7:30a.m. I hated it, really hated it, so much that I would show my displeasure to Pipo by complaining nonstop all day. This was the method of choice if you wanted to get a Visa and travel to Spain. It was so excruciating, but I had no choice; Pipo needed me and I was not going to makes things worse by refusing to go with him. I was the happy-go-lucky guinea pig who tagged along with Pipo as his interpreter and filled all the required documents for the upcoming trek. My biggest gripe was you had to spend all day there going from one line to another and filling out all these long forms that took away so much time that it literally zapped out all your energy. In addition, I had to constantly engage in a Q&A format interpretation for Pipo and the many different examiners who requested the information vital to our impending trip. Everything had to be just right, or no visa. I could not stand all the waiting, and most of the people who worked there were very condescending and arrogant toward all of us. They had very little patience, and this was self-evident to me because of my many visits there.I found the people arrogant.

After enduring these tedious frustrations in the past, Pipo agreed to apply for citizenship and avoid going through this messy process again in the future.

I also promised him to do everything in my power to help prepare for the exam. The exam itself would cover basic historical, constitutional, and governmental working knowledge of the processes and laws of the United States. This was an area quite familiar to me since I was in high school at this point in my education, and it would come in handy in mitigating Pipo's anxieties in his journey of becoming a citizen.

Years later, I became a political junkie, watching the nail biter 1968 presidential election with family and friends until the early morning hours, as well as many hours of C-SPAN when it was launched on March19, 1979. The marathon election was called for Richard Nixon, and it impacted me so much that I have feverishly watched each subsequent election without missing a beat. These two events and my time with Pipo gave me the motivation I needed years later when I enrolled in college. I loaded up heavily in political science courses because of my keen interest and reservoir of knowledge I had obtained through these experiences in this field. Plus, the countless hours I spent in concert with Pipo helping him study the little book that the Department of Justice and the Immigration Service issues to every prospective citizen served as the last straw for me in influencing me to obtain my bachelor's degree in liberal arts years later. It put a real fire in my belly that could not be ignored.

I gave Pipo this one caveat: he needed to answer me in English, no Spanish, or very little in the beginning, and if I was going to use Spanish with him, it would be for a clarification only. He reluctantly promised to follow my instructions fully. I put this harsh demand on him because I felt it would improve his chances of succeeding—you know, a kind of a tough-love approach that has been proven to work in the past.

This material in this little book was written in a straightforward format; first you were given the question and then the answer, a classic, simple Q&A approach, or so I thought. But it was like me taking the test in hieroglyphics or Mandarin Chinese—not so easy. It was going to be an uphill climb for both of us. In my case I had to be very patient and understanding with him, and he had to be willing to listen and comprehend very careful this material fully. I also was helping my mother at times, but since she knew a little English, her studies were going very well. Pipo, on the other hand, was struggling with everything. It was like a toddler learning his ABCs and pronunciations for the first time. I would ask him the simplest questions; for example, I asked him in Spanish and I repeated several times. "Who was the first president of the United States?" He looked at me in a perplexed demeanor and paused for a few seconds. I said, "Dale! Dale! (Come on! Come on!)"

He said, "No me a pure! (Don't hurry me!)" He then responded in Spanish, "El primer presidente de los Estados Unidos es George Washington Bridge (The first president of the United States is George Washington Bridge)."

I said, "No! No! No! It's George Washington, not bridge. The bridge name in George Washington signifies a tribute to him by naming el puente en su nombre (the bridge in his name)."

"Oh, lla comprendo (Oh, now I understand). That connects New Jersey and New York over the Hudson River."

I kept asking him the easiest questions first, like how many stars in the US flag and what do these stars mean and so forth. Plus, who is the governor of New Jersey and how many years was he elected for (a single term) and how many senators are elected in each state and how long are they elected for. I also asked him the minimum age requirement for president, senator, and congressman. I kept this rapid-fire tactic until I though he was making progress. I kept tutoring him about a half hour a day on most days, sometimes longer if he was up to it. I was convinced he was making positive inroads by measuring his current level of information with where he was when we began.

In all fairness to Pipo, he did get one initial question correct. I asked him, "Pipo, who is the president of United States?" He answered me, "The president of the Unites States is Gerald Ford." We both laughed out loud, thinking if you don't know who the current president of United States is, you are living on a different planet. For a split second, I marveled at the possibility he would say Richard Nixon, who had to resign the presidency after the Watergate scandal in August of 1974. And if he did say former President Nixon, I wouldn't have blamed him anyway because of insatiable news media were in full blitz mode in those days covering this story and could not get enough. It seemed every TV channel, newspapers, magazines, and whatnot were covering the fallen Nixon, leaving the current President Ford overshadowed. I told Pipo in a jubilant, excited voice, "You are correct!" and applauded him at the same time. I followed up with this related question: "How many years is he elected for in each term, and how many total years is he able to serve?"

He said, "I don't remember, Miguel," as he tried to look at the book for the answer.

I said, "No looking at the book and no cheating, Pipo."

Pipo replied to me in a harsh tone, "How is anyone going to remember all this stuff without going to the book?"

I said, "Pipo, there is nothing wrong with going to the book to refresh your memory. But when I am with you I expect you to answer my questions as best as you can without it. This will provide a good barometer for me and will allow me to concentrate with you on your weak areas more fully. Yes, study the book by all means on your own time."

He said, "Yes, I will do that. Just give me the book now and I'm going to study by myself and not bother you anymore from this point on. You are not patient with me and I can't take the abuse of you raising your voice at me any longer. You should go now and go and play with your friends and do your thing and just leave me alone. It's quite apparent to me that your desire is to be somewhere else and not with me."

I said. "Pipo, I would never, ever raise my voice at you. I just feel you are not picking this stuff up quickly enough, and I'm getting frustrated."

Sometimes Pipo did reveal his temper, but when he did it was tough love in reverse direction to me, as when I was young and he would take the belt from his waist and let me have it. Well, I was trying to let him have it for his own good, but he did not see it that way and broke rank with me for the duration for the upcoming exam. It was a very unfortunate situation because I really loved my hero, Pipo, and wanted to spend time together so he could pass this important test. But I lacked a balance of sensitivity and prudence, and it was a critical mistake in retrospect to push too hard and too fast, and it backfired on me.

As the days followed after my calamity with him, I noticed Pipo doing very well and looking much rejuvenated as I frequently went past him in our home. It seems every time I saw him, he was busy studying, whether it was in bed, sitting by the lookout window monitoring our cars, or any other place. He was 100 percent committed to the task at hand. This empirical observation by me was music to my ears. I just loved what I was seeing. On several occasion he even called me over and asked me to fire away some questions, and I was pleasantly amazed at how much he had improved since I left him alone. My mother, on the other hand, was doing very well and answering most questions correctly that I threw at her, mostly in the evening. In my humble opinion, I figured she was a shoo-in to pass when called to report for the exam. With Pipo it would be more of a squeaker if he did pass. I sure did not want him to repeat the five negative results of his driver's license escapade. Especially in that bicentennial year of the founding of our nation, it would be a nice, memorable event for all of us if both of them passed.

In late spring of that year, Pipo and my mother received notification from the Department of Justice to report to the federal building in Newark for the interview process in becoming a citizen. My mother was scheduled a week earlier than Pipo, so we all accompanied her for moral support and crossed our fingers as she went inside the room to be interviewed. It was very crowded, as always, as we waited for her to return. After only twenty minutes she reappeared with a glow and a jubilant face and told us, "Passe! Passe! (Pass! Pass!) And in two weeks I report to the federal court building to take the oath of citizenship, the last hurdle in cementing my allegiance to this great country that gave us the opportunity to make a life for ourselves and our family. Thank God for this new land we call the good old United States of America! Amen!"

After hearing this great news, it was Pipo's turn to face the music a week later, hoping for identical results. My mother and I did everything possible to take Pipo's nervousness away while he waited to be called. But he still remained very antsy to the very last moment before being called for the interview. I told Pipo as his name was called to go in there and try to duplicate what my mother did a week ago. He said, "Hijo, es el tiempo ahora (Son, is now the time)?" As he walked in with the interviewer, my mother and I rushed to him and gave Pipo a big hug and kiss. We both waited nervously for Pipo to come out with a positive and a smiling face. Thirty-five minutes had elapsed before Pipo walked out of the room without any positive energy that would indicate a successful outcome. Pipo quickly told us that the interviewer spoke too fast and he was not able to understand any questions at all. I felt so bad for him that words alone could not do justice to my disappointment for my hero. I looked over at his letter and I read the comments, which said, "Gerardo Garcia (Pipo) lacked the basic knowledge of English and could not answer any of my questions satisfactorily. This failure by Mr. Garcia resulted in not approving his citizenship at this time. He is eligible to come back and retake the exam in the future."

My mother and I told Pipo in the lobby not to be somber because he would pass very soon. I also said, "I am very proud of you, no matter what just happened or anything else. You are my *padre* (father). I love you dearly." This genuine comforting was all we could do for Pipo to try to get back his high spirits, which were always his hallmark. A few days later Pipo was to take this positive feeling of ours and embark directly on enrolling in an agency that catered toward people, just like my father, who lacked English but had the knowledge in their native language to answer all the questions correctly. He paid $300 for this intense four-week course with them. After the completion of this course, I was in disbelief at how well he was answering all my questions in English and in Spanish, with no problems whatsoever. I did this in a rapid fashion at various intervals throughout the week. However, my questions this time with Pipo were more in a dialogue structure, not any previously robotic format that proved not to work, and not just about the Constitution.

I said, "Can you name the governor of New Jersey?"

He would say, "The governor of New Jersey is Brendan Byrne."

I kept asking questions while he smiled. "What is your name and where do you live?"

He said, "My name is Gerardo Garcia and I live in Newark, New Jersey."

These were the questions I felt were going to make the difference in the upcoming test, because it was quite evident to me that he for sure knew the material to pass this time.

He reported this time more confidence than ever before to the Federal Building with my mother, Aunt Genoveva, and me at his side to get this monkey finally off his back on this second try. When Pipo was called, I made a fist as I look at him and told him, "I'll be waiting outside for a victory party for you, Pipo!"

He responded, smiling in a cheerful and humble way, "Otra vez mas (one more time)." In the meantime, aunt Genoveva and my mother were praying for Pipo to finally pass and become a citizen. As the door whipped open from the test office, I could not stand the anticipation as I was engulfed with lots of butterflies in my stomach when I saw Pipo walking in our direction. He had a mixed demeanor and I couldn't figure out with certainty if he did pass. Well, that was very much short lived, because he said quickly, "The only questions she asked me this time were what was my name and where did I live. Plus, she asked about my work and so forth and a couple of from-the-book questions on the Constitution, and that was it. All in all she was very polite and attentive—a very nice black woman. Then finally she said, 'Congratulations, Mr. Garcia, you are ready to take the oath of citizenship at the federal court in two weeks. Again, congratulations, and I welcome you as a new citizen, Mr. Garcia.' "

These were the types of questions that I had thrown at Pipo constantly, and it paid off big time. I was the happiest person in the world upon hearing those magical words from Pipo. It was a big relief for Pipo. We were so happy for him, knowing how hard an effort he put into this long process and that he was now able to just take it easy and permanently reduce his stress once and for all. This occasion was a monumental mark in our lives in this country, because the 1976 presidential election between President Ford and Governor Carter was the first time they'd had the pleasure to vote in their new adopted country. Needless to say it was a very upbeat ride for us as we drove back to our Landfill apartment that afternoon.

Pipo and my mother took the oath of citizenship a couple of weeks apart in the summer of 1976 as I waited impatiently outside of the courthouse for each of them, waving a small America bicentennial flag as they came out of the courthouse. Man, what a joyous scene that moment was for me. It has been and it will always be a crystallizing moment for me. It was so hard trying to keep my watery eyes dry as I drove home with them, waving Pipo's flag out my window.

The moral of the story was not only my parents becoming *gringos*, but my refusal to become a citizen with them in 1976. My mother had told me numerous times to fill out all the required application forms simultaneously with them, but I told her many times, in a loud, defiant voice, "No! No! And no! I will not do it. Don't mention it to me anymore." My reason, I thought at that time, was a sound one. I was burned out with many family members and friends who were asking my mother for my help time after time. Each time, I had to fill out a barrage of forms and be an interpreter for them and submit myself constantly to the abuse of those lazy people in the Federal Building that I knew so well, so I was not going to go through all the crazy paperwork again. But in 1976 my parents decided to travel to Spain again for the second time, and guess what? I was not a citizen, and I had to go back to the line of fire to get my visa if I was going to do any travel to Spain. I had to go! However, this time the shoe was on the other foot and the tables were definitely turned on me. This gave Pipo the ammunition to fight back against me for the many times I complained about accompanying and helping him in filling forms and unfortunately wasting many entire days with him. Pipo said, "I don't get it, *hijo* (son). All of this could've been avoided if you had just taken it upon yourself to apply for citizenship with us back then. Why didn't you just listen to what we told you? You know, it was for your own good. You were just being lazy and you know it. Look at me, almost sixty-seven years old and speaking no English, and I did what I had to do. Now we are here, when you know so well all of this should have been avoidable."

I was so upset at myself for being so stupid and having tunnel vision, and my shortsightedness came back to bite me in the butt, with Pipo having the last laugh at my expense in a fun and good-humored way between father and son. Oh, the citizenship thing, it wasn't until December 27, 1983, when I finally became a new American. I am so proud and honored to have citizenship bestowed on me, just like Pipo and my dear mother, Maria. God bless America!

CHAPTER 31

Turning Up the Heat

Over the years, I pulled many practical jokes on poor Pipo, but one's one clearly stands out above the rest. It took place in 1977, an electrifying year in America, especially in the New York metropolitan area, where the "Son of Sam' took center stage as a serial killer who held the city hostage with fear until he was apprehended that summer. During this time also we had the blackout, which, unlike the 1965 and 2003 blackouts, resulted in citywide looting and other disorder, including arson. It was a city in flames. This time was also when disco music really took off, led by movies like *Saturday Night Fever*, with John Travolta; *Thank God It's Friday*, with Donna Summer, the queen of disco, making her acting debut and singing her signature song, "Last Dance"; and *Looking for Mr. Goodbar*, about a woman's search for a liberated life of promiscuity, starring Diane Keaton. She also won the Academy Award for best actress and best picture for *Annie Hall* that same year. But the biggest phenomenon on the big screen was none other than *Star Wars*. It shattered all the records, eclipsing *Jaws* as the number one movie of all time. It seems like everything was happening at the same time all over the place. With the epicenter located at Studio 54, the famous club where the rich and famous danced the night away. This residue of positive energy was infectious and addictive to all of us who were young. But it was a sour-note time for me because my favorite baseball player, Tom Seaver, was traded to the Cincinnati Reds in June. I still don't forgive the Mets for that stupid and ill-conceived decision to let him go. He was and still is considered by baseball gurus and by Mets fans alike as the club's best player ever. Period! There is no debate on this matter. It's no coincidence why he was and still is often called "The Franchise" and "Tom Terrific" as his patented nicknames. However, across town, my arch-nemesis, the New York Yankees, captured a World Series title by beating the Los Angeles Dodgers, led by Mr. October himself, Reggie Jackson, who hit a record-breaking five home runs in the series. This feat set a record for most home runs in one World Series. However, what made Reggie Jackson shoot to the stratosphere as a baseball legend was that he hit three home runs during the clinching game six of the series on the very first pitch each time. Three pitches, three home runs...an amazing and unforgettable performance that catapulted him to stardom and made him the toast of the town, with a company even naming (can you believe it) a candy bar after him. Only in America!

Encapsulated with all these major events and others was the intense heat we were facing in the metropolitan area and its surroundings at this time. The temperature rose to over one hundred degrees with no signs of letting up any time soon. I recall specifically the week of July 18, 1977, when the temperature reached 104. As I drove around Newark and neighboring towns, I could not help but notice so many young and old people trying to keep cool by opening fire hydrants. This was quite apparent because of the heavy traffic backup on the local streets; this common practice was a welcome relief to the masses who had no other way to stay cool. However, this scenario also hampered motor traffic, slowing it to a snail's pace, which resulted in a dangerous situation as we tried very slowly to get through with our vehicles without hitting them. It was quite a difficult task at times because you were not able to have a clear 360-degree view due to the intense water pressure spraying on your car. Plus, you had those individual who wanted to have a free car wash at the expense of others who wanted just to pass quickly through. This repeated itself continuously, corner block after corner block, without any signs of letting up until the heat is dissipated. In the meantime, this led to many unavoidable, tinderbox confrontations with the police to unclog the streets, and with drivers, in addition to the fire department patrolling and closing the valves of all these hydrants because of low water pressure, which was causing an urgent public safety concern. It was a losing battle of wills between all parties involved.

In the midst of this scorching heat, I decided to play a prank on Pipo without him noticing it, just for fun. I wanted to keep it clandestined and foolproof if at all possible, so I could use it with family and friends in the future as well. I was going to incorporate this extreme heat condition and make it even hotter in my 1970 Ford Torino. I did a trial run just to see how effective this was going to be before I tried it out with Pipo. First, I was going to make sure my power windows were not operable at all, so the windows would remain permanently closed. Then, I was going to turn on the heat in the car and then slowly turn it up and up until it reached the maximum temperature available. My plan was to have the heat on already by the time Pipo entered the car. This would give me the normalcy I needed at the beginning of my stunt to carry it through without Pipo being suspicious. As I drove around with the windows closed and the heat turned on to maximum, I was gasping for air; it was intolerable inside my car. I contemplated aborting my plan altogether because I thought it was too severe, and it clearly crossed the line as far as I was concerned. So I decided to modify my plan by not to increasing the temperature in the car at all. I just kept it at the lowest level to avoid a potential health risk to all of us.

I decided to try to convince Pipo to accompany me in my 1970 Ford Torino to pick my mother up at work and then go food shopping at Pathmark. But before I did, I came up with a phantom story that my car was not running right and I needed him to come with me to check out the problem firsthand. This gave me enough cover and credibility to deflect Pipo's thinking somewhat from the rise in temperature in the car as I drove slowly. Plus, I took the much longer and more time-consuming routes as we began to sweat unmercifully. At this time I was trying my very best not to lose my composure and break out in an uncontrollable, loud laugh that would reveal to Pipo my agenda. So, I tried my darnedest to have him concentrate on mechanical problems with my car. I said, "Pipo, my car is totally falling apart; as you can see, my windows are not working. In addition, can you hear *el ruido* (the noise) underneath?"

Before he responded, Pipo took his handkerchief from his back pocket to wipe his soaking face as he shook his head in response to the troublesome sweat rolling into his eyes and his not able to see anything as I talked to him about the car. One thing about the entire Garcia family, from generation to generation, is that we are predisposed to sweating profusely. It's clearly in our DNA composition. Then, while Pipo wiped his eyes from all the sweat, his handkerchief was obviously no match for it, so I gave him a roll of paper towels and napkins that I was also using myself to help. During this time we heard on the radio that the temperature had hit 104 degrees. Upon hearing this weather news, Pipo said, "This car is about to melt! It is so hot in here that I can't even put my hands on the console, windows, or anywhere inside the car because it burns my skin."

I said, "Pipo, si mucho calor aqui a dentro (Yes, it is too hot inside)," as I wiped off the sweat from my eyes. At this time I mentioned to Pipo that the heat was so intense I could not grab the steering wheel anymore. I said, "I'm going to pull over to the shoulder so I can open the trunk and put on my thick winter gloves to protect my hands from burning." While I was making this remark, I grabbed his hand and tried to place it on the steering wheel to make him notice I was not faking it, but he quickly pulled back his hands. After I pleaded with him just to place them there for a split second, he did. After pleasing me, I then quickly opened the car door and stepped out. The outside ambient temperature felt like a freezer even though it was in the triple digits.

It must have been about 150 degrees inside our car on that particular day. Even if it wasn't, it had to be in the vicinity. As I came back with my gloves on, I was clearly overplaying it with Pipo and having a good time with him. Man, I was having so much fun with my ploys and trickery; it was good acting on my part. I just wanted to continue a little longer before I decided to pull the plug. As I came back to the car, I noticed a bunch of trucks and cars on the shoulders of the road with their hoods open and white smoke coming out from overheating. I said, "Pipo, look at all these cars smoking as we pass by them." It was a daunting sight, and it gave me more ammunition to use.

Then he said, "Miguel, check the gauge and see if the car is okay or if it is getting hot."

I said, "Pipo, it looks like the needle is all the way to the right, and I don't think it could go any more."

He said, "What? Let me see." As he leaned over toward me and looked at it, wiping his eyes, he hollered at me and said, "This car is about to overheat and the radiator is going to blow up. Stop the car right now."

I said, "Pipo, we are close to picking up mother; let's wait till we get there so we can open the hood while we wait for her to get out of work. This will give my car time to cool in a safe and less-trafficked area."

He said, "Go and try to make it. Hurry up before the car stalls and we get stuck with these big haulers zooming by us."

Suddenly, I floored the car as the smoke started to fizzle out from the front hood. Man, this car was inflamed and ready to burst wide open if I didn't make it in the next twenty seconds or so. Luckily we were able to make it to my mother's company at Port Newark just before imminent doom. We both got out of the car, Pipo opened the hood, and we saw the thick smoke bursting out from underneath the radiator cap as it boiled over. Pipo said, "Miguel, get away from here—stand back twenty feet in case the cap blows up and hits you in the face. I will try to slowly turn it and leave it on safe mode until it cools off."

"Okay!" I said. "You don't even have to tell me anything, Pipo. I know better. I won't come any closer."

Fifteen minutes later my mother came out of her air-conditioned work area and right away flipped when she saw what was happening to my car and the high temperatures on that day. She said to Pipo, "Why did you not come in the Granada on the hottest day of the year? You came in this car? I want to know why! I just cannot believe it for the life of me. We have a new car and you bring this car. Are you insane? What were you thinking? This serves you right." She was furious, and guess what? She was correct. It was not Pipo's fault, but mine alone. I said, "Mima, it was my idea to bring my car so Pipo could check for a mechanical problem. He did not want to use my car at all."

Then, she quickly responded, "Are you going to listen to him or follow common sense and dignity? Come on!"

Pipo, at this time, was focused more on the car's condition than my mother's rambling escapades. She said, "I am not going inside this car if I see any smoke coming out. I am not going to blow up with the rest of you. Do I make myself crystal clear?"

"Yes, Mother!"

After twenty minutes the car was cleared by Pipo to drive back home. This allowed me and my trickery to continue all the way home with an extra twist to embellish even more. I was going to use my mother and Pipo against each other in the car with the heat turned on. It was going to feel like the longest twenty minutes of commuting in eternity. I was more than ready, salivating like a puppy to witness the fireworks take hold as soon we entered the car. My biggest obstacle, again, was to retain a natural demeanor with them.

The car was a little cooler as we took off because we were in the shade while we waited for my mother. However, in no time the car was getting warmer in the stop-and-go traffic. It was up my alley having this slow pace, because it gave me the luxury of putting the attention on them instead of me. I heard my mother start yelling, "What's going on with this car's air conditioner?"

I told her, "This car has a leak in the AC unit and it's not working. I made an appointment to get it fixed next week."

Then she said, in a very loud voice, "Open the windows before I suffocate in this car."

I said, "Mother, the motor that controls the power windows is not working either."

Then she really snapped at Pipo and said, "I am about to pass out here inside. If you don't open this door right now, I'm going to break the window and jump out."

Pipo's reply, as he looked back at her, was, "Calmate! Calmate! (Calm down! Calm down!)"

She insisted that the door be opened. I asked Pipo to crack the door slightly and I would do the same thing on my side because of the burning heat and the continued stoppage of traffic. We both did this to allay my mother's threat of jumping or cracking the window. My quick ideas worked for a while, as I kept Pipo busy concentrating on my fictitious mechanical problems at hand. It was so hot that Pipo and I took our shirts off .He remained in his sleeveless undershirt and I was shirtless, while my mother was soaked and complaining to Pipo about these unacceptable conditions.

Pipo did everything possible to keep her cool by using a magazine as a fan. She went on a rampage, saying to Pipo, "I'm not going all the way home in this car that falling apart. Nothing works. I work too hard to be exposed to these conditions, and this is not acceptable to me now, tomorrow, or next week. Stop this car right now; I'll get a taxi or ride the bus with the comfort of having air conditioning in it all the way home."

Then Pipo said to me, "Pull over at the next gas station to get some cold sodas or water before we overheat ourselves." As soon as I stopped the car at the Sunoco gas station, Pipo jumped out of the car and let my mother slide out of the front door, and she immediately went to the ladies' restroom to freshen up with cold water. Pipo told me while waiting for Mother to return, "This car of yours is going to my mechanic as soon as we get back and drop your mother at home! Do you hear me?"

I said, "Pipo, it is too hot to do it today. Let's take the car tomorrow." In reality there was nothing wrong with the car at all. It was all a fabrication on my part, and I didn't want anything to do with a mechanic, because he would find out that the problems were tampering and not real. This would spoil my fun and get Pipo angry at me, which was not a good idea. So I had to come up with a quick, credible excuse to avoid this tinderbox scenario, which I did before getting home. As all of us got in the car, I couldn't help but rejoice on drinking a simple Pepsi beverage. It was the best soda in my life, as it quenched my thirst, and by the looks of Pipo and my mother, it also helped them alleviate their dehydrated mood as well. It was an energy booster that relieved the previously polluted atmosphere of my mother sounding off at us. During this time, about ten minutes before getting home, I decided to stop my prank and open the windows to avoid more confrontations. I told Pipo I was getting scratched by some wire on my left leg underneath the dashboard and that I intended to pull over the car and check it out. This was the only escape plan plausible enough to redeem me with them. I intended to implement this action in seconds to restore the windows' ability to go down and let air in the car. Even though it was hot air, it provided much-needed circulation in the car. I told Pipo, "I found a loose wire. Can you give me the flashlight from the glove compartment?"

"Okay, here it is," he said. I was doing my very best to look serious in trying to figure out what the wire was connected to. After three minutes of this shenanigan, I finally told Pipo I had found the problem and I was reconnecting the wire where it belonged. Wow, what a genius I was; I fixed a perplexing issue that was bothersome to all of us. This good Samaritan act brought me many kudos from my mother and Pipo, because now the window was open and we could finally breathe fully.

This prank was just a way for me to get closer to Pipo and to my mother through what were surely my infantile games. That same week I tried it again with Pipo, aunt Genoveva, grandfather Domingo, Pepilla (his second wife), and my mother as we drove to a picnic area. However, this was in my father's car, so my only move was to put on the heat as high as possible, of course indiscreetly, as we drove to our destination. Wow, it was another scorcher of a day; this incredible heat wave was causing great discomfort. I could see the displeasure in their faces as I increased the heat in the car. But upon seeing my poor grandfather Domingo, in his late eighties, through my rearview mirror, I felt so bad and quickly shot down the idea for good. During this terrible heat wave episode, I also realized that anyone can go too far with a joke at times. The most important thing to remember is to be fully attentive to know the limits of any endeavors, because it may lead or might be manifested in an unexpectedly dire outcome. This heat prank by me against Pipo and my family was also used in reverse during the record-breaking low temperatures we also had in the 1970s. Yes, I loved Pipo so much; that is why I turned up the air conditioner in the car to tease him continuously. In retrospect, I believe with all my heart that Pipo had become aware of my shtick toward the end and let me get away with it. Who was playing who, I wonder? We were both trapped, facing the same hostile, confined environment. I rate this one as advantage Pipo. I would be back for more!

CHAPTER 32

The Car Engine Didn't Stop

Pipo had a profound passion for automobiles and the meticulous maintenance and upkeep of these essential, everyday machines. It's a passion that my brother, Gerardo Jr., and I both shared and adhered to so intensely in our father's footsteps, without missing a beat. I must admit candidly, though, that my brother's passion was on a higher plane than mine. But nevertheless, I caught the bug as well, and I have surely never waivered one bit, thanks to Pipo.

However, one particular car memory from 1983 stands out. (That was the year my beloved Mets reacquired Tom Seaver from the Cincinnati Reds after a six-year exile. Unfortunately, it was short lived—they lost him again that same year to the Chicago White Sox because he was left unprotected. What can anyone expect from an organization that has proven time after time throughout the history of the franchise to be oblivious to making intelligent decisions? This folly by the Mets was the genesis of losing my fanaticism toward my favorite childhood team, and it has never reignited again. But enough about my frustration with this idiotic proclivity and just blame it on my being a simple fan who gets really despondent and needs to vent and escape the so-called real world for a fleeting moment.) In 1983 a new purchased car went haywire and I was privileged to be at an arm's length from Pipo when it transpired. It was quite a scene, and I was dumbfounded, as was Pipo as well ,and this time it was not a fabricated prank by me or anything like that. It just evolved and evolved organically with none of my fingerprints on this silly and weird episode. My only involvement was to add a twist of sarcasm at Pipo's expense and to try to solve this really heartwrenching dilemma without delay.

The culprit was none other than my mother, Maria, and, to a lesser extent, my brother, and it reinforced the decision to trade our 1976 Ford Granada for a 1983 Ford Escort. I was from the very beginning opposed to this conclusion, as was Pipo. First, Pipo was not a young man anymore and I did not wanted him to be worried or consumed with a monthly car payment. I thought that was a big mistake, and I made my point crystal clear to them. It was a losing proposition on my behalf from the very inception. They had made up their mind to dump the old car for a brand new one at all cost. My mother's argument was that Pipo was spending too much money on repairs and that her check was eaten alive, and this unfortunate practice had to be halted at once. End of debate! This argument, I believe, was a smokescreen. I think she wanted to buy a new car and had to justify it somehow, so she upped the ante of normal repairs to a higher level to convince Pipo of her rationale. My mother had absolutely no knowledge of anything to do with the internal working mechanics of a car. Plus, she had never even had a driver's license or driven a car on her own, yet she was lecturing Pipo and me about cars. What a bizarre argument she was unveiling, but nevertheless, her stern and uncompromising position would prevail this time with Pipo instead of mine. I just felt sick to my stomach when Pipo told me to go with him and my mother to Riverside Ford, were we purchased our old car in 1976, to trade it for a new one. I had so many good times in this car with the family and friends. I remember of course all my pranks and all of that, as well as speeding with my friends and having my first serious girlfriend and driving her home on that very night we met and so forth. I told Pipo, "It was a bad decision, and I'm not going to take part in any of it, especially going with you and mother to the Ford dealer. Since it was mother's idea, she should go with you, not me." Pipo was very apprehensive that day, because he knew in his heart that the old car was working fine, but his hands were tied by my mother's stubbornness. He wanted peace with her, so he quietly took all frustration inward to avoid any donnybrook affairs that remained very much on the surface. Very smart moves by Pipo at that time, or any time, because he knew you can never win an argument with a woman (which I was too young to realize and take in at that time). However, it was a terrible economic decision and detrimental to Pipo's comfort zone and mental disposition. It proved from the outset to be truly unwarranted and damaging to all of us, but no one greater than Pipo.

The decision was made to purchase a new car with my mother, brother, and Pipo going to the so-called circus of decisions and negotiations in choosing a model without me. However, the next day I reluctantly accompanied Pipo alone (my mother and brother had to work) Riverside dealership to bring home the new 2003 Ford Escort model that they had chosen. In those days it took a day or two to complete all required paperwork and give the car an extensive cleaning before driving away. Well, it was Pipo and I, the two of us, again involved in the world of automobiles that we both cherished. This time we were swept away in our little universe as we picked the car up and drove home. He first insisted that I break it in and drive home, but I refused. I said, "Pipo, you know I loved the old car and didn't want to part with it, but you did."

So he took his keys out of his pocket and opened the door to sit behind the wheel as he flipped the ignition key. The engine started with no signs of any problems yet, and we were ready to embark as I looked over one last time out the window to our old 1976 Ford Granada parked in the lot. As we pulled away, I told

Pipo, "This new car is too small. It feels like you're trapped in a toy car."

He said, "Miguel, never mind that! I can't find the signal switch to make turns! I'm going to stop the car right here before we leave the lot and try to get to know where all the buttons are located, because I have no idea what's what or anything, Okay?"

I said, "Espera un Segundo (wait one second) and I'll step out of the car and go to your side and try to get us familiar with all these new control buttons while you stay behind the wheel for now, so you can remember things better."

Then he said, "Vamanos (Let's go!) Esta bien (Okay)." It took about twenty minutes using the manufacturer's owner's manual to fully embrace all of the controller's functions and locations. Nervously and apprehensively, Pipo and I finally departed the dealership on our way home. During our little seven-mile voyage home, I reiterated like a broken record that I did not like the car at all. This car was not stylish, plus it lacked the horsepower needed to get into the flow of the highway and possibly avert an accident in high-speed traffic. It was troublesome and notice-able to Pipo as he tried to accelerate after numerous traffic light stops with no kick. As we got closer to home, I kidded with him about everything you could think of why this car was not a good choice. But you know, there is something about driving a new car for the first time. Pipo was extra attentive on this ride and paid little attention to my discouraging remarks. It looked like he just wanted to get home as quickly as possible and put the car in the garage in one piece. And who could blame him? I also was extra careful and cognizant with my new T-Bird as I drove it home for the very first time. This approach was the norm, but what distinguished this from the others was going to take place shortly.

Even though we arrived safe and sound at our Landfill apart-ment home, this car was about to give Pipo, known for suffering terrible migraine headaches, his biggest one yet. He told me a couple of blocks away from home how glad he was to procure one of the vacant garages from our apartment's owner, Checky. The garage was about five feet away from our apartment's back entrance on Pulaski Street. You could not get any closer to our apartment even if you tried. It was just so perfect and very convenient for Pipo. No more worries of having this new car vandalized or stolen, as were the previous ones. However, this calmness soon turned to a train wreck as we approach the front grey wooden door of our garage. He stopped the car five feet away on top of the sidewalk to get out and open this big old door as I remained standing outside the car to make sure he didn't hit the right-side concrete wall as he went in. This garage was extremely narrow, so to get in and out you had to get as close as possible to the right side of the wall. He had about a foot of space left to wrestle himself out of the car. Apparently, he had it figured out, from what I saw him do on that particular first day of using the garage. What he did was lay these layers of cardboard alongside the wall earlier in the week in anticipation of this event, so when he exited the car, the door would be protected, and also his clothes, from getting any type of damage. I was flabbergasted when I saw Pipo hold his stomach in as he opened his door and slid out of the car. He then leaned against the cardboard-covered wall and slid out like a jet. He then quickly closed and locked the garage door while I was waiting for him near the small steps to our rear entrance to the Landfill apartment. All of a sudden he called me and said, "Miguel, come here and listen to the sound coming from inside the garage. Put your ears to the door and listen to what I hear."

I said, "I hear a sound like the car engine is on! Did you leave the keys inside the car and forget to turn off the car?"

He said, "No! I have the key with me!"

I said, "What about the second set of keys…do you have those, too?"

He said, "Look, I have both sets in my hand."

I said, "Maybe in these new cars you did not turn off the ignition switch all the way when you pulled out the keys."

He said, "This is strange. It has never happened to me in my lifetime before!"

"Pipo, there is always a first time for anything and everything, and this is just that."

At this point he reached for his garage keys in his pocket and opened the door to check out the noise. He said, "Miguel, come, do you hear the engine?"

I said, "Yeah, it is still on. Go and shut it off."

As I stood next to him while he sat inside the car trying to turn it off, he said, "Let me know when the sound is gone!"

"Okay, Pipo," I said. He then put the key in the ignition and turned it several times without shutting off the car. I said, "Pipo, what are you doing? The car is still on. Have you forgotten how to turn off the car?"

Obviously, I was being a wise ass with Pipo at his expense. This was the ultimate prize for me—to make Pipo happy in identifying the cause of the problem with this stubborn car. At this time, Pipo's blood was reaching its boiling point in more ways than one. First, I was irritating him by hacking away like I always do. This bizarre incident had no precedent as far as I was concerned, and like a salivating, hungry, insatiable dog waiting for his bone to eat, Pipo was my bone and I was determined to have lots of fun with him. After several times trying to shut it off, he gave up and asked me to give it a try myself, which I did, but after multiple attempts my results were no different than Pipo's. So I told him that something was very wrong with this car and if we didn't fix it soon, it was going to simply run out of gas.

With this caveat, Pipo told me, "Miguel get the car out of the garage right now! I don't know what to do with this car anymore!" After backing up the car, Pipo and I went to the front and tried to open up the hood, but it was so hot that we had to get a pair of gloves from the house to continue. I said, "Pipo, how many times did I tell you not to trade the old car? Now tell me. I warned you not to do it, and look what is happening. This car is a lemon! A big lemon and nothing more. You spent all of this money for what? You tell me. We cannot shut this car off."

Shaking his head desperately, he said, "For the life of me, how could I ever agree to purchase this junk of a car?" In Spanish several times he said, "Me cago en la leche! Me cago en la leche! Y me cago en la gran leche! Y en el dia que nazi!" (It literally means to shit on milk and not to have been born; It is an old saying in Spanish.) He said, "I am ruined! What am I going to do now?"

I said to Pipo, "We have to cut this engine off somehow. This car is going to blow up. It's too hot and the paint is going to melt if we don't act quickly. At this time we started to draw a crowd around us; most of them were from the neighborhood. We all could not figure out for the life of us this puzzle. One guy even suggested disconnecting the battery to cool off the engine and save gas. Another told Pipo to take it back to the dealership and get the car replaced immediately. In the mean time, I was conversing with a bunch of people about this mind-boggling fiasco. You could hear the whispering and the laughter in the background, but for Pipo it was no laughing matter. He had spent his hard-earned money and did not warrant any hindering from anybody.

At the apex of this event, I counted about fifteen people around us giving their opinions without a positive resolution. You know the old sayings about opinions? They are a dime a dozen and worthless. Well, that was so true in this case, because it made it worse for anyone to really take charge alone and just focus on getting the car fixed. Man, it was a circus environment, and Pipo was up to his ears in advice until a Spanish friend of his who is a mechanic stumbled in and saw Pipo downtrodden. He asked, "What's going on with all of this commotion with this '83 Escort?" We told him that it was Pipo's brand new car and it was driving *loco* (insane) because the engine was superhot and not able to turn off. He shook his head in disbelief and said, "These little cars are nothing but problems. I've had a few over at my shop with engine and transmission problems. They get too hot and they overheat very fast. You have to stay on top of them more so than the other cars with the six- and eight-cylinder engines. I wouldn't touch any of these cars for that same reason."

Upon hearing this bad news from his confidant in front of him, it reinforced my credibility with Pipo. He asked his friend his professional opinion on what to do with this car. He said, "Gerardo, take the car back and get a different model. That's what I'd do if I was you." In the meantime, he disconnected the battery to cool the motor for ten minutes. This action by Pipo's buddy turned out to be the magic bullet that shut down the engine after nearly two hours. He explained, for future reference, that these particular four-cylinder models tended to heat up higher than the typical eight cylinders and not to be alarmed if it happened again in the near future. "These fans were supposed to cool off the extra heat in the small engine, but your car did not respond to factory specifications, so have it checked out," he said.

The next day my father returned the car to the dealership to have the car put on a diagnostic machine. Come to find out, a wire was defective that ran from the motor to the fan. After the repairs my father kept the car for the sake of my mother, knowing that it was a true lemon. Two years later my father passed away. We kept the car in the family and it went to my brother. Two years later my brother called to say the motor ceased and asked what I wanted to do with it. My first impression was to keep the car in Pipo's memory, but I was so angry over the way the car was purchased, I told him to just sell it. Pipo and I proved to be right for not wanting to buy the lemon, but my mother had to keep up with the Joneses.

CHAPTER 33

Going to the Ballpark

What could be finer than going to a ball game with your father and sharing those fleeting, cherished moments together? Well, if there are any finer moments, I can't really think of them. There isn't any other place I want to be than at the ballpark eating a hot dog and watching my favorite team. It was a state of nirvana for a youngster like me back then, watching all of my heroes come alive in person while I was sitting next to Pipo.

Over the years my father took me to a number of games, but two games stand out above the rest. First, the excitement and anticipation of going to my very first game ever was a dream come true. The second was the return home of Tom Seaver, pitching against his former team, my New York Mets. However, on that night, I was fervently rooting for Tom Seaver to win and not my beloved Mets. It was the night of June 11, 1981, just one day before the lockout that canceled 713 games. This game was played on March 30, just a couple of months after President Ronald Reagan was shot and wounded just sixty-nine days into his presidency. And a couple of weeks later we were all injected with a national morale booster that lifted our nation's spirits on the very heels of the failed attempted assassination of Reagan. Eleven days later the first space shuttle, *Columbia*, blasted off into orbit. Not to be out done, the royal telecast of the wedding of Charles and Diana captivated a world audience and became front and center as the most popular program ever broadcast.

Unlike the first time, we took no mass transit and drank no Coke; I took my 78 T-Bird car and we both drank watered-down, high-priced beer, to my father's chagrin. Tom Seaver—my favorite, "the" player—pitched a great game in a 5–2 complete-game victory, which is not the norm in today's babying of pitchers and not letting them finish what they started. This game had no extra-inning drama like the first one, but it was just as sweet because Pipo and I were able to sit comfortably behind the Mets' third-base dugout together for most of the game. This vantage point was a godsend. It facilitated my picture-taking mission as the players came in and out of their dugout. It was the perfect close encounter of the third kind. I was so ecstatic, pointing out each player to Pipo and giving meaning to their statistics in layman's terms while he listened. He appeared this time more relaxed and less tired than the first time as he and took it all in. Besides my picture taking, I also videotaped this game, and you are able to see my hands reach over the dugout as Tom Seaver walked in. I have watched this last frame numerous times on my VCR over the years to remind me of the game with Pipo and now more so, because good old Shea Stadium was demolished and replaced by Citi Field in 2009. These historical structures in America at large are not preserved and treasured as they are in other parts of the world. This is unfortunate and shameful; hopefully this trend will stop soon, so future generations will benefit from the past firsthand and not by photos or video reels only.

During our trek to the stadium, I missed the Shea exit from the Van Wyck Expressway and ended up at Flushing Corona Park, where I first saw the magnificent Globe of the 1964 World's Fair years early. I drove around the park for about fifteen minutes before I found my way back to the stadium parking lot, but not before it left an unmistakeable, lasting impression, sharing time and space literally with Pipo, since this park was all about the future and the coming new technology encroaching on us. I had discovered an unyielding appetite, for some unknown reason, for planes. This hunger dates back to our sojourn in Mexico City in the late '60s when Pipo took the time to read to me stories about the coming of the jet age. They were feature in *Life, Look, Reader's Digest,* and other magazines with stunning photographs that came to life as he turned the pages. This on this trip and others were directly linked and manifested from my happy childhood experiences, when Pipo had the central role in shaping my well-being. This park will always have a living presence for me and my father because it traces the best times of my life.

I was big fan of America's number one pastime back then, and I don't think the word "big" was enough to really justify how devoted I was to this sport. I ate, drank, and slept nothing but baseball in those formative years. Pipo, on the other hand, had no knowledge of it and couldn't care less about baseball and my Mets. He was never any type of sports aficionado and spent very little time playing or even watching it on television. His favorite sports growing up in Spain were wrestling and bullfighting, and later on in Cuba and in America he became a boxing enthusiast.

However, I used to try to get him from time to time to play catch with me in the street or in the neighborhood parks. When we did play, I would throw the ball extremely hard to him just to get his reaction. It was so much fun for me watching Pipo constantly dropping balls, even the perfect chest-level ones that hit his glove dead center but still popped out. I think he was more concerned with getting hit in the face by these hard balls than anything else. He looked like he was more in a preventive mode of survival, which made for good theater for me, as well as my friends and family who were privy to this enclave of uncontrollable laughter and humor.

Over the years Pipo complained to me that I spent too much time glued to the television watching the Mets and not enough with schoolwork. He and my mother were correct; I lived and died with every pitch during the game telecasts. I would on most evenings run full speed home from the school playground, where I played basketball and other sports with my many friends, to catch the game as it began. The broadcast at the time was on WOR Channel 9 in the New York metropolitan area. It was my daily ritual during baseball season growing up with America's national pastime, as so many others did.

The year 1972 was full of unabashed, incredible firsts similar to my own. You had the Watergate break-in, Nixon's trip to China, his reelection landslide, the Munich Olympic tragedy, Apollo 17, the last manned lunar landing, and the debut of the TV show *M*A*S*H*. Not to equate or dismiss the importance and the magnitude of those historical events with my own, but for a young man devoted to following the Mets, it was not a stretch in my own mind. I was also very mindful about world current affairs, and I followed those critical events that shaped our world with a strong conviction of being an informed citizen. Despite the fact that I spent so many hours following not only baseball but other sports as well, this fixation, in retrospect, was definitely overplayed by me. It did stifle my educational development during those crucial years when I knew I had the potential to excel in the academy.

Well, after strong arming Pipo for a year or so to take my mother and me to a game, he finally decided to surprise me himself in the kitchen of our apartment at 94 Garden Street. He called me over and said, "Vamos aver la pelota tu y yo (We are going to the game, you and me)."

I said, "No tu esta jugando conmigo…no es verda (No, you are playing with me; it's not true)."

He said, "Miguel, si es verda preparate y dime que dia! (Mike, it is true, and be prepared and tell me the date)." Wow, I jumped for joy and grabbed him by the leg and would not let go for anything while my mother laughed and smiled at my happiness. A few minutes later I got up and gave him a big hug and kiss, and I rapidly went to the sports section in the *Newark Star-Ledger* in my room to look for the Mets home schedule. I decided the best date to go was Sunda,y May 7, 1972, for the game against the San Diego Padres. I quickly informed Pipo of my decision.

The night before the game, I was so excited I couldn't sleep at all. I woke up Pipo at 6:00 in the morning that day to get an early start for the 2:05 p.m. game. He said, "Go back to bed! It's too early, let me get more sleep."

"No, you don't understand. We have to be there early at the ballpark to get good tickets and watch batting practice. Plus, I have a better chance of catching a ball during batting practice than in the game. Also, you are able to get closer to the players and meet them as they line up signing autographs near the stand Pipo," I said.

Well, we finally left at 9 in the morning for the game after eating a big Spanish omelet prepared by my mother for breakfast. We took a taxi to Newark Penn Station, then we got on New Jersey Transit to New York Penn Station with a quick transfer at Times Square, then finally on the New York City Number 7 subway lines to Shea. As we approached the stadium, I was engulfed by the sheer magnitude and beauty of Shea Stadium as I looked from inside the train window on my immediate left. It was as if I saw an oasis appear out of nowhere in the middle of a crowded urban setting. I was so much in awe of what I was seeing, I kept pointing for Pipo to look at the stadium as the train slowly pulled into Shea Station. We both quickly ran down through a turnstile maze to the footprints of the stadium and looked for the box office to purchase two tickets for the game. I still have, after all these years, those original tickets from that game in excellent condition in my collection. None are more valuable than those because it was an unforgettable experience I shared deeply with my father. The purchase price on those tickets listed for $4.50 each in 1972. Today they have inflated to such a high level that the average fan could not afford to go to games like my generation was able to enjoy back then. "Wow" is definitely the operative word for how times have changed.

Well, to my surprise we were very fortunate to pick up field-level seating. I guess it was because we were the first ones in line that morning. Plus, it also gave me the opportunity to relish this magical structure and its surroundings a little longer; including the giant globe—the Unisphere across the horizon, a relic from the 1964 World's Fair—that immediately attracted my attention. Since we had nothing to do prior to the stadium opening, we just walked and mingled around with other diehard Mets fans outside of the stadium. It was a sea of orange and blue as the Mets fans proudly wore their team colors.

At first when I got there, I wanted also to buy a bunch of souvenirs, but in the end, I settled for a yearbook, a scorecard, and an official Mets cap. Not too shabby, if you ask me.

It was a dream come true for me to see all my heroes as we entered the ballpark, but none greater than my father.

I immediately ran to the stands to catch a glimpse of the field for the first time as Pipo trailed behind me. What I saw was right out of fairyland—the field was so pristine, certainly like no other field I have ever seen anywhere, especially in our local neighborhoods. We both stood up next to each other and just went bonkers admiring the sheer beauty of this park as the jets flew by above us in the clear, sunny, blue sky. The weather, thanks to God, was picture perfect on that day. It was a wonderful blessing from the beginning to the very end. When one of my heroes, Tommie Agee, hit a tremendous and climactic two-out, two-run, walk-off home run to deep left center field in the bottom of the tenth inning to beat the Padres by the score of 8–6, the place went berserk, with so much pandemonium and joy as we celebrated this sweet victory after trailing by six runs going into the bottom of the eight. It was just simply an amazing comeback by the Mets and a fitting ending to my first game ever in a big-league park. In retrospect, I give all the glory and kudos to our Lord and Savior for making it happen on his terms. I know he had everything to do with this split-second moment frozen in time with Pipo and me at a ballpark called Shea Stadium. This priceless memory has never left me one bit since that spring day, and I have continued to cherish it ever since. I will always be indebted to our Creator for making my dreams come to fruition in spectacular fashion with my father. That euphoria of watching my boyhood hero come through in the clutch in front of both of us was truly a gift preordained.

What I remember equally as much was our interaction with each other during the game with Pipo. Doing things like going to the concession stand and getting something to eat…there's nothing better than ballpark hot dogs; they taste so good. I can't explain why, but they do, along with some fries and a Coke. I also was trying to explain and convey to Pipo the rules and the markings on the field—a difficult task, but when you are eating the best hot dogs in the world, it is not that hard to do.

One pertinent question that he asked me that was paramount for him to know was, when is the game over? I said, "You see that big scoreboard behind the fence on right center field with numbers from one to nine on it?"

He said, "Where? I don't see anything!"

I said, "Pipo just look to the very top of the scoreboard! Do you see now?"

He said, "Yes, I see it now!"

"Well, the game ends when all the boxes underneath one to nine are completely full, either with zeros or other numbers in them. Do you understand?"

He said, "Yes, now I understand…well, it is not as simple as wrestling or bullfighting, when you really know when the game is over for good!" He then gave me a bit of a good-humored chuckle when he commented that his favorite sports did not have the action of baseball, which I adamantly admitted was true. However, the underlying point was crystal clear to me: I had the same lack of knowledge in those sports as he did with baseball. My explanation was not complete, and I omitted key information that came back to roost when Pipo ask me this revealing question: "You said the game is over after all nine innings are full; is that correct?"

I said, "Yes!"

"Then why is the game not over now, even though all nine innings are full?" he said.

I quickly replied, "That's because the teams have the same score and it has to go to extra innings until one teams has more runs than the other. And since the Mets are the home team, they have a better chance to win the game if the Padres fail to score a run in the top of the tenth, because the Mets bat last. You got it now?"

He said, are you telling me that it is not over until someone scores a run, and if nobody does, it's not over until is over?"

"Yes, Pipo, that is what I'm saying!"

"Well, we could be here for a long time," he said. I think Pipo was getting a little tired and wanted to depart for home, and who could really fault him for that? Tommie Agee's home run was music to my father's and my ears for different reasons. When he hit it, everyone got up from his or her seat and started screaming, "Mets win! Mets win!" Pipo grabbed me by the arm and said, "Miguel, what happened?" I said, "The game is over, Pipo!" Upon hearing this news he started to clap, jump, and mimic the crowd with a standing ovation himself because it was finally over "for good," as Pipo would say about his childhood sports. And off we went.

CHAPTER 34

At the Jersey Shore

"What are you doing this weekend?"
"Well, I'm going down to the shore!"
If you were from the New York metropolitan area, this lingo was the common vernacular used to describe a fun time at the Jersey beaches. It was no different for our family to escape the city heat for a day or a weekend stay just to cool off.

The New Jersey coastline consists of 125 mile of beaches, beginning with Sandy Hook and ending with historic Cape May. In between these two end points, you had great beaches like Long Branch, also famous for the world's largest haunted mansion attraction, a place Pipo and I visited and were scared out of our socks in doing so as we went along in this maze of darkness and weird howling sounds. I grabbed on to him tightly from behind throughout this teeth-chattering time as a young boy, and I survived with my hero. Years later, I came here many times with friends and repeated this adventure numerous with much courage and lived another day to tell about it. On one of these visits, I purchased an official black T-shirt from the mansion that said, "I Survived the Haunted House in Long Branch."

The crazy thing about this T-shirt was that I received so many compliments on it back home in Newark. I remember one particular late Sunday evening hanging out with friends in front of Tony's Pizzeria on Pacific Street when they decided to go to a hot club called Fountain Casino. It was a club owned by the same man that owned Tony's Pizzeria, our hanging-out core spot for the Pacific Street boys. Since I had no intention of going anywhere that night, I was dressed very casual with my Haunted Mansion shirt and jeans. After much arm pulling by my buddies, I decided to go with them, leaving behind my father's 1976 Ford Granada in the opposite empty lot and hoping it would be there upon my return home. Earlier that evening, I had persuaded Pipo to switch cars with me because I did not want to take a chance with my Thunderbird getting vandalized or stolen, since it was an attention getter. Nevertheless, to get into the club I was given a black leather jacket by my buddies to pass the entrance dress code, which I did. Once inside, I loosened up and opened my jacket as wide as possible, when suddenly this cute girl named Josie spotted me near the dance floor and opened my jacket even wider to see what was underneath. As she opened my jacket with a beautiful smile, she said, "Nice shirt," and the rest is history. I grabbed her hand innocently and everything clicked right after that moment. She became my girlfriend by the end of that night, but not before I watched her dance from afar on the dance floor. Man, she was by far the best dancer I saw. She was just magic on the dance floor while all of my friends watched in envy. At closing time I told Josie that my friends had left me behind and I needed to get home to Newark. This innocent lie to her was just a genuine manifestation of how much I liked her and wanted to be with her a little longer. And apparently she had the same proclivities and feelings I had for her. She convinced her best friend to drive me all the way to Newark, while en route I got a couple of nice, sexy, first smooches from her. When we eventually arrived, I was so relieved to see Pipo's car still in one piece in the lot. I took a huge chance with Pipo's car, and I was fortunate to dodge a real bullet and not have it stolen because of my negligence. Oh, I was able to convince Josie to let me drive her back home to Perth Amboy, New Jersey, but not before I extended our time together a little longer by parking by the waterfront one block away from her house at her request. It was picturesque as the early morning sun rose, reflecting the calm water of the bay on that Christmas Eve day in 1979. We both watched and cuddled up to keep us warm, as if the world was standing still for us only—without any worries or cares to think of. How good it is to be young and innocent! Amen to that!

Well, I got home at 11:00 a.m. that day, and believe me, I received an earfull from Pipo and my mother for not calling and letting them know my whereabouts, since I never had stayed out all night before.

That shirt was my lucky charm. I wore it proudly until it fell apart in the late '80s. It will be forever linked to Pipo, his car, and Josie and me extending the boundaries of youth, just like my father had done in his own life.

Unfortunately, a massive fire occurred on June 8, 1987, destroying the entire pier and boardwalk. But it has not destroyed my fond memories of the Old Long Branch every time I visit the new and rebuilt upscale Long Branch, with its fancy décor, shops, restaurants, and bars. I hope in the future they will bring back some of the old charm that made this place so much fun for the young and old alike. A good starting point would be to bring back the mansion. Is anybody listening out there? One last nugget before I forget. Its true how things come in a full circle, and this is no more apparent than the time, years later, that Pipo, Josie, and I were standing outside the mansion together and I was thinking how it all started with Pipo and that shirt and my girlfriend. And, yes, it is only fitting, naturally, that Josie and I went inside the mansion together in the summer of 1980 while Pipo and my family remained outside walking on the pier.

Not to be outdone by Long Branch was Asbury Park, with its prominent, golden history of being the premiere vacation destination in America years earlier, and also famous for its native son Bruce Springsteen performing at the Stone Pony club. All these area beaches and other cities were vying with Atlantic City and the Wildwoods to be the premiere place to go and be seen by the rich and famous in there heydays, similar to what South Beach is today in Florida. We went to those places sparingly because of the longer travel time to get there. However, our favorite spot was going to Seaside Heights; it was only about seventy-five miles away from Newark. The best way to get there was to take the Garden State Parkway to exit 82 and drive about eight additional miles to cross an old wooden drawbridge that connected the island to Toms River over the Barnegat Bay. This had nightmare underpinnings because the bridge had only two lanes, one each way. This created traffic backups for miles on end, especially coming back home, when it was double the delays; it always seemed like everybody was trying to leave at the same time. You could see from the distance at the elevated apex part of the bridge that cars, one after another, were barely moving, and you knew by just watching the scene it was going to be a long, long wait till we got there ourselves. This bridge was also very noisy and scary as you passed by it, and you could see the mood in the car become very quiet as we climbed up toward the top of the bridge. Then, my brother would begin making jokes about how the bridge was going to come down, and as we passed by, we would hear the wood underneath squeaking and turning and ready to split open as the ocean lay below. My mother hated this part of the trip so much that my father had to control her and cover her eyes on just about every passage. Honestly, even as young boy, I was also concern as I looked down to the very long drop down to the water. But the good news was they were building a new span next to this old bridge, and it opened in 1972 to finally end this bottleneck. The old bridge was rebuilt and it open up again in 1976 and now serves as the northbound route to the Toms River, while the new bridge is the southbound span that connects to Seaside Heights.

Having tackled the bridge problem once and for all, and putting it behind us, we faced an even more daunting challenge of major traffic jams on the New Jersey Parkway. The traffic delays were of legendary magnitude and lasted for several hours of sitting in traffic with the engine completely off to save fuel and prevent overheating. As you crawled by in traffic, you saw many vehicles broken down or abandoned on the side of the road. The two culprits were cars just running out of gas and overheating. This compounded the primary problems of sheer volume on the roads, accidents, and—my brother's biggest grievance, along with many millions of driver and nondrivers alike—the dreaded and despised tolls and collecting booths. This was the most idiotic way of collecting money you can ever imagine on one of the most congested highway in the country. Every fifteen to twenty miles or so of driving, you had to slow down and pay a quarter while you waited and waited for the cars in front of you to drop their quarters properly inside the electronic basket. And God forbid if you missed, because the New Jersey State Police would be waiting for you to pull you over and ticket you. This created at times a mess as people got out of their cars and looked high and low for their rolling quarters because they did not have any others and did not want to pay a fine for nonpayment. I'm happy to report this circus atmosphere regarding the toll booth has ended; it was finally put to rest in the early 2000s. Good riddance!

In the late '60s and early '70s, on our many trips to Seaside, my brother always complained vigorously to us in the car concerning the weather and why it always seemed to rain when the Apollo program mission was in space and bringing back contaminants from the lunar landing, affecting the earth's atmosphere with days of rain ruining the summer. Whether this was true or not, it was sure raining a lot when those babies were up there doing their thing. He was so adamant about his belief that he had Pipo and the rest of us believing there was a true, direct, cause-and-effect link between the two.

At Seaside, my mother and aunt Genoveva always made sure that we loaded up the car with plenty of good, homemade Spanish food. aunt Genoveva was a beloved person whom we all loved beyond any words that could ever attempt to show or describe our adoring affections. She was absolutely endearing to my brother and me growing up, as well as to my mother, who she raised when her mother died. She was also a charismatic person who attracted attention and had a large network of family and friends, similar to Pipo. Having said that, she was also a fabulous cook, and everyone who came to our home for the holidays and special days was treated to fine cuisine. She also owned her own restaurants in Spain and in Cuba, so she knew her craft very well, because people always came back for more at her eateries. She spoiled my brother and me big time with loving care, food, and with the finest hard-to-find toys in Cuba during the revolution. One of the best times was that when it was time to eat, she would call us by shouting our names and giving us the hand signal. But even though I enjoyed the ocean a lot, good food ruled the day—any day, for the matter; it never took long to convince us otherwise.

The trips to the beach were a direct association with those same good times I had with Pipo from my earliest recollections of being born in Cuba. In Seaside, I played many hours in the water with Pipo at his urging. He normally took it upon himself to go in first most of the time in the morning and spend about two hours in the ocean with me. Unlike Cuba's warm waters, which are so clear that you can see all the way down to your feet, the water at Seaside was cold and it ws hard to see beyond a couple of inches down from your leg. At first dip, the body's natural defense mechanism is to self-protect by shivering. The Jersey water gives you this shocking, chilling effect as you enter it. When I saw Pipo in the water knee high, I quickly ran after him and shouted and said, "Entra! Entra! Entra en el agua! (Go in! Go in! Go in the water)." He looked at me as other swimmers jumped in hard and splashed ice-cold water on his back.

I really enjoyed the waves with Pipo. He would fortified himself solidly with his feet buried in the sand as the waves unleashed their force against him. I then would do my best to knock him down by grabbing his feet so he could fall and I could jump on top of him. He would try to push me away constantly because he knew my tricks. The best time was after we all ate and everyone fell asleep soundly except me. And who could blame them? The food was delicious and the large proportions were exuberant and filling. My favorite was the Spanish omelet with potatoes and chorizos (sausage); the steaks and sandwiches of Serrano ham and cheese were also delicious.

When I got older, I too succumbed to sleep underneath the Jersey sun. But as kid it was only natural that I wanted to keep on playing; I was not tired and needed no sleep in the afternoon, especially at the beach. As my father slept, I kept digging next to him a hole in the sand until he rolled over and went in tho hole, which was then full of water. Other times I just covered his whole body with sand and he couldn't get out without help from my mother or brother. In the afternoon Pipo and I stayed in the water for hours until my chicken mother finally came in and joined us in about three feet of water. These family gatherings in the summer months at the Jersey Shore over the years with Pipo and my family were full of pleasure and activities, whether we were in the water playing a trick on Pipo or walking on the boardwalk and stopping for some soft ice cream while we sat on the benches, people watching. It was a feeling of being grateful to God in my own head, taking it all in, and knowing that times move forward and that our voyage is short and we would be coming in to dock soon, so lean back and enjoy it.

As I got older, I still played with Pipo in the water, and I kept splashing him with the ocean's cold water no matter how old I was. This silliness has never left me. Sharing those enduring times with Pipo in the water was fantastic. And speaking about fantastic, Pipo often took me on those wild rides in the amusement park section on both ends of the Seaside piers. He was not intimidated or hesitant about getting on any of those speedy rides to please me. As a matter of fact, he used to welcome them, for some reason. Some of those rides went over the ocean as they spun, spun, and spun before they came back over the pier. After these exhilarating rides, my mother and I often would stop and get a bite to eat with Pipo. I loved boardwalk shore food. My favorite was Italian sausages with onions and peppers, cheese steak, and pizza, and when I got older I shared with Pipo beers instead of a Pepsi, since Pepsi was the official soft drink for many years until it was replaced by RC Cola. We also played games on the boardwalk, and Pipo did much better than me, winning prizes, including a figurine of my favorite superhero, Batman.

My brother accompanied us on many of these trips even after he got married, with his first wife, Maria Elena, and his daughter, Barbara, and his son, Gerry, as well as his in-laws on some of these trips with us. However, in the later years, it was me doing the driving and getting frustrated on the Garden State Parkway, just like my brother and Pipo did back then.

Years have passed, but the spirit of Pipo lives, and his enduring persona, even with no English to speak of, was constantly able to draw people to him no matter what setting it was. This was no more obvious to me than in the sixteen years of going down to the Jersey Shore with him. This innate gift, given to him by our precious and loving God, was not only a gift to me but to those who met him as well. Even my ex-girlfriend Josie has confided in me many times how she loved my father and how much she misses him. I shared the same sentiments with her, in that her own father, Anthony Santana, became like a second father to me after the passing of Pipo. I spent numerous hours with him in dealing with my great loss. He was wonderful, simple, humble, and cut from the same cloth as my own father. He also left a profound legacy of devotions to public service. This is a fruitful reminder to us all that a humble, good, simple person is something we all should strive to be. This universality is the ultimate—to touch someone's life and make a real difference is the ultimate purpose of existence. In my own journey, the torch is lit up and the flame of what I learned from Pipo's wisdom will never be extinguished. I have emulated him to change the lives of others for the better.

CHAPTER 35

Dancing and Poetry

My father, Pipo, was a happy man who loved to party and have a good time doing so. His favorite pastime, among his arsenal of choices, was dancing; it was his true passion, hobby, and favorite activity to do, bar none. He picked up this passion first while growing up in his birthplace of Valle De Las Casas Spain and in the surrounding villages. After many long days of hard manual labor helping his parents and siblings at the farm, he would go to local festivals in a cascade fashion to escape that world for a short time while he learned to improve his dancing skills. After leaving home and joining the military, he was able to polish his dancing even further. The port city of Ferrol, where he was stationed, was known as a party town with many dance halls to cater to the large number of enlisted personnel. He loved this atmosphere of beautiful ladies who loved to dance just like he did. Plus, his former naval friends who were great dancers themselves were still around and living there after their military days were over. He also owned a bar in this energetic city, where people came in from all over for a few drinks and some conversation before going dancing. Often they would drag Pipo with them to the clubs for a night of fun.

This zest for life continued even more so when he immigrated to Cuba. He suddenly fell in love with Cuba's upbeat sound, which contained a unique African twist from this gorgeous Caribbean island paradise. However, by this time his dancing was more confined to family events and social gatherings, as he married and had two kids. In Cuba it was more of the same. My father knew the dances from both Spain and Cuba quite well, as he practiced them all. However, his favorites were *el paso doble*, the Argentine tango, and *danzon*, sprinkled with some sizzling Spanish poetry to top it off. The danzon is one of my personal favorites, along with *el son*, because it captures brilliantly the best that Cuba has to offer in its music, people, and culture, which also includes numerous great dances like the congo, bolero, Cuban salsa, mambo, rumba, timba, and others to enjoy.

He also loved to dance on top of a table with a long neck beer bottle placed in the center as he shuffle his feet back and forth in a stomping sound and motion, similar to a flamenco dancer, without hitting the bottle. This dance was a crowd pleaser that family and friends often requested Pipo to perform. And perform he did, with his lightning-speed footwork that blurred the bottle while he dazzled all of us skillfully until he dismounted by jumping to the floor. Then, five seconds later, he would again rattle the crowd, who thought the dance was over, by jumping back onto the table for a twenty-second finale with an even faster foot and hand speed than before, finally landing again on the floor to the charged applause of all us. He often tweaked this dance to make it fresh each and every time he was asked to dance it.

El paso doble dance mimics the sound, suspense, and action of a Spanish bullfight. It has an element of intense, heartfelt emotions of life and death as it unfolds and is beautiful to watch.

The Argentine tango, on the other hand, originated from the ordinary man in the *barrios* (inner city) perspective of hard times into a seductive and romantic dance. Danzon is a very elegant Cuban dance and an important part in Cuba's rich musical history up to the present day.

Pipo was also inspired by Spanish poetry big time. It gave him an equal, alternative element to complement his love for dancing. His verses were powerfully delivered, full of heartfelt emotions that made people weep in happiness as they both together uncovered their most hidden feelings. These sharing snapshots of his humanity and vulnerability were what made Pipo so much admired by everyone who met him.

While Pipo did love to dance, he seldom ever participated in any dance contest or any runoff, formally or informally. He said, "Dancing is a celebration and is not supposed to be work; we have plenty of work already, so why add more? I come here to celebrate with friends and new acquaintances, not to compete with them in any manner. I couldn't care less about that kind of stuff. I come to these social gatherings to dance and only dance, with no another agenda whatsoever. I live for the moment and enjoying it to the fullest." He often commented to me on the importance of balancing life and work appropriately. In America, life and work are very much unbalanced, and Pipo got caught in this insane web himself in his later years by working so many hours to make ends meet. This mentality of "live to work," instead of "work to live," in America must be changed for the betterment of our family, society, and our country. Even though the United States is the best country on the planet, it has lots of areas where it needs many improvements. A good start would be to mandate an employer to give every employee four weeks of vacation per year, similar to what Europe has at the present time. Since Pipo worked so many hours in America, it deprived me of the golden opportunity to spend more time with him and learn so many more things in life, including dancing. This is an incredible loss for me, as well as for others who shared my frustrations as I look back to those days and think of what could have been, with that type of question always lurking in my mind. In the long run, for America to flourish once again, we have to go back to the family value tree approach of providing a sustainable living wage to all

Americans as we have done in the past and stop the insanity of couples working four combined jobs just to pay the bills.

In my childhood years in Cuba, our homes in Jobabo and, to a lesser extent, our last one in Victoria De Las Tunas were pack to the hilt with family and friends from the neighborhoods that came to celebrate with us many times during the year. During this time, I caught a few glimpses of Pipo strutting his passion on the dance floor. I would watch curiously from afar and often saw his signature smile as he popped in and out of the dancing area to go greet our guests. Our parties were legendary in scope in our town, and everyone knew about them. For the most part we welcomed as many as we could fit unless someone started to look for trouble. That incredible Cuban sound, together with the traditional roasted pork that produces a watering-mouth effect in people, was difficult to rest for any length of time. This aroma tended to circulate around our entire home before it slipped out into the streets, adding more fuel to our parties. This after-effect culminated in forming these enclaves of people gathering outside our home, dancing in the street and becoming an extension of our festive party themselves. What made this fall-out always so pleasant, with no signs of any disturbance ever, was that Pipo would often come out of the house and invite them to come in for as much food and as many beers as they wanted. Since Pipo owned a spirits distribution company, he never worried about running out of alcohol at his parties any time soon. Most of these people who were African Cubans respected my father so much that they invited him and our family to their parties in the countryside for a day or two of relaxation, good food, and Afro Cuban music, with a beautiful backdrop of palm trees underneath the breathless Cuban blue sky that I still vividly remember as if it were yesterday. In reality, it was not so new for him after all; music and dancing were always fertile ground for him. Home is a transient state that is to be shared with loved one, not owned in any physical sense of the word. It is universal in our human existence, and we should spend more time embracing it. But we don't, and that's too bad! Pipo had it right all along.

It was awesome to get away back then in those remote places and see my father in this new, unspoiled natural terrain. These frequent getaway excursions were what the doctor, if you will, prescribed in Cuba to recharge his battery for more fun times ahead in the countryside and upon coming home for him and the family. It did an amazing job replenishing the body, mind, and spirit with even higher vigor—unless you got poison ivy, which my mother and I did once, and that was not fun as we itched and scratched ourselves to more pain. On the other hand, Pipo was literally immune to it and never came down with it. I guess it had a lot to do with my mother and me running away from the party and exploring the field while Pipo was reciting poetry and dancing. Plus, during the afternoon he slept in a hammock underneath two palm trees, sucking in the tropical breeze. Again, I have to hand it to Pipo for his uncommon common sense, which my mother and I surely lacked.

In Mexico City I witnessed Pipo do amazing things during our times in the refugee mansion, provided to Cubans by a wealthy woman. His innate ability to make new friends was a godsend when we celebrated Noche Buena (Christmas Eve) and New Year's. During our time in that city I always accompanied Pipo everywhere he went, and I was constantly amazed at how often he was offered a job by the store vendors, but he could not accept any jobs because the Mexican government prohibited it. And when it came time for Pipo to pay, they did take not his money, no matter what Pipo said. This was never more clear than our holiday celebration in the refugee mansion, when his new friends came in unexpectedly loaded with their supplies so we could enjoy the holiday spirit with a big celebration. We had more than enough of all types of food and beverages to ring in the festivities, just as if we had never left Cuba. We also had a traditional roasted pig being cooked slowly and cases of Corona beer, all provided by them since we had no money to speak of. The most memorable was the bash itself and Pipo dancing non-stop with this refugee community and the locals. There had to be over four hundred people in the house and in the spacious green garden and this tall tree in the center of the front yard. We celebrated like the Rockefellers. They were the most memorable two parties I ever saw, and only a week apart from each other. What made them even better was that we were a community with no motherland to speak of anymore, and we really rallied behind each other with immeasurable affection in a time of uncertainty.

This uncertainty was absent for me to a large extent because Pipo was always on my side; even at this event he stopped dancing, and quickly came running toward me from the dance floor to cheer me on as I hit the piñata and broke it in two. I then suddenly dove to a crowded floor full of kids and adults to get candies, toys, and whatever was inside this stuffed animal. I picked up some lollipops and gave one to my hero, and he unwrapped it and put it in his mouth and went back to the dance floor as I looked at him from a distance, enjoying himself again.

In America Pipo and my mother still celebrated many holidays and special events with family and friends from the old country; these parties were more modest in scope than those in the past but were never absent. Sometimes we traveled to their homes, or other times they took place at churches, banquet halls, or on trips. My father's passion was contagious and it was fun to be near him. I remember a few trips that I tagged along with them that are hard to forget. On our trip to Spain in 1976, we took a Madrid-at-night tour of the city that made multiple stops at restaurants, shops, and shows. At one particular show in a fancy cabaret, he was ready to go up on the stage and recite a poem in front of about six hundred people. But my mother and I talked him out of it. It was more me than my mother, because I grabbed his arm and would not let go. I did not want to get embarrassed, for some stupid, selfish reason I had. I think it was just being a teenager and the senseless proclivities that come with it. Anyhow, by the time he broke loose from me, someone else beat him to the stage. But the night was still young!

The next and final stop was a flamenco show in a small, intimate setting which was very crowded because of people from the tour. To my surprise, we sat in the very front, which I hated. I did not want to be in a position where I would be dragged to the stage and make a fool out of myself. I remained cognizant of this possibility during the duration of the sultry performance. My worst fear came to fruition when they asked for volunteers to come and join them up on stage for a performance. While I lowered myself on the seat, Pipo got up and off he went with them. I lowered myself even lower as Pipo stood between these two female dancers while the male dancer stood near the guitarist and the others in the group. Well, I knew my father was a great dancer in his own right, but he was sixty-seven years old by then and I thought he was too old. The female dancers began first by doing a solo and a duet as the male dancer came in and out of the group. As he came in and out, my father replaced him, improvising the male dancer's previous moves with his own, to the delight of everyone watching him as they clapped and stomped their feet in a constant, unified beat as they (and I) cheered him on with applause and singing. This went on for about fifteen minutes to the delight of the professional performers themselves and those of us who watched him, like so many people previously who fell in love with his humble spirit inside, not his skills as a dancer. He was past his prime but nevertheless his brittle bones could not deny him a great time in his beloved mother country of Spain one more time. And it showed profusely up on stage, just like it showed in his younger days in celebration of life.

In our vacations in Spain, Pipo took advantage of the opportunity to get together with old friends and rekindle those fond memories by dancing, mostly with my mother, in the exact villages where he once danced, and this was heartwarming to me to watch.

Another trip was to Niagara Falls in Canada, where we went on a tour with our Immaculate Heart of Mary Church in Newark in 1977. What I regretted was not going in the same bus with Pipo and my mother at that time. This was because, unbeknownst to me at that time, one of my best friends, Frank, was going on this same trip with us and I wanted to be in the same bus with him for two main reasons: first, on the bus my parents boarded there were much older people, while the bus with Frank was younger, which I thought was more fun for the long travel ahead; and second, it was full of cases of Michelob beer, as Frank's father, an older brother, and some friends were ready to party big time along with my best friend and me. After a big stink with my parents, I threatened them with not going to Canada. Reluctantly, they caved in and agreed to let me ride with Frank and his parents.

Many people stopped me cold when we returned home to tell me how animated and wonderful my father was on the bus ride. They played all types of games in the bus. One of the games was Pipo running down the aisle, holding his pants up and baring his white chicken legs while everyone tried to pinch him if he got the answer wrong on a quiz. Other times he began singing familiar songs as others feverishly joined him in the singing. He also told great stories and recited many moving Spanish poetic verses from the front of the bus using a mike as the bus rolled on. It was Pipo at his best, making the ride seem a lot shorter than it was. It captured the hearts of young and old who witnessed it.

The only time I saw Pipo on this trip was at the old 747 Club and hotel across from the Buffalo airport, where we stopped for breakfast but instead slept in for the night because of the seven hours' delay we encounter when our bus was got lost and returned to Elizabeth, New Jersey, to connect to the other bus. This created a furor on our bus, with Frank's father and others threatening to go home after stepping out of the bus and coming to the hard realization that they were still in New Jersey, half drunk and very tired. We thought 100 percent we were in Canada but ended up just five miles away from where we left. What type of driver would get lost that long without the foggiest idea where in the world he was driving to? This was their simple question put to the driver and the lady in charged of the trip. She said, "The driver is not from this region of the country and has very limited experienced following directions clearly in pitch darkness." What a crazy, unexpected twist to this traveling circus. Her frugal remarks almost caused a riot to break out while waiting on Elizabeth Avenue for the lost bus to arrive so both buses could depart together without getting lost a second time. Well, cooler heads did prevail an hour later as the lost bus and my parents finally arrived and met with us outside before departing again—but not before a few penetrating jokes and some sarcasm, such as "we could've flown to Cuba and come back in less time,: were heard out loud in the middle of the crowd. These types of outbursts threatened to cancel the trip altogether. My father then explained to all of us what had happened from the driver's perspective, including Frank's father, who was the most vocal in his grievances.

Anyway, we left immediately after eating breakfast to visit the Canadian falls, Space Needle Tower, wax museum, flower garden, and others. I was walking around like a zombie without any sleep and wet because of the mist of the falls. I could not wait to get back to the hotel and go to sleep. Upon getting back to the hotel, we had a big dinner in the dining hall with everyone, concluding with a live band playing Latin music into the early morning hours. In the hotel room, I told my parents while they were changing clothes to attend the party, "I'm not moving from this bed and going anywhere tonight."

Pipo then shook his head and said, "You are eighteen years old and you are tired? I'm almost four times your age and I'm not tired. I'm looking forward to all of it. Come on, let's go! Your friend Frank, his brother, plus his girlfriend is going to be there asking why aren't you there!" He almost change my mind, then moments later, after my parents left for the party, I heard Frank knocking on the door hard, loudly calling my name to open the door, but I resisted and ignored him, then fell asleep. The next day, I found out how much fun every body had at the party, and that Pipo was again a marathoner on the dance floor with my mother and friends. Plus, he told great stories and recited poetry in between sets.

On our first trip to Spain, we visited many bookstores looking for a special book that he was not able to find in America or any other place previously. He also had written to family members in Spain in the past to have them try to locate this much-sought-after book without any luck or success in finding it. However, things were about to change for the better. In Madrid, the capital city of Spain and the epicenter of Spanish culture for centuries, if you needed to find anything related to Spanish, you were in the right place to find it. And find it we did, in a bookstore that catered to history and language, located in an older part of Madrid. This find was music to my father's ears. His eyes lit up like a Christmas tree when the store owner gave the book to him. Needless to say, he purchased it for 150 pesetas (before the Euro currency was in place). Finally, Pipo had found his beloved treasure, this little paperback book that contained eight hundred pages of nothing but the best Spanish poetry in history, called *Las Mil Mejores Poesias De la Lengua Castellana*, third edition (*The One Thousand Best Poems from the Castillean Language*). This anthology is a must read for anyone who loves the Spanish language and its inner beauty.

My father carried this book all over with him, throughout our initial trip to Spain, and it never left his sight. It came in handy, especially on long train rides. He often read before he retired for the evening.

Today, as I look at and read it, I can't help but notice so many folded-top-corner pages, serving as bookmarks for Pipo's favorite poems. It also is extra special knowing I'm touching those exact pages with my fingers that my beloved hero, Pipo, once did. This was mind boggling for me because I saw him spend so much time reading and rejoicing with this book now in front of me. It's like I could see him reappear in front of my eyes and tell me, "I'm here near you, don't worry about anything. I'll take care of everything just like before." This strong feeling is very powerful and it comes to light whenever I grab this book of his that he cared about so much.

I had my former wife, Virginia, read to me before going to sleep some of his favorite poems from the book, and I tell you I was emotionally connected to him right there. I did not want her to ever stop, but she succumbed each time; she couldn't keep her eyes open anymore and succumbed to sleep.

My father's passion for poetry has certainly imparted a curiosity over the years in my own manifestation of being pulled to poetry without ever realizing the influence he had on me. This was no more evident than when I enrolled in college and fell in love with the world of literature, history, philosophy, theology, etc. In addition, I was drawn to the folk music of the 1960s and to those songwriters who were poets first but who happened also to be musicians. But it did not stop there; I would go to other venues of interest to fill my needs. These included book signing, lectures, television, radio, and today the Internet, a one-stop shop, if you will, to keep you well fed for a lifetime.

Below are two of Pipo's favorite bookmarked poems from the book *Las Mil Mejores Poesias De la Lengua Castellana,* third edition. I asked my mother, Maria, to pick only a couple of poems among the many that best captured his aura and spirit. The poems below are in Spanish on purpose to prevent and preserve the essence of the original meaning, which would be lost in an English translation.

Author: Anonimo (Anonymous)

(Probablemente de Santa Teresa de Jesus
Soneto a Jesus crucificado

No me mueve, mi Dios, para quererte
el cieloque me tienes prometido,
ni me mueve el infierno tan temido
para dejar pore eso de ofenderte.
Tu me mueves, Senor, mueveme el verte
clavado en una cruz y escarnecido,
mueveme ver tu cuerpo tan erido,
mueveme tu afrentas y tu muerte.
Mueveme, en fin, tu amor, y en tal manera,
que aunque no hubiera cielo. Yo te amara,
y aunque no hubiera infierno, te temiera
No me tienes que dar porque te quiera,
pues aunque lo que espero no esperara,
lo mismo te quiero te quisiera.

Author: Jose Marti
(1853–1895)

"Cultivo la rosa blanca…."

Cultivo la rosa blanca,
en mayo como en enero,
para el amigo sincero
que me da su mano franca.
Y para el cruel que arranca
el Corazon con que vivo,
cardo ni ortiga cultivo;
cultivo la rosa blanca.

CHAPTER 36

Leaving the Corner/Konner Laundromat

The corner Laundromat was a stone's throw away from the back window of our Landfill apartment on the corner of Pulaski and Elm Street. Pipo looked after this business establishment from 1978 to 1985 for three different owners during this span, as if he owned it himself. In the beginning, he would just open and close the Laundromat for a fellow Spaniard in exchanged for free open parking spots for our three cars behind the building. This arrangement continued for a couple of years afterward until the second owner asked him if he was able to work about thirty hours a week, plus continue to open and close the shop, like before. He immediately said yes and accepted this expanded position gladly, without any hesitation whatsoever. This was the perfect platform for Pipo because he was a people person who brought out the best in them, which resulted in higher volume and more profits. In addition, regular users tended to take better care of the machines out of respect for my father. They also provided a watchful eye in Pipo's absence, preventing random vandalism or loitering by hooligans who subscribed to the seek-and-destroy mentality very prevalent in those days. These acts were the norm by a minority few, but created much havoc in property damage if the building was left unattended for a relatively short amount of time; it also decreased the quality of life due to unfettered intimidation, which cannot be tolerated by any business if it is going to remain solvent in the future. This establishment was running on all cylinders without skipping a single beat, thanks to Pipo at the wheel. This wheel I'm referring to was his nurturing and helping people help themselves by providing a secondary, unsanctioned place to come together. This unintended cultivation by Pipo was similar to a barber shop where people come in not just for a haircut, but also to socialize. It was a meeting place to unwind and relax in good company and engage in protracted, enjoyable conversations. This atmosphere was so conducive that the owners also stopped by after work and just hung out to shoot the breeze with everyone, past closing time.

Pipo was in his natural environment at this establishment in his later years in life. It was also therapeutic because it kept him very busy and constantly connected to people. This distraction served him quite well emotionally, and secondly he felt productive, earning a weekly paycheck to do with as he pleased. He loved playing the state lottery Pick 3s and Pick 4s, especially when he won. Unfortunately, he never won a substantial amount of money to travel the world in his leisure time. What he tried to do was to fight off my mother's insatiable wishes that he spend his small winnings on her, without any prolonged success in achieving that goal. My mother also did not like the fact that he was spending too much time there and constantly nagged him to come home. This place was my father's only escape that he had left, which my mother failed to realize. This was evident to me because more often than not, when I came home after high school, I would stop by the Laundromat and talk to Pipo and help out him with some lifting and trouble shooting. I just had to stop by and check out how he was doing as much as I could. At times, he'd ask me to stay in the shop while he went to pick up my mother at work in Port Newark. During this one-hour stay, I noticed how often customers would tell me how much I looked like my father and how nice a gentleman he was. These were the words I kept hearing day in and day out in. Man, I had big shoes to fill, which I knew too well from previous experiences. This man seemed like he was universally liked by everyone, and everywhere he went.

One thing my father had was character, and you knew from the outset where you stood. He despised lying, cheating, gossiping, stealing, laziness, excuses, etc. What he liked was to put in an honest day of work; this was his gold standard and he never waivered one bit in his life, which is why I am writing this manuscript about him: so others will learn what I have learned about passing along a sense of decency, a good work ethic, and, most importantly, carrying my father's invisible banner of helping others in time of desperate needs. My father had a tough life, like most of us. He also was cognizant of harsher circumstances in the third world, where people are starving to death by the millions every year. In comparison he was the richest person in the world and blessed to be so fortunate. And under this umbrella type of thinking and attitude, he kept marching forward, dispensing what little he had in terms of economics but made up one-hundred-fold by his kind, giving spirit. These were his central, core values that I have inherited and have taken action on in my own lifetime, implementing them as a tribute in his lasting, eternal memory.

However, this era of his and ours in the city of Newark was coming to an end since our arrival at the old North Terminal Newark Airport. Our main concern was our rent. It was increasing 100 percent at the Landfill apartment on the corner of Lafayette and Pulaski street beginning in a month. This was not acceptable to my parents, so they decided to move to another apartment in Newark. But out of the blue my mother got the idea to buy a house instead of renting an apartment. This threw a curve ball to all of us, but none more so than Pipo. This new idea of buying a house did not sit well with Pipo and me at all; it reminded me of her fiasco with the new Ford Escort purchased two years earlier. Anyway, I think my mother took advantage of this situation to lobby hard and try to convince Pipo and me why this made a lot of economic sense. I was pretty much neutral in the beginning, but I started to have second thoughts because I was aware Pipo was too old to be burdened with a high mortgage and the money we needed for the down payment and the closing cost. In addition, Pipo was very happy working at the Laundromat and did not want to leave. Working there was fun for him and gave him a natural buffer to fight off stress or any negative thinking. I raised this issue with my mother several times, but it went in one ear and out the other. She dismissed it completely and did not want to hear it anymore. She just said, "Gerardo spends too much time for little money."

I responded, "Mom, he enjoys being at the Laundromat because it give him a social life."

In my view, he was too old to pay a mortgage and handle the upkeep of a house. "It's going to kill him, you watch," I said. "He is only getting a small Social Security check plus the money from the Laundromat. How will he make the bills?"

She was stubborn and never relinquished any possibility of changing her mind to look for a rental apartment in Newark. She was determined to buy her first home in America, no matter what obstacle came her way. My mother's argument from an economics point of view was stellar and difficult to challenge from that perspective in the long run. My concern in the short run was for Pipo's psyche and our family's getting highly in debt if we decided to purchase a home.

A few weeks went by before we found a two-family house two miles away in Harrison, New Jersey, on 400 Cross Street. The divide between these two cities was the Passaic River. This city had a large influx of immigration from Ireland at the turn of the twentieth century. This was apparent as soon as you went over the Jackson Street Bridge and drove a half a mile to the center of town. Today the city is very diverse with a very large Hispanic population. This small town is in the middle of a transformation, going from an industrial base to a leisure base economy. In 2010 the new Red Bulls Stadium and major league soccer will open their doors and put Harrison on the world soccer stage, domestically with the Red Bulls team and hosting many high profile teams in international friendly matches.

Harrison was the only city in the running for our first new home for two main reasons: my niece, Barbara, and my nephew, Gerry, who lived there, and my mom wanted to be closer to them so Pipo did not have to drive to pick them up.

Well, everything made a lot sense except the financial part as the particulars were coming to focus. The sale price in 1985 was $92,700, with a $22,700 down payment, financing $70,000 for thirty years. We also had to come up with the additional $6,500 for closing costs. Our monthly mortgage payment with taxes and insurance was about $790 per month. It doesn't seem like a lot of money today, but back then, it made you gasp for air to hear those numbers. I could see Pipo's face become white as a ghost; even gung-ho mom had a perplexed demeanor, unusual for her persona. I remember sitting with them at the dining room table in the Landfill apartment, going through the numbers, and coming to the conclusion that we needed to borrow money from family and friend to qualify. This reality was leaving a sour taste in my mouth and in Pipo's. Even with my $11,000 in savings, we still had to borrow another $11,000 from family and friends to make it work. First we went to our cousin Lupe and her husband, Luis, to borrow the first $5,000 and then to three close friends for the last $6,000. This was a large sum to have to pay back within six months of borrowing. We were on the take and nobody felt any worse than Pipo, because he never liked to ask people for money, not because he was indigent or anything like that, but because he just personally felt it was not a smart move to be in debt to someone who works just as hard as you with many of same obligations. He hated putting people on the spot and asking for loans, knowing quite well everyone in his circle had limited resources. Even with those fortunate friends who were somewhat affluent, he remained steadfast in his refusal to approach them asking for money. And this house loan was no different. If we were going to get the money needed to finance this house, it was at my mom's beck and call, period.

At the Penn Federal Savings Bank on Wilson Avenue in Newark, Pipo accompanied me to withdraw my entire savings to purchase our first home in America. Money to me is just a tool—a conduit to enhance people's lives—and I didn't really have any remorse in emptying my account to zero. I have never been in love with money or stingy with it. What I am guilty of is being too generous with my hard-earned sweat, if you will; this has put me over the years in a very precarious financial situation with those people who have demonstrated no gratitude to me. A simple phone call once a year is more than sufficient for me. I don't care or want their money. Let the record show in this manuscript that all loans of mine are absolved and completely wiped out officially, forever, in the name of Jesus.

The bank tellers gave us a whole stack of $100 bills, because they were a lot easier to count and the tellers would be less prone to make a mistake counting them. This gave me a quick idea to confuse and rattle Pipo halfway into the counting of the money. As he counted the bills, I echoed his counts with him softly for about ten bills in a row, and then I would jump ahead or behind his counts to break his concentration. After four times abruptly losing his count, he said, "Miguel, me cago en la leche! Por facor callate la voca! (Mike, I shit on milk)." This was an old Spanish saying. "Please shut your mouth!" I was trying not to break out in a big laugh. After all, this was serious amounts of money in cash back then, and we needed to be correct with our counts. I told Pipo to line up the money on top of the table in the bank in stacks of ten. He said, "Tu esata loco? Con tanta gente mirando? Cuando vamos a fuera no roban todo el dinero (Are you crazy? With so many people looking at us? When we go outside they will rob us)." He was very nervous having all this cash in his pocket, and it showed; he could not wait to get home to put it inside the safety deposit box. I surveyed the outside of the bank first for any unscrupulous-looking characters waiting on us. These people preyed on the unsuspecting leaving the bank. Often they worked in teams of twos and threes, so you had to be careful carrying significant amount of cash. Well, lo and behold, we made it safely to our home and stashed all the cash in a safety deposit box for the upcoming closing.

We closed in March of 1985, and we left Newark for the first time since we immigrated to America in 1968, one of the most tumultuous years of violence in our history that almost ripped apart the fabric of this nation. After a tiresome two days of moving and organizing all our possessions, we finally settled down in our new home in Harrison.

The novelty of our new home quickly dissipated on many fronts. First, we were swamped with one repair after another. The most costly was with tenants that came with the house on the second floor; they literally destroyed their bathroom, wall and floor and everything that went with it. It seemed every time they took a shower, we had a massive water leak in our apartment, affecting and possibly compromising the entire structure of the ceilings. We quickly determined it was their fault and asked them to leave or expect a significant rent increase to help with the $3,000 in repairs we faced. A week later, to our surprise, they moved out without any notice and left us with no rental income. This was a bitter pill to swallow for the whole family, and it hit Pipo the hardest. His demeanor started to change in the following days, as he was figuratively scratching his head, thinking how long it would be before we depleted our emergency savings. This internal turmoil was continuously impacting his spirits negatively, unlike anything I had ever seen with Pipo before. This unprecedented characteristic was noticeable to family and friends as it intensified.

I believe I have been given an innate, special gift by God to be able to decipher and know certain unexplainable complexities and to know something without the knowledge of how I know. Don't tell me how, but I just know! This mystery has been a puzzle to me since I was born. Intuitively, under this backdrop, I was able to recognize and know certain things about what Pipo was thinking, feeling, and wanting without him saying anything as he lay in bed. In other words, I was connecting to his soul full of anxieties and worries about life and beyond.

Before Pipo left to pick up my mother, normally at 3:30 p.m. every day, at her job in Port Newark, he'd usually lie down on the bed with both hands underneath his head, looking up to the ceilings or into the small backyard garden, dismayed. He would leave the bedroom door open.

During some of these moments, I would come over and talk to him as I passed by his bed, to cheer him, but it did not work. On several other occasions, I would jump into the bed for some fun and diversion, to see if I could get a spark from him, but again nothing. But one time when I lay down next to him, I said, "Pipo, yo se lo que tu esta pensando siempre en esta cama y entodos los lugares...Tu quiere ser joven otras ves padre eso lo que piensa, es verda? (I know what you are thinking always in this bed and every place...You want to be young again, don't you?)"

He responded, "Si hijo yo quireo ser joven otra ves. los anos se me fueron tan rapido (Yes, I want to be young again, the years went by so fast!)" This was his most hidden secret that he revealed to me only. He said, "Miguel, youth is the most precious gift we have, and I feel so terrible for you because I have ruined yours, son." He was looking very melancholy during this time.

I told Pipo, "What are you talking about? You have not ruined me! Stop saying those things! You are getting me very upset, Pipo! Yo te quiero mucho (I love you very much)!"

He said, "Te quite todo tu dinero que a trabahado tan duro hijo para comprar esta casa eso no esta bien y meduele mucho hijo.Un dia te var dar quanta lo que yo te a dicho hoy (I took your money that you work so hard for to purchase this house, and this is not right, and it hurts a lot, son. One day you are going to realize what I told you today)."

I said, "Pipo," touching his forearm as I lay next to him in bed, "money is not important to me and I don't care for it. What I care is about you and only you, so stop dwelling on money, plus all this talk about ruination, it's a bunch of garbage. I have a well-paying job, no car payments, and my credit card charges are very low. Plus, I'm able to give you more money for the mortgage payments every pay week and still have more than enough for me. Since I have good credit and very little outstanding debt,

I'm going to apply for a loan to pay back the money we borrowed from the family and friends. I promised you that, Pipo!"

He said, "Hijo tu tiene que aser tu vida (Son, you have to live your life)."

I said, "I am living my life; I just want to do this. It's no big deal, Pipo! You know when I go to clubs and hang out with my friends, I waste money on stupid things like buying rounds of drinks and so forth. Helping you gives me the most satisfaction ever!"

He said, "You gave us $11,000 that I could never repay you, son!"

I said, "Pay me back? Pipo, what kind of talk is that? The money is in the house; it has not left us, so forget about it for good!"

In this new house, I never felt like it was a true home, like the other three apartments in Newark. And I did not like the neighborhood; for one thing, the parking situation was a horror show, much worse than previously thought. This small town was very congested and most homes had no garages or driveways to speak of, so practically everyone had to find parking and fend for himself on the streets. What made it even more of a lunacy was the early street cleaning at 5:00 a.m. on the main streets of Harrison Avenue and Fourth Street (now named after Frank E. Rodgers Harrison, who served the city for fifty years as mayor, one of the longest in American history). It drove Pipo insane, he refused to moved his car after 6:00 p.m. This town was ticket hungry, known for giving many parking summons. I even saw police officers getting out of their homes in pajamas, half asleep, I kid you not, writing tickets late in the evening. This nightly episode was in full force because each corner in the city had these yellow lines painted too far back, taking up valuable space to park. This ample corner space was a mouse trap to increase city revenue. Many drivers would park there after circling the block for hours as a last resort, hoping to get lucky and not get ticketed. It was so bad that one of my best friends moved out of the city because he incurred $1,350 in tickets in two years, an amount which he had to pay to be admitted to the police academy. This problem affected many of our family and friends and kept them from visiting us. On one occasion, a good friend of mine, whom I had informed earlier about these practices but who had shrugged them off in disbelief, got ticketed by an off-duty police officer wearing Mickey Mouse pajamas, and he never came back to visit our house again. Fortunately, after an outcry of protest by the community, the street cleaning hours were pushed back to 9:00 a.m., and the yellow lines were repainted closer to the corners years later.

Pipo became more withdrawn as the days passed by, without any signs of recovering to his former self. It was obvious he missed the corner Laundromat, his stomping ground, a place to be with friends and customers alike and earn some money for his discretionary spending. In this new environment he had little spending money left after paying the bills, which limited his natural self to the very end. In retrospect, I was correct and my mother was also correct. Unexpectedly, nine months later, without notifying me, she put the house on the market and sold it in less than a week for an incredible $159,000, nearly $70.000 in profit. Then she decided to return to Newark and purchase a brand new townhouse on Chestnut Street, but not before making another $30,000 in profits from the sell of the townhouse, after we sold it. Two years later her impulses took over and, against my wishes, my brother convinced her to fiddle with the idea of moving to Miami before they settled back to Harrison once again at 429 William Street in a two-family home. This location became our home for twelve years before my mother decided to once again sell it because of issues with a tenant which got very ugly. Her timing to sell this home came at the right time, just before the housing bubble burst. We sold this home for $450,000, a $220,000 profit which we used again to return to Newark and purchase a brand new townhouse at Valsumo Lane off Ferry Street, where we currently live. Over my time at William Street, I got married and divorced and, unlike my mom, lost money on my very own home at 118 Clyde Avenue in Hope Lawn, New Jersey.

I have to give high kudos to my mom for her savvy real estate decisions. She never lost in this arena. However, it came at a high very price from the original inception of the idea. I would give up everything in the universe to have had Pipo around me for a few more precious moments. As I'm writing this sentence, I look above my laptop to my favorite picture ever in happier times, showing me taking in Cuba's Guardalavaca beach resort with Pipo, Mom, and my brother; I am wearing a tire tube proudly in those unforgettable days in our youth! Well, I was correct in predicting the decaying of my hero's dynamic spirit that had been unshakable in the past, while my mother was proven correct as well in large economic gains. Pipo's armor of enjoying life to the fullest was punctured by three main nemeses greater than any war he had faced before. First, he was facing the reality of aging; secondly, sickness; and, finally, at his advanced age, he was economically drowning in his mind.

My father, for his age, was still very strong and had a dynamic natural flair with people, but it was less so. This flair sometimes attracted ladies and got him in trouble with mom. She did not hold back her loud disapproval in private, and on some occasions in public. I found these outbursts by Mother comical because Pipo was not a spring chicken anymore.

Toward the end he was not feeling like his usual self and began to have problems with his prostate. His concerns for my future woes and the magnitude of the household financial situations in those days played a pivotal role in his final days.

CHAPTER 37

1974 Vacation in Spain

This was my inaugural trip to Spain, and my parents' first in twenty years away from the mother country. This was a long time in coming. They save their pennies, literally and figuratively, for six years in America for this most anticipated trek. I, on the other hand, did not want to go with them. As a young fifteen-year-old teenager, I wanted to hang out with my friends all summer. My mom had other ideas and prevailed in the end. She told me it would be good for me to come learn a different culture, where our ancestors came from. "You will have a better time with us than staying back home in Newark; trust me, you will see." I was not buying any of that crap. Reluctantly, I had no choice but to go with them. And it was a good thing I went to Spain, because this trip exposed me to my Spanish heritage, which I had not known before. This exposure has grown over the years and has never left me since, in contrast to my brother, who never went in his formative years and thus has not been enriched as I have. I am forever glad that my parents forced me to go with them on this trip, because on the following trips, I needed no convincing; it was I who anxiously wanted to go.

The day of departure to Spain had arrived, a fitting July Fourth send-off on our nation's 198th birthday celebration. Our biggest concern was transporting fifteen bags, mostly presents, to our family. It was hard to fathom the logistical nightmare of what we were about to face shortly. Airliners today will nickel and dime you to death for every piece of luggage you take on board, changing rates continuously and charging passengers all sorts of fees. I should know; I am a proud employee of United/ Continental Airlines, the best-run airline company in the business today, bar none, so I happen to stays up to date on industry news. The airline industry is one of my passions and hobbies, and I am happy to have been professionally associated with it since 1999.

It started with the exhausting first leg commute, a taxi ride to Newark Airport to connect to a shuttle helicopter flight over to JFK International Airport before heading toward Barajas International Airport Madrid with a stopover in Malaga. In 1974 Newark Airport was a small, domestic airport with virtually no international flights. Carrying this much luggage was making Pipo and me thin skinned with Mom as we struggled picking up these many heavy bags. One caveat to keep in mind is that in 1974 luggage had no wheels to roll it as we do today. It was pure lifting as far as you can go, then drop it down, rest for a few seconds, and repeat the cycle until you get there. Not much fun if you ask me! Today in modern society we are indeed spoiled with so many amenities that make our lives easier. Let me tell you, Pipo and I were drenched in sweat carrying all those bags while wearing suits. Proper attire while traveling was the norm and was required, just like having a visa to go internationally on board an airliner. It was so uncomfortable parading around in those wet clothes in the middle of the summer, especially at JFK, where we almost lost the bags, transporting them from the chopper to an airport transfer shuttle bus taking us to the Iberia Airline ticket counter. Luckily for us the bags were found and returned to us at the check-in counter. We bit the bullet this time, but Pipo knew we were not out of the woods just yet. We would be tested for sure soon enough on Spanish soil, traveling to different regions using various modes of transportation.

We finally boarded the "big bird," my favorite aircraft, a Boeing 747 jet, the biggest commercial plane in the world. A few years earlier, on January 21, 1970, I had witnessed on television its maiden voyage as Pan American World Airways took off from JFK to London, the beginning of the jumbo jet age, blasting off into history. It left a positive impression in me, so naturally I was eagerly waiting to step foot on this giant city of a plane for the first time. I just couldn't wait much longer as I let Pipo and my mom board the plane first. Once inside, I was in awe at how immense this plane was and wondered how in the world it would get up in the air! I kidded with Pipo and Mom, once seated, about bringing too many bags onboard, making the plane too heavy to fly. I said to them, "Look around. All the seats are full. There have got to be over four hundred people on this plane, plus bags, freight, gas, and the plane itself. There is no way this plane is going to take off, just like it happened to us leaving Cuba for Mexico on two aborted takeoffs from Cabana Aviacion Aerolinias. Do you remember?"

At this time my mom was getting nervous as we taxied for takeoff, hearing the massive four engines growl like a hungry lion ready to attack its prey. Suddenly, this big city sprinted full speed forward down the runway and blasted off into the evening's bluish, dark sky as we all looked out the window. "Man," I told Pipo, "what power those engines must have to lift us up so fast." He acknowledged me in a half smile, shaking his head in amazement and in bewilderment. Most of the plane ride I was looking out the window and seeing all these little ships in the ocean. In reality these were huge freighters, but they didn't look that way from an altitude of thirty-five thousand feet. As we entered the airspace of the Iberian Peninsula, we started to see many picturesque valleys and mountains below. This caught the eye of Pipo profoundly. He had a glazed look in his eyes watching his home turf after a twenty-year hiatus. These farms and fields in the countryside sights were breathtaking; it looked like a giant blanket laid down across the plain, with different colorful patches on it. Slowly, as the big 747 jet was descending, we were able to see old, small villages coming into focus. All this time, Pipo kept pointing to me as we approached the capital city of Madrid for our landing. It was a perfect touchdown as everyone clapped, no one more so than Mom.

The first thing we did after rounding up our bags, no easy task at Barajas International Airport, was to exchange our American dollar currency for Spanish pesetas. These were funny-looking bills, I thought; the denominations were different and larger than ours, according to their note value. They filled Pipo's front pocket in his trousers when he put the stacks of bills in. He had to bind them with rubber bands to make them fit. He commented to us that next time he would exchange less to avoid this situation again. Pipo and Mom made sure to carry most of their money in American Express travelers' checks instead of cash to avoid the possible pitiful of losing our money and destroying our six-week vacation. This was a great lesson for me to learn in the years ahead about having your money secured if the worst happens.

At the airport curbside, it was difficult to convince a taxi to stop and take us to a hotel in central Madrid, and who could blame them upon seeing a pile of suitcases bigger than their cars? Our odyssey was in full gear in beautiful Spain. It wasn't until Pipo decided to pay extra for the baggage that we were able to catch a taxi to take us where we wanted to go, which was a decent hotel, because we had made no reservations at any. My father asked the taxi driver to take us to one that he was familiar with in the past. He took us to three hotels, but there were no vacancies. They were all booked solid, because the summer is the high season for tourism. At this point, I was ready to go to any park and look for a bench to go to sleep on providing someone else did not think of it first. We finally drove to a hotel that had vacancies, but it was run down, in a bad neighborhood, and not to my mom's liking, so we decided to continue in our hunt for a better hotel after nearly two hours had elapsed. The driver then took us to a hotel called Santander about three blocks away from the Puerta Del Sol the center of Madrid. We all walked in, hoping to strike gold with a room. My mother went to the front desk to inquire about the availability. The front desk person was also the owner of the hotel, an older woman in her fifties. She said, "We are booked solid for the entire summer, but we have a last-minute cancellation in a suite. It's the most expensive room in the hotel and the largest; it takes almost the whole top floor. If you are interested, I will lower our normal rate and give it to you at that discounted price. Do you want to take it?"

In those days the dollar was king. My parents said, "Give us a minute to talk it over." They went away from the front desk in the lobby near the entrance door to discuss the numbers. It was a quick decision; they accepted the room for one week then and for five days later on when we came back to Madrid for departure. This was music to my ears; we had our hotel to relax and go to sleep, but not so fast. We still had to bring the suitcases into the rooms; it was a time-consuming process because the elevator was old and weight restricted. It was hand operated, and it had all these steel devices, including the gate. Plus, our suite was located at the end of the hallway about 150 feet away.

Once inside the room we were all flabbergasted at how spacious and beautiful the room was. One of the first things my mother did was to open all the windows and to look down on the streets. She said to Pipo and me, "Look how beautiful this corner view is!" After making my mother happy, we took turns taking probably the best showers ever. This shower revived me, giving me a boost to go out into the city with my parents for the first time for a night of fun. But nighttime in Spain did not come early; it was still daylight at almost 11:00 p.m. Can you believe it? Madrid at night is extra special. I was dumbfounded at how alive the city was; everyone seemed to be enjoying himself or herself in the many crowded outdoor cafés, munching away on traditional tapas and wines. Unfortunately, I was having a Pepsi with mine while my parents were having wine and beer with theirs. As we walked around town, I noticed the large penetration of American movies playing in theaters. Big posters were plastered all over promoting movies like *The Sting, American*

Graffiti, A Touch of Class, just to name a few. In the midst of all this Americana, I felt as if I was home. We continued to explore Madrid that first night until 2:00 a.m. This is usually the beginning hour for nightclubs across the city, but not for us on that night. We caught a taxi and returned to our hotel for a night of much-needed sleep. We fell asleep to the sound of passing cars below and slept and slept until a hard knocking finally woke us up. Pipo was half asleep when my mother yelled at him to see who was at the door so early in the morning. Pipo said, "It's a lady from the hotel with breakfast for us."

My mother replied, "I did not order anything."

My father opened the door and, to the delight of all us, the lady brought in three king-size complimentary breakfasts, which were included as part of our renting the suite. The breakfasts had danishes, fruits, churros, chocolate, coffee, omelets, etc. It was so extravagant we felt guilty in not even coming close to finishing it. One would've being more than enough.

My mom checked the time and said in disbelief, "It's almost 1:00 p.m. We've got to get going!" We visited in the first week in Madrid all the major tourist attractions, plus we traveled to Toledo for a day trip, about sixty miles south of Madrid. This most historical city was on my mother's radar screen from the time she planned our trip and it could not have been passed up. We visited many of the old, famous structures, including the Alcazar of Toledo and the cathedral that rises above the magnificent skyline. My favorites were the Monasterio de San Juan de Los Reyes, a Franciscan monastery; the Bridge of San Martin; the medieval castle of San Servando; the Bridge of Alcantara; and finally saw the fabulous view from a hilltop of the town looking down toward the Tagus River and its ancient surroundings. This was the most memorable moment with Pipo and mom as we stood there over an hour admiring the beautiful landscape with each other. The only reason we did not stay any longer was because I was thirsty due to the high temperatures and also a little bit hungry.

In Madrid our sightseeing adventures were in high gear, and who could forget Pipo with me in Retiro Park Lake rowing and paddling in front of Alfonse XII statue while my mother watched from a distance? This was lots of fun because, being the practical joker that I was, I let my father do all the rowing at his expense. He moaned and groaned several times to stop my shenanigans and threatened to stop rowing and leave the boat if I didn't cut it out soon. All in all I had a great time sharing a magical moment together in Madrid's sun-bathed heat. We then strolled around this popular park and watched many entertainers and vendors do their things while we sipped a cold Pepsi in the garden shade.

Another great place we went was the Plaza Major. This place on Sunday mornings becomes a flea market for a few hours, where vendors come and peddle their items. I was able to buy some coins and stamps to add to my collection, having Pipo pay for them. This was a large, open complex where people came to socialize in the many bars, sharing a bite and a drink and sitting outside people watching. Great place to relax! At this time, I was starting to get used to this Spain thing with my parents, which I never thought I would.

Just outside Madrid, about thirty miles northwest, away we went to two complexes that are must-see for any one traveling to Spain. These were the Valle de Los Caidos (Valley of the Fallen) and El Escorial. The first one has the most amazing large cross in the world sitting on top of a rock mountain that takes your breath away. It is the tallest memorial cross in the world. This place was built on the order of Dictator Francisco Franco to honor those who died during the Spanish Civil War. It is also housed his tomb after his death in 1975. Underneath lie the basilica and abbey. The second was a mausoleum for the Spanish monarchy. Here you were able to see all the past kings' tombs in this former palace and monastery complex. These two sites I visited with Pipo and mom were a lesson to me that has grown over the years. We listened carefully to the guides as the tour unfolded. Pipo again attracted a loyal following among our tour group with his storytelling and humor. Even the guide was engrossed with his innocent humor and entertaining personality, while mom and I walked away mystified and I thought to myself, "I bet you all these dead corpses in this castle were listening to Pipo as well." I even extended my irrational thinking verbally to mom, and her reply was, "I think you are right. This is ridiculous, son, having all these strangers congregating in a circle as he walks. He has more people next to him than all the kings here." Well, that was Pipo at his best; he certainly was the real king amongst the kings there on that day, as far as I'm concerned, in a palace most fit for a servant and a humble man like my father, Pipo.

Before leaving Madrid my father bought me powerful binoculars that I wanted so badly; this came on the heels of losing a valuable roll of film at a photo shop, or possibly it was erased passing through the metal detector machines at the airport. On this roll I had all my photos of my graduation from Lafayette Street Elementary School in Newark. I was heartbroken and blamed my mother because of her insistence on finishing that roll of film in Spain instead of developing it back home. Well, to appease me somewhat, she convinced Pipo to reach in his pocket for some heavy moola for this expansive toy. He was shell-shocked at first upon hearing the price tag but reluctantly agreed.

Our next destination in Spain was the province of Galicia in the northwest region of Spain. But before we left we had to round up the fifteen bags and call for a taxi big enough to fit them all in. Once again, after a small hiatus of worrying about the bags, we were facing the pain of being prisoners of our own making. We were fortunate that the front-desk person allayed our fears quickly, calling for a large cab to takes us to the Atocha train station. On that first visit to Madrid I was struck by how small the cars were. In America, I was used to seeing nothing but big cars on the road. That was not the case in Spain in 1974. In present-day America our cars have shrunk and are more in line with theirs. Times have dramatically changed since I first stepped foot in Madrid.

At the station, before we boarded, I asked Pipo to buy me a couple of magazines for the road at the newsstand near the track. I grabbed the *Economist* and *Time*. My mother picked *Hola*, a popular Spanish magazine, while Pipo snatched the local paper and, of course, lottery tickets. We hopped on a Renfe train, the equivalent of Amtrak in the States, and off we went for a ten-day excursion and visit with family. Nothing finer than a train ride with family; I always love the train, and this was the first long train ride with Pipo and Mom since those overnighters to Havana when I was very young. As the train left the station, I could not help but notice the many bullfighting and flamenco posters scattered all over the place, particular in newsstands across Madrid. These practices were still alive and kicking in modern Spain; to anyone traveling, bring back a piece of this as a souvenir depicting the essence of Spanish culture.

On the train I took turns alternating with Pipo between facing forward or backward by the window. The views were spectacular as the train zoomed by the many villages and farms. I was glued to the window, looking with my new binoculars at the horizon as farmers cultivated the fields. Pipo also took an interest and started to borrow my binoculars to get a closer look at these farmers. Even my mother put down her favorite magazine and took part in enjoying the view. I spent most of the trip looking out the windows with my binocular. Other times I would come out of our cabin compartment with Pipo, walking the hallway as we made our way to different passenger cars. Most of the people we met were locals getting home from work in the bigger cities. We arrived at the Friol Train Station, an old-looking brick structure with a lot of age on it, similar to the ones we saw on our way there. They all seemed very desolate.

We took one of the very few taxis in town to my cousin Angelita's house in Gia, about seven miles away. On our way there we were very cramped in the taxi; we had bags in our laps and could hardly see anything in front of us. Pipo was in the front and mom and I were in the back. Seven miles into our trip, the driver veered to the left and left the paved road for a dirt road full of mud. We saw nothing but cornfields and all types of vegetable plants of on both sides of the road. About a mile into it, we entered a small village with homes made of dark clay with hay on the roof. I did not like what I was seeing. However, when the taxi pulled up to Angelita's house, I was pleasantly surprised. Her house was made out of brick, not like the other ones. Plus, it had a store in the front and a small bar with a black and white television. "How about that?" I said to myself. Our cousins met us outside with the biggest smiles and reddest cheeks I've ever experienced before. They helped us with the luggage and set the bags up in our bedrooms in the second floor. After a quick sit-down to get to know each other, especially me, for the first time, and a little bit of homemade Serrano ham and cheese with burgundy wine, we all got a tour of the place. It wasn't too bad; in the back they had a bunch of livestock: pigs, chickens, etc. They had a huge barn full of hay for the animals. For a village it was not so primitive like other ones I saw on our trip. The bad part was the lavatory. It had no toilet, just a hole. My cousin Angelita said, "The reason I have no toilet is a hole is much cleaner to maintain. In addition, part of the house is a public facility and is used by many customers." This was going to be our central home for the next ten days. It would serve as the launching pad to visit the historic city of Lugo and La Coruña, the beautiful beach city of Riazor, where they famously claimed "no one is a stranger."

Angelita, her husband, her son, and grandfather made us feel at home from the moment we arrived. My cousin Jose Antonio, three years older than me, did not leave my sight for the entire stay. He introduced me to his friends and took me to various parties. I also helped him in the fields with collecting hay for storage to feed the animals. He even let me drive the tractor with a full load on it, so I had to be extra careful not to jerk it or speed up and shift the load, losing it all. But the most fun was riding on top of the ten-foot-high stacks of hay, drinking Strella de Galicia beer, and returning home with a good day of work behind me. When I got home, I couldn't wait to tell Pipo what I did all day. He listened and smiled as Jose Antonio told him the good job that I did with him. On many trips, I accompanied my cousin Jose Antonio to nearby villages in his car to hang out with his friends and party. We drank wine, beer, brandy, cider, coffee, etc., and ate great food with beautiful local village girls that were humbly gorgeous and innocent in nature. Each year I visited, I had a great time with him. In the house, I enjoyed the big, long dinners typical of Spain, and in my cousin's house it was no different. Dinner started at eight in the evening, lasting often easily past midnight. My father's natural storytelling was the main culprit, but the others, including me, did not lag behind either. You include fine wine and other spirits into the mix with a cortado (a small cup of coffee with a little bit of heated, foamed milk on top) and you have a recipe for a wonderful, lasting conversation.

In Lugo, we visited other cousins and took a tour of this great old Roman city, founded before the birth of Christ. My father and my mom kept telling me about this *muralla* (wall), and I said, "What's the big deal?"

Pipo then said, "This wall was built by the Romans on the highest hill terrain of the city for protection against the arch-nemesis. It surrounds the entire city without any break in between, a great monument and an amazing construction." We took many photos outside this wall on the first trip, appreciating the sheer magnitude of this work of art. I took so many snapshots that Pipo said to me, "Basta! (Enough!)" I was driving him crazy and making him dizzy, as only I could do.

We then entered the old city inside the wall and visited the market plaza to stop for a quick bite before heading toward the cathedral. We then went back to my cousin Consuelo's house and met up with her husband, Manolo, and her only son, who was either separated or divorced and living with them. Everyone had a great time telling stories in this modern house, which housed a lot of cheeses. The entire house smelled like a cheese factory, so it was difficult to ignore; it was making me sick to my stomach, feeling like wanting to puke if I stayed there much longer. For some unexplainable reasons my parents were immune to this penetrating odor. I just decided to go outside for some fresh air. An hour later, they all walked out of the house to show us the massive construction projects changing the face of the city outside the wall. She pointed out the new superhighway behind her house that took part of her land to build and the many who lost their property altogether for little compensation. They shouted, "This is not right what they are doing."

A short time later, other cousins stopped by and accompanied us to see the new Lugo. To my eyes' delight, I saw a pretty girl coming with them. We got introduced as distant fourth cousins, which is a good thing because we hit it off nicely, and you never know. I spent the whole time with her instead of hearing this and that coming out of the elders. I was not interested in anything else but her, as she was about me. She continually asked all types of question about American music, movies, and what I did. I knew I had surmised correctly that she liked me when I heard how much she liked my maroon velvet jacket and she straightened my collar standing in front of me, three inches away from me. This Spain thing was getting better and better, to the boiling point, if you asked me. In the meantime, Pipo and Mom called me out to come next to them, so grudgingly I went over there and I said, "Que pasa (What's up)?"

My mom said, "Que te parese de Españas a hora (What do you think about Spain now)?" while Pipo smiled in the background. I smiled back to them and I was happy to return to my new friend. The last stop in this new Lugo was the new bridge, not yet open to traffic, so we walked to get there. It was quite high when you look down at the river below. We spent about an hour looking and taking photos at the landscape surrounding the hilly countryside. Plus, I was not in a hurry to leave anytime soon. I had everything I wanted right beside me; who could ask for anything more? Well, the tour ended, and we went back to Gia shortly on a taxi, but not before I got a very nice double kiss on the cheek from this pretty lady. I saw her briefly one more time before leaving Spain and again two years later before losing contact.

Well, in Gia my parents and I were invited to a feast in a nearby village to soak it all in one more time before departing for La Coruña late the following afternoon (after having time to rest up from the previous evening's partying). Every village has its annual festival, and in Gia it was around August 15, which conflicted with our travel plans to visit other places, so unfortunately we had to skip that year. But two years later on our visit we more than made up for it by partying for two nights, led by Pipo dancing to many traditional folk songs. I, on the other hand, was two years older and better able to discern more possibilities when hanging with Jose Antonio and his friends. My cousin was very well liked in the village and knew everybody. He and I became very close and he introduced me to many people wherever we went. He was the best in all my time in Spain.

We all went back to the party. I had to raise the ante somewhat; some of the local boys had a little too much to drink and did not take too kindly to me dancing with "their" ladies. They would constantly break in on us in a wild type of way and try to provoke me, asking who I was. I would ask in rebuttal, "Who are you?" These confrontations went on verbally on and off; however, they never went any further. Plus, my cousin was a whisker away if trouble arose. Pipo and Mom were too caught up in their world and never realized what was happening with me. I'm glad for them because they were having such a great time dancing while family and friends watched intently.

In La Coruña we stayed about three days in one of my favorite places, along with Madrid, where I would love to relocate someday permanently. It is called little Madrid, full of energy and never boring. It has what Madrid lacks, beautiful beaches; among the many, Riazor and Orzan are the most well known. It has a beautiful harbor full of fishing boats, cruise ships, and yachts. In additional, the view from beach toward the city is spectacular as you look at all the buildings with nothing but windows; it's a glass city encircling the beaches. As a matter of fact the whole city was designed with this type of structure, which gives it uniqueness. A small paradise located near the westernmost part of the European continent, it was labeled "The End of the World." Nothing existed beyond this point, was the prevailing thought in earlier times. Well, to those who have visited La Coruña, you can honestly say, who needs the rest of the world when you have this hidden treasure?

In the city we spent three days visiting a couple of my cousins, Pepe and Jose. Pepe had a tapas restaurant and invited us to eat and drink at his establishment. He also showed us around the city, every nook and cranny of it. On the days he was not able to be with us, we decided to go to Riazor beach for a fun time in the water and catch some sun on Spanish beaches for the first time. Once there, my mother, Pipo and I walked around first in the sand until we saw these rock boulders sticking out of the ocean as the waves smashed into them hard. One caught our attention; it was shaped like a pyramid adjacent to one of the naturally formed stone pier that were very prevalent in this area. Sitting by this rock, my mother got hit by a high wave that really soaked her. She immediately ran for cover and returned to the sand and tried to dry up.

My father, Pipo, decided to go in the water, and before he went in, my mother warned him not to go. She said, "The water is ice cold," as she shivered.

Pipo responded, "Vamos, no se tan covarde (Come on, don't be such a chicken)."

She then put on a coat on the beach, to our amusement. She said, "Nunca avisto una playa tan fria com esta (Never seen a beach so cold as this one). Esta gente aqui son como oso que viven en el polo norte (These people that live here are just like the bears who live in the North Pole)."

My father had a smiling, amused face as he watched my mother talking all that nonsense. Then, being the instigator that I am, I quickly told Pipo, "Mira por toda la playa mi madre es la unica aqui con un abrigo puesto. Que le pasa ella esta loca oh que (Look at the entire beach, and my mother is the only one here wearing a coat. What's the matter with her, is she crazy or what)?"

My father said, "Es verda lo que dice Miguel ahora que miro todo el mundo tiene ropa de playa puesto a ropa de plata, meno tu. Es un rediculo! It is true what Mike said; now that I look at it, everyone here has his or her beach clothes on except you. It's ridiculous)!" I was laughing all this time.

She then said, "Dehame en Paz! Vallan ustedes si quieren (Leave me in peace! You go if you want)!" With this in mind, my mother, trembling, got up from the small rock on the beach, yelling, "Te van a frizar cuando salgan (You are going to freeze when you come out)!" As we made our way closer to the water, I felt the frigidness of the moistened sand. Courageous Pipo— or stubbornness, either way, take you pick—tiptoed in the water first; I had his flank. These waters were not like the Caribbean we were used to in Cuba. They felt more like the Arctic Ocean waters imbedded in an iceberg. These northern waters were radically different in temperature and it caught us by surprise. I could not help but splash him when I saw him turn his back on me. He then turned around, jumping like a wounded mammal ready to dispose his prey—me, that is. I ran so fast that I did not feel the coldness anymore. We stayed in the water for about an hour; our bodies had adjusted to the water's cold temperature. We both had a good time playing with the waves and each other and remembering Cuba. Coming out of the water was even worse than being in the water. It was late in the afternoon and the cold breeze had picked up steam, leaving us in a state of trembling and shivering just like mom had. This time, mom was doing the "I told you so" routine on us; while Pipo began to wrap a beach towel around himself, he shortly began sneezing nonstop, to the delight of my mom. We then left immediately for the hotel to get warm as fast as we could. We all drank hot chocolate to the delight of our freezing bodies. Pipo and I learned our lesson quite well, the hard way; these natives had thick skin and we did not.

In this city we did a lot of walking, going to places of interest such as the Plaza de España, Deportivo soccer stadium, Tower of Hercules, etc. We had a ball.

Now it was time to return to Gia before departing to Gijon to see more family members the next day. We took a taxi to the train station to jump on the train to Gijon, but Pipo was persuaded by the Galician driver to let him take us all the way in his car. He told Pipo he'd do it cheaper, plus we would not have to worry about dealing with thirteen bags of luggage on the train. This was a convincing argument that could not be dismissed by my parents. It was a very uncomfortable ride and a dangerous one, too. We had bags on the top, back, and floor of the taxi, and on our laps. It was about a six-hour trip, because it was slow going as we climbed up the curvy mountains. The heavy fog was thick, with no visibility whatsoever; you could not see oncoming traffic more than fifteen feet in front of you. I remember large incoming buses trying slowly to pass us on this narrow road with no barriers to prevent us from falling thousands of feet below. It was a very scary ride; if we had known about it, especially my mother, we would've taken the train. The worst part was that once we arrived, we learned our cousins were vacationing in Valle De Las Casas in the province of Leon, my father's birth place and our very next stop in our traveling circus. We went there to surprise them and they surprised us. We decided with much trepidation to go back to Gia. However, my mother was very worried; it was apparent by her facial expression. On the way back the driver was exhausted, trying to fight falling asleep as best as he could. I saw my mother, next to me in the back seat, not saying much, just praying while Pipo and I talked to the driver to keep him from falling asleep often. At one time my father had to take quick action and turn the wheel to the right or face instant death by falling off the tall mountain. My mother had had enough of this falling-asleep taxi driver after he kept insisting that he was fine to keep going. He finally pulled over to drink a large container of coffee and also takes one for the road. This gave us a chance to stretch our legs, eat a little snack, and, most importantly, relax. The driver was rejuvenated and we finally made it home without a physical scratch. I'm not so sure mentally. Today these dangerous roads have been eliminated for the most part by superhighways that go through the mountains. Thank God for that!

The next day we boarded a train to the city of Leon en route to Valle De Las Casas and Prado De La Guz Pena. After a quick ride to the heart of the city, we made multiple stops before we wound up in a bed-and-breakfast type of establishment for a one-day stay before we looked for better accommodations the next day. The next day we got a taxi to take us to a hotel that my uncles from America used when traveling in this region and highly recommended. In addition, the owner, Geronimo, of this five-star hotel called Hotel De Luna in the heart of the city is the same one who sold Pipo a chicken and livestock farm twenty-plus years earlier in Gerafe, seven miles away from the city. He had become a wealthy person in the intervening years. Upon getting to the hotel, I was awestruck by how beautiful this area was. It was like being in Times Square in New York City. It was that great.

At the hotel front desk, my father inquired if Mr. Geronimo was available. The attendant asked for my father's name and left to look for Mr. Geronimo. In less than a minute, Geronimo walked in and bear hugged Pipo for about a minute and then shook my mother's and my hands. We talked for an hour in the lobby, and then he lead us to the front-desk person, to whom he gave one caveat: "Give him the best suite in the hotel!" He also told my father we were welcome to stay there as long as we wanted. My father was given a substantial discount for this spacious and most luxurious hotel room in which I have ever stayed. When we first walked in, we were in awe of how elegant this one-of-a-kind suite was. It had seven rooms, all in immaculate condition. The refrigerator was fully stocked with beers, sodas, juices, and water. The bedrooms were king size and the suite also had a Jacuzzi and sauna. This was a luxurious room of the highest quality.

As I opened the windows to look outside, I saw this mammoth movie theater structure at the opposite corner below, playing the American movie *The Odessa File*. When I called my mom to come over, she told me Geronimo also was the owner of the theater. I was able to persuade my parents to come to the theater with me that night. It didn't hurt that the theater was across the street, either. The movie was excellent and nobody fell asleep watching this time. In Madrid it was difficult to keep my parents awake from the beginning to the end. These movies were dubbed in Spanish and sometimes you could see the actors move their lips and no voice coming out. It was weird; I was always used to watching movies, and anything else, for that matter, in English. We stayed about three days in this great city. We also visit my cousin Anita at her house; her husband had passed away a year earlier. We spent a whole day together, with Anita taking us all over the city. One thing that stuck out was the imposing beauty of the cathedral, an impressionable structure that stood out among many.

We then took a taxi ride to Valle De Las Casas, about a forty-minute car ride from the city of Leon, to visit aunt Rosario. This was the birthplace of my father, his parents, and nine siblings, his dearest and most anticipated stop on our trip. Upon getting there, I did not like the primitive living conditions and did not want to stay there at all. I just wanted to leave. I complained and complained while my father tried allaying my fears by tricking me into coming inside that house as the taxi took off. When we got inside, it was pretty much like if I had been in the 1700s in colonial America: no modern amenities whatsoever. We had no electricity, no running water, and no bathroom to speak of. The bathroom was two hundred feet away from the house, behind some bushes and a tall tree. Can you believe it? No wonder my father joined the navy to get out of there. It was tough living conditions that I had never experienced before. I had to make the best out it for the next ten days of misery unless I got eaten by the many wolves and coyotes scanning the area for their prey. I made sure I went to the bathroom in the daylight to avoid any wild animal attacks. I did not wanted to be caught with my pants down, if you know what I mean. It was always very dark in this village; you could not see anything out there, let me tell you. The best thing about this place was my father showing me the many trails, roads, fields, and people as we both walked the entire town. As always, he would attract a large crowd of his past friends who had stayed back or returned on their vacations. Either way it was never boring having Pipo at my side. We visit the village square, which had this water fountain where the whole community would come for water. Nearby you had a little general store to purchase food and household items. We visited the cemetery to pay respect to my father's mother, who had passed away two years earlier. At the tomb, I clearly remember Pipo's watery eyes as he paid respect to his beloved mother. We stood there about twenty minutes with aunt Rosario and others until he said, "Vamonos (Let's go)!" As we departed, I went over to Pipo to try to cheer him up by changing the conversation with small talk.

A day later, while walking the terrain, Pipo pointed out Peña Corada, a multiple-peak mountain standing in the foreground. He said, "As as young child, I would always be within view of this mountain while working in the fields or riding my bike, being chased by a flock of coyotes and wolves going and coming to work."

I think that by expressing his sentiments to me, he was lamenting his youth without saying so. But I was too young to understand fully the scope of those words or to grasp his real meaning. However, it did not take away from the fact that I was spending quality time with Pipo where he grew up, as father and son. This was the most satisfying moment we shared together.

At Prado De La Guzpena, a small village with a smaller population than Valle, about two miles away, we visit my aunt Guadalupe for four days. We all had a great time, none greater than Pipo. aunt Guadalupe was very dynamic and loving and couldn't do enough to make our stay as pleasant as possible. In this house, they did have lights, but they turned them off to save energy, which was not okay with me, because it was pitch dark and I could not fall asleep for the life of me. I would get up in the middle of the night, turn the lights on in the hallway, and leave my door cracked open. This was the only way I could fall asleep. But a few minutes later, Pipo or my aunt would get up and turn the lights off again. This cat-and-mouse game went on until I fell asleep. I loved this town. I hung out with all my many cousins around my age and younger, playing games late into the evening. One day, we missed dinner time, and my mother went looking for me near Peña Corado with family members and miraculous found us. I was having a good time climbing the mountain that my father did so many times. My mother scolded me and we returned to my aunt's house for a late dinner. The previous night at dinner, I got stuck at the very end of the table for almost four hours without being able to come out. Once Pipo started storytelling, it went on forever. I think this is a trait of all the Garcias; they all seem to inherit this gene, from what I could see.

We then boarded a train to Balmaseda to visit Pipo's younger brother uncle Justi and aunt Josefina. This was a long train ride in the evening to Basque country near France. We had great accommodations in our cabin, plenty of room to stretch out and to lie down, since we were the only ones in the cabin. During this trip, I noticed many sailors traveling on the train, as Pipo and I walked the hallways or just stood up by the windows talking to each other. He conversed and mingled with the soldiers as they squeezed by us. He got to know them fairly quickly as they hit it off quite well, and the rest is history, as they say. They told stories and sang many songs about the mother country, like "Que Viva España" ("Long Live Spain"), embracing as if they were in a fraternity. Many people on the train took notice and came out of the cabins or opened their doors to join in on the festivities. I was having a ball witnessing my father light up this train with everyone in it, one car at a time. Even the conductors joined in the singalong. Some of the passengers missed their stops altogether because they got caught up in that magical moment. Most of these were soldiers coming home from military bases and maneuvers. They had to catch a cab or a bus back to return to their original drop-off destination. I will never forget the fun and the excitement on everybody's face, none greater than my father. He too was in the navy, so he had a lot in common with these young cadets. In his youth, he had taken this same trip or similar ones many times serving his country. This spontaneous outburst of clean camaraderie by Pipo reminiscing about his youth was a welcome imprint on this vacation. Not to be outdone, he jumped out of the train just before it came to a full stop to buy, at the station deli, some boiled ham sandwiches for us. This time, I jumped off and chased after him, unlike in Cuba Camaguey train station, where he went solo to buy sandwiches and had to run as fast as possible to get back on the train while it was moving.

We had a little quiet time in the cabin eating and discussing uncle Justi and the city of Balmaseda as the train rolld on to our final vacation spot before returning to Madrid to leave for America, our home sweet home. We took a taxi ride to my uncle's apartment. Apparently, the driver knew my uncle very well in this small city; my mother gave him the address to take us to this location in front of a river, and my father's eyes lit up when the taxi driver said, "Oh, you are going to Justi Garcia's home?! He is a good friend of mines for many years." My father told him that he was his brother from America that he hasn't seemed in over twenty years, and that we were coming to surprise him without any notice. Upon hearing this news the driver immediately stopped the car and introduced himself to Pipo and told us that he was at our disposal any time we need him for anything. He refused to take Pipo's money and also helped us with carrying eight heavy bags to the second floor of the apartment. Our load was cut almost in half from the original fifteen; things were looking better from my perspective, hoping but not counting on one less bag when leaving. Well, we shall wait and see about that, with my mother's insatiable appetite for shopping!

Uncle Justi, my father's youngest brother, was the only one I'd never met before, since he always lived in Spain. My first encounter with him was one for the ages. We knocked at the door, and we were met by aunt Josefina and my cousin Elena; her older sister Pili was working as well as my uncle Justi. First thing my father said was, "Where's Justi?!" My aunt said, "He is working at the movie theater about four blocks away!" My father was going to rush to the theater to see him, but my mother and aunt Josefina suggested for me to walk in the theater unannounced and look for him myself. At first, I thought it would be better for Pipo to go with me for this happiest occasion and the big surprise, but he then decided for me to have the honors. And what an honor it was for me. After a couple of wrong turns and asking for directions, I managed to get to the theater. I purchased one ticket and went in and sat down for ten minutes, looking at a very entertaining American western movie. When I saw an usher and asked him for Justi Garcia, he pointed to a man near the back exit door helping a customer. I approached him and said, "Estoy buscando por Justi Garcia (I'm looking for Justi Garcia)."

He said, "Si yo soy el (Yes, I am him)."

I replied, "Yo soy el hijo de Gerardo Garcia. ("I'm the son of Gerardo Garcia)

He commented, "Como (What)?" He could not believe I was his brother's son standing next to him after traveling such distance. When it finally sunk in, he hugged me, picked me up in the air, and left the theater in a flash for home to reunite with his brother. Wow! At the house Justi took out his best cigars, which he was saving for a special occasion, and started to smoke them. My father did smoke them cigars, but he drank the very best brandy he had. They talked for hours, catching up on a twenty-year-plus hiatus. The first night, we went to sleep at four in the morning; we picked up where we left off the following day by spending all day walking around the city and meeting many friends. My father and uncle Justi were like teenagers, walking in a carefree way, enjoying each other's company; words alone don't do justice to how happy they really were. These moments don't come too often, and I think intuitively they both knew that. I was so happy for them; they really love each other a lot. This manifestation of affection was greater than with his other siblings, with the possible exception of his older sister Guadalupe, whom he so loved.

The following day my mother, aunt Josefina, and Pilli went out to shop while my cousin Elena, around the same age as me, took me under her wing to meet her many friends in town. And, boy did she ever do that! Her friends took a strong liking to me, showing me everything around the town. They took me to nightclubs, pool halls, and to their private social club, where they congregated planning outings. Among the many places that I went, attending a soccer game in Bilbao about fifteen miles away was the most enjoyable for me. The game was between the Athletic Bilbao and the West German team that captured the World Cup a few weeks earlier. The best thing about this match was not only the home team winning the game 5–3 on the same day President Nixon resigned the presidency of the United States of America—man, what irony!—but the most fun I had with them happened before the game, especially with Jose Mari and Richar, both of whom became my very best friends as a direct result of spending so much time together. We went to a secluded vacation house next to a river for some relaxation and partying. We had, plenty of wine and food mixed with beautiful ladies, telling jokes, singing, dancing, and playing cards. We acted foolishly in this reclusive oasis the night before the big game. The next day we left early, loaded with wine inside of a drinking boot. This is the tradition in Spain of drinking wine without touching your mouth. Once inside the stadium we settled in the standing-room-only section, the rowdiest and most dangerous area. This was because it was mostly young people who just kept drinking and drinking until they passed out. We were almost squashed to death several times. The last was the worst; as the game ended and we tried to exit the stadium, a large wave of people pushed against us, and luckily for us it just carried all of us through the doors instead of pinning us against the steel and concrete wall. We were very fortunate to walk out alive. Two years later, just like in Gia with my cousin Jose Antonio, I had an even better time with them.

Back at uncle Justi's apartment, we had many one-on-one times, both mom and I, listening to Justi talk about how much he loved his brother Gerardo, my father. He was a very likeable person in the same way as my father. This was apparent to me from the very outset of meeting him. On the last day the whole family went out to eat to a local restaurant that my uncle knew well. At this establishment, I watched Pipo and my uncle trade blows in storytelling all night, leaving me and everyone around us laughing our butts off. It was an enriching, classic moment when time itself froze for all of us witnessing those two. Those nine days flew by so quickly; I couldn't wait to return and continue this wonderful life with my new friends and family, which we did in 1976. On our long train trip back to Madrid, aunt Josefina loaded us down with delicious Spanish tortillas, steak sandwiches, and Serrano ham and cheese sandwiches. She made so much food that Pipo this time did not jump out of the train to pick up anything. We just read and looked out the window for most of the time and caught a little sleep here and there. Well, Pipo concentrated on his beloved poetry book for most of the trip, ignoring me and my silly, horse-playing, annoying tactics.

In Madrid, we spent the last couple of days making my mother happy shopping at El Cortes Ingles, the biggest and most popular store in Spain, similar to what Macy's is in New York City.

At the Barajas Airport before departing, Pipo got lost getting us ham and cheese sandwiches. We had to page him and look for him along with the police. We rapidly walked the entire terminal concourse to try to find him quickly, because boarding was about to begin and Pipo was nowhere to be found. When he showed up near the Iberia Airline ticket counter, he was steaming and blamed us for walking away and leaving him alone searching for us. He was right; my mother and I did wander off, looking intently for souvenirs in the various gift shops and losing track of him.

We boarded the big bird to fly back to America just in time for the seven-hour flight to JFK Airport. I spent most of this time looking with my binoculars out the window while my parents read and watch a movie

Once we arrived at JFK, my brother, Gerardo, picked us up at the curb with the eight bags, instead of the fifteen we took off with. It should have been six, but my mom stashed a bunch of hams, cheeses, wines, and liquors in a bag, hoping to get it past US Customs. She was a nervous wreck as she helplessly watched inspectors open a couple of suitcases and find nothing. The others were opened but not searched completely. Those were the ones where she hid the food and the wine. After passing through Customs, she hurried Pipo and me outside as fast as possible, thinking that someone would come and check her bags. We were astonished at the amount of stuff she had when we got home and opened up the suitcases. My father and I shook our heads in disbelief when she put all the items on the table for us to see. My father said, "Tu iva pagar todo eso en multa oh ir la carse (You were going to pay all the fines or go to jail)." My mother knew my father would never approve of any of this and kept him in the dark.

I quickly noticed upon hitting American roads again how big the cars were here. I mentioned it to my brother as we left the airport road and drove onto the belt parkway. He just laughed it off, thinking I was crazy. Pipo had to come to my rescue and vouch for me. Thanks, Pipo!

This vacation, I spent more time with Pipo and my mother than I had since our stay in Mexico City six years earlier. I am so grateful to my mother for her insistence on my taking this trip with them. It made my life richer because of many new friends I met and the places I went. Thank you, Mother!

CHAPTER 38

Farewell

This is the most difficult chapter to write, for the obvious reason of reliving all those uncharted waters and feelings of deep pain that came with Pipo's unexpected passing. It was by far my darkest moment in life, and it is impossible to measure it. It is a commonality that we all share, but we hope it will never come to reality with our loved ones as they age, though we know it will. Death is an eventuality I try to not to think about, because it is always heading toward us from the day we are born. We can never run away from it, so why worry and make yourself depressed or sick? My father, Pipo, lived a complete life with so many adventures in between when "the Boss of Bosses" called him up and told him it was his time to leave. I was stunned by this early calling, but who am I to challenge or ask and seek an answer to the ultimate question, "Why now, God?!" I I just wanted a little more time with him, because he was still very strong and active and could've lived easily another twenty years.

I believe writing this book serves as a dual cathartic experience in finally liberating me of any hidden sentiments or resentments as a direct result of that overwhelming, unexpected moment of impact taking refuge inside of me for many lost years. I firmly believe my own quality of life suffered enormously, which took me a long time to come to grips with. I encourage anyone reading this book to take stock in discerning his or her internal shortcomings by either keeping a journal or writing a book. This self-therapy has been a blessing to me, a magic drug, if you wish, similar to penicillin, curing my ills and shortcomings and opening up the floodgates, letting me live life with the same zest as Pipo did from his youth to the very end.

My mother said, "Gerardo, tu tiene que ir a ver al medico, porque el medico desea averte y vamos ir hoy (Gerardo, you have to go see the doctor, because he wants to see you and we are going to go today)." They went to see his personal physician, Dr. Cabaleiro, for a checkup. He did not find him very well. He told Pipo to go to St. James Hospital in Newark for a series of tests. On Tuesday they went to the hospital for the tests and the results came back positive for prostate cancer. They found something abnormal in his colon and suggested that he be operated on as soon as possible—the very next day—to prevent any possibility of it spreading to other areas of the body. Well, the operation was a success, thanks to God. Immediately after performing the operation, Dr. Ponce came out to the waiting area to notify my mother, brother, and me of the good news. He said, "Everything went well. He should be awake in an hour; you could see him then." When Pipo awoke, we all kidded with him. His physician, Dr. Cabaleiro told us he would be going home on Saturday, the twenty-seventh of July. This was welcome news to Pipo and all of us. I was going to be the one to pick him up at the hospital. I could not wait for my hero to return to us. But it was never to be.

My father was a very special man. He took care of his family, which was the most important thing for him to do. As time was passing by, we noticed that he didn't look good. He had problems with his blood pressure, and the doctor gave him some medication to take, but he didn't want to take it because it made him go to the bathroom too much, so one night he ended up in the hospital. The doctor came to the emergency room to see what was going on. My mother and my brother were there with him, so when the doctor came in, Pipo said to him, "What's going on?"

"Why is your blood pressure so high? The medication that I gave you should not have allowed your blood pressure to go up. So are you taking the medication?"

My father, with a straight face, said to the doctor, "Yes, I am." Well, my mother had told my brother that he wasn't taking the medication, but my father didn't want the doctor to know that he wasn't taking the medication, because he didn't want the doctor to scream at him.

But my brother, Gerardo Jr., said to my father, "You know, Pipo, you are lying. You are not taking the medication because it makes you go to the bathroom too much, so why don't you tell the doctor the truth? You are lying to him." My father, according to my brother, didn't know what to say. We had never called my father a liar; that was the first time, and I think it took a lot for my brother to say that, but he was worried that something could happen to him. Well, the doctor jumped all over Pipo about that. He was sent home a few hours later with the instructions that would have to take his medication or he would end up in the hospital, and my father hated hospitals, so he promised the doctor that he would take it. With my mother in charge of making sure that he would obey the doctor's orders, the doctor said go home.

Months passed by and everything looked good until one day when my mother took my father to the doctor because he wasn't feeling well. They checked him out and said he needed to do other tests, so my father went and had the tests done. After a few days the results came back, and he got a call from the doctor to come to the office to see him. Well, the results were not good. He told my father that there was a growth in the colon and he needed to have surgery right away. We didn't know anything about this until my mother told us about it, and we all felt like the entire world was coming down on us. The surgeon was called and everything was set up for the operation. We talked to the doctor and he said there wasn't anything to worry about, everything would be fine.

Tthe day of the operation came. It took a few hours and we were all praying that everything would come out okay. After the surgery, the doctor came out and said everything was fine and he should be home in a few days. When he walked into the room, we all felt a sense of relief that everything had come out okay. My mother stayed with my father all day, and he wanted her there every day, but my mother had to go to work, so she called my brother to talk to him. My brother called Pipo and said, "Don't worry about it. Look, mom has to go to work, and as soon as she gets out of work, she'll come straight to the hospital,"so he said okay.

While at the hospital, my father was on a very strict diet—nothing by mouth, just liquids. My mother was there when this nurse came in with a tray of food for him—some scrambled eggs and bread and other things—and he started to eat some when my mother realized that something wasn't right, so she called the nurse back. The nurse realized that she had made a mistake, and she took the tray away, but not before my father had a couple of bites. His doctor came in a few minutes later, and my mother told him what happened, and he went to the nurses' station and started screaming at them. After a few hours, my father threw up something black, but after that he told my mother he was fine, so my mother went home that night.

In the middle of the night we get a phone call to come to the hospital, that Pipo wasn't doing too well, and that we should come. They had called my brother, who lived far away from the hospital, and they told him to come, too. My brother got in his car and that night he was speeding so much that he broke the speedometer in his car. When he got to the hospital, he went to the emergency room and told the nurse he had gotten a phone call that Pipo wasn't doing too well. He said that the nurses looked at each other and the security guard, and my brother knew that something wasn't right. My brother went to the fifth floor of the hospital, and he got out of the elevator. He said he saw all those machines outside Pipo's room and he knew something bad had happened. He walked in first with my mother as I was the last one to arrive. My father was already dead. They had already put him in a plastic bag. He was dead. My brother came and grabbed my father so tight and cried so much that the doctor had to check his blood pressure. We were all looking at Pipo. There he was, gone; the father that we all loved so much was gone forever, and we weren't going to have him anymore. Right then we knew that this was going to change our lives forever, because he was loved by so many people.

Now we had to leave that hospital and go tell my grandfather and my grandmother and aunt Genoveva. All of them were very old. My grandfather and grandmother were in their nineties, and my aunt Genoveva was in her upper eighties. As we went to see my grandfather at his house, when we told him the news, his remarks were that he just lost his brother, his son, his best friend. Both he and my grandmother were devastated. Now he had to go home and tell my aunt, and she was devastated. After all this, we had to make funeral arrangements, which my brother took care of. The next day was the first visitation, and my brother walked in first to make sure everything was fine so my mother could have some peace knowing that everything was okay. Many family members and friends came to the funeral the next day. We buried my father and said our last good-byes to the father that we loved and that we would never see again. That was a very devastating loss to all of us and to the people that loved my father so much. It was so devastating, this loss, that my grandfather died four months later, followed by my grandmother three months after my grandfather had died, and eight months later my aunt Genoveva died. There was our family almost all gone in less than a year and half, but they are all together, all buried near each other. Twenty-four years after his death, we still miss him. We go to his gravesite and we still all cry like it was yesterday, but we stay strong because my father used to tell us to be strong and be good men. We know that he's in heaven with the rest of our family, and he's looking down on us and still watching out for us. The only thing that we can say is, "We love you, Pipo. You were the best."

Dr. Ponce stressed to Pipo to rest as much possible, No lifting or any strenuous activities that would affect the IV, he said. Don't do anything foolish. If you need help going to the bathroom, call a nurse. Don't try to do it yourself and break the IV connections. My mother also reiterated forcefully the doctor's orders to Pipo, because she knew Pipo could be very stubborn and not follow directions that were for his own good. She stayed with Pipo for two straight days without going home, keeping him at bay and well taken care of. The next day he had a lot of visitors come in to see him and became very tired. He told my mother to go home and get some rest herself. She had spent a couple of days with no sleep in the hospital with Pipo and decided to go home since he was doing fine. Pipo told my mother that he was going to sleep, so if he did not pick up the phone, not to worry about it. Everything was going well with Pipo.

On the Tuesday the twenty-third, about 4 in the afternoon when going to work, I got this strong feeling to go see my father at St. James Hospital. This impulse came to me on McCarter Highway, also known as Route 21 in Newark. Since I had stayed all day with Pipo after the operation, I knew his condition was stable. I did not fear anything bad happening to him, since the doctors assured me of his release from the hospital Saturday morning, just four days away. I was a happy camper on this good news. So when I got this awful feeling to stop by to see him, I almost ignored it completely, because he was doing well.But the feelings t was so intense, it compelled me to stop by his bedside and talk to him. I did not care if I was late to work or not for my shift starting at 6 p.m. When I arrived at the hospital my father was sitting on the bed with my mother sitting on the chair opposite from him. I remained standing in front of him, talking up how good he looked. But in reality he looked pale and fragile, not his usual self. My mother overheard him say, "Tengo mucho dolor en el lado (I have a lot of pain on the side)." She basically shrugged it off as simply the fresh wounds of the operation. I, on the other hand, was concerned about his severe pains. He did not look right for some reason. He asked me, "What time do you have to be at work?"

I said, "A las seis de la tarde (At six in the afternoon)."

Then he replied, "Son las cinco y vente de la tarde vas a llegar tarde al trabaho bête ahora. (It's 5:20 in the afternoon. You are going to be late for work, go now)!" I told Pipo to walk with me in the hallway. He had the IV connected to him as he walked and chatted with me to the end corner of the hallway. From this location, we could see clearly from this big window my 1978 Thunderbird car parked on the opposite side below on Elm Street. I told him not to leave this area until I got in my car and took off for work. He said, "Esta bien higo (Okay, son)." I gave my father a big hug and a kiss and went to work. When I came down from the building, I stopped outside on the sidewalk and looked up for about minute, waving to my hero as he looked down smiling and waving to me. He was wearing that white hospital garment that all patients wear. I ran to my car, pulled out from the curb quickly, traveled no more than twenty feet forward to the intersection, and stopped the car right there, where he could see me clearly. It had to be from only about twenty feet away, close enough where I could see his eyes and face. I gave my hero, not knowing what was about to come in just eight hours, the biggest salute ever. He then saluted me back with a big smile, waving his hands high to each side as I disappeared from his view. This was the last time I saw my hero alive. I am proud to have had the chance to give the final, ultimate salute to a worthy steward who meant so much to me. Every time I travel through the St. James Hospital area (due to budget cuts in 2008, the hospital was decommissioned), I look up and see my father still standing behind the big window, smiling and waving just like that day.

At five minutes past two in the morning, my supervisor at Alcan Ingot & Powders, 901 Lehigh Avenue in Union, New Jersey, called my department to tell me about an emergency phone call. I went to the guard house to take the call. The security, for privacy reasons, transfered the call to an enclosed pay phone on the side of the building. I got the phone and my brother's second wife, Carmen, told me, "Go to the hospital right now!"

I asked her, "What happened to Pipo?!" She wouldn't say anything but to just go! My brother already had left, joining my mother at the hospital. My mother had called Moises and his wife, Teresa, who lived around the corner from our house on Cross Street in Harrison, New Jersey, to take her to the hospital. Moises was very much more than family to Pipo and my mother as well as me since the papellitos days. I ran across the factory yard, into the parking lot and driveway in deep desperation, saying to myself, "Oh God, no, don't let this happen." I was in a blur. I felt like my life was sinking out of my control. I knew in my heart that something bad happened to Pipo. I drove this seven-mile distance on fumes, spiritually speaking, hoping to control my emotions and not crash. I was expecting the very worst. When I got to the hospital, I parked in the same spot as I had eight hours earlier. But the front entrance door was closed, so I ran to the emergency entrance in the rear. I told them that the door was closed and I needed to see my father. They asked me for his name and let me in to his room. When I got there, I saw my mother and brother crying outside the room. She said, "Esta muerto! Esta muerto! Esta El cuerpo esta muy frio! (He's dead! He's dead! The body is very cold!)"

I ran over where he was and couldn't believe what I was seeing. He was motionless in the bed, white as a ghost. My mother and brother suspected he had been dead for a while. I tried to not to cry watching over my father's body in front of my mother, but it was impossible. So I left the room immediately to call my longtime school friend, David, from my Lafayette Street school days and beyond. On the way out of the room, I was outraged on seeing two nurses, a female and a male, laughing right outside my father's room. I felt like I needed to say something to them, but I decided not to because I knew for a fact I would lose my temper and would've taken action for their lack of sensitivity.

David was a very philosophical and studious person who helped me cope for nearly one hour in my grieving on this terrible night. That night and the following days, our home was inundated with family and friends, who tried console us with their support. One of my good friends, Al, who had chosen me to be his best man in his wedding in two weeks' time, stopped by with his fiancée, Vicky, and allayed quickly any commitment to his wedding. All my friends showed up, including the Vidal brothers, Robert, John, and Freddy, who helped me in the upcoming weeks by taking me to clubs to distract me somewhat from my great loss.

Pipo's body was sent to Galante Funeral Home in Newark on Pacific Street, less than two blocks away from our first apartment in America that we had labeled "the North Pole." At his casket, I put inside his suit blazer pocket a St. Anthony picture from the Cathedral of Guadalupe that he bought for me when I was eight years old. I also promised in front of his casket to keep the same commitment of being there for my mother as I did for him.

Before and during the funeral, my brother told me and the family that my father's death could have resulted from multiple errors by staffers at the hospital. This was a plausible possibility, because there was another man sharing the room with the same name as my father. He could've had been administered the wrong drugs in an ongoing emergency situation that was occurring. The person in the room said that my father had gone to the bathroom and something happened while he was there. He doesn't know what exactly happened during the time when he fell sick. Pipo was rushed to his bed with a bunch of nurses screaming as they worked on him. A few minutes later they open the curtain and came out with a defeatist look in their face. It was apparent that my father had passed away, as they closed the curtain once again and transfered his roommate to another room to leave us alone with my father when we arrived.

As a youngster, I almost lost my leg in this same hospital because they failed to detect an inchlong piece of glass from my bike mirror that was left behind inside my knee upon stitching me up after a bike accident. I was, from the very first moment of hearing that this operation was going to take place at this hospital, concerned about my father's well-being. I did not think he was going to get the best medical care possible at this hospital. I really did not have a good taste in my mouth at all. I even fought with my mother about it. But she told me that the surgeon and his personal physician worked at this hospital and they would monitor him closely. She took their biased advice to have the surgery there. I told her, "I have bigger issues with the nursing staff than the doctors, or have you forgotten what almost happened to me twelve years earlier? As you recall, these people in the emergency room butchered my operation. As you recall, I had to go under the knife and get operated by my cousin, Dr. Casanova, six months later upon him finding a piece of glass traveling inside my knee. Well, I haven't forgotten, and I've got the scars to remind you of that."

She said," Si yo me recuerdo (Yes, I remember)." Having made my point crystal clear to her, I decided to move on. I knew quite well that all of us would be next to Pipo while he recovered from surgery, especially my mom, since my brother and I would be working intermittingly during his hospital stay.

It was a tough time at Galante Funeral Home. My mother was crying her lungs out while friends and family tried to calm her down. Among the many who were there, Lalli, Feliz, and Angela were at her side during the entire funeral and in the days ahead. She was in shock because Pipo was doing so well earlier in that day.

The official cause of my father's death was a pulmonary embolism due to an air bubble in his bloodstream. He essentially drowned in his own body. (Pipo passed away July 24, 1985. His passing coincided with President Ronald Reagan's prostate surgery.) Now the question back then, and now, was how did this happen? Was it the incompetent staff at the hospital that might have induced this incident? These issues and questions permeated the entire funeral for friends and family alike. I was constantly approach by family and close cronies to take legal action to possibly unwrap a potential cover-up at the hospital. I was so adamant that these people literally killed my father that I decided to contact Gerry Spence, the famous cowboy lawyer. He was one of the best lawyers around, constantly appearing on television and well known to me in having won 150 cases in a row. I wanted the whole truth about what happened to cause my father's passing. I was not going to leave any stone unturned or cranny unchecked. I asked my brother to write a full, detailed account about the circumstances that lead to his death as best as he knew so I could send it to Mr. Spence as soon as possible. The letter also included the official autopsy report that said nothing unusual was the determining factor in the cause of my father's passing. This report, to my brother and me, was a bunch of bull, merely protecting the hospital from any lawsuit.

Three weeks later we received a letter from the office of Gerry Spence indicating that these types of cases required an extensive commitment of time and resources and are very difficult in the end to win. In addition, he had a heavy schedule and would not be able to find the time necessary to represent our plight 100 percent. He had passed on the case, but mentioned I should pursue it with another firm. I did not want to hear that. I just wanted him to come in on his white horse, figuratively speaking, to seek justice. I was so disappointed with his reason of not taking the case that I refused to watch him on television. Every time he appeared on one of these talking head shows, I immediately switched the channels. I refused to give this man my time of day from that point on, a policy that still remains in effect to the present time. It's a good thumbs down for him, because he comes across on television as a good-natured fellow in helping the little people. But in reality, he just cares about being in the spotlight and rubbing shoulders with the big, influential moguls, accepting cases that are sure-bet winners, less marginal in difficulty to continue his amazing winning streak, fueling his own propaganda of marketing his intellectual property by increasing book sales, and charging a premium rate for speeches.

At my mother's request, I stopped my diligent pursuit of justice. After she and the doctors had spoken at length about what transpired, they convinced her that what took place was one in a million, but it does happen. All surgeries, small or big, have this risk. We take many precautions by using various methods to minimize this remote possibility from occurring. His personal doctor, upon hearing about Pipo's death, immediately concluded that it had to be the air bubble in his blood that caused the embolism. He confided to my mom how devastated he was about what had happened to his longtime patient and friend. He explained fully how ironic it was for Pipo to be affected by this adverse reaction, a low-level, minuscule risk at best. I remain unconvinced, but had to move on with life's complexities, which included additional financial support and whatnot.

During the viewing I walked outside to the curbside often to get some air and to break up tension as my friends and family took turns talking to me. However, most of the time I just sat near my mother, aunt Genoveva, grandfather Domingo, Pepilla, and others. During one of these times, my brother came and whispered that our uncle Fidel and his wife, aunt Clara, had just arrived from Florida. "They are in the lobby; come with me," he said.

I rushed to greet them with a big hug and a kiss. I was so happy to see my uncle Fidel, whom I always liked so much when I was in Cuba. My brother, standing next to me, said, "Bro! He looks just like Pipo, doesn't he?" Man, he was a spitting image of my father. We talked for a while as I greeted guests arriving to pay their respects to my father. I was overwhelmed and very happy indeed to see my uncle Fidel for the entire three days' duration of my father's funeral. He provided me a spiritual uplift, because when I saw him, I saw my father in him. I made sure I was never more than an eye's view from uncle Fidel whenever I felt I was about to lose it.

I was taken outside the funeral home and across the street to a Cuban deli for some refreshments by Anthony Santana Sr., who was like a second father to me. He was the father of my ex-girlfriend Josie, who had called me earlier to comfort me. She was not able to make it to the funeral, but her wonderful mother, Josephine, was able to come in her place. The owner of this establishment, whom I knew somewhat from before, took out a couple of beers from behind the counter and gave them to us upon listening to my woes. We spoke about politics (which is one of my favorite pastimes) and made small talk for about twenty minutes, which helped me greatly since he was involved in politics all his life and had run for mayor of Perth Amboy (I had worked on his campaign). This lasted until my cousin Luis came to notify me to come back inside because Father Francisco was about to perform the eulogy. He was my favorite priest growing up in Newark while I attended Sunday masses with Pipo and Mom at Immaculate Heart of Mary Church on Lafayette Street, where I also did my first Communion. His voice was very intimidating, full of stern warnings about one's commitment to serving God fully. He was a Franciscan, very rigid in making sure we stayed on the straight and narrow path. His words at the funeral home, and then more so at the church for Pipo's mass, brought me back to those days in church, standing between my hero and my mom, listening to his homilies on each Sunday morning. I felt so secure in knowing that God's love was all over us on that day. I listened to Father Francisco's words as if they were coming straight from God himself, while staring at my father's coffin on my left, near the altar.

The huge cross hanging from the ceiling with Jesus on it also caught my attention. This very same cross, as well as the many Bible pictorial stories that are permanently painted on the front wall, behind the holy altar, was impossible to ignore. I took refuge many times during my father's funeral mass. As a youngster, I spent so much time looking up at these various holy images during mass. It was if I was having a private conversation with Jesus and he was telling me everything would be fine.

On Saturday morning we arrived at the Galante Funeral Home for our last viewing of Pipo before the mass and the burial. My mother, brother, and I kneeled together for the final time looking at Pipo before the casket was closed. My feelings and emotions hit uncharted territory as I promised Pipo to keep things in order down here. This included looking out for my dear mother intently and never abandoning her, no matter what. After a few minutes of silence, we all leaned over, gave my beloved father a good-bye kiss, and left weeping.

We started the funeral procession about 10:45 a.m. toward the Immaculate Heart of Mary Church about two blocks away. It went up Pacific Street and made a right on Elm Street, going against the traffic, and a quick left on Congress Street, which was also one-way against the traffic, and finally another right onto Lafayette Street, where the church was located in the middle of the block.

I helped with taking the coffin out of the hearse and putting it on the flat bed and rolling it in. We left it in the front of the church for the entire mass. Father Francisco administered the mass while my cousin Lupe, the daughter of my father's oldest brother, Manuel, and his wife, Marciana, read one of the readings. It was only fitting since she was very much loved by my father. In addition, she had always volunteered her time at the church since she arrived from Cuba in the 1960s.

From the church we went to the cemetery, but before we left, I told the driver and owner of the funeral to go pass by our former homes in Newark and in Harrison. We went ten blocks down Lafayette and made a right on Pulaski Street, and there at the very corner sat our Landfill apartment, where we shared so many great moments. On the following corner on Elm Street appeared the Laundromat, where he felt so alive; people came out and saw me out the window and started to cry, knowing quite well this was my father in the car, saying one last good-bye. Nine blocks down we passed by St. James Hospital, the last place I saw my father alive. Then we went over to North Arlington Cemetery, about ten miles away from Newark, but not before we went by our home at 400 Cross Street in Harrison.

This day of his funeral we had a torrential rain storm that never let up. Someone, I believe it was my mother, said that when it rains so heavily, the spirits of the departed are at peace, and I believe this was true in Pipo's case, because I'd never seen rain fall that heavily for the whole day as it did that day. We were all soaked as we put the flowers on top of his casket and prayed for his soul. After the burial we went back home to Harrison for an all-day get-together with the many friends and family.

It took me almost ten years from the date of his burial to visit him again at his tomb. My mom and brother were always after me to visit Pop with them every time they went. The reason I never went was because I felt my father's spirit was alive and kicking near me, and going there would make me depressed. At the encouragement of my ex-wife, Virginia, after numerous pleas with me, I finally caved in and went to the cemetery to make her happy, but in all reality it was my mom's wish for me to go. It also gave me a chance to visit the plots of grandfather Domingo, aunt Genoveva, and Pepilla, who are also buried in the vicinity. This back section of the North Arlington Cemetery has an amazing view of the New York City skyline far into the horizon, about twenty miles away. Over the following years I have gone there several times on my own and with mom.

During this time frame, I was following two news stories closely with a keen interest. The first one was President Ronald Reagan going to the hospital for prostate surgery, just like Pipo. But unlike my father, he made a complete recovery and lived many years more; like I thought Pipo would do also. The other big story was my baseball idol, pitcher Tom Seaver, approaching his three hundredth win, a feat he accomplished against the New York Yankees on August 4, 1985. This was a memorable moment for me. It distracted me a little bit from the so-called real world, taking the edge off a rough period in my life. Thank God for sports!

One thing that I did right away was get back to work; I only took two days off because I wanted no idle time to think about my loss. I also knew that my father wanted me to do so, and that's what I did. At my job at Alcan in Union, New Jersey, I started to think about my future and what my father had said four months earlier about ruining me. I never thought for a minute that he had done such a thing to me, but it did focus me on pursuing my dreams. The first thing I did was to register at Middlesex County College in Edison, New Jersey, for a class. In high school I did not apply myself at all. I did just enough to pass and get my high school diploma. Even though I was an avid reader of many periodicals and newspapers, I truly lacked focus in this area of my life. Having said all this, my first class was Psychology 1. I purchased the textbook two months before class started. I was so enthusiastic with this new world of knowledge I had not known before that I began reading this whole book. Once I started going to class, I felt I belonged in this new environment. Many of the students were about the same age or a couple of years younger because I was going at night; they tend to be a little older than the day students. Thanks to God! I was holding my own with the workloads and grades with these students, even after working about eighty hours a week, while most of them did not work or had only a part-time gig at best. I fell in love with this brave new world, if you will, quoting from the title of Aldous Huxley's famous book published in 1932. It was an awesome change in my life, but a change that I pursued with vigor, just like my father pursued his frontiers in leaving his homeland several times and going to different countries that did not speak his native tongue. If he could do it, why can't I go back to school and get my education? His hurdles were a lot higher than mine to jump. With his strong inspiration always present, I managed to complete my bachelor's degree after many bumps in the road.

In the intervening years after his farewell, my hero was and still is a big presence in my life. He was my guide all the way through the completion of this manuscript, having his two hands firmly placed on the steering wheel in between mine. It reminds me of those days in the Port Newark parking lot where he taught me how to drive his car for the very first time, saying, "I have your back, son, now and forever. Just listen and follow my instructions."

Dad, I'm happy to report I have followed those instructions with your humble love and dedication. Thanks for being there for all of us in the flesh and in the spirit.

In retrospect, this was not the hardest chapter to write; it was the easiest one, because it was the most liberating to me.

Again, Pipo, te amo para siempre! Tu hijo, Miguel (I love you forever! Your son, Mike).

CHAPTER 39

Final Thoughts and Words

My grandfather Domingo captured it best when he told me, "Your father was the greatest man I've ever met!" I never heard any bad words said about Gerardo, ever. And who could argue with my grandfather? He was nearly one hundred years old. He was almost a centenarian and still in full control of his faculties. God bless him!

This conversation took place the day after the funeral at his apartment, called La Casa Chiquita. It had earned this name because it was very narrow with no depth, and it was very tiny. His wife, Pepilla, was standing nearby as we started to talk about Pipo and his life stories, and suddenly he began to weep uncontrollably, like a young child. I then immediately rushed next to him and hugged him for about five minutes without letting him loose, trying to comfort him as much as I could. I had to remain strong and in control for his sake, but all my control quickly evaporated into the ceiling as he cried out loud and said, "Le voy echar mucho menos, yo no se que voy hacer ahora (I'm going to miss him so much, I don't know what I'm going to do)." I could feel the deep pain behind his words as he lamented the loss of Pipo. My grandfather's words were so emotionally charged that we remained together, embracing as the tears poured and fell to the floor endlessly. Pepilla huddled with us from behind in her own grief over Pipo's death. My father always kept a close eye on my grandparents, and his care of them never waivered. I decided to take it upon myself to take over his frequent visits, grocery shopping, and whatnot. However, it became very difficult for me with two jobs and going to school and so forth. I felt so bad not spending enough time with them and letting my father down as their caretaker. They had nobody else except for my mother and me. My brother was not able to visit them because he lived far away in Parlin, New Jersey, with his wife and kids. Pipo would always talk to us about not visiting them often enough and how bad they felt. In retrospect, I really regret my negligence; it should be a reminder to all of us to visit our grandparents and parents, because as you and they get older, their universe starts to shrink at a faster pace than yours. The moral of the story is you too will get old soon enough; just wait and see if you are lucky.

What my grandfather Domingo told me is a microcosm of what so many family and friends have said about my hero, Pipo. There is not a day that goes by since he left us to be with God that I don't think about him and what he has meant to me. In reality, he never left; he is still alive and kicking next to my mother, brother, and me in spirit. He awaits us, along with aunt Genoveva, grandfather Domingo, Pepilla, family, and friends at the door of heaven, where he is having infinite great times knowing it's a matter of milliseconds before we eternally unite once again....

I wrote most of this book at my townhouse in Newark, New Jersey, at 53 Valsumo Lane, Princeton University, at the Frist Campus Center in SB1, our office, and in the Albert Einstein Lecture Hall in room 302, and, finally, at Roosevelt Park in Menlo Park, New Jersey, where we frequently picnicked.

About the Author

Mike Garcia is currently employed at Princeton University in Printing & Mailing.He also worked in the Frist Campus Center, where he began as an operations assistant in 2002. He is also working at United/Continental Airlines in Newark Liberty International Airport in airport operations since 1999.

He was born in Camaguey, Cuba, on March 1, 1959. He left Cuba in 1967 through Mexico with his parents and immigrated to America, settling in Newark, New Jersey, in 1968.

After many years living away, in 2004 he came back to his beloved city of Newark, where he grew up.

He attended Middlesex Community College in Edison, New Jersey, and received his bachelor's degree from Thomas Edison State College in the liberal arts field.

He has spent countless hours volunteering his time, service, and, more importantly, showing his compassion, especially with new immigrants who lack basic knowledge of US immigration laws. He also stresses the importance of furthering their education in order to achieve the American dream of upper mobility more quickly in their newly adopted homeland, so they can live much richer lives.

He enjoys bike riding and taking long walks. In addition, he is a huge fan of the University of Nebraska Cornhuskers football team and of high school sports. His favorite pro sports teams are the Pittsburgh Steelers, New York Mets, New York Knicks, New York Islanders, and F.C. Real Madrid.

One of his hobbies is visiting old castles, universities, monasteries, museums and churches. He is also an avid reader of philosophy, psychology, political science, theology, history and going to the movies.

Above all, he loves the simplicities and purities of life best.

My father entire immediate family with his parents and nine siblings. My father is the one standing in front of the baby.

This photo taken in Port City of Ferrol, Spain. It was founded by my mother Maria in Pipo's wallet. She believes is his daughter before they met.

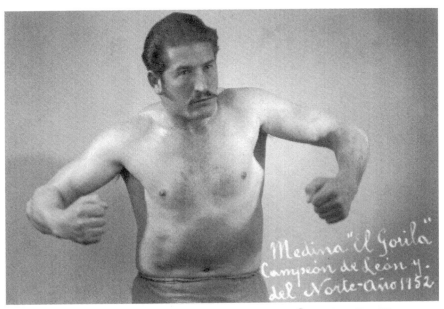

My father's nephew Benedicto, known as The Gorilla.

My brother Gery on his pony in Cordez, Spain with aunt
Genoveva and my parents.

My parents with aunt Genoveva in Gerafe, Spain with my
brother and Aurora in 1954.

My father and his brother Justi in the navy in Spain.

Mom & Dad wedding day photo on August 15, 1951.

Pipo, signing his life away.

My Parents cutting their "Wedding Cake" with family.

My parents with my Cousin Micaela and Felisa at a dance in La
Colonia Espanola in Jobabo.

Pipo, holding my brother Gery with mom, standing next to him
in one of many family celebrations in Jobabo ,Cuba.

My parents in The Colonia Español in Jobabo, Cuba on
January 6, 1951.

Jobabo River in Cuba. Pipo and mom with friends and family living it up.

Mom and dad at the Batey De Jobabo, Cuba in front of Antonio
Lopez's home.

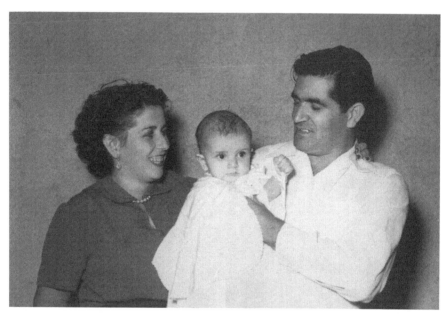

My mother and father with my brother at a dance in the
Colonia Espanola in Jobabo.

Candido (friend) follow by his oldest brother Manuel and his wife Marciana, brother Fidel with wife Clara and my parents and brother Maecelino.

In our Jobabo home, celebrating my brother's birthday with family & friends.

My Parents with aunt Marciana on the side of their spacious
home in Victoria De Las Tunas in Cuba.

My brother and I on his 7th birthday in Jobabo.

My father keeping busy, driving his truck in Jobabo, Cuba.

With our in-housekeeper Catalina, my brother Gerry, aunt
Genoveva, Pipo and me in the beautiful beach resort of
Guardalavaca, Cuba on September 31, 1964.

Our family on vacation in Guardalavaca Beach Resort in 1964.

My aunt Genoveva, me, my brother and in-house keeper
Catalina in Guardalavaca Beach Resort, Cuba.

In the aftermath of Hurricane Flora with my aunt Genoveva
and brother in front of our home in Jobabo, Cuba. I had a
great time in this tree, playing with friends.

Me, looking proudly at my brother Gerry in front of our
Jobabo home. One of my aunt Genoveva and my mother's
favorite photos.

My original passenger ticket from Havana Cuba
to Mexico City to Miami.

My parents and I in the North Pole apartment home
in Newark, New Jersey in 1968.

Celebrating my brother's birthday with the whole family, just like we did in Cuba at the North Pole apartment in Newark, New Jersey.

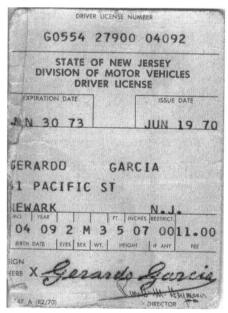

My father's first drivers license in America.

At my brother's wedding at our 94 Garden Street apartment
in Newark, New Jersey in 1972 (our second apartment in
America).

My father and I in Lugo, Spain in the Plaza Santo
Domingo in 1974.

Photo of our cousins in Lugo, Spain on top of a new bridge, not yet open to the public in 1974 with Pipo.

My parents in Riazor Beach in La Coruña, Spain in 1974.

My father In Valle De Las Casas in 1976 with his sisters
Rosario & Radigundis.

My father and I in Chili Riazor beach in La Coruña, Spain.

In Valle De Las Casas in the birthplace home yard of Pipo and his nine siblings) with my parents and family, As well with my beautiful cousin next to me.

At my uncle Justi and aunt Josephine home in Balmaseda, Spain in 1974.

My father, mother and I watching a wonderful flamenco show that my father went up to the stage floor and dance with the dancers to the crowds delight in Madrid, Spain on August 8, 1976. The tour was called "Madrid in the Evening" that we book from our Hotel Santander, where we usually stay.

Pipo and I in 1976 at the Retiro Park in Madrid, Spain.

My first baseball game ticket with my father Gearrdo (Pipo).

Helping my father dig out our 1970 Ford Torino from the big snow storm of 1969 in front of our apartment at 41 (North Pole) Pacific Street in Newark, New Jersey.

My father and I on my 20th birthday in the landfill apartment on 362 Lafayette Street in Newark, New Jersey.

At the Landfill apartment with aunt Genoveva with my nephew Gerry, my ex-girlfriend Josie, my brother, mom, grandfather Domingo and Pipo.

At home in the Landfill apartment at 362 Lafayette Street in Newark, New Jersey with family and friends.

Pipo taking good care of my 1978 Thunderbird below. Behind the Laundromat that he worked. Also, a bird's eye view from our so called landfill apartment.

Pipo wearing my favorite teams colors to please me; including a baseball signed by Tom Seaver, my favorite baseball player.

Mimicking my father Pipo holding my favorite autograph baseball of Mets Great Pitcher Tom Seaver.

My father in the Landfill apartment on Lafayette Street in
Newark, New Jersey in 1976.

Pipo and I in 1983 at the Landfill Apartment on Lafayette Street.

St. James Hospital in Newark, New Jersey. This was last place
I saw my father alive from the second floor corner window
waving and saluting me as I look up. I also saluted and
waved back to him as well. As I was leaving to go to work
on the faithful afternoon.

Made in the USA
Charleston, SC
02 July 2012